THE SELF IN ANXIETY, STRESS AND DEPRESSION

ADVANCES
IN
PSYCHOLOGY
21

Editors

G. E. STELMACH

P. A. VROON

NORTH-HOLLAND
AMSTERDAM · NEW YORK · OXFORD

THE SELF IN ANXIETY, STRESS AND DEPRESSION

Edited by

Ralf SCHWARZER

Free University of Berlin
Berlin
Federal Republic of Germany

1984

NORTH-HOLLAND
AMSTERDAM · NEW YORK · OXFORD

ISBN: 0 444 87556 5

Publishers:
ELSEVIER SCIENCE PUBLISHERS B.V.
P.O. Box 1991
1000 BZ Amsterdam
The Netherlands

Sole distributors for the U.S.A. and Canada:
ELSEVIER SCIENCE PUBLISHING COMPANY, INC.
52 Vanderbilt Avenue
New York, N.Y. 10017
U.S.A.

Library of Congress Cataloging in Publication Data
Main entry under title:

The Self in anxiety, stress, and depression.

    (Advances in psychology ; 21)
    Consists chiefly of rev. papers originally presented
at an international conference entitled "Anxiety and
self-related cognitions," held in the summer of 1983 at
the Free University of Berlin, West Germany.
    Bibliography: p.
    1. Self-perception—Congresses. 2. Self—Congresses.
3. Stress (Psychology)—Congresses. 4. Anxiety—
Congresses. 5. Depression, Mental—Congresses.
6. Cognitive therapy—Congresses. I. Schwarzer, Ralf.
II. Series: Advances in psychology (Amsterdam,
Netherlands) ; 21.
BF697.S435 1984   155.2   84-10261
ISBN 0-444-87556-5 (U.S.)

PRINTED IN THE NETHERLANDS

PREFACE

The problems addressed in this book are related to self-referent thought and emotional states and traits. This is a topic which receives more and more attention. Viewing emotions and actions from a cognitive perspective has become a common and well-accepted practice. The chapters deal with specific empirical problems in research on stress, anxiety and depression which can be solved or clarified by investigating the role and functioning of the self in the face of taxing or threatening environmental demands. The organized knowledge about oneself based on previous experience can be seen as a moderator of self-regulatory processes and coping attempts. Self-awareness and the expectancy of self-efficacy are key variables in the determination of instrumental actions and emotional states. Social anxiety and test anxiety as composed of worry and emotionality are central constructs in this realm of psychology and play a crucial role in the development of stress, helplessness and depression. Appraising a situation as ego-threatening is a common source of anxious arousal. Here, the appraisal of the self as competent or invulnerable is most influential in coping with threat. The development of learned helplessness and dispositional depressive mood is characterized by self-related cognitions, by an unfavorable attributional style and, partly, by distortions of reality. Vulnerability towards psychic disorders can be determined by perceived lack of resources within the person such as self-regulatory competence or by lack of environmental resources such as social support. The intention of this book is to further the idea of self-related cognitions as an integral part of emotions and actions. Processing information about oneself initiates or impairs instrumental behavior like effort or persistence in a variety of settings dependent on the specific circumstances.

The point of departure for the preparation of this book was an international conference entitled 'Anxiety and Self-Related Cognitions' which was held in Summer 1983 at the Free University of Berlin, West Germany. The meeting itself was financially supported by the Deutsche Forschungsgemeinschaft, the Free University and the Senator für Wirtschaft und Verkehr. Most of the chapters collected in the present volume are written by the speakers who delivered a revised paper for publication. Some additional chapters are submitted by invitation of the editor.

I wish to express my thanks to the contributors for the spirit of industry and cooperation displayed in fashioning their chapters. I am also deeply indebted to my coworkers Matthias Jerusalem, Manfried Kuliga, Hans-Henning Quast, Arne Stiksrud and Mary Wegner for their support in organizing the conference. Special thanks go to Helga Kallan who retyped the majority of the chapters and who coped successfully with the new word processor. Finally, I am grateful to Dörthe Belz, Joachim Faulhaber, Peter Kalehne and Anja Leppin who were responsible for the bibliography.

Berlin, February 1984   Ralf Schwarzer

TABLE OF CONTENTS

The Self in Anxiety, Stress and Depression
R. Schwarzer (Editor)
© Elsevier Science Publishers B.V. (North-Holland), 1984

THE SELF IN ANXIETY, STRESS AND DEPRESSION:
AN INTRODUCTION

Ralf Schwarzer

Free University of Berlin, Federal Republic of Germany

Many heterogeneous scientific approaches are directed to the self claiming to gain insight into the functioning and the hidden structure of human thinking, feeling and behavior. The present author favors an information-processing view which leads to assumptions about the development of the self, its cognitive dimensions and its relationship to some emotional or motivational concepts like anxiety, stress and depression. The key to understanding this interdependence is the 'self-related cognition'. Research projects on self-concept, anxiety, stress, coping, depression and helplessness share the idea that self-related cognitions are highly influential and deserve more attention. The following sections of this chapter contain statements about these research topics from the above-mentioned perspective. This chapter serves the purpose of introducing the reader to the empirical findings gathered in the present book.

THE SELF

Self-concept. Self-concept can be conceived of as the total of self-referent information which an individual has processed, stored and organized in a systematic manner. It can be defined briefly as a set of organized knowledge about oneself. For scientific purposes the self-concept can be used as a hypothetical construct with a multidimensional structure. Shavelson and Marsh (1984) subdivide the general self-concept into an academic, a social, an emotional and a physical self-concept, each of which can be further subdivided. A relatively stable hierarchy of cognitions represents the way how the individual sees himself and also delivers the categories for self-perception and self-evaluation.

With respect to self-worth, the 'self-concept of (academic) ability' is most important in our society (Covington 1984, Meyer 1984). Several factors play a role in developing such an image of oneself. First, direct and indirect information from the social world outside are relevant. Parents, peers and teachers provide evaluative feedback to one's performance in a variety of situations. If they praise the individual in response to an accomplishment, the person may be convinced of his competence. However, feedback does not always have a straightforward effect. Indirect communications like punishment can also lead to a positive self-concept under certain circumstances (Meyer 1984, Rustemeyer, this volume); or emotions can be transformed into self-related cognitions:

If the teacher expresses pity, the student may feel dumb; if
she expresses anger he may feel lazy, etc. (Weiner 1982). The
individual infers from others' communication to their perception and attribution of causes,and appraises this information
as self-relevant. Second, the person relies on self-perception
and self-evaluation by monitoring his accomplishments and
attributing it to ability or to other causes. Also, memory
scanning provides a selective retrieval of information on the
self. The processes involved are self-reflective and comparative. Standards for comparison are based on social norms, or
individual norms or on absolute criteria (Rheinberg 1980,
1982). The most powerful and efficient way of obtaining information about one's ability is by social comparison. This
procedure allows a quick review of one's relative standing
with respect to one or more target individuals who are characterized by 'related attributes' (Suls & Miller, 1977). In
classroom environments and many other settings these social
comparison processes yield results about an individual's rank
position within a reference group (Hyman & Singer, 1968).
Student self-concept of ability is developed mostly by school
group effects (Jerusalem, 1983). Self concept stability and
continuity over time is thoroughly discussed by Silbereisen
and Zank (this volume).

Self-focus. The focus of attention is a key variable in
information processing (see Claeys, this volume). Directing
the focus to the self leads to a self-preoccupation which
increases self-knowledge on the one hand, but can impair the
ongoing action and debilitate performance on the other. The
theory of objective self-awareness (Wicklund, 1975) states
that self-focus makes certain aspects of the self more
salient, and it motivates to reduce discrepancies. In an
emotional state self-awareness leads to more affect. Buss
(1980) distinguishes between private and public self-awareness. Private self-awareness is present when persons look into
themselves, investigate their feelings and attitudes and
ruminate about their identity. Public self-awareness is
present when persons feel they are being observed by others or
being evaluated. Then they worry about their public image.
Self-awareness as a state is distinguished from self-consciousness as a disposition, both bearing a private and a
public component. This has implications for self-presentation
and for social anxiety (see Asendorpf, see Jones & Briggs,
this volume).

Self-focus is often contrasted to task-focus, implying that
the direction of attention is the major determinant of task
persistence and accomplishment. However, studies by Carver and
Scheier (1981, 1984) have proven that this dichotomy is too
simple and misleading. At the trait level a high degree of
self-consciousness makes the person prone to a high frequency
of self-focussed attention. At the state level self-focus can
be induced experimentally by the presence of a mirror or any
other technical device which gives feedback of one's face,
voice or behavior. Also it can be induced naturally by anxious
arousal. The person perceives bodily changes like increased

pulse rate, blushing, sweating etc. which leads to self-focus and interruption of the on-going action.(It remains unclear, however, if either self-focus or interruption come first.) Self-focus, then, facilitates performance for low anxious and debilitates performance for high anxious people. This important statement in the work of Carver and Scheier raises the question of anxiety definition. If one equates anxiety with perceived arousal there would be no disagreement with the statement. But if anxiety is defined as a cognitive set of worry, self-deprecatory rumination and negative outcome expectancy combined with emotionality then their statement would be questionable.

Carver and Scheier redefine anxiety as a coping process starting with self-focus. Self-focus leads to an interruption of action and provokes a subjective outcome assessment. At this point the authors claim the existence of a "watershed" with respect to the content of the self-focussed attention: For some persons this state of self-awareness leads to favorable, for others to unfavorable outcome expectancies. The first group will shift to more task-focus, invest more effort, show more persistence and will gain more success. The second group will withdraw from the task mentally and will be preoccupied with self-deprecatory ruminations. Therefore they will invest less effort, are less persistent and probably will experience failure. The first can be defined as a low anxiety group, the second as a high anxiety group. A feedback loop makes the high anxious persons more prone to perceived discrepancies and interruptions of action by arousal cues. The key variables in this model are self-focus and outcome expectancies. Worry, here, is not the primary cause of performance decrements, it is only one element in a maladaptive coping procedure based on mental withdrawal and unfavorable expectancies. Self-focus gives way to a cognitive process where one's own coping ability is under scrutiny.

Self-efficacy.The notion of outcome expectancy or "hope vs. doubt" is similar to Bandura's (1977, 1982) concept of self-efficacy. This can be defined as a perceived action-outcome contingency attributed to one's ability. In our own model this is called "competence expectancy" (Schwarzer, 1981).Perceived self-efficacy can be acquired by direct, indirect or symbolic experience (Bandura 1977): Mastery of tasks provides information about one's capability to handle specific kinds of problems; observing similar others performing well on a task leads one to infer the same capability to oneself; being convinced verbally to possess the necessary coping strategies may also be sufficient to perceive oneself as competent.

Self-efficacy is partly responsible for the selection of actions, for the mobilization of effort and for the persistence at a task. People who are assured of their capabilities intensify their effort, whereas people who lack self-efficacy may be easily discouraged by failure. In a recent experiment Bandura and Cervone (1983) have studied the interplay of goal setting, performance feedback, self-dissatisfaction and self-

efficacy. It turned out that combining a personal standard
with performance feedback of progress toward it was a better
prerequisite for motivation than goal setting alone or
feedback alone. Subgoals and standards had to be explicitly
quantitative, challenging and temporally proximal in order to
serve that purpose. In addition, perceived negative discrepancies between what to do and what to achieve created self-
dissatisfactions which served as motivational inducements for
enhanced efforts. High self-dissatisfaction with a substandard
performance and strong self-efficacy for goal attainment made
an impact on subsequent effort intensification. This finding
sheds light on the role of self-doubts in motivation. Self-
doubts are defined as a perceived negative discrepancy between
the current performance level and the desired goal attainment.
In applying acquired skills goals are hard to attain if one is
plagued by self-doubts. The process of acquiring a new skill,
however, is stimulated by self-doubts or slightly negative
self-evaluations. Self-efficacy may be more important in the
execution of established skills than in the learning of
unfamiliar tasks. "In short, self-doubts create an impetus for
learning but hinder adept use of established skills" (Bandura
& Cervone, 1983, 1027).

This construct of perceived self-efficacy or competence
expectancy could possibly be defined as part of anxiety.
Bandura postulates an "interactive, though asymmetric,
relation between perceived self-efficacy and fear arousal,
with self-judged efficacy exerting the greater impact " (1983,
464). For him perceived self-efficacy and anxiety are
different concept, the first being the more influential for
performance prediction. However, his definition of anxiety is
not a cognitive one. Instead, it is something like fear or
perceived arousal, in other words: he refers to nothing but
the emotionality component when talking about anxiety.
Therefore his findings indicating a superiority of self-
related cognitions over "anxiety" is in line with those who
claim the same hypothesis for the worry component of anxiety.
The question raised by the findings of Bandura (1983) and
Carver and Scheier (1984) and many others seems to be a matter
of definition: Which theoretical concepts described in the
process of coping shall be subsumed under the heading of
anxiety ? I prefer a broad conceptualization and suggest to
use variables like perceived self-efficacy (hope vs. doubt),
self-deprecatory rumination (worry) and mental withdrawal
(escape cognitions) as constitutive cognitive elements of
anxiety as a state and as a trait. Subdividing anxiety into
more than the usual two components is in line with the
findings of Irwin Sarason (1984), Helmke (1983) and Stephan,
Fischer and Stein (1983).

Self-serving bias. Many people take credit for good actions
and deny blame for poor outcomes. This is a well-known self-
enhancement strategy in order to protect the self-esteem. It
has a functional value for the maintenance of one's self-
concept. Mild depressives were found to rate themselves in a
realistic way, whereas nondepressed people tended to overesti-

mate their capabilities. Normal individuals have a tendency to make greater self-attributions for their own positive behaviors than for their own negative behaviors. One can easily distort any outcome by use of several kinds of self-serving bias. Evaluating oneself too positively may strengthen one's self-esteem and may make less vulnerable towards depressive disorders (Alloy & Abramson 1979, Lewinsohn, Mischel, Chaplin & Barton 1980). Realistic self-evaluation may be unfavorable for one's mental health. On the other hand, illusions of control may lead to an underestimation of academic demands und seduces people to select too difficult tasks which result in unexpected failures. Distortions of reality seem to be characteristic for highly self-reliant persons. In two experiments (Schwarzer & Jerusalem 1982) we gave students working on an intelligence task fictitious feedback and found statistical interactions between self-esteem and success vs. failure. It turned out that high self-esteem students attributed their presumable success to their ability but did not attribute their presumable failure to a lack of ability.

However, sometimes people accept responsibility for negative outcomes and deny credit for positive acts. The reason for such a 'counterdefensive attribution' may lie in a motivation for a favorable self-presentation. A positive public image requires modesty; therefore private thoughts about one's competence or morality are to be suppressed in favor of less positive statements which in turn serves the needs for public esteem. This is especially the case in situations where the subsequent behavior of the person is under scrutiny. People who accept undue credit for positive outcomes could experience an invalidation of their unrealistic statements by a subsequent failure. Such public invalidation would be associated with embarrassment and pose a threat to one's public image (Harvey & Weary, 1981). Therefore self-serving biases can be located at the level of covert self-perception or at the level of overt self-description depending on the kind of situation and on the state of public or private self-awareness.

ANXIETY

Test Anxiety. Anxiety can be defined as "an unpleasant emotional state or condition which is characterized by subjective feelings of tension, apprehension, and worry, and by activation or arousal of the autonomic nervous system" (Spielberger, 1972, 482). Test anxiety is a situation-specific state or trait which refers to examinations. As mentioned before, this may be confounded with social anxiety when the test is taken in public or when social interactions are part of the performance to be evaluated. Test anxiety theory has a long tradition which makes this phenomenon one of the most studied in psychology (Morris & Ponath, 1984; Tobias, 1984). However, as paradigms shift in our general psychological

thinking, this has a strong impact on the investigation of
specific phenomena, too. The cognitive approach to emotions
and actions has given rise to new concepts which are fruitful
in understanding and explaining the subjective experience of
anxiety in specific situations. The first three volumes of the
new series Advances in Test Anxiety demonstrate the far-
reaching consequences of cognitions of the worry type for our
scientific knowledge (Schwarzer, Ploeg & Spielberger, 1982,
Ploeg, Schwarzer & Spielberger, 1983, 1984).

Tests are mostly regarded as general academic demands in
schools or in higher education but also can be conceived of as
highly specific demands, as discussed in mathematics anxiety
(Richardson & Woolfolk, 1980) or sports anxiety (Hackforth,
1983). Such demands - if personally relevant for the individual - can be appraised as challenging, ego-threatening or
harmful (Lazarus & Launier, 1981). The appraisal of the task
as ego-threatening gives rise to test anxiety if the person
perceives a lack of coping ability. This second kind of
appraisal is most interesting for the study of self-related
cognitions. The individual searches for information about his
specific competence to handle the situation. The coping
resources looked for could be one's ability to solve the kind
of problem at hand or the time available and the existence of
a supportive social network (see B. Sarason, 1984). Perceiving
a contingency between the potential action and the potential
outcome and attributing this contingency to internal factors
is most helpful in developing an adaptive coping strategy.
This confidence in one's ability to create a successful action
can be called self-efficacy (Bandura 1977). A lack of
perceived self-efficacy leads to an imbalance between the
appraised task demands and the appraised subjective coping
resources and results in test anxiety which inhibits the on-
going person-environment transaction and decreases performance. This is a case of cognitive interference (I. Sarason,
1984). The individual's attention is divided into task-relevant and task-irrelevant aspects. The presence of task-irrelevant cognitions can be regarded as a mental withdrawal (Carver
& Scheier, 1984). People who cannot escape from an aversive
situation physically because of social constraints or lack of
freedom to move, do so by directing their thoughts away from
the problem at hand. Task-irrelevant thoughts can be divided
into self-related cognitions (like worry about one's inability
or failure) on the one hand and those which are totally
unrelated to the task (like daydreams) on the other. This
mental withdrawal from the threatening demands equals the test
anxiety component which debilitates academic performance. The
perception of discomfort and tension is the other component.
Autonomic arousal may accompany this state or trait but need
not. Mental withdrawal is maladaptive in a specific situation
because it contradicts any kind of problem-centered coping
action. However, in the long run there may also be a certain
adaptive value because the person may learn to distinguish
such situations from those which are easily manageable and
therefore avoids to select wrong situations or too difficult
tasks.

There are many causes which make a person test anxious. The individual history of success and failure combined with an unfavorable attributional style (Wine, 1980) and no supportive feedback from parents, teachers and peers may lead to a vicious circle which develops a proneness to scan the environment for potential dangers ("sensitizing"),to appraise demands as threatening and to cope with problems in a maladaptive way.

The assessment of test anxiety has to consider these theoretical advances and ,therefore, requires measures for separate components. Such a satisfactory measure for example is the Test Anxiety Inventory (TAI) by Spielberger (1980) which is now available in several languages (see Spielberger & Diaz-Guerrero 1976,1982, 1984). Another new instrument ,called "Reactions to Tests", is introduced by I. Sarason (1984). Advances in research and assessment are published annually by the International Society for Test Anxiety Research (Schwarzer et al. 1982; Ploeg et al. 1983, 1984).

Social Anxiety.Social anxiety can be defined as consisting of (1) negative self-evaluations, (2) feelings of tension and discomfort, and (3) a tendency to withdraw - in the presence of others. This is a pattern of cognitive, emotional and instrumental variables which may occur simultaneously, but need not. Shyness, embarrassment, shame and audience anxiety are different kinds of social anxiety. Shyness is a general social anxiety applicable to a variety of social situations. Embarrassment can be seen as an extreme state of shyness indicated by blushing. Shame occurs when one sees himself as being responsible for negative outcomes or for failing in public. Audience anxiety is characterized by a discomfort when performing in front of an audience (stage fright) which can lead to an inhibition of speech. This is closely related to test anxiety because the individual is afraid of being under the scrutiny of others. Both kinds of apprehension in face of tests and social interactions share this aspect of evaluation anxiety (Wine, 1980). Social anxiety is more general, whereas test anxiety can be conceived of as very specific with respect to written exams. In the case of oral exams and any other tests performed in public, test anxiety as well as social anxiety are adequate variables to be taken into account. Test anxiety researchers have usually neglected this social aspect or have defined test anxiety in a manner too broad to be of use.

Whether social anxiety can be subdivided into these four emotions has not been finally agreed on. There may be more or less facets. Buss (1980) has made this differentiation popular, but now undertakes a conceptual change by conceiving embarrassment as part of shyness (Buss, 1984). Some authors don't make any distinction at all and prefer to accept social anxiety as one homogeneous phenomenon. In contrast, Schlenker and Leary (1982) conceive shyness and embarrassment as separate facets of social anxiety. This question requires further theoretical efforts (see Asendorpf, this volume).It is

useful to distinguish state shyness from trait shyness in
accord with the widely accepted conceptualization of state and
trait anxiety (Spielberger, 1966). The state of anxiety refers
to the acute feeling in the process of emotional experiencing.
The trait of anxiety refers to a proneness to respond with
state anxiety in threatening situations. This proneness is
acquired during the individual's history of socialization.
Shyness is characterized by: public self-awareness, the
relative absence of an expected social behavior, discomfort in
social situations, an inhibition of adequate interpersonal
actions, and awkwardness in the presence of others. Buss
(1980) claims that public self-awareness is a necessary
condition of any kind of social anxiety. In this emotional
state the person directs his focus of attention to those
aspects of the self which can be observed by others, like
face, body, clothes, gestures, speech or manners. At the trait
level public self-consciousness is the respective variable.
Persons high in public self-consciousness are prone to
perceive themselves as a social object and tend to think and
act in front of an imaginary audience. The direction of
attention to the self can be understood as a mental withdrawal
from the social situation at hand, leading to a decrement in
social performance. Self-related cognitions are part of the
complex emotional phenomenon of shyness or social anxiety in
general.

The anxious individual worries about his social performance,
is concerned with his public image, perceives inability to
cope with social demands, is apprehensive to behave inadequa-
tely, permanently monitors and evaluates his actions and is
preoccupied with himself as a social being. The emotional
component refers to the feelings of distress, discomfort,
tension and the perception of one's autonomic reactions in the
presence of others. For example, blushing when experiencing
embarrassment is a source of information which can lead to a
vicious circle (Asendorpf, this volume). The "emotional component" can be seen as a "quasi-cognitive component" because it
deals with information processing on feelings and arousal.
Finally, the instrumental or action component refers to
awkwardness, reticence, inhibition of gestures and speech, a
tendency to withdraw from the situation, and the desorganiza-
tion or absence of social behavior. Both shy and polite
people can be very similar in behavior but differ in cognitions and feelings: non-shy, polite individuals are relaxed,
calm and direct their attention to the situation, whereas shy
individuals do not.

Causes of shyness can be theorized in different ways.
Schlenker and Leary (1982) propose a self-presentational view:
Shyness occurs when someone desires to make a favorable
impression on others but is doubtful of the desired effect.
Embarrassment occurs when something happens which repudiates
the intended impression management. There may be a discrepancy
between one's own standard of self-presentation and one's
actual self-presentation. When such a discrepancy is expected,
shyness will result, and when it is actually perceived,

embarrassment is experienced. This can be seen as a two-stage process at the state level of social anxiety. A person who expects falling short in impressing others will be shy. If this anticipation becomes true, the person is embarrassed. Buss (1984) mentions a number of other potential causes for shyness, such as feeling conspicuous, receiving too much or too little attention from others, being evaluated, fear of being rejected, a breach of privacy, intrusiveness, formality of social situations, social novelty etc. With respect to common stress theories social anxiety depends on the appraisal of the social situation as being ego-threatening and the appraisal of one's own inability to cope with it.

The development of shyness can be traced back to two sources (Buss, 1984). The "early developing shyness" appears in the first year of life and is better known as stranger anxiety or wariness. Novelty, intrusion and fear of rejection are the immediate causes. Since there are no self-related cognitions at that time, this is a fearful shyness, whereas the "later developing shyness" can be regarded as a self-conscious shyness. It first appears in the fourth or fifth year of life and is associated with acute self-awareness and embarrassment. Both kinds of shyness contribute to the complex phenomenon of shyness during the individual socialization process. Fearfulness as an inherited trait and public self-consciousness as an environmental trait may be two sources of trait shyness, which attains its peak degree during adolescence (Buss, 1984). Low self-esteem and low sociability may be two additional causes. In a field study with 94 college students, we obtained satisfactory correlations between shyness and self-consciousness (.39), audience anxiety (.39), general anxiety (.36), other-directedness (.36) and self-esteem (-.62) (Schwarzer, 1981). These may be rough indicators of trait associations.

Other findings show that shyness is negatively correlated with number of friends, frequency of social activities, closeness to others, social satisfaction, self-disclosure to friends, dating frequency, dating satisfaction (Jones & Briggs, this volume). The data suggest that the inhibitory effect may be greater for males than for females. Shyness can be regarded as inhibition, tension, and anxiety preoccupation in the presence of an audience. Shy people tend to be less friendly, outgoing, warm and talkative. Other indicators of shyness are identified as self-consciousness, loneliness, communication apprehension, and feeling inadequate with superiors. One possible cause for shyness may lie in a more accurate memory for negative feedback from social sources. Shy people may have a reduced capacity to gather and to correctly process social feedback.

There are few measures designed to assess trait social anxiety. In analogy to test anxiety research, separate worry and emotionality scales have been constructed (Morris et al. 1981). However, these scales do not distinguish shyness from embarrassment, shame and audience anxiety. On the other hand, the specific shyness scale of Cheek and Buss (1981) does not provide a separation of cognitive and emotional components.

Evidently there is a lack of operationalization compared to
the obvious increment in theoretical efforts during the last
years. A complex measure of social anxiety which satisfies the
needs of the present approach should consider the four kinds
of social anxiety and the state-trait distinction as well as
the three components (cognitive, emotional and behavioral),and
also provide as many subscales. The distinction between a
cognitive and an emotional component bears treatment implications: Self-related cognitions could be modified by a restruc-
turing and attention training, whereas tension and nervous
feelings could be treated by systematic desensitization.

STRESS

Cognitive appraisals. Stress research is no longer directed
either to environmental stressors on the one hand or to
personality dispositions on the other. Instead, stress is
regarded as a complex phenomenon which occurs and develops in
the person-environment process (Lazarus & Launier, 1978).
Cognitive appraisals are key factors in the emergence and
experience of stress. First, an encounter is evaluated as
irrelevant, as benign-positive or as stressful. Those stimuli
which are felt to be stressful are further appraised as
challenging, threatening or harmful. Challenge refers to the
potential for mastery, personal growth or positive gain.
Threat refers to the anticipation of danger, and harm or loss
refer to injuries which have already occurred. The person
processes information about the environmental demands: He
constructs a cognitive 'situation model' (Schwarzer 1981).
This has been called 'event appraisal' or 'primary appraisal'
(Lazarus).

While being confronted with a stressful encounter the
individual also constructs a cognitive 'self model' as a
potential response to the 'situation model'. This has been
called 'resource appraisal' or 'secondary appraisal' (Lazarus)
not implying a temporal order. The person checks his material,
social, physical and intellectual resources required for
overcoming the situation at hand. When the ongoing action is
interrupted by a stressful encounter the focus of attention
shifts to the self making those aspects salient which are
relevant for dealing with the encounter efficiently (Carver &
Scheier, 1984). One's coping competence or self-efficacy or
one's external resources are under scrutiny. There is a rather
stable body of knowledge about one's resources but in
stressful encounters the person becomes more aware of it than
usual. The 'self model' contains cognitions about the
subjective availability of appropriate actions or action
scripts, that is a set of expectancies and adaptive routines
for a variety of demanding situations. Believing to be
competent or invulnerable is rather general, therefore such a

cognitive 'self model' partly determines which situations are selected, which actions are chosen, how much effort is exerted or how long one persists. If a specific 'situation model' taxes or exceeds one's specific 'self model' the specific person-environment transaction is experienced as stressful. Persons with a weak 'self model' are highly vulnerable towards environmental demands and are prone to get in trouble.

Coping. The process of coping is the more or less adaptive response to both kinds of appraisals. The individual strives to regain the predominance of the 'self model' over the 'situation model'. Coping can be more problem-centered or more emotion-centered (Lazarus 1980): The person may direct his efforts to the problem which causes the inconvenience or he may focus on his emotions trying to cool out the arousal or to regulate self-cognitions (palliative coping). Four coping modalities have been stated: Information search, direct action, suppression of action and intrapsychic coping (Lazarus & Launier 1978). Information search leads to a different view of the situation and implies reappraisals. Direct action is an attempt to control the environment. Suppression of action is adaptive when any impulsive action would cause more harm and when waiting patiently is successful as it is in the 'delay of gratification paradigm' (see Toner, this volume). Intrapsychic coping addresses reappraisals and other internal processes like denial, reattribution or self-serving cognitions. Further influential variables in the coping context are the degree of uncertainty or unpredictability of the event, its level of threat, the existence of conflict, and the perception of helplessness or vulnerability.

Critical life events. Recently, research on stress and coping has turned to observations in natural settings and has focused on the experience of life events (see Filipp, Aymanns & Braukmann, 1984). Different kinds of life events are distinguished from each other: 'Normative' events occur to a majority of people in a certain age or time period like exams, marriage, birth of offspring, death of parents or other close persons, and transitions in the professional career. 'Nonnormative' events are less predictable and happen to a limited number of people, like accidents, earthquake, disease, joblessness, divorce, conflicts and tension. Minor chronic problems are the 'daily hassles' which also may cause severe stress in the long run. Preventive actions can be aimed at developing coping competence for a variety of encounters. However, prevention seems to be limited to normative events. In any case, a generally strong 'self model' would be supportive whereas vulnerable individuals have to suffer more from daily hassles. Four or more dimensions can be distinguished with respect to the content of life events: loss and separation (death or severe illness in the immediate family, divorce), autonomy and intimacy (tension with a loved one, arguments with the boss, peer pressure, religious problems), academic pressure (amount of homework, anticipated failure of an exam, work load, deadlines), and financial obligations (lack of money, paying bills, job search, installment loans). Life events can be very stressful and are accompanied by emotions like anger, anxiety, grief, depression and by health problems like sleeping and eating disorders which impair the readjustment process. On the other hand, successful coping with these encounters are followed by personal growth. The individual acquires skills and strategies and experiences an enrichment of the self.

Social support. One protective factor can be seen in the availability of other people and the potential support by them (see B. Sarason, 1984). It is part of one's resources or 'self model' and serves as a buffer against stress. The development and maintenance of such a social network can be influenced by situational and by personality factors. Moving to another place or the loss of a relationship would be situational factors whereas sociability or social anxiety are dispositio- nal factors of influence. Social networks do not explain psychological outcomes but the closeness and by this the frequency and intimacy of social exchange or the involved activities are causal determinants. Three fundamental types of social exchange can be distinguished. (1) Help. A helping significant other can provide tangible support (material aid), appraisal support or emotional support. Help functions in reducing stress or threats to well-being, and the outcomes are feelings of less stress and a higher quality of coping. (2) Companionship and intimacy. These serve no direct and instrumental function but involve activities which people enjoy like shared leisure, discussion of common inerests, affection, humor, self disclosure etc. Social ties have a beneficial function. They provide a positive input to well- being and to self-esteem by giving pleasure and stimulation. The affected outcomes are satisfaction, happiness, quality of life and less boredom, loneliness, sadness and depression. (3) Behavior regulation. People experience feedback and modeling in the conduct of life by roommates, colleagues and other close persons. They learn to comply with social norms or rules like traffic rules, seatbelt use, alcohol and cigarette consumption, dental care, formal interactions, shopping and other daily life activities by receiving feedback and by observing models. Their role behavior and social performance in general are prompted by significant others. Outcomes of this are structural inputs to daily affairs. Due to a lack of prompting, people living by themselves behave differently than those living in a social network due to a lack of prompting.

Generally, social support is regarded as a buffer against stress. However, the topic is broader and more complex. It is necessary to ask for the adaptational value of social contexts or for the impact of social relationships on coping efficiency. The social environment is part of the environmental demands to be appraised as subjectively relevant. If relevant, the social environment can be appraised as stressful or as benign-positive. The first one turns out to be social stress and the second one to be social support. The pure existence of a social network is not supportive per se. If a person is already stressed by another event, she or he will probably perceive offered help as social support.

Otherwise unrequested help can be perceived as obtrusive or as self-dehumiliation. The focus on the supportive aspect of social networks concerns only one side of the coin. Often the social situation is stressful by itself. The social network of a student, for example, consists of parents, siblings, peers and teachers who provide feedback, rewards and punishment. Sometimes this is supportive, sometimes it is not. The social network of peers in the class serves different functions simultaneously. It is a reference group providing the yardsticks for successes and failures. Since social comparison is the basic procedure for achievement evaluation, the best social support of peers would be to perform worse than the one who needs support. Coping relies on information from a social source. Poor achieving peers provide helpful information without knowing about it. A poorly performing, ill, handicapped or unhappy person can serve as the salient source of information that leads the coping process into a successful direction. This is valid if the source person is similar on 'related attributes' like age, sex, social class or others. A patient in hospital can facilitate his well-being by comparison with those who have to suffer more. Also, it is possible to invent significant others, for example an 'imaginative audience', and use them for comparisons.

The starting point of coping within a social network is information from a social source; the processing of this information can be done by social comparison; if it leads to a favorable outcome it is regarded as social support, if not, it is regarded as social stress. Unrequested help can have detrimental effects because the individual attributes the following success externally. If the responsibility for efficient coping is external, the person may feel grateful but also incompetent. The hidden costs of such kinds of social support are often underestimated. Helping someone to cope with his problems is more supportive in the long run if the subject is taught to solve the problem by himself. Model behavior can be supportive in this way, especially the 'self-disclosing coping model'. Another example for the psychological meaning of support can be studied whithin the concept of 'risky shift'. Activities which would be too difficult, threatening or risky for an individual are done much more easily by a group. Diving into the social context leads to a diffusion of responsibility. The person looses his normal level of self-awareness and becomes more action-oriented. Responsibility of actions and negative outcomes is shared with others. The focus of attention is on actions and social approval. Therefore the social environment of gangs, drug abusers, and alcohol drinkers is supportive and results in maintaining the problem behavior. Smokers who never stop smoking are likely to have a strong social network of smokers, nonsmokers who never start smoking should have a strong social network (of nonsmokers) as well. The anonymous alcoholics are a typical example for social support in coping with a temptation. Reduction of self-awareness by social interaction is a basic mechanism of an efficient social network. Social networks are not identical with social support. They can be supportive or stressful depending on the circumstances and the perception of their actions.

Stress and health. Behavioral medicine deals with bodily symptoms and complaints as a result of risky behaviors, inappropriate life styles or unfavorable health beliefs of people at risk. Smoking and substance abuse are typical examples. Chronic stress may contribute to the likelihood of myocardial infarcts and other diseases. Research on coronary prone behavior has found a population at risk called 'Type A individuals' (see Falger, this volume). These are persons characterized by impatience, competitiveness and anger. They strive for self-imposed but diffuse goals, are highly alert, are involved in a variety of challenging activities under time pressure, tend to speed up their accomplishments and respond to interruptions by others with anger, aggression and hostility. They feel stressed by meeting deadlines and other professional demands. Many encounters in their transactions with the environment are decoded as stressful and personally relevant. These are appraised as challenging or threatening. The demands tax or exceed the 'self model'. Type A individuals represent the active, involved and assertive socialization type who is more successful and receives more rewards than his counterpart, the Type B individual. However, this way of self-realisation has its price.

DEPRESSION

Contents of cognitions. The cognitive components of depressives are stated as a negative view of the self, the environment and the future (Beck 1972, 1976). Most depressions are reactive and are based on the experience of loss or harm. For a subset of them the theory of learned helplessness provides the best explanation (Seligman 1975, Abramson et al. 1978, Garber & Seligman 1980): The depressive person has acquired an expectancy of behavior-outcome independence and, by this, developed a state of passivity, sadness, hopelessness, and low self-esteem. Perceived loss of control and perceived loss of social reinforcement are causal determinants in the development of depression. People experience a decrement in self-esteem when failing to maintain or to attain the desired standard or feedback. Their degree of perceived self-efficacy or coping competence is reduced; this is accompanied by selecting less demanding tasks, investing less effort and less persistence which in turn results in poor outcomes and less satisfaction. The internal and stable attribution (lack of competence) of social or academic failures or non-contingencies contributes to this unfavorable process. According to Fry (this volume) the following thematic contents of depressive cognitions were found: Thoughts of hopelessness, self-criticism, dependency, inefficacy, unfavorable stress appraisals and self-reports of cognitive failure. A maladaptive thinking style, negative self-statements and increased self-focus can be seen as characteristic for depressed people. For mildly depressed this is in line with reality. A lack of self-serving bias in perception and self-description makes them vulnerable and causes them to fail to protect themselves and to maintain a positive self-esteem. They miss the 'warm rosy glow' which is typical for healthy normals with a slight illusion of control (Alloy & Abramson 1979; Lewinsohn et al. 1980). For severely depressed the self-appraisal is much worse than reality. It is unclear if depressive cognitions are the cause or the effect of depression or both. A critical life event can result in maladaptive coping and depressive thoughts. This may be true for most victims but especially for those who were predisposed by such cognitions in earlier days. On the other hand, depressive cognitions can be a starting point for inappropriate social behavior resulting in the loss of a social network and subsequently in a loss of social reinforcement which finally completes the state of depression.

Learned helplessness and academic performance. In the achievement domain the development of learned helplessness and depressive mood may follow a theoretical model with four stages (Schwarzer, Jerusalem & Stiksrud 1984). This model is built for the special case of continuous failure only whereas in natural environments intermittent successes would be more likely. The basic idea is that an achievement setting represents a stressful situation evoking 'situation models' and 'self models'. The question is which cognition is the dominant one within the set of appraisals. The first unexpected failure might cause a challenge to be dominant. If this happens repeatedly, the person will feel more threatened than challenged, but will still persist with the task. Later, when the next failure is already expected with a high degree of likelihood, the person will experience loss of control, feeling less threatened because the loss is certain. Challenge decreases and loss increases from one point in time to the next. Threat first increases and then decreases with continuing experience of failure. The highest degree of threat is located where there is complete uncertainty about the next outcome. Different cognitive appraisals lead to different emotions and behavior. Challenge leads to curiosity, exploration and productive arousal. Threat leads to anxiety, and loss of control to helplessness or depression. Four stages can be distinguished. The first is the reactance stage where the person is challenged by one or several failures, but still has confidence in his or her ability to cope with the demands. High self-efficacy is combined with productive arousal and the tendency to explore the nature of the task. When failures mount, threat surpasses challenge appraisal, and anxiety becomes the leading emotion. This combination of anxiety with productive arousal can be called "facilitating anxiety", because the person is still self-reliant and persists with the task. The emotionality component would be higher than the worry component in anxiety. At the culminating point there is complete uncertainty about the next outcome. The threat appraisal will be combined with less challenge and more loss of contol. This is called "debilitating anxiety", because self-related cognitions distract from the task. The person worries about the performance, is afraid of another failure,

has self-doubts and is no longer confident in his or her
competence. Finally, loss of control is dominant, replacing
the appraisal of threat. The student becomes helpless and
gives up trying. The next failure is almost certain. There is
some empirical evidence supporting this model (Schwarzer et
al. 1984).

In sum, there are many theoretical links among anxiety, stress
and depression and the self which can be explored by the
empirical study of self-related cognitions. Attitudes,
emotions and actions of the individual are guided by self-
referent thought.

The Self in Anxiety, Stress and Depression
R. Schwarzer (Editor)
© Elsevier Science Publishers B.V. (North-Holland), 1984

SELF-IMPOSED DELAY OF GRATIFICATION IN CHILDREN:
THE DEVELOPMENT OF SELF-REGULATORY BEHAVIOR IN STRESSFUL SITUATIONS

Ignatius J. Toner

The University of North Carolina at Charlotte, Charlotte, North Carolina, U.S.A.

The demands of daily life in our world are diverse. The hectic life-style of an individual living in a busy industrial city may bear little resemblance to the simpler, more relaxed pace of living in a smaller rural community. Nevertheless, to function successfully in most societies, individuals must typically learn to plan their behavior in order to set, aim for, and reach long-term goals even in the most stressful of situations. People must recognize the importance of considering the needs of others and modifying their own desires and actions to compliment the actions of those around them. Further, they must accept that some goals, whether immediate or distant, may be blocked and so they must learn to tolerate the frustrations inherent in group functioning.

In success-oriented societies where the emphasis is on productivity and achievement, individuals are very often required to exercise high levels of self-regulation to function effectively and meet the expectations of both the culture and the immediate social group. For example, on leaving high school, the adolescent may reject the possibility of embarking on an immediately avialable career to become committed to a four-year college course of study, in the hope that the eventual professional opportunities will be more varied and desirable. Likewise, he or she may turn down the offer with better prospects for promotion and self-fulfillment. Since such dilemmas recur throughout our lifetimes, it is not surprising that the ability and/or willingness of people to control, evaluate, and adjust their own behavior has generated a substantial amount of interest in philosophers and psychologists alike.

Just as they serve as agents of societal norms for others, people are also instrumental in control over their own personal world. Very young children, however, often seem ill-equipped to deal with the complex external demands placed upon them. When confronted with the choice between an immediately available but less valued reward and a delayed reward of greater value, the young child may seem unable and/or unwilling to set aside momentary pleasures to wait for the delayed gratification. It seems that the young child often displays an inability to organize his/her behavior to cope effectively in such stressful dilemmas. The young child is often captivated

by the immediate pleasures of the external world and relies on
these temptations to dictate his/her behavior. In this way,
although perhaps fully responsive to the directives of parents
and peers, the child will often experience difficulty inhibiting emotions, actions, choices, and judgments when left to
his/her own devices.

Throughout the course of early development, there evolve
gradual yet profound changes in the child's ability and willingness to regulate and impose self-control on actions,
decisions, and emotions. Eventually, by late childhood, such
self-control is quite noticeably more like that of adults.
Where previously, controlling influences had bombarded the
young child from all angles of the external world, the older
child typically has become fairly adept at selecting those
aspects of the environment which he/she deems acceptable as
controllers of his/her behavior. Lessons from the external
world are not forgotten but eagerly attended to and internalized so that the child becomes increasingly more likely to
impose his/her own controls on impulses in future similar
situations. Reliance on the external world and its immediate
enticements is diminished. Likewise, the older child's behavior has become more organized. Distant goals may be set and
often achieved, plans of behavior may be constructed and
retained in mind while the necessary behaviors are coordinated
which will effectively attain these long-range objectives.
This increasing mastery of self allows the child to inhibit
behavior, choice and judgment more effectively and reliably.
In fact, learning when it is appropriate to inhibit or tho
express specific behaviors, choices, and judgments is a primary outcome of successful socialization.

Given that major changes in childhood self-control are seen to
occur relatively early in life, it seems logical to inquire
into what specifically determines the degree to which individuals master control over themselves. How can such control be
measured and why do dramatic differences clearly exist between
children in their exhibited levels of self-control ? We focus
our description and explanation of the phenomenon of the
development of childhood self-regulation by attempting to
understand a particularly significant form of self-control,
self-imposed delay of gratification in stressful situations.

SELF-IMPOSED DELAY OF GRATIFICATION

Excited at the prospects of buying a new toy, two young children approach their parents and, in return, are each confronted with a choice. Each may either buy the toy with borrowed
money or wait until the following week to buy the toy without
jeopardizing the ability to select other options for investment. One child decides to retain future options and does
not borrow to buy the toy. The second child has also been
tempted by the more immediate pleasures and decides to get the
toy immediately, giving little thought to next week's possible
needs. Clearly, although both children were given the same

choice under apparently similar conditions, each has chosen a distinctly different course of action. In an attempt to determine why this might happen, researchers have concentrated upon identifying factors which may influence children's ability and/or willingness to defer immediate gratification in favor of delayed rewards.

The research on self-imposed delay of gratification has divided naturally, illustrating that successful delay of gratification is not a unitary process but rather is comprised of two distinct phases. Further, while studies of the first phase dominated research before 1970, studies of the second phase dominated research since that time. In the first phase, the individual makes a <u>choice</u> between the immediate or delayed reward. If the person chooses to delay gratification, he/she then enters the second phase -- that of <u>maintaining</u> delay behavior through the waiting period. To investigate factors which influence delay choice, researchers have typically presented individual children with real choices. The child might be offered one piece of candy immediately versus several candies in the future. Regarding the second phase of self-imposed delay, more is required of the child than merely stating a preference. Now <u>patience</u> must be demonstrated while waiting for the deferred reward. Returning to our previous example, the child who has decided to refrain from buying the toy must now wait until the next week to get his reward. In both research settings and in the real world, this waiting is often made all the more difficult when the child knows that he/she may terminate the waiting period before the prescribed time has elapsed and settle for a lesser reward. In this chapter each of these phases of delay of gratification, and the factors that influence them, are considered separately. A major reason for this separation is that the stated willingness of children to defer gratification is not necessarily predictive of the actual waiting behavior of these same children (Toner, Holstein, & Hetherington, 1977). The child who decides to defer gratification may or may not be able or willing to actually wait for that delayed reward. Just as a child may agree to abide by rules but yet may ultimately break them, or may set a target level of achievement which may be abandoned unfulfilled, so too an individual's stated preferred course of action regarding self-imposed delay of gratification is not necessarily indicative of subsequent behavior. While the choice to defer gratification is necessary to adequately defer gratification, this choice is not sufficient to achieve the goal.

CHOOSING IMMEDIATE VERSUS DELAYED REWARDS

A child's stated preference for an immediate or delayed reward is a choice influenced by many factors. Some of these influences exist as part of the particular situation which presents a choice between rewarding outcomes. Other factors exist as characteristics of the individual's own personality and life history and so are brought by the child to each situation

encountered. Thus, both situational and personal forces
interact to produce actual behavior in delay choice situations. This is certainly no simple process. The converging
influences of situation and the person often make the understanding of delay decisions in the real world most difficult.
Nevertheless, it has been possible to learn much about the
dynamics of childhood delay of gratification choices by investigating the potentially significant influences in isolation.

<u>Situational Influences on Delay Choice.</u> Walter Mischel (1966)
and his colleagues have identified three major aspects of any
given self-imposed delay of gratification situation which most
likely will influence children's choices. First, the more
confident a child is in the availability of the delayed
reward, the more he/she will consider choosing the delayed
rather than the immediate reward. A second factor which the
child takes into account is the relative value he/she attaches
to the immediate and delayed rewards. The child is more likely
to choose a delayed reward if the subjective value of that
delayed reward is greater than the value of the immediately
available reward. The greater the discrepancy in subjective
value, the more likely will be the delayed choice. Third,
Mischel noted that the perceived duration of the delay interval is considered by the child. Longer delays make immediate
choices more likely. It is clear that all of these considerations are usually taken into account by older children contem-
plating self-imposed delay of gratification. As we shall
see, the child's ability to deal with all of these factors may
well depend on the level of cognitive sophistication of the
child. As in the classic conservation problems posed to
children by Jean Piaget, some children are not likely to
consider all relevant information when making judgments and
this may not take advantage of opportunities available to them
to obtain future benefits.

Reward probability, relative reward value, and length of delay
interval are clearly critical considerations in the delay
choice situation. Beyond these factors, other situational
features may dramatically affect a child's stated preference.
For example, children who observe a model choosing either an
immediate or a delayed reward may often state similar preferences (Bandura & Mischel, 1965). In addition, external
persuasion may also affect children's willingness to defer
gratification. Staub (1972) examined the effects of various
persuasion techniques on seventh grade boys and girls. He
demonstrated that the children were more likely to choose the
delayed, more valued reward when they were told by an authority figure that the waiting time would seem short, that they
could trust the researchers, and that individuals who wait for
delayed, more valued rewards were likely to be considered as
more intelligent and able by parents and teachers. The
strength of these techniques of verbal persuasion was reinforced by the fact that the children's changes in choice behavior
persisted over a two-week period. Interestingly, one of the
techniques used by Staub had no effect on children's choices.
When the authority explicitly recommended that children choose

the delayed reward without offering reasons or arguments to justify the recommendation, the children remained uninfluenced. Thus, the situational characteristics that involve behavioral and /or verbal pressure from authority figures can influence delay choice in children.

Finally, in a recent study, Kanfer, Stifter and Morris (1981) investigated the influence of choosing for the benefit of others on decisions by preschoolers in a delay of gratification situation. The child's choice of waiting or not waiting for a delayed reward was affected by whether his/her choice would benefit another child. Children who chose only for themselves, for both themselves and an anonymous child beneficiary, or for a friend were more likely to state a preference for delayed rewards than were children who chose for an anonymous child or for a classmate alone.

In sum, the specific characteristics of any situation involving a delay of gratification choice play a large part in determining children's decisions. However, even in identical situations, different children may consider and respond to these characteristics in markedly different ways. Personal characteristics of individual children influence their self-imposed delay of gratification decisions by interacting with the situation.

Individual Differences in Delay Choice. Washburne (1929), noting that "all children are irresponsible but that bad children are even more so (p.1)", conducted one of the earliest investigations to identify the personal characteristics of children which might affect their delay choice. Delinquent and non-delinquent children were presented with three hypothetical and two actual choices between immediate and delayed rewards. On the basis of his findings, Washburne concluded that "a consistent choice of 'now' appears to indicate delinquency in children over 12 years of age, and more or less misbehavior in children between 8 and 12 (p.18)." He contended, albeit dramatically, that delay choice is a direct indicator of character or degree of moral rectitude. While Washbure sensationalized his data in overstating a correlational result, nevertheless the study does serve as a vivid illustration of the influence of individual differences in delay choice. It is now believed that personal individual differences are most noticeable in their influence on delay choices of different children when the conditions surrounding the delay choice situation are either uniform or ambiguous.

One difference between individual children is their relative chronological ages and, indeed, the percentage of choices of delayed rewards that children make increases with age. In view of this relationship between age and delay choice, several researchers have attempted to establish the existence of a "critical age", after which the child who has previously chosen immediate rewards for the most part is now more likely to decide to defer gratification in similar situations. Mischel and Metzner (1962), while noting that a major change from immediate to delayed choices often occurs at around age ten years, stressed that the "critical age" could be located at virtually any age be manipulations of situational characteristics. In view of this, it may be best to conceive of the developmental changes in delay choice behavior as part of a gradual process. With increasing experience and cognitive maturation, children become more likely to make delay choices in situations where delays are longer, rewards less distinctive, and the availability of rewards less assured. Further, older children become more able to consider several aspects of the delay situation simultaneously in determining their choice. Children who more consistently choose deferred rewards, where lesser immediate ones are available, tend to possess other qualities which enhance their ability to function as efficient and productive members of society. Specifically, when compared to children who more often choose immediate rewards, these children are also more likely to resist the temptation to violate rules when unsupervised, to perform better at school,to have higher scores on intelligence tests, to be more socially responsible and mature, and to display stronger needs to achieve success in a variety of situations (Mischel, 1966). It should be stressed that the willingness to defer gratification should not be assumed to cause or be caused by these personal characteristics. American society has developed such that it depends upon the expression of all or several of these attributes by its members for its continued existence. Consequently, it is perhaps more accurate to consider preference for delayed rewards and the expression of these other qualities as the multiple outcomes of successful socialization.

Cultural Differences in Delay Choice. Societal values differ sometimes radically throughout the world and it may well be that consistent preferences for delayed rewards are not adaptive in all societies or even in all strata of Western cultures. A good example of a cultural norm different from industrialized societies is found. Unlike findings in Western industrialized societies, older children in the particular culture do not make more delay choices than do younger children. On the contrary, the older and more intelligent the aboriginal child, the more likely he/she is to select rewards that are immediately available (Bochner & David, 1968). That culture seems to be structured such that it encourages its members to choose immediate gratification when possible. Being nomadic people, the conservation of resources for later use would create a burden. Hence, the behavior which has evolved as being the most suited to this lifestyle seems to place emphasis upon the immediate consumption of resources. Clearly, the choice to delay is only valuable relative to the cultural demands placed upon the individual.

Even within Western societies, group differences may exist. For instance, there has been speculation that middle-class children are usually more instilled with a sense of the benefits of deferring gratification than are lower-class children. The underlying assumption is that, although gratification may be temporarily delayed, middle-class children have learned from experience that the rewards for postponing gratification will eventually be forthcoming. Lower-class children, on the other hand, may have learned that the eventual availability of delayed rewards is by no means certain. While such social class differences in delay choice behavior have been found, these differences are not necessarily resistant to change. Walls and Smith (1970), for example, constructed a series of experiences for lower-class children which were designed to raise their expectations that future rewards would be likely to be made available to them. These experiences led to a reduction in the difference in delay choice behavior between socially advantaged and socially disadvantaged children. Initially, children from lower-class homes may have been demonstrating a highly adaptive response to their life situations by opting more often for immediate gratification. When these children were convinced that this behavior was not always the most adaptive strategy, they appeared quite willing to defer gratification. It is clear that lower-class children might not typically choose to delay gratification as often as middle-class children. It is equally clear that these lower-class children can choose to delay gratification when they are convinced of the benefits of delay.

The Wise Choice. How do children themselves view delay choices? Nisan and Koriat (1977) presented children aged five and six years with the choice between small immediate and larger delayed rewards. The children were also asked to guess what choices a "smart" child and a "stupid" child would each make in the same situation. The children said that the "smart" child would be more likely to choose to delay while the "stupid" child would prefer immediate gratification. Interestingly, the children themselves stated fewer delay choices than they expected of the "smart" child. An incongruity certainly seems to exist between what children perceive as a wise choice and the choice that they themselves are able or willing to make.

Summary. Delay versus immediate choice behavior by children depends on a variety of interacting factors. The probability that future rewards will be available, the relative value of immediate and delayed rewards, the amount of time that must be endured before securing the deferred reward, and social pressure from others to make particular choices all contribute to the decision that a particular child makes when confronted with a self-imposed delay of gratification choice situation. In addition to these situational factors, some personal characteristics of the child seem to influence his/her decisions. The age, degree of successful socialization already achieved, level of cognitive maturity, culture, and social class are often important determinants of the child's choices in delay of gratification situations.

Patience: Waiting Behavior in Self-Imposed Delay

When a child states a preference for an immediate or delayed reward, this is but the first step in self-imposed delay of gratification. If the child chooses the immediate gratification, there is no second step since no further self-control is required. However, if the child chooses the deferred gratification, the child must then actually wait until the delayed reward becomes available. This maintenance of delay is a form of patience and is the second step in self-imposed delay of gratification. As previously noted, although some children are more likely to choose to delay through waiting period than are other children, any child's decision to wait or not does not necessarily predict his or her actual waiting behavior. A child who consistently decides to defer gratification may or may not be better able to wait for deferred outcomes than a child who consistently chooses immediate rewards or who is inconsistent in choices between immediate and delayed rewards. The ability and/or willingness to actually wait for deferred rewards is surprisingly independent of the ability or willingness to choose deferred rewards and, like delay choice, is affected by an array of situational and personal factors.

Early Research on Patience in Children. In the pioneering study of the influence of situational manipulations on delay maintenance behavior in children, Mischel and Ebbesen (1970) explored how variations in the waiting child's attentional activity might affect how long that child would wait for a delayed reward. Their method for measuring young children's delay maintenance behavior was as follows: Each child was asked to sit alone at a table and informed that if he or she successfully waited for the experimenter's return, a valuable reward would be given to him/her. The reward was a packet of a snack food. Each child was also given the opportunity to terminate the wait for the experimenter before he came back but the child understood that this would mean that he/she would then receive only one piece of the snack. The setting was not the same for all of the preschool children who participated in the study. Some of the children spent the time waiting for the experimenter with nothing on the table in front of them while other children waited with the reward available for them to see while waiting. This difference in setting significantly affected the amount of time children waited for the experimenter. Preschoolers waiting with the reward before them did not wait as long before terminating their delay as did preschoolers waiting without the reward available at the table. It seemed that when the children could see what they were waiting for but could not have it immediately, this made them more frustrated and made waiting more aversive to them. Mischel and Ebbesen wrote of those children in the experiment who successfully waited with the rewards present on the table as follows: "Instead of focusing prolonged attention on the objects for which they were waiting, they avoided looking at them. Some children covered their eyes with their hands, rested their heads on their arms, and found other similar techniques for averting their eyes from the reward objects. Many seemed to try to reduce the frustration of delay of reward by generating their own diversions: they talked to themselves, sang, invented games with their hands and feet, and even tried to fall asleep wile waiting -- as one child successfully did (p. 335)."

It appears that learning not to think about the delayed reward may be an important lesson in developing the ability to defer gratification. Yet the relationship between the presence of delayed rewards and the ability to wait for them is not quite so simple as at first seems the case. Mischel, Ebbesen, and Zeiss (1972) found that preschool children who were expressly told to distract themselves from the delayed reward, which was present for them to attend to, were able to wait longer for these rewards than were agemates not given the instruction to distract themselves. However, not all distracting thoughts were equally helpful in facilitating delay maintenance behavior. Children thinking about "fun things" were far more patient than were agemates who focused on "sad thoughts" while waiting. Further, even when deferred rewards were not physically present for the waiting child, if the child thought about the absent delayed reward, his/her patience was like that displayed by children who attended to delayed rewards physically present during the waiting period. Finally, even when the delayed reward is present for the waiting child, the way that the child thinks of that reward can influence the degree of patience that child will demonstrate. For example, when children imagine delayed candy rewards as pictures or as other nonconsumable objects (e.g., imagine marshmallows as round, white clouds), children can actually demonstrate a high tolerance for delay. On the other hand, thinking about the delayed rewards as real, consumable things usually lead children to terminate their delay maintenance after a relatively short period (Mischel & More, 1973; Moore, Mischel, & Zeiss, 1976). The way in which a delayed reward is thought of is sometimes more influential than whether that reward is physicaly present or not for the waiting child.

Recent Research on Patience in Children. While Mischel and his colleagues have used one type of waiting situation for assessing delay maintenance behavior in children, Toner and his colleagues have devised a somewhat different method to study patience in children. This method involves the child playing a game in which candy rewards accumulate throughout a waiting period. The child is told that one piece of candy will be placed on the table in front of him/her after every specified period of time (e.g., every thirty seconds) and that the experimenter will continue to put the candy on the table until the child takes the candy or tells the experimenter to stop. Once stopped, the game cannot be restarted. Thus, unlike the waiting task designed by Mischel, children in the studies conducted by Toner and his colleagues gain some benefit from waiting brief and intermediate periods of time. These children might not get all of the possible rewards but they can still get more than the minimum amount. While this technique certainly differs from the earlier one, the results from the studies in which it is featured are remarkably consistent with the results from the studies conducted by Mischel.

Self-Verbalization and Self-Control. Toner and Smith (1977), using the candy game technique, sought to determine whether what a child might say aloud during a test of patience might influence how much patience that child would demonstrate. Noting the success of self-verbalization techniques in altering other behavior in children (e.g., Meichenbaum & Goodman modified impulsive problem-solving behavior in children, 1971), the experimenters randomly assigned preschool girls to one of four treatment conditions for the study. While all girls would play the candy game under the same rules, each girl would be instructed to say one of four specific utterances while playing, each utterance corresponding to a treatment condition. Each girl was tested individually. Preschool girls who were instructed to speak of the goodness of waiting or to speak of something unrelated to the task at hand waited a longer time before terminating their delay. When left to their own devices, that is, when the preschoolers were not instructed to make any particular statements while waiting, these children did not wait very long before stopping the game. When first- and second-grade girls were tested in precisely the same way, a similar pattern of results was found with one notable exception. When these older girls were left to their own devices, they waited quite well. It appeared that preschool girls focused on the delayed rewards when not instructed to do otherwise while older girls spontaneously engaged in more distractive thought. This possibility was given credence in a followup study. Toner (1981) found that, when preschoolers were given a choice as to what to say during the candy game, two-thirds selected a statement focusing on the goodness of the delayed reward over a statement focusing on the goodness of waiting.

What children say while waiting clearly can influence how long they wait. Further, younger children can show just as much patience as older children when provided with strategies to help them distract themselves. When such help is not provided to these young children, they seem likely to employ a very inefficient strategy in trying to cope with the stress of the delay of gratification situation.

In an interesting extension of research on the effects of self-verbalization on self-control, Toner and Ritchie (in press) administered the task in which possession of accumulating candy rewards was made contingent upon the child's decision to stop any further accumulation. However, the children they tested could not overtly self-verbalize. Hearing-impaired children who did not have functional overt speech manually signed assigned statements when engaged in the test of delay maintenance behavior. The hearing-impaired children, who under instruction, periodically signed statements about the goodness of the delayed reward, waited longer before terminating the waiting period than did similar children who

signed other statements.   This finding was unlike that reported in other studies in which non-handicapped children   verba-
lized similar statements (e.g.,   Toner,   1981;   Toner, Lewis &
Gribble,   1979;   Toner & Smith,   1977).   Thus, caution must be
used   in predicting the reaction of hearing-handicapped   children   to   techniques   which   have been shown to   facilitate   or
impair self-control in non-handicapped children.

Labeling and Self-Control.   Often children behave in accordance   with the expectations of others.   Patience may be one   of
those   behaviors   which   is   especially   susceptible   to   such
demands.   Toner,   Moore   and   Emmons   (1980)   investigated   the
effect of being labeled by an adult as "patient" on children's
subsequent   delay maintenance behavior.   The   adult   informed
some   randomly   chosen   kindergarten,   first- and   second-grade
children that she believed that they were patient because   the
could   "wait for nice things when (they) can't get them   right
away."   This remark proved highly influential even though   it
was part of a longer discussion with the child.   Children who
heard   this remark about themselves consistently waited longer
before   ending   the candy game than did children who   did   not
hear the label.   In fact, not only did the children labeled as
patient wait significantly longer than unlabeled children when
the adult who labeled them monitored their performance as they
played the game,   labeled children waited longer when an adult
stranger   who knew nothing of the label monitored the   child's
performance on the game.   Most significantly, labeled children
waited   much longer than unlabeled children even when   playing
the   candy   game   in an unsupervised setting   where   a   machine
dispensed the candy rewards.

In   a   recent   followup   investigation   involving   Scottish
preschool   children,   Ritchie and Toner (in press) found   that
labels   can influence patience in children as young   as   three
years of age.   In addition,   these researchers found that the
power   of   a label given directly to the children could   overcome   any   bias an adult tester might have about the children.
The only children influenced by the expectations of adults who
tested   them   were the children not directly   told   beforehand
that they were patient children.

In another recent study,   Toner and Hagan (1983a) explored the
process   by   which labels about   children provided   to   adults
(but   not to the children themselves) achieves   its   outcomes.
Adults   were given information   about children whom they   were
to instruct.   These adults were then individually video taped
(while   alone) presenting rules for a task which would   assess
the   child's patience.   The information provided   beforehand
focused   on the age and on the patience or friendliness of   the
child   who   would view the tape.   Instructors told that   the
child   was patient were more likely to read the rules verbatim
than   were   instructors   given   the   task-irrelevant   label
(friendliness)   about   the child.   Further,   for   instructors
expecting a 5-year-old to view their tape, those told that the
child   was   patient took more time   initially   presenting   the
rules   than did those told nothing about the child's patience.

For instructors expecting a 10-year-old to view their tape,
those told that the child was patient took significantly less
time presenting the rules than did instructors told nothing
about the child's patience. The instructors' predictions of
their child's self-control were affected by the label. Instructors expected more patience in older children. In addition,
these predictions by the instructors were not related to any
particular behavior they demonstrated on the video tape.
Thus, information provided to adults about a child beforehand
influenced both their expectations and their performance when
interacting with the child.

In a followup investigation, Toner and Hagan (1983b) sought to
determine the influence of various instructional behaviors,
determined in part by labels concerning children's age and
patience, and of adult expectations on the subsequent reactions of children in a test of self-control. Both the ability
of the children to comprehend the content of the instruction
and the ability and/or willingness of instructed children to
display self-control on the task assessing their delay of
gratification behavior were measured. Older children instructed by adults expecting a patient viewer did indeed demonstrate a higher level of delay and, in general, older children
understood the rules more fully and waited longer than did
younger children. Surprisingly, it was also found that adult
expectations regarding children's behavior were more predictive of the children's rule comprehension than of the children's actual delay behavior.

Thus, children's self-control can be substantially altered by
either directly labeling them or by divulging a plausible
label to adults who interact with the children. While the
results presented here focus on self-regulatory behaviors in
young children, it appears likely that similar findings would
emerge if other childhood behaviors were studied as well.

A Child's Eye View of Patience. With all of the research
activity focusing on establishing the relative effectiveness
of different strategies on childhood self-imposed delay of
gratification, only quite recently have investigators turned
their attention toward the issue of the child's own developing
understanding of these processes. Harriet and Walter Mischel
(1983) systematically explored how well children understand
the strategies which best assist them in deferring gratification. They noted that: "Children begin to under-stand two
basic rules for effective delay of gratification by about the
end of their fifth year: cover rather than expose the rewards
and engage in task-oriented rather than in consummatory ideation while waiting." Further, just as Toner found that younger children prefer to speak of the delayed rewards while
waiting, Yates and Mischel (1979) demonstrated that preschoolers prefer to view the real rewards rather than pictures of
these items and thus they experienced great difficulty in
maintaining their delay. Children older than these preschoolers tended to prefer pictorial representations as if they had
learned to avoid placing themselves in circumstances of atten-

ding directly to items of great temptation. Mischel and Mischel also noted that four-year-olds tend to create "self-defeating dilemmas" for themselves by preferring to attend to delayed rewards while waiting for them. These findings once again support the notion that the low levels of patience often noted with younger children are not always due to an inability on the childrens's part to demonstrate self-control. Instead, these younger children seem more likely to use inefficient strategies in situations requiring patience compared to their older counterparts.

SUMMARY

Self-imposed delay of gratification is at once a simple and multi-determined phenomenon behavior. The ability or willingness to postpone immediate rewards for the sake of greater delayed rewards is best understood as having two phases which corresponds to a cognitive and a behavioral aspect. The cognitive component is most clearly shown in the statement of preference between immediate and delayed rewards. This statement is determined by a variety of considerations --both situational and personal. The second phase is patience or delay maintenance behavior. Once a decision to wait has been made, the individual is now faced with the prospect of following through on a course of action dictated by the delay choice. This phase of self-imposed delay of gratification is also influenced by a number of situational and personal factors. As in the case of delay decisions, these influential factors do not work independently but rather these factors interact. Thus, the prediction of a particular child's decision to delay or not and the prediction of whether that child will actually wait if the decision to delay is in fact made are most difficult predictions indeed. While absolute predictive accuracy is virtually impossible, nevertheless, psychologists do understand some of the factors involved in determining delay decisions and patience. In recent years, the resurgence of interest in this topic has led to a great deal of research effort and we have witnessed the development of a guiding theory of how and why children decide and behave as they do when confronted with one of the most common yet stressful dilemmas of their daily existence. To wait or not to wait, that is the question.

FOOTNOTE

The author gratefully acknowledges the assistance of Fiona Ritchie in the preparation of this chapter.

The Self in Anxiety, Stress and Depression
R. Schwarzer (Editor)
© Elsevier Science Publishers B.V. (North-Holland), 1984

SELF-FOCUSED ATTENTION AND THE DEVELOPMENT OF SELF- AND OTHER-SCHEMATA:
IMPLICATIONS FOR THE SELF IN DEPRESSION

Willem Claeys

Laboratory for Personality Research, Catholic University of Leuven, Belgium

In order to explore the structure and the content of the self-concept in depressed persons, several authors (Davis, 1979a; Kuiper and Derry, 1980, 1981, 1982; Derry and Kuiper, 1981; Kuiper, Derry and MacDonald, 1981; Eelen, 1981; Kuiper and MacDonald, 1982; De Loore, 1982; Ingram, Smith and Brehm, 1983) employed a modified version of the Craik and Tulving "depth-of-processing" paradigm (1975). In this procedure the subjects are asked to freely recall information (e.g., trait words) that has been previously presented under different orienting tasks. When the aim is to investigate the self-concept, one of the tasks, of course, is the self-reference task (e.g. Does the word describe you? Yes or no). The most frequently employed additional tasks are a semantic task (e.g. Is the word meaningful? Yes or no), a structural task (e.g. is the word written in capital letters? Yes or no) and a phonemic task (e.g. Does the word have a rhythmic sound? Yes or no). In some of the investigations different persons function as referents, e.g., the self, a familiar- other person, an unfamiliar - other person, "people in general", etc.

When in unselected samples of normal (nondepressed) subjects trait adjectives (or behavioral episodes) with nonpathological (nondepressed) content are used, it has been repeatedly found that the adjectives or sentences previously rated under the self-reference task, are better recalled than the adjectives or sentences previously rated under a semantic task, a structural task or a phonemic task (see e.g., Rogers, Kuiper and Kirker, 1977). This phenomenon is referred to as the "self-reference-effect" and has been interpreted by several authors (a.o., Rogers, Kuiper and Kirker, 1977; Rogers, 1981; Kuiper, 1981) as evidence for the assumption that, in normals, the cognitive representations of the self are structured as a well-organized schema, i.e., as an elaborated (rich), integrated (strong), differentiated and stable (enduring) cognitive structure.

When the subject-sample consists of clinical (severe) depressives the self-reference effect does not always appear. Davis (1979a) found that during the initial stage of clinical depression, the patients (with a mean Beck Depression Inven-

tory (B.D.I.) score of about 28) did not recall self-referent
information better than information presented under a semantic
task.   This finding led Davis to conclude that short-term
clinical depressives do not possess a stable and well-organized self-schema.   This conclusion has been corroborated by
Davis (1979b) and Davis and Unruh (1981) using the multitrial
free recall method in order to assess the "Subjective Organization" (S.O.) of self-descriptive trait-terms in short-term
clinical depressives.

The statement that short-term clinical depressives do not have
a well-organized and stable self-schema is at odds with Beck's
(1967) conviction that clinical depressives possess a stable,
negative self-concept.   Kuiper and Derry (1981), in an attempt
to reconcile Davis' findings with Beck's position, argue that
the failure to find a self-reference effect in short-term
clinical depressives is due to the fact that in Davis' study
only words with nonpathological (nondepressed) content were
presented during the trait-ascription task.   Starting from
their "content-specificity" hypothesis Kuiper and Derry expect that, when the new information consists of depressed
words so that these words are compatible (congruent) with the
negative contents of the self-schema, a self-reference effect
will also be found in short-term clinical depressives.   In
their study, clinical depressives (with a mean B.D.I. of about
22) did not show a self-reference effect, except for yes-rated
depressed words.   This finding is a partial confirmation of
their hypothesis.   More recently, however, it has been demonstrated (De Loore, 1982) that in clinical depressives(with a
mean B.D.I. of about 26) no self-reference effect was found
whatever the answer-category (yes or no) chosen during the
trait-ascription task and whatever the evaluative tone of the
trait words (positive or negative).

The question arises whether the findings with short-term
clinical depressives also hold for less pathological forms of
depression.   This question must be answered negatively in the
light of the results of recent studies.   In all studies
(Kuiper and Derry, 1982, experiment 1 and experiment 2; Kuiper
and MacDonald, 1982), except one (Kuiper and Derry, 1980), on
mild depressives (with a mean B.D.I. of 11 through 14),
enhanced recall of self-referent words was found for both
depressed and nondepressed contents.   In medium depressives
too (with a mean B.D.I. of about 20) a clear self-reference
effect (Kuiper and Derry, 1980) was found for both depressed
and nondepressed words.   Thus, unlike short-term clinical
depressives, mild and medium depressives seem to possess a
well-organized and stable self-schema with both negative and
positive contents.

It is puzzling why the absence of a well-organized self-schema
is only found in short-term clinical depressives and not in
long-term clinical depressives (Davis, 1979a, 1979b; Davis and
Unruh, 1981).   This variation of the strength of the self-
schema as a function of the duration of (clinical) depression,
proved to be unrelated to the severity (depth) of clinical

depression (Davis, 1979a, 1979b; Davis and Unruh, 1981). The first explanation Davis (1979a) offered for this phenomenon existed in the assumption that the reappearance of a well-organized self-schema was a consequence of "much experience in the misconstruing of reality to fit negative expectations (p. 101)". A very similar explanation has been given by Kuiper and Derry (1981) who state that "only after reconsolidation of the self-schema to accomodate to new depressed content, the prior efficiency of this cognitive structure would return (p. 277)." This explanation implies that the reorganized self-schema in long-term clinical depressives should consist of negative contents. However, since the increase of recall of self-referent information with duration of clinical depression is found for words with nondepressed content in Davis' study (1979a), this explanation is not very convincing.

More recently, Davis and Unruh (1981) proposed an alternative explanation for the reappearance of a well-organized self-schema in long-term clinical depressives. They argue that "it is possible that the strength of the self-schema, is, in part, mediated by the length of time an individual has been in psychotherapy, a process that fosters <u>self-reflection</u> (p. 132)." This alternative explanation does not require that the newly developed well-organized self-schema in long-term clinical depressives should consist of negative contents. Moreover, if this explanation is correct, one has to assume not only that enhanced self-reflection (induced by psychotherapy) results into the reappearance of a well-organized and stable self-schema in clinical depressives, but also that the absence of a well-organized self-schema in clinical depressives who do not have benefited yet from psychotherapy, is due to their lack of self-reflection.

The assumption that variation in the strength of the self-schema in clinical depressives reflects variation in the habit to be self-reflective, elicits the question whether there is any empirical evidence (reported in the literature outside the realm of psychopathology) indicating that self-reflection fosters the development of a stable and well-organized self-schema. As to this question, Markus (1977) has claimed that the crucial factor, fostering the development of an articulated self-schema in a parti cular behavioral domain, is the amount of attention the person has spent in the past to his/her own behavior in that domain. Markus writes that "self-schemata ... represent patterns of behavior that have been observed repeatedly ... If a person has not attended to his behavior in this domain, then it is unlikely that he will have developed an articulated self-schema (p. 64-65)." Buss (1980) reformulates Markus' statements in terms of "private self-consciousness" theory by claiming that "it is a reasonable guess that people high in private self-consciousness tend to have many self-schemata simply because they think about themselves so often ... Self-schemata are the cognitive structure of such thoughts that result from prolonged attention to the private aspects of oneself (p. 95)." The link between degree of private self-consciousness and the

existence of elaborated self-schemata has also been   made   by
Turner   (1978a;   1978b;   1978c;   1980) and by Franzoi (1983).
Unfortunately,   only one empirical study (Hull and Levy, 1979)
directly   bears   on   this   issue.   Hull   and   Levy   demonstrated,
with the Craik and Tulving incidental-recall methodology, that
people with high scores on the   "Private   Self-Consciousness
Scale" (Fenigstein, Scheier and Buss, 1975) recall significantly better trait words previously rated under a self-reference
task than do people with low scores on the scale.

HYPOTHESES

The   main   aim   of the present study is to   gather   additional
evidence   for   the   link   between   dispositional   self-focused
attention (as measured by the   Private   Self-Consciousness
Scale) and the strength and stability of the self-schema
(operationalized as the amount of   incidental recall of   trait
words   previously rated under a self-reference task during the
Craik and Tulving procedure).   Like Hull and Levy (1979),   we
expect   that   people   with high scores on   the   Private   Self-
Consciousness   Scale   (high-PSC   subjects),   as   compared   to
people with low scores on the same scale (low-PSC subjects),
will   have   an   enhanced   incidental   recall   of   self-referent
information.   In the light of Duval and Wicklund's assumption
(1972)   that the focus of attention is bipolar (i.e., either
focused on the self or focused on the environment), we also
expect   that   low-PSC   subjects,   as   compared   to   high-PSC
subjects,   will have a higher incidental recall of trait words
previously rated with respect to another person, especially a
person   the   subject   has frequently met in   the   past   (e.g.,
father, mother, best friend, etc.).   Thus we find a significat
disordinal interaction between degree of PSC (high versus low)
and   referents   (self   versus familiar-other   person)   on   the
incidental recall of trait words (our   first hypothesis).

As a second hypothesis, we expect the appearance of a significant   interaction between degree of PSC and degree   of   public
observ   ability of   the behaviors referred to   in   the   trait
terms.   This prediction is derived from the "content specificity" hypothesis formulated by Kuiper and Derry (1981,   1982).
These   authors state that enhanced incidental recall of   words
presented   under   a   self-reference task or under   an   other-
reference   task   during the Craik and Tulving procedure,   not
only depends on the degree of organization of the self schema
or   of   the   other-schema,   but   also   on   the   compatibility
(congruence) of the content of the new information (e.g.,
trait   words) with the contents of the self-schema   or   other-
schema.

The   distinction   we   make between trait words referring to
covert (lowly observable) behaviors and trait words   referring
to   overt   (highly observable) behaviors is important for   the
following two reasons.   First, the Private Self-Consciousness

Scale (Fenigstein, Scheier and Buss, 1975) is primarily a measure of dispositional attention to own covert behaviors (own feelings, motives and thought processes), since only a minority of the statements concerns the dispositional attention to the self in general (i.e., without specification of the kind of behaviors: covert or overt). Thus it can be assumed that not only the self-schema will be more developed in high-PSC subjects than in low-PSC subjects, but also that in high-PSC subjects the self-schema contains relatively more contents derived from previous observation of own overt behaviors, whereas in low-PSC subjects the self-schema contains relatively less contents referring to own covert behaviors than contents referring to own overt behaviors. Second, it is a matter of fact that the covert behaviors of other persons can only be known by the observer in an indirect way (e.g., by interpreting possible expressive movements, accompanying these covert behaviors, or through probably very rare verbal reports the familiar-other person gives about his/her covert behaviors). Thus it can be assumed that besides the fact that the (familiar) other-schema will be more developed in low-PSC subjects (supposed to have a high dispositional other-focused attention) than in high-PSC subjects, in both low-PSC subjects and high-PSC subjects the (familiar) other-schema will contain relatively less contents referring the other's covert behaviors than contents referring to the other's overt behaviors.

In line with the hypothesis that amount of incidental recall of new information (e.g., trait words) varies, in part, as a function of the compatibility (congruence) of this new information with the contents of the self-schema or of the (familiar) other-schema, we expect recall differences as represented in Figure 1.

Figure 1 indicates that not only a significant disordinal first-order interaction between degree of PSC and referents (self versus familiar-other person) is expected (hypothesis 1), but that also a significant first-order interaction between degree of PSC and degree of public observability of trait will be found (hypothesis 2). The latter interaction then would support the expectation that in low-PSC subjects highly observable traits will be better recalled than lowly observable traits, whatever the referent (self or the familiar-other person), whereas in high-PSC subjects the difference between recall of lowly observable traits and recall of highly observable traits (when the recall data for both referents are combined) is expected to be almost zero.

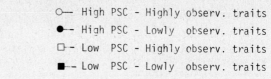

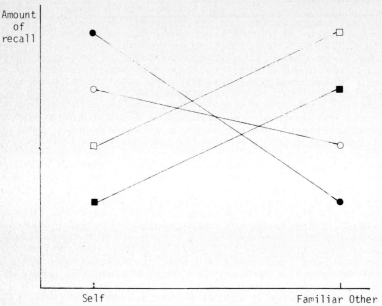

Figure 1

Expected incidental recall of trait words as a function of degree of PSC (high versus low), referents (self versus familiar other) and degree of public observability of traits (high versus low).

METHOD

Subjects. In order to test our hypotheses, 70 (male and female) Dutch-speaking first-year students at the Department of educational sciences of the University of Leuven (Belgium) served as subjects.

Material. Forty-eight trait adjectives (40 target adjectives, plus 4 recency and 4 primary buffers) were selected from a pool of about 400 trait adjectives generated by last-year high-school students during a free-format self-description task used in a previous study in our laboratory. The selected trait adjectives represent a broad range of possible characteristics.

One of the criteria used in selecting the 40 target words was to ensure that they represented, in an equal amount, the five main basic factorial personality dimensions, identified by Tupes and Christal (1961), starting from Cattell's "reduced personality sphere" (1957). The five dimensions are: friendliness, extraversion, emotional stability, conscientiousness, and culture. In addition, out of the 8 adjectives referring to a particular personality dimension, 4 were representative for one pole of this dimension, and 4 were representative for the other pole of the dimension.

Assessment of the public observability of the traits. A public observability index for each trait word was derived from observability ratings provided by another sample of University students. The public observability of the traits was assessed following the Kenrick and Stringfield (1980) procedure. Sixty seven University students were asked to rate the 48 trait adjectives for self-description on 7-point rating scales. Immediately after, these students had to indicate, for each trait adjective, on 7-point rating-scales, the degree to which their own position with respect to the trait could be derived from their publicly observable behaviors in the past. An "observability index" for each trait word was provided by averaging the observability ratings across the subjects. Using the medium split, half of the trait words were considered as referring to easily observable behaviors in the past. An "observability index" for each trait word was provided by averaging the observability ratings across the subjects. Using the medium split, half of the trait words were considered as referring to easily observable behaviors, and the other half of the trait words were considered as referring to lowly observable (private, covert) behaviors. Examples of easily observable traits are: active, orderly, brusque, nervous, and examples of lowly observable traits are: oversensitive, reliant, unconscientious and philosophical.

Assessment of the social desirability of the traits. Half of the adjectives refer to socially desirable characteristics, the other half to socially undesirable characteristics. The degree of social desirability of a trait was determined by 3 judges. A trait was considered as socially desirable or as socially undesirable when the 3 judges were in complete agreement. The social-desirability index of a trait word proved to be unrelated to its observability index.

The social desirability of the traits was controlled for, since divergent conclusions have been formulated in the literature concerning the impact of the evaluative positive tone of the new information on subsequent recall of this information, when the Craik and Tulving depth-of-processing paradigm is used with normal (nondepressed) subjects (Bower and Gilligan, 1979; Derry and Kuiper, 1981; Kuiper and Derry, 1982; De Loore, 1982).

Tasks. There were 4 rating tasks: "describes you ?", "describes your father ?" (a familiar-other person), "describes Martens?" (i.e. the Belgian prime minister, a less familiar other) and "describes the extravert ?" (a semantic task). The subjects were instructed that, during the semantic task, they were not allowed to think of a particular person they consider as highly extraverted, but to think of the abstract concept "extraversion". In the light of our hypotheses, it is not expected to find any difference between high-PSC subjects and low-PSC subjects as to the recall of words previously rated under a semantic task.

The subjects answered a question by encircling yes, no or depends-on-the situation. Nisbett, Caputo, Legant and Maracek (1973) found that the depends-answer category is more frequently chosen when describing the self than when describing other persons. The use of the same answer categories (yes, no and depends-on-the situation) in the present experiment was an attempt to replicate the Nisbett et al. findings. The subjects were told that "depends" signifies "sometimes yes and sometimes no", rather than "I don't know" (see Lord, 1980).

Procedure. Following the Craik and Tulving procedure (1975) adapted by Rogers, Kuiper and Kirker (1977) each subject had to judge each referent with respect to a series of adjectives. A numbered task list informed the subjects which of the 4 possible questions they were to answer for each trait adjective as it was shown. Each subject rated 12 adjectives under each task. Four task orders were generated to ensure that, over the 4 lists, each adjective was rated under each task.

The subjects participated in groups of 15 to 20. All subjects saw the same 48 trait adjectives projected as slides on a screen with order constant. Each of the 48 traits consisted of the following sequence. The subject heard first a tape-recorded neutral tone and, one second later, the tape-recorded voice of the experimenter pronouncing the number of the question the subject had to read on the task list. Three seconds later a trait adjective appeared on the screen for 8 seconds. When the projection stopped, the subject was allowed to answer the question on the task list by encircling yes, no or depends within a time limit of three seconds. Immediately after, the subject heard the neutral tone again, which announced the beginning of the second trial, etc.

After this rating task the subjects were asked to write down, in any order, the adjectives they had rated. Five minutes were allowed for recall.

Thereafter the subjects were asked to indicate on 7-point scales (with end points of (1) "not at all confident" and (7) "extremely confident") how confident they were in their answers during the rating task, separately for each of the 4 tasks. On other 7-point scales the subjects had to indicate how difficult it was to perform each of the 4 rating tasks. These confidence- and difficulty ratings were asked, since in the literature on the self-schema in depressives it is suggested that uncertainty in self-description is an indicator of a disorganized self-schema (Davis, 1979a). Note that these confidence- and difficulty ratings refer to each task as a whole, and not to each trait word separately (Kuiper and Rogers, 1979, 1979; Davis and Unruh, 1981; Ferguson, Rule and Carlson, 1983).

Finally the subject filled out the Dutch version of the Self-Consciousness Scale (Fenigstein, Scheier and Buss, 1975).

Data Analysis. The data were treated statistically by analysis of variance (ANOVA). In addition, several a posteriori multiple comparisons of means, using the q-statistic (Kirk, 1968) were performed. Rating data and recall data concerning the 8 (4 primacy and 4 recency) buffer items are omitted in the statistical analyses.

RESULTS

Trait ascription during the orienting tasks. The mean number of target words in the yes-, no- and depends-answer categories were 2.7, 2.8 and 4.5 in the self-reference task; 3.2., 4.3 and 2.5 in the father-reference task; 3.0, 4.2 and 2.8 in the Martens-reference task, and 2.8, 3.6 and 3.6 in the extravert-reference task. This result is clearly in line with the Nisbett et al. (1975) findings.

Confidence ratings and difficulty ratings. Two-way analyses of variance (with one within-subject variable: tasks; and one between-subject variable: Levels of PSC) were performed with the data on the confidence ratings and on the difficulty ratings (Table 1).

Table 1: Mean confidence ratings and mean difficulty ratings as a function of degree of tasks (referents) and private self-consciousness (PSC)

Tasks (referents)

	Self	Father	Martens	Extravert	All tasks

Confidence Ratings

PSC

| High(n=39) | 6.03 | 5.54 | 2.68 | 3.49 | 4.42 |
Low (n=31)	5.65	5.45	2.48	2.87	4.11
All Subject	5.84	5.53	2.60	3.21	

Difficulty Ratings

PSC

| High(n=39) | 2.05 | 2.31 | 5.15 | 4.69 | 3.55 |
Low (n=31)	2.09	2.29	5.45	5.03	3.77
All Subjects	2.17	2.30	5.24	4.85	

For each kind of data there is a significant main effect of tasks (referents) ($p < .001$). Aposteriori multiple comparisons of means, separately for the confidence ratings and the difficulty ratings, indicate that, except for the comparison of the self-reference task with the father-reference task, all means differ significantly from each other at $p < .05$ or better.

No significant main effect of PSC appears for difficulty ratings ($F(1,68) = 2.17$, $p = .146$) but does appear for the confidence ratings, ($F(1,68) = 4.76$, $p < .05$) with high-PSC subjects being more confident than low-PSC subjects in their rating of words, whatever the referent. There is no interaction effect at all between task and PSC on the difficulty ratings, ($F(3,204) < 1$) nor on the confidence ratings ($F(3,204) < 1$).

Recall data. Table 2 displays the recall of trait words as a function of tasks (referents), as a function of degree of PSC of observability of traits. A three-way analysis of variance (with 2 within-subject variables: task and observability of traits, and 1 between-subject variable: degree of PSC), reveals that there is no significant main effect of PSC $(F(1,68) < 1)$ and no significant main effect of observability of traits $(F(1,68) = 2.77, p = .101)$ but that there is a very strong main effect of tasks (referents) $(F(3,204) = 23.75, p$ significantly differ from each other at $p < .05$ or better. Thus not only recall of words rated under the self-reference and father-reference tasks is significantly higher than recall of words rated under the Martens-reference and extravert-reference tasks, but there is also better recall of self-referent words than of father-referent words $(p < .01)$ and better recall $(p < .05)$ of Martens-referent words than of extravert-referent words.

Table 2: Mean number of words recalled as a function of degree of PSC, of tasks (referents) and of degree of observability of traits

Tasks (referents)

	Self (1) (2)			Father (1) (2)			Martens (1) (2)			Extravert (1) (2)			All
PSC	H.O	L.O	Sum	H.O	L.O	Sum	H.O	L.O	Sum	H.O	L.O	Sum	words
High	1.6	1.7	3.3	1.2	1.2	2.4	.9	.9	1.8	.7	.7	1.4	8.9
Low	1.4	1.2	2.6	1.7	1.3	3.0	1.1	.9	2.0	.8	.7	1.5	9.1
All	1.5	1.4	3.0	1.4	1.2	2.7	1.0	.9	1.9	.8	.7	1.5	9.0

(1) H.O signifies highly observable traits

(2) L.O signifies lowly observable traits

Among the four possible interactions, only two of them are statistically significant, exactly those which are expected from our hypotheses. The resemblance of Figure 2 (representing the obtained results) with Figure 1 (representing the expected results) is striking.

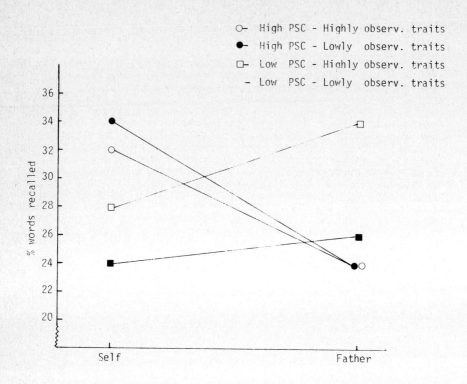

Figure 2

Incidental recall of trait words as a function of degree of
PSC (high versus low), referents (self versus father) and
degree of public observability of traits (high versus low).

As predicted (hypothesis 1), a strong interaction effect between PSC and tasks (referents), $(F(3,204) = 4,27, p < .01)$ is found. This interaction effect is primarily due to differences between high- and low-PSC subjects as to the recall of words rated with respect to the self and as to the recall of words rated with respect to father.

High-PSC subjects recall significantly better self-referent words than father-referent words $(t(38) = 4.99, p < .001)$, whereas low-PSC subjects recall significantly better father-referent words than self-referent words $(t(30) = 2.55, p 0.05)$. Figure 2 clearly illustrates the existence of a so-called "self-reference effect" in high-PSC subjects and of a "father-reference effect" in low-PSC subjects. Moreover, as predicted, high-PSC subjects recall better self-referent words than do low-PSC subjects $(t(58) = 2.05, p < .05)$, while low-PSC subjects recall better father-referent words than do high-PSC subjects $(t(68) = 1.83, p < .10)$.

Our second hypothesis is also confirmed, since a significant first-order interaction effect between PSC and observability of traits is found $(F(1,68) = 4.13, p < .05)$. This interaction is primarily due to the fact that in low-PSC subjects highly observable traits are better recalled than lowly observable traits, whatever the referent (especially for self and father), whereas in high-PSC subjects the recall of lowly observable traits is higher than the recall of highly observable traits for self-referent words. This implies that the difference in recall of self-referent words between high- and low-PSC subjects is particularly strong for lowly observable traits (respectively 34% and 24%), and the difference in recall of father-referent words between high- and low-PSC subjects is particularly strong for highly observable traits (respectively 24% and 34%).

An additional finding is that in both the high- and low-PSC subjects, whatever the referent, socially desirable words are better recalled than socially undesirable words. The total recall of socially desirable words and of socially undesirable words are, respectively, 1.53 and 1.46 for self; 1.47 and 1.22 for father; .99 and .91 for Martens and .88 and .70 for extravert. These results are clearly in favor of an interpretation in terms of the Pollyana principle (Matlin and Stang, 1978). In order to know whether the better overall recall of socially desirable words than of socially undesirable words is dependent on the answer category (yes, no or depends) chosen by the subject, a different analysis of the recall data was effectuated, existing in the calculation of "adjusted recall" scores.

Adjusted-recall scores. Adjusted-recall scores were obtained as follows. For each subject the number of recalled adjectives in each of the 12 cells of the design (4 referents x 3 answer categories) was divided by the frequency of his/her ratings in that cell, to form 12 proportions, i.e., recall scores adjusted for varying frequency across cells. When a subject assigned no adjectives to one of the cells during the rating task, the entry was fixed by reference to row and column effects (see Lord, 1980).

Comparison of the (adjusted) recall of yes-, no- and depends-rated words reveals that in both PSC groups, with respect to the self-referent task, yes-rated words are significantly better recalled than no-rated words and depends-rated words. The mean adjusted recall of trait words for yes-, no- and depends-rated words are respectively, .36, .25 and .26 for self; .26, .26 and .27 for father; .19, .19 and .18 for Martens and .15, .20 and .08 for extravert.

One might suggest that the superior recall of yes-rated words presented under the self-reference task supports a "self-enhancement" hypothesis. This explanation of the phenomenon can be discarded, since the superior recall of yes-rated words under the self-reference task is found for both socially desirable words and socially undesirable words. The mean adjusted recall of yes-, no- and depends-rated words under the self-reference task are respectively, .36, .29 and .23 for socially desirable words and .37, .22 and .30 for socially undesirable words.

CONCLUSIONS AND IMPLICATIONS

Focus of attention and the organization of self- and other-schemata. The reported disordinal interaction between degree of PSC (high versus low) and referents (self versus father) on recall of trait words is partly due to the fact that people who report, with the PSC scale, that they use to attend to own behaviors, have a significantly higher recall of self-referent information (trait words) than have people who report, with the same PSC scale, that they have paid little attention in the past toward their own behavior. Thus the Hull and Levy (1979) findings are replicated in the present study. Assuming that enhanced recall of self-referent trait words reflects the degree of stability and organization of the self-schema, this result is clearly in favor of the hypothesis that the strength of the self-schema increases as a functio of habitual self-reflection.

The just mentioned disordinal interaction also implies that low-PSC subjects, as compared to high-PSC subjects, show in enhanced recall of (familiar) other-referent information. This phenomenon has as yet never been demonstrated by other investigators, but is not surprising in the light of the assumption that the dispositional focus of attention is bipolar, i.e., either focused on the self or focused on the (predominantly social) environment. In other words, in low-PSC subjects, stable and well-organized other-schemata develop, especially when these other persons are familiar ones.

Since the recall differences as a function of referents are found following a "within-subject design", one might object that it is not allowed to offer separate explanations for the between-group difference in recall of self-referent information (in terms of strength of the self-schema) and for the between-group differences in recall of father-referent information (in terms of strength of the father-schema). This objection is legitimate if one can assume that the individual's total capacity to recall words is fixed, i.e., that hightened recall of words rated with respect to one referent necessarily results into lowered recall of words rated with respect to the other referent. However, the latter assumption is not supported by the results of studies on group differences in incidental recall, where, in addition to the self-reference task, a structural task and a phonemic task are given to the subjects. In those studies, between-group differences (between high- and low-PSC subjects in Hull and Levy's (1979) study; between depressives and normals in Davis (1979a) study and in De Loore's (1982) study) in recall of self-referent information are not accompanied by (opposite) group differences in recall of words rated under the other tasks. Anyway, it would be informative to check whether the present results replicate when, in each PSC group, one half of the subjects is submitted to the self-reference task and the other half to the father-reference task.

Evidence for the content-specificity hypothesis. The reported significant interaction between degree of PSC (high versus low) and degree of public observability of traits (high versus low) on the recall of trait words results from both the fact that in low-PSC subjects self-referent and father-referent trait words concerning covert behaviors are less well recalled than self-referent and father-referent trait words concerning overt behaviors, and the fact that, in high-PSC subjects, recall of self-referent trait words concerning covert behaviors is higher than the recall of self-referent trait words concerning overt behaviors. Thus it can be concluded that new information which is congruent with the content of the self-schema or the other-schema is better recalled than new information which is less congruent with these schemata. This result lends strong support to the content-specificity hypothesis formulated by Kuiper and Derry (1981). As to the recall of father-referent words in high-PSC subjects, highly observable trait words are not better recalled than lowly observable trait words. This is the only result which is not in line with the content-specificity hypothesis.

Self-focused attention and self-confidence. An unexpected finding in the present study is the significant main effect of degree of PSC on the confidence ratings, with high-PSC subjects being more confident than low-PSC subjects in rating trait words, whatever the referent. One possible explanation of this phenomenon is that degree of confidence in judging a referent reflects degree of organization (associative richness, strength and differentiation) of the memory contents concerning whatever referent. However, since the overall confidence in rating trait words does not result into a better overall recall of trait words, this explanation is not very convincing.

An alternative explanation of the phenomenon exists in accepting that the overall confidence in rating words reflects higher "clarity" of own mental contents (memories, attitudes and opinions) concerning whatever event, object or concept. The degree of clarity of own mental contents is supposed to be higher in high-PSC subjects than in low-PSC subjects (Buss, 1980). However, it can be assumed that clear mental contents are easily retrievable contents, and that newly encountered information (e.g, words presented in the Craik and Tulving incidental-recall procedure) will be subsequently retrievable to the extent that it becomes associated with existing easily retrievable contents of memory (Greenwald and Pratkanis, in press). The absence of any difference in the overall recall of trait words between low-PSC subjects and high-PSC subjects makes also this alternative explanation rather far-fetched.

Another alternative interpretation of the high confidence of high-PSC subjects, as compared to low-PSC subjects, in rating trait words, might be that it reflects degree of global esteem and, thus that high-PSC subjects are characterized by a higher global self-esteem than are low-PSC subjects.

Finally, it is possible that high-PSC subjects strongly "belief in traits", and that their higher confidence in rating trait words is a consequence of this belief.

Focus of attention and clinical depression. Davis and Unruh's (1981) assumption that in clinical depressives the absence of a stable and well-organized self-schema is due to their low degree of self-reflection is in accordance with our finding that normal (nondepressed) persons, who are characterized by low dispositional self-focused attention, have a poorly organized self-schema (operationalized as low incidental recall of self-referent information during the Craik and Tulving procedure).

The suggestion that clinical depressives (at least before any psychotherapeutic intervention) are characterized by a lack of self-reflection (i.e., a lack of self-focused attention) must sound revolutionary in the ears of clinicians who use to describe clinical depressives as "innerdirected" (e.g., Arieti, 1959; Arieti and Bemporad, 1980) and as characterized by "self-referential thoughts" (e.g., Beck et al., 1979). However, a more detailed analysis of the clinicians' description of the personality of clinical depressives teaches us that the notions "inner-directedness" and "self-referential thinking" must not be confounded with the notions "self-focused attention" or "self-reflection".

Arieti (1959, p. 434; 1980, p. 138) uses the term "innerdirected" to indicate that <u>clinical</u> depressives, before the onset of their illness, are very attentive to the expectation of (dominant) other persons and of the internalized authority figures (the Superego or Self-Ideal) with respect to themselves. Describing the personality of the person at risk for clinical depression, Arieti (1959) states that the "necessity to please others and to act in accordance with the principles that he has accepted, makes him unable really to get in touch with himself. He does not listen to his own wishes; he does not know what it means to be himself (p. 434). Arieti concludes that the clinical (severe) depressive, through psychotherapy, "must learn and relearn to ask himself what he wants, what he really wishes ... He must learn to listen to himself and to reduce the overpowering role of the Thou (1959, p. 450; 1980, p. 227)". In other words, the exaggerated attention to the expectation of others and of internalized others has made the clinical depressive unable to attend to his "real self". Psychotherapy, then, is expected to foster the patient's focus of attention on the real self.

Beck et al. (1979) have claimed that clinical depressives are characterized by "self-referential thought". By this expression it is meant that the clinical depressive gives "egocentric" interpretations of objectively neutral events. E.g., people talking in the distance may be seen as self-directed so that the patient's experience of the world is interpreted by thoughts of being thwarted, deprived and depreciated. It is evident that this morbid search for self-relevant information in the outer world can only be successful through hightened attention focused on the environment (and away from the self).

Since the results of the present study suggest that the absence of a well-organized self-schema cooccurs with the presence of well-organized other-schemata, one may wonder whether in clinical depressives too a poorly organized self-schema goes together with well-organized representation of the (erroneously interpreted) behaviors of other persons.

In order to answer this question, it is necessary to submit <u>short-term clinical</u> depressives to a modified Craik and Tulving procedure where, in addition to the self, also other persons (e.g., family members) function as referents during the trait-ascription task. Moreover, since the clinical depressive is described as very sensitive and reactive to the expectations and demands of the internalized authority figures (the Self-Ideal), it can be expected that he has developed well-organized representations of these demands. Therefore, it might be revealing to insert, in addition to the (real) self and other persons, the "ideal self" as a referent in the Craik and Tulving procedure.

NOTE

The author owes large debt of gratitude to Paul De Boeck, Martine Corijn, Wouter Van den Bosch, Bert De Cuyper and Kris Parmentier for their technical assistance and for their helpful comments.

The Self in Anxiety, Stress and Depression
R. Schwarzer (Editor)
© Elsevier Science Publishers B.V. (North-Holland), 1984

DEVELOPMENT OF SELF-RELATED COGNITIONS IN ADOLESCENTS

Rainer K. Silbereisen and Susanne Zank

Technical University of Berlin, Federal Republic of Germany

In the past, adolescence has been seen as a time of rapid, crisis-laden changes ("Sturm und Drang:" c.f. Muuss, 1975, and Wylie, 1979). This view has persisted despite the fact that adolescents only rarely report such crises (c.f. Coleman, 1978).

A closer inspection reveals that theoretical and methodological weaknesses in the verifying studies are responsible for the distorted picture: (1) the concept of change has not been sufficiently differentiated; (2) the research designs have not been satisfactory; and (3) the envisioned models of self-concept have not been adequate.

(1) Concept of Change. "Change" in developmental psychology is discussed in rather precise terms. The developmental function signifies change in mean values of age groups over time. Questions of qualitative change are subsumed under continuity/ discontinuity, usually depicted as similarity between factor structures at different points in time. Finally, quantitative change is considered under stability/instability. The changes in an individual's relative position over time are expressed in the degree of correlation among repeated measurements.

Studying about 2,000 3rd to 12th graders, Simmons, Rosenberg and Rosenberg (1973) found substantial group differences in several aspects of self concept. They interpreted these - incorrectly - as an indication of instability; at most, their cross-sectional data reflect the developmental function. Monge (1973) factor-analyzed extensive semantic differential scales on "My Characteristic Self" and compared the factor structures for grades 6, 9 and 12. From their close similarity, he deduced - inappropriately - continuity: the continuity of development is not defined with cross-sectional data; it is also liable to be confounded with stability.

Brunke and Hörmann (1984) studied more than 300 students between the ages of 15 and 21 twice at three-year intervals; competence self, emotional self and social self were differentiated. Unfortunately, the items were chosen for maximal

continuity over time, so that this question can not even be
raised.
(2) Research Designs. Only longitudinal designs permit discussion of all the aspects of development. This type of
study, however, is extremely rare. With regard to developmental functions, it may be assumed that an increase in self-
esteem occurs between adolescence and the early adult years:
In their longitudinal study, O'Malley and Bachman (1983) found
for example a yearly increment of 10% of the first measurement's standard deviation. This and two further studies
(McCarthy & Hoge, 1982; Center for Human Resource Research,
1981) represent the current state of findings on mean change
of self-concept development.

On stability, too, there are really only two substantial
studies: O'Malley and Bachmann (1983) again, and Dusek and
Flaherty (1981). In both studies, the stability coefficients
(retest correlations) were about .40 to .50, and lower at
larger intervals.

Dusek and Flaherty (1981) are the only authors to report
extensive findings on continuity/discontinuity of the self-
concept. They found predominantly continuity over three years
for school children in grades 5 through 10. In any case,
dramatic qualitative breakthroughs were not found.

(3) Aspects of Self Concept. Unfortunately, the half dozen
longitudinal studies are not actually comparable. One case is
concerned exclusively with self-esteem (various variants of
the Rosenberg-scale, as in O'Malley & Bachman, 1983), another
with semantic differential scales for "adjustment", "achieve-
ment/leadership", "congeniality/sociability" and "masculinity/
feminity" (Dusek & Flaherty, 1981) -- just to give examples of
the diversity.

Once comparability in self concept is assured, other problems
occur. The Brunke and Hörmann (1984) study might have been
compared with Dusek and Flaherty (1981), had the German
authors not limited themselves to the 'Gymnasium' (academic
high school) students, i.e., they did not sample from the
normal population.

The Problem. Investigating developmental function, continui-
ty/discontinuity and stability/instability of self concept in
German young people requires a random sample of the entire
population. This was possible as part of the Berlin Youth
Longitudinal Study (c.f. Silbereisen and Eyferth, in press), a
six-year longitudinal study of Berliners between 12 and 18
years old in which two cohorts are investigated according to a
sequential design. Only results from such a "normative-
prospective" sample may properly be compared with those of
O'Malley and Bachmann (1983) or Dusek and Flaherty (1981).

As regards the differentiation of the self concept, Filipp's
(1979) theoretical position provided the point of departure:
Self concepts are related to certain aspects of experience and

behavior. They are cognitive representations of the results of processing information about the self which has been gleaned from various interpersonal sources. Thus, in line with recent research in the psychology of memory (c.f. Flavell, 1981), "knowledge about one's self" may be seen as threefold: (a) knowledge of results, i.e., self concepts; (b) knowledge of precessing modalities affecting for example encoding or recall of information about the self, i.e., metacognitive experience concerning the self; and (c) knowledge concerning sources of self-relevant information such as one's father or boyfriend, i.e., metacognitive knowledge concerning the self.

The present research is a first attempt to study systematical- ly the development of these three aspects of self concept in young people. Some restrictions apply to the study as it presently stands:

The categories of knowledge about one's self are self-esteem, transgression proneness and social relationships. This selection (together with other categories not relevant here) is determined by the Berlin Youth Longitudinal Study's parti- cular concern to investigate the development of drug use and possible alternatives among young people (for the theoretical background c.f. Kaplan, 1980). The presently available data pertain to three school grades only, with retests after one year (grades 5/6, 8/9 and 9/10). Finally, for metacognitive knowledge concerning the self, only supplementary cross- sectional results are available.

METHOD

Questionnaire. The questionnaire consisted of three sections (a) self-concepts (= knowledge about products of self-related informatin processing) concerning personal future, trans- gression proneness and self-esteem; (b) self-related meta- cognitive experiences (knowledge about self-related informa- tion processing) concerning encoding, processing and recall; restricted to social relationships; (c) self-related metaco- gnitive knowledge about sources of self-related information. Sources are father, mother, same-sex friend and girl/boy- friend; content is related to self-esteem and transgression proneness (older sample only).

Self-Esteem, Transgression Proneness, Interpersonal Awareness. During the first wave of the Berlin Youth Longitudinal Study (Silbereisen and Eyferth, in press), the self concept questionnaire was administered to 810 Ss (average age 11.5 years) of a younger cohort as well as to 605 Ss (average age 14.5 years) of an older cohort; in all, to 1,415 people.

Means, item-total correlations, and stability coefficients were calculated for all self-concept and metacognitive experience scales (separate analyses for each of the two cohorts led to identical results. Because of inadequate psychometric quality some scales have not yet been included for the present study: all these scales were revised success- fully during the second wave (not to be reported here) of the Berlin Youth Longitudinal Study.

Ultimately, the three scales self-esteem, transgression, proneness and interpersonal awareness were chosen. Their psychometric criteria are shown in Table 1; (translated) item formulations are depicted as well.

With one exception (item 6), the magnitude of the item-total correlations is acceptable. The minimal length of the scales in mind (4 items only in each case), internal consistencies (alpha-coefficients) meet the requirements, too; .66 (self- esteem), .58 (transgression proneness), and .73 (interpersonal awareness).

The items were rated by the Ss using 4-point scales (never applies, coded as 0; usually doesn't apply, 1; usually applies, 2; always applies, 3).

Sources of Self-related Knowledge. Included in the question- naire were items where the S was asked how important/per- sonally relevant he/she would evaluate statements from mother, father, same-sex friend or girl/boyfriend such as, "How can you be so low" (self-esteem), or "You couldn't care less about what's allowed" (transgression proneness). The items were rated on four-point scales (totally unimportant, coded 0; usually not important, 1; usually important, 2; very impor- tant, 3).

Samples. For longitudinal analyses, a subgroup of 226 stu- dents was drawn from the entire group: (a) 86 students from grade 6 (formerly 5; five elementary school classes, attrition rate from first to second data gathering 18%); (b) 42 students from grade 9 (formerly 8; one "secondary modern"/junior high class and one comprehensive school class; attrition rate 28%); and (c) 98 students from grade 10 (formerly 9; 3 'Gymnasium' and three comprehensive school classes; attrition rate 26%). Attrition rates may be overestimated because data for some of the Ss have not yet been recorded.

For additional cross-sectional analyses, the data on 184 sixth and tenth graders (second wave of the Berlin Youth Longi- tudinal Study) were read; these files contained their ratings of sources of self-related knowledge.

Table 1

Content and Psychometric Criteria of Items
(n = 1,415)

Scale	Arithmetic Mean	Item-total Correlation
Self-esteem (alpha = .66)		
(1) I want to change myself in many ways	1.4	.45
(2) Sometimes I wish I were different	1.3	.51
(3) Sometimes I think I'm not worth very much	1.7	.43
(4) I'm satisfied with myself	1.9	.38
Transgression proneness (alpha = .59)		
(5) I can imagine that I might steal something sometime	.6	.41
(6) Sometimes I enjoy telling a lie	1.3	.23
(7) I often think adult rules and regulations are bad, and I don't always want to observe them	1.8	.36
(8) Sometimes I really feel like doing something forbidden	1.5	.44
Interpersonal awareness (alpha = .73)		
(9) I get curious when other people talk about me	2.0	.59
(10) I would like to know what my friends think about me	2.2	.54
(11) When my classmates are talking about me I pay attention and like to know what they're saying	2.1	.61
(12) I'm very interested in what my parents say about me	2.0	.36

Table 2

Factor Loadings for Self-esteem, Transgression Proneness, and Interpersonal Awareness, Differentiated by Grade and Year

	Factors											
	Self-esteem						Transgression Proneness						Interpersonal Awareness					
Class	5/6		8/9		9/10		5/6		8/9		9/10		5/6		8/9		9/10	
Year	82	83	82	83	82	83	82	83	82	83	82	83	82	83	82	83	82	83
Item																		
1	.74	.53	.77	.65	.65	.53												
2	.68	.75	.50	.65	.79	.74												
3	.32	.69	.53	.61	.54	.42												
4	.56	.68	.54	.55	.58	.52												
5							.50	.44	.50	.56	.53	.43						
6							.05	.50	.22	.23	.15	.24						
7							.55	.71	.40	.72	.48	.62						
8							.48	.72	.98	.76	.83	.85						
9													.07	.58	.65	.58	.69	.75
10													.53	.70	.70	.61	.37	.59
11													.83	.78	.81	.79	.73	.85
12													.74	.57	.75	.37	.24	.33

RESULTS

Continuity/Discontinuity. The 12 items on self-esteem, transgression proneness and interpersonal awareness were analyzed into principal components and Varimax-rotated -- separately for each wave. Guided by eigenvalue-diagrams, the analyses were terminated after extraction of three factors in each case. The portion of extracted variance equals 56% and 60% for the first and second wave, respectively of the youngest group; 57% and 57% for the intermediate, and 53% and 54% for the oldest group. The loadings are shown in Table 2.

For clarity's sake , all items theoretically not related to a certain scale were omitted. Anyway, only a few of these coefficients were substantial at all (The order of factors in Table 2 is not in each identical with the Varimax-solution). The most prominent quality of the loading matricess is their distinctness: A clear, simple-structured three-factor solution. Even self-esteem and interpersonal awareness are independent, although conventional wisdom associates them.

Furthermore, the loading patterns among grades (cross-sectional) as well as between waves (longitudinal) are so similar that continuity of self-concept changes (in the present realm) will be assumed for the steps to follow (more thorough analyses of the similarity of self-concept structures have to use procedures such as LISREL (c.f. Jöreskog & Sörbom, 1984).

Stability/Instability. Because of the highly similar loading patterns, retest correlations may be interpreted as stability coefficients. These coefficients are shown in Table 3. The calculations were done using the raw sums of all the items per scale.

Table 3

Stability Coefficients (Pearson Correlations)

| | Grade | | |
Self-concept	5/6	8/9	9/10
Self-esteem	.37	.42	.45
Transgression Proneness	.52	.56	.46
Interpersonal Awareness	.42	.23	.41

On the average, stability coefficients are .43. With one exception (interpersonal awareness in grades 8/9), differences between grades are not substantial. All coefficients are significant with p .01.

Differential change of self-concepts. With grade (only 5/6 and 9/10 because of otherwise too extreme differences in sample size), sex and year (1982 and 1983, i.e. longitudinal measurement), a multivariate analysis of variance (MANOVA) was calculated. Dependent variables were sum scores in self-esteem, transgression proneness and interpersonal awareness.

The main effect of sex as well as all interactions are not significant. Differences between grades, however, are significant ($F = 12.5$, p .001). As univariate F-tests show, this effect is due to self-esteem ($F = 23.5$, $p < .001$) as well as interpersonal awareness ($F = 11.4$, $p = .001$). Means for all significant main effects are summarized in Table 4.

Table 4

Self-concept Means Differentiated by Grades and Year

Grade	1982	1983	Average Rows
5/6			
Self-esteem	1.5	1.7	1.6
Transgression Proneness	1.3	1.2	1.2
Interpersonal Awareness	2.1	2.3	2.2
9/10			
Self-esteem	1.7	2.1	1.9
Transgression Proneness	1.3	1.3	1.3
Interpersonal Awareness	2.0	1.9	2.0
Average columns			
Self-esteem	1.6	1.9	
Transgression Proneness	1.3	1.2	
Interpersonal Awareness	2.0	2.1	

As is shown in the table, self-esteem is higher among the older cohort (1.6 vs. 1.9) whereas interpersonal awareness is lower (2.2 vs. 2.0).

The longitudinal comparison (main effect years) is significant as well (F = 5.05, p = .002). This effect, however, is due to the self-esteem scale only (F = 14,8, p < .001 in univariate testing). According to Table 4, self-esteem is higher after a one-year interval (on average 1.6 vs. 1.9).
Data from grades 8/9 were not included in the MANOVA. Nevertheless, respective means are included in Table 4 as well. As for self-esteem, the means follow the general trend of grades 5/6 (1.4 vs. 1.8 in 1982 and 1983, respectively); for interpersonal awareness, averages are similar to those for grades 9/10 (2.1 vs. 2.0). As in the other grades, there are no differences in transgression proneness.

Age-related differences in sources of one's self-concept. Data concerning sources of self-esteem were analyzed using a univariate analysis of variance with three factors:
grade (6 and 10, respectively), sex, and source (mother, father, same-sex friend, opposite-sex friend). For the older group only, 'sources of transgression proneness' were also analyzed (with sex and source as factors). The dependent variable is the importance/personal relevance ratings of the respective sources.

With self-esteem, the main effect of source is significant (F = 3.39, p = .018). Furthermore, two interaction effects are significant: source x grade (F = 4.94; p = .002) and source x sex (F = 13.22; p = .001). In Table 5 the respective means are summarized.

As shown in the table (column averages), mother/father are rated as more important by the younger adolescents (2.5/2.4 vs. 2.1/2.0); reversed for same-/opposite-sex friend (2.0/2.2 vs. 2.3/2.5). The source x sex interaction reveals differences in importance of same-sex vs. opposite-sex friend (row averages): among girls the boyfriend is less important than the same-sex friend (2.3 vs. 2.4); among boys, however, the opposite is true: the girlfriend is rated much more important than the same-sex friend (2.4 vs. 2.0).

Concerning transgression proneness, only the source x sex interaction is significant (F = 2.83; p = .04). The means in Table 5 show that this marginal significance stems mainly from a difference among boys: their same-sex friend is definitely a less important source for "ethical standards" than all the other interpersonal sources for boys and girls.

Table 5

Average Importance of Mother, Father, Same-sex and Opposite-sex Friend
as Source of Self-esteem and Transgression Proneness,
Differentiated by Grade and Sex

	Source											
	Mother			Father			Friend same sex			Friend opposite sex		
Sex of S	f	m	average	f	m	average	f	m	average	f	m	average
Self-esteem												
Grade 6	2.5	2.5	2.5	2.4	2.5	2.4	2.2	1.8	2.0	2.3	2.2	2.2
Grade 10	2.0	2.2	2.1	1.9	2.1	2.0	2.6	2.1	2.3	2.4	2.6	2.5
Average	2.3	2.3		2.2	2.3		2.4	2.0		2.3	2.4	
Transgression Proneness												
Grade 10	1.8	1.8	1.8	1.7	1.8	1.8	1.9	1.5	1.7	2.0	2.1	2.0

DISCUSSION

Longitudinal change is evident in self-esteem and in inter-personal awareness. The rise in self-esteem corresponds to O'Malley and Bachman's (1983) findings. It is not yet possible to say just how far this increase is in fact curvi-linear (c.f. cross-sectional comparisons 8/9 with 5/9 and 9/10). Since the age groups do not overlap, our results cannot be compared directly with Brunke and Hörman's (1984), either. Nevertheless, it now appears likely that the general decline in self concept (competence self, social self) they report is in fact specific to their sample: unlike O'Malley and Bachman (1983) and the present study, Brunke & Hörman (1984) have studied 'Gymnasium' students exclusively. Our older group included both comprehensive school and 'Gymnasium' students, and the younger groups are fully representative for the age population.

The decline in interpersonal awareness, too, conforms to the picture of increasing self-confidence: as adolescents grow older they become less interested in others' (parents' or classmates') opinion of them. It may also be that they are less likely to see themselves as central to others' thoughts. Elkind and Bower (1979) called this youthful egocentrism and report a decline with increasing age which conforms to our data.

Our stability coefficients fall within the expected range: O'Malley and Bachman (1983) found a one-year stability for self-esteem of about .50; Brunke and Hörman (1984) found about .59 (four-year interval); Dusek and Flaherty (1981) found .36 for grades 5/6 and .44 for grades 9/10 (averaged over four self-concept aspects). Our average of .43 is the more impressive considering the length of our scale: all the other studies mentioned have at least twice as may items per aspect of self concept as we do.

In view of the brevity of our scales, the consistency co-efficents .66, .58 and .73 (self-esteem, transgression prone-ness, interpersonal awareness) are satisfactory.

The fact that no change occurred on the transgression prone-ness scale is not surprising considering the fact that the Berlin Youth Longitudinal Study has realized random sampling. In contrast to findings in studies on selected (problem behavior) groups, norm infringements as revealed in our self ratings do not increase with age. The general population of young people is not characterized by "lax" moral attitudes.

The result that self-concept development is not only fairly stable but that its course is continous as well conforms to that of Dusek and Flaherty (1981).

Of course, it goes without saying that the intuitive comparison of factor analyses is still unsatisfactory. Taking the present factor patterns as evidence of

continuity is further justified by a comparison: Claar,
Boehnke & Silbereisen (1984) investigated the development
of motives for prosocial behavior among 12 to 18 year old
German and Polish young people.   The sample was comparable with that of the present study.   Quite unambi-
guous discontinuities were found.   These were obvious in
simple factor patterns as well as in LISREL models.

From another perspective, however, discontinuity was found.
Analysis of the sources of information about the self show
that young people age-typically perceive differences in the
significance of mother, father, same-sex or opposite-sex
friend for their self-esteem.   The general tendency of older
youths to attach more importance to peers in forming their
self-esteem is not surprising.   However, as the data on
transgression proneness show, there are also differences among
peers: the male friend would seem to have no "ethical"
significance to boys in this sense, quite in contrast to the
girlfriend.

NOTE

The research was supported by a grant from the Deutsche
Forschungsgemeinschaft (German Research Council) entitled
"Berliner Jugendlängsschnitt" (Si 296/1-1,2,3,4; Silbereisen
and Eyferth as principal investigators). We wish to thank
Karin Scherrinsky for her careful organization of the data
files and Hans Otremba for his help with the data analysis.
Our special thanks go to the youths and their parents who are
participating in the study. The senior author is responsible
for the present paper.

The Self in Anxiety, Stress and Depression
R. Schwarzer (Editor)
© Elsevier Science Publishers B.V. (North-Holland), 1984

REFERENCE GROUP, LEARNING ENVIRONMENT AND SELF-EVALUATIONS: A DYNAMIC MULTI-LEVEL ANALYSIS WITH LATENT VARIABLES

Matthias Jerusalem

Free University of Berlin, Federal Republic of Germany

The development and change of self-related cognitions and self-concept can be conceptualized within the framework of a transactional stress-model, as proposed by Lazarus & Launier (1978). In everyday-life we have to cope with a variety of situational demands, where subjective appraisals are made by evaluating one's personal resources with respect to environmental tasks. Self-related cognitions refer to subjective competences, that have been acquired by learning experiences and determine the appraisal process of a situation as being stressful or not. We experience stress, when the situational demands tax or exceed our subjective competences. Slight discrepancies challenge us, whereas larger discrepancies are experienced as threatening or even loss of control going together with a decrease in self-esteem. These cognitive processes turn into different kinds of cognitive, emotional and action oriented coping behaviors. Success or failure in the reduction of stress finally provides us with new experiences, that again influence the development and change of self-concept. On the other hand self-related cognitions - understood as structural elements of the self-concept - are responsible for cognitive appraisals and actions in future situations.

Such a transactional model makes it necessary to analyze the relationship between self-related cognitions and self-concept in more detail. There are interindividual differences in self-related cognitions concerning their influence, kind and process, which are not only determined by situational differences. There are also dispositional differences to take into account. These dispositions represent situation-specific cognitive structures based on learning experiences. They can also be understood as the momentary cristallization of self-related cognitions, that might be changed or reaffirmed in future situations. On the one hand the interrelation between concept and cognition can be considered as an inductive process of cristallization (development and change of the dispositional structure). On the other hand we can speak of a

deductive process insofar as there is an individual preference
for particular kinds and intensities of self-related
cognitions, that occur in specific situations with certain
probabilities. Taking this perspective of a "helical
interaction" has certain consequences for diagnosis: Neither
we should make disposition oriented assessments of concepts
only, nor we should just restrict to process oriented and
situation oriented assessments of cognitions. Both have to be
done in longitudinal analysis.

The same holds for the present study which is dealing with the
development and change of academic self-concept of school
children. Socialization in school takes place as a process of
person-environment transaction. The student tries more or less
hard to cope with academic demands within a social setting.
Self-evaluation is a cognitive process which determines the
way the child sees himself as a student. Academic self-concept
is an effect of socialization in an achievement-related
context. Everytime the student evaluates himself he delivers a
contribution to his academic self-concept which may be more or
less time stable and differentiated dependent upon the
personal history of success and failure in school (Burns,
1979, Epstein, 1979, Heckhausen, 1980, Schwarzer, 1981, Winne
& Marx, 1981).

With regard to the academic self-concept we have to
differentiate several levels of fluid transitions between
concept and cognition. The most general level can be
represented by a concept of ability in the sense of talent.
This could be constituted by a kind of average across
individual successes and failures in a variety of achievement-
related situations. Perceptions of ability that are more
situation-specific are describable as expectations to cope
with particular situational demands, that is expectations of
self-efficacy. The situational specifity is increased further,
if perceptions of personal competence are applied to concrete
school subjects. With an increasing specifity of self-related
cognitions a change in self-evaluation is more likely to
appear.

The transactional character of the individual self-evaluations
can be represented by the fact, that self-related cognitions
and situational aspects are always involved together in this
process. Thus, self-concept development in school should not
only be seen on the background of the subjective learning
history. Moreover, at the same time the daily learning
environment provides a further basis for self-evaluations of
academic performance with respect to teacher feedback and
social comparisons between peers: Situational factors which
contribute to these evaluations are the reference groups, the
rank position in the class, and the perception of the
classroom climate including the teacher's reference norm
(Schwarzer, 1983, Schwarzer & Jerusalem, 1983). In this
context self-awareness seems to be a personality disposition
which also has a considerable impact on self-concept
development: Both situational and personality factors have

proven to be important in the development of anxiety and helplessness (Schwarzer, Jerusalem & Schwarzer, 1983). In the following sections these different aspects are to be discussed in more detail.

SOCIAL COMPARISON PROCESSES AND REFERENCE GROUP EFFECTS

Judgments of performance quality must be anchored to some standard of reference. The teacher uses information provided by the perceived achievement distribution of the class at hand. The peers do the same. They compare an achievement product with all other products in class, because students within a class are rather similar to each other with respect to related attributes: Age, living circumstances, learning history, and every day experiences are shared in common. By this, evaluations and self-evaluations are based to a large degree on social comparison processes (Crano & Crano, this volume, Festinger, 1954, Levine, 1982, Suls & Miller, 1977, Suls & Mullen, 1982).

Social comparison processes lead to a self-evaluation that can result in positive or negative emotional states like pride or achievement anxiety. It has to be taken into consideration that information about oneself needs not focus upon social comparison but can also focus upon temporal comparisons (Albert, 1977) which uses information about the individual behavior across different occasions or time periods. A third reference norm is concerned with absolute standards of achievement as can be found in criterion-referenced testing. It is very unclear until now to what degree individual differences in preferring one of these reference norms exist. But it is rather clear that social comparison processes are predominant in achievement-related social environments like schools (Jerusalem & Schwarzer, 1982, Rogers, Smith & Coleman, 1978).

Social comparisons can be seen as limited by social contexts. In this sense academic self-concept is highly dependent on the choice of reference groups available in the perceived environment. For a student there are different reference groups at his disposal in the school environment. He can compare himself with others in his class, across some classes with all members of the school or across schools with his own age-group etc. There are many possibilities to select a certain number of similar individuals in order to establish a reference group for one's self-evaluation. But the freedom of choice is limited by the reality which confronts the student every day. He has to survive in that class to which he was assigned for a long-term period. This is the dominant social context for his daily experiences (Strang, Smith & Rogers, 1978).

Evaluations by teachers and peers take place which are
concerned with the achievement distribution in this limited
reference group. In consequence self-evaluations will be
dependent on the same context. Of course there will be also
other comparison processes with other reference norms or other
reference groups. These processes will take place in a
reflective mood when the student worries about his
achievement level and about his social significance. There
seems to be a rank order in the occurrence of comparison
processes which has social comparisons within classes on the
top followed by other comparisons in dependence on individual
differences between the students.

The social limitation of these cognitions has consequences for
the distribution of self-concept in the school environment.
Those students who are in the upper part of a reference group
should have a high academic self-concept and vice versa. From
the researcher's standpoint there are many groups with
different levels of achievement and prestige. The distribution
of self-concept is not equivalent to the distribution of
achievement and prestige. Instead one can sometimes find more
variation within the groups than between them. If we compare
a high achievement class with a low achievement class we will
find an overlap of the two distributions of self-concept
scores. So it is understandable that students of low ability
in good classes feel worse than students with high ability
in poor classes, even when there is a great difference in
achievement. Students with high achievement in poor classes
feel like "big fishes in a small pond" and students with low
achievement in good classes feel like "small fishes in a big
pond" (Davis, 1966). The former effect is called "relative
gratification" and the latter is called "relative
deprivation" (Pettigrew, 1967). These two effects are the main
subject of reference group theory.

There is some empirical evidence for this theory but it is not
sufficient until today to explain all differences in self-
concept. Especially the chain of cognitive events including
the perception of an achievement distribution and the self-
evaluation by social comparison processes is not proved.
Closely connected with this problem is the question of
causality: Do positive perceptions of ability improve on
performance (self-enhancement) or is it more likely that
learning successes and higher rank positions in class
determine the development of academic self-concept (skill-
development)?

Our own investigations within the German school system gave
some further support for the theory. In this school system
after primary school there are three levels of academic
education which can be chosen in view of ability and previous
achievement of the pupils: Secondary School (Hauptschule),
Middle School (Realschule) and Grammar School (Gymnasium). In
addition, at some places Comprehensive Schools (Gesamtschulen)
are established where all kinds of students are taken
together. For the students this is a transition from an

achievement-heterogeneous social context to an achievement-homogeneous social context. For some of them this means a dramatic change in social comparison processes. If they have been at the bottom of the former distribution they now find themselves together with other poor children from other schools in one class. Therefore the environment becomes less threatening. If they have been on the top of the former distribution they now are confronted with other bright children and more competition in school. In this way the school system provides reference groups and is partly responsible for the development of self-concept. Corresponding reference group effects could be demonstrated within a longitudinal study in high and low track schools (Schwarzer & Jerusalem, 1983). Entering a low track institution after having been mainstreamed for four years in primary school had for instance a positive impact on the self-concept of poor students.

This means that in the long run self-evaluations should become equivalent to the perceived rank within the new, limited frames of reference in secondary education. Students who rank below the median of their class worry about their competence and perceive test situations as threatening. Those above the median see themselves as superior and are more likely to appraise academic demands as challenging. But this effect is only valid if, first, social comparison processes dominate over temporal and criterial comparison processes. Second, the social comparison processes must be limited to the range of the actual class members, and third, the academic self-concept must be dependent on achievement-related cognitions in the school environment. If, for example, success and failure in school do not contribute to the self-evaluation because there are other involvements with greater subjective significance we cannot expect an influence on self-concept in school. But even when all these prerequisites are given, reference group effects alone are not able to predict all differences in academic self-concept. There are further subjective perceptions altering in dependence on a change in social context. Therefore we have to take into account perceptions of the learning environment with respect to their relative influence on self-evaluations, too.

SELF-AWARENESS AND LEARNING ENVIRONMENT

Cognitions related to certain aspects of the daily learning environment are assumed to contribute to the development of self-concept in school. From the student's point of view these cognitions represent subjective interpretations of situational social cues that can lead to a variety of further cognitions and emotions. It is of the utmost importance that these perceptions of class climate to a certain degree determine, whether achievement situations are appraised as a challenge, a threat or even a harm to one's self-esteem (Lange, 1982). If students perceive their classroom and their lessons as pressing, demanding, competitive and anonymous, then an increment in test anxiety and a corresponding decrease in academic self-concept are likely to occur. Later, when coping attempts have failed often, yet stronger self-doubts and even helplessnesss might take place. The teacher as an evaluating person represents another situational factor: Perceiving teacher feedback as norm-oriented and being compared with others is threatening. Perceiving feedback as individualized, however, is more supportive and encouriging.

Perceived achievement pressure means a cognitive appraisal of academic demands in school. Students interpret the lessons with respect to their own competences and coping abilities. Those who believe that a lot is demanded and that they have to work very hard to meet these standards, are perceiving achievement pressure. The accumulation of many tests in close distance to the next school reports as well as the uncertainty concerning the kind, difficulty, frequency and timing of exams represent aspects of this perception. The experience of achievement pressure should be accompanied by appraisals of threat and by feelings of anxiety that in the long run have a diminishing effect on self-esteem.

Perceived anonymity refers to the closenesss of social relationships and, as a consequence, to the amount of available social support (Quast & Schwarzer, this volume). It also can be characterized as perceived lack of orientation and social safety. The student has no friend to find recognition with and he doesn't know where he is belonging to. He is feeling superfluous in a bureaucratized learning factory and is not sure whom he can ask for advice and to have trust in. The environment seems to be a machine of rules, laws and automated routines without human relations. These children find themselves in a difficult and threatening situation, because they have to solve all problems with their own coping resources - a situation that can harm the subjective quality of school life to a large degree. At the same time this burden hinders the effectiveness of coping outcomes, achievement results and competence expectancies.

Achievement feedback is a further possibility to influence self-related cognitions of ability. Within this process the teachers mainly use two different comparison qualities to communicate their judgments: Social comparisons and intraindividual comparisons. Both represent different reference norms (Rheinberg, 1980). The social norm emphasizes interindividual differences of abilities. Individual progress and changes in achievement over time are less important. This feedback behavior stabilizes the rank distribution in class and is especially threatening for those who are not on the top of this distribution. Furthermore social comparisons between the students are enforced, that is social standards are a contribution to more competition, achievement pressure and anonymity, too. The feedback which refers to intraindividual changes in performance over time brings up a motivational advantage. In comparing students' achievements longitudinally with their former outcomes effort is more emphasized and success or failure are no longer judged in relation to others' performance only. Thus, learning situations are more likely to be appraised as challenging, and learning motivation is raised. As a result self-evaluations are raised, too. Therefore it makes a difference for self-evaluations, whether the children see themselves confronted with individual or with social standards of judgment (Ames, 1984).

One important point concerning all our previous considerations has to be added yet. Self-evaluations are always connected with self-awareness. So the focus of attention must shift to the self. This occurs usually when oneself is evaluated by others or when events occur which are not expected (Wicklund & Frey, 1980). In school those situations are created every day: Performances are evaluated and grades are sometimes not in line with expectations. Beyond these situational aspects there seem to be interindividual differences in the degree of self-awareness. This dispositional aspect can be understood as an individual characterization with respect to the frequency and intensity of actually occuring self-related cognitions. Children who focus their thoughts more often on the self are at the same time more likely to worry about their competence and to stress their own weak points. However, children who concentrate their thoughts more on task oriented topics should act effectively and evaluate themselves in a positive way. This means, a lack of self-bias is predicted to evoke better self-evaluations in academic settings and vice versa.

In the following these theoretical considerations shall be empirically reflected within a longitudinal study that is concerned with the change of academic self-concept over time. Self-evaluations, achievement, self-awareness and subjective perceptions of the learning environment enter into a structural analysis that is testet for correspondence with our theory.

METHOD

In September 1980 we began to follow-up a sample of 622 students who were first identified at the transition point between primary and secondary school: The longitudinal study covers the age range from ten to twelve, or the grade levels five and six. The data were collected in all four German types of school (see above). During two years five measurement points in time took place, three in grade five and two in grade six. Our central research questions can be summarized as follows: How stable is the academic self-concept that the children have already built up in primary school? Are there any reference group effects in such a way, that self-related cognitions change in dependence on the achievement distribution in secondary school? What is the causal relationship between achievement and self-concept? Are there debilitating effects on self-concept development by high degrees of self-awareness and negative perceptions of the new learning environment in the long run?

Measures. Using a multiple indicator approach there were three measures to assess the academic self-concept. The first is a German translation of the Rosenberg self-esteem scale consisting of eleven items (Rosenberg, 1979). The second measure is a self-concept of ability scale developed by Meyer (1972). This scale consists of ten items which are designed to focus on how the student sees himself as a learner in comparison to others. The third measure is a self-efficacy scale developed by ourselves with respect to the self-efficacy theory of Bandura (1977, 1980). The 13 items contain statements like "Regardless of what's coming, I'm usually able to do well on a test" or "If I work hard in school, everything works accordingly to plan". They are designed to assess the personal perception of contingencies between one's own action and a positive outcome. So this can be seen as a measure to assess the degree to which the student believes to have control over his learning environment.

The achievement was operationalized by the students' math grades that were asked for the last four points in time. The first of them refers to the grades in primary school which the children recalled retrospectively. This had to be done because the first relevant grades in secondary school were obtained somewhat later: The first school reports were given after the second measurement point. The end-of-year-report took place between measurement points three and four. The achievement-related rank position in class was determined by the relative standing of an individual within his reference group based on the math grade.

Self-awareness was measured by a scale containing private and public items (Fenigstein, Scheier & Buss, 1975, preliminary German form by Filipp, unpubl.). The perceived achievement pressure is measured by a scale containing twelve items like "In our class there is not enough time to work on all the tasks which are required". Perceptions of anonymity are assessed by seven items like "In our school it is hard to find real friends". The teacher's reference norm is measured by a scale consisting of ten items like "Our teacher also praises poor students when monitoring their individual progress". This scale is designed to assess the perception of an individualizing teacher behavior, that is for example, giving feedback from an intraindividual reference norm.

Analysis. We have specified a structural model according to the structural equation approach by Jöreskog (1977). Within this causal modeling each observed variable is used as an indication for a latent variable. The three academic self-concept measures for instance serve as indicators for the

latent variable "self" . Our structural model contains five
latent self-concept variables over time, as part of a causal
network of related variables. The self-concept at measurement
point one, achievement at point two, self-awareness, class
climate and teacher's reference norm represent independent
latent variables, all others are dependent ones. The analysis
of the model was performed by LISREL IV (Jöreskog & Sörbom,
1978), a program that combines confirmatory factor analysis
and path analysis and allows to test the goodness of fit. It
provides maximum likelihood estimates of the factor loadings
and of other free parameters. The procedure is designed to
test if the model fits the data. Information about the fit can
be obtained by three advices: First, a chi-square test of
goodness of fit is available which, unfortunately, is
dependent on sample size. Models that are based on large
samples are likely to be rejected. Second, a matrix of
residual coefficients is offered that represents the
difference between the observed correlation matrix and the
reproduced correlation matrix. Third, reliability coefficients
proposed by Tucker & Lewis (1973) and by Bentler (1980) can be
calculated which are good estimates of data fit.

RESULTS

In the final analysis 298 students with complete data
remained. The resulting coefficients of the measurement
models, that is the factoral loadings of the observed
variables on the corresponding latent variables are depicted
in Table 1. These coefficients are sufficiently high in degree
and in line with our expectations. Thus, the measurement model
is confirmed and the selected variables can be seen as valid
indicators of the hypothesized constructs.

The structural model including all other LISREL-estimates is
described in Figure 1. A significant chi-square value of 861
with 214 degrees of freedom implies a missing model fit. But
this result could be expected because of the sample size and
the complexity of the longitudinal network. However, the
coefficients of Bentler (delta=.76) and Tucker & Lewis (R=.77)
indicated a model fit that is satisfactory for
further interpretations of the structural path coefficients.

Looking at the last point in time, self-concept can be traced
back to several antecedents. It is mainly determined by
previous self-concept measures, that is, there is a
disposition that remains very stable over time. This
consistency over time can be seen by the auto path
coefficients between .67 and .89. These coefficients can be
understood as retest reliabilities at the construct level.
However, this stability is becoming weaker during grade six.
One of the co-determinants of self-concept is represented by
the learning environment variables. There is a direct effect

Table 1: Lambda Y-Matrix of factoral loadings
         (Standardized LISREL IV solution)

	SELF1	SELF2	SELF3	SELF4	SELF5	MATH2	MATH3
Esteem1	.73						
Ability1	.71						
Efficacy1	.56						
Esteeem2		.72					
Ability2		.86					
Efficacy2		.62					
Esteem3			.69				
Ability3			.85				
Efficacy3			.70				
Esteem4				.68			
Ability4				.81			
Efficacy4				.67			
Esteem5					.65		
Ability5					.77		
Efficacy5					.63		
Math2						.96	
Math3							.76

	MATH4	MATH5	AWARE	CLIMATE	REF.- NORM
Math4	.71				
Math5		.86			
Self-Awareness			.54		
Pressure				.68	
Anonymity				.93	
Ref.- Norm					.62

of school climate (-.17) and of teacher's reference norm(.33). In view of the fact that the indirect effects are -.17 and .09 respectively, the total effects sum up to -.34 for class climate and to .42 for teacher's reference norm. According to theoretical considerations both aspects are highly connected (-.51). The perception of achievement pressure and anonymity impairs the self-concept, whereas the perception of individualized evaluations by the teacher improves it. Within this context the reference norm seems to be the more important perception of the learning environment with respect to its influence on academic self-concept.

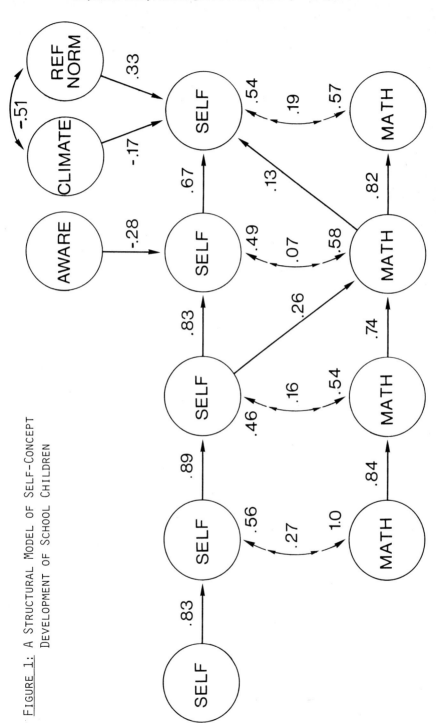

FIGURE 1: A STRUCTURAL MODEL OF SELF-CONCEPT DEVELOPMENT OF SCHOOL CHILDREN

Self-awareness can be regarded as a further impact on the
stability of self-concept development. There is a direct
effect on the fourth measurement point in time (-.28) and an
indirect effect on the last one (-.19). The higher the self-
awareness, the lower the self-concept. This may be related to
the hypothesis that self-rumination and self-monitoring
distracts from coping behavior, whereas action orientation or
task-related cognitions serve to prevent helplessness and
maintain a satisfactory self-concept.

The results concerning the influences of the reference groups
and the causal relationship between achievement and self-
concept are a little bit more complicated to demonstrate. This
is because of the dominance of indirect path coefficients and
the timing of school grades in secondary school. At
measurement point two the students still referred to their
math grades in primary school. The indirect effects on self-
concept at point three (.37) do not yet reflect the influences
of the new achievement environment. But looking at point four
and five there exists an increasing impact of the new
achievement distributions from .19 to .37 on the self concept.
Especially interesting is the increase in importance of math
grades after point four that is additionally demonstrated by
the direct effect of .13. At this time the end-of-year-reports
just had taken place. This event can be considered as the
first relevant and officially documented feedback of relative
standing of each student within his new class. Correspondingly
the stability of math achievement increases from point four to
point five (.84). By these coefficients the stronger impact of
the student's stabilized rank position in class on his self-
evaluations is demonstrated. This is in line with reference
group theory. On the other hand we have to regard the opposite
direction, too. The math grade in the end-of-year-report is
influenced by the self-concept at the former point to a large
degree (.44). This means, achievement can also be seen as
dependent on previous self-concept scores. Later on this
influence is decreasing again. From point four to point five
it amounts to .24. As a result, before point four self-concept
seems to dominate the individual rank positions, after point
four the opposite causal relationship is favoured by the
model. But these facts are not contradictory. They can be
brought in line with our theoretical considerations. Skills
and social ranks are usually seen as strong predictors. On the
other hand, self-enhancement leads to skill-development, and
in turn to better self-evaluations. In other words, with
regard to these data primary school grades predominate self-
concept values that determine the achievement in secondary
school. The new rank distributions are again precursors of the
future self-concept development. This complicated reciprocal
causal relationhip cannot be completely untangled by our study
because we did not focus on micro-processes in the person-
environment transaction. All the above mentioned variables
together explain 71% of the self-concept variance at the last
point in time.

CONCLUSIONS

It can be concluded that subjectively different socialization conditions in secondary school have a strong impact on the stability of childrens' academic self-concepts. The self-concept is determined by 'itself' to a large degree, that is by self-related cognitions established as a result of all previous experiences in achievement-related contexts (Shavelson & Marsh 1984).

But in the long run changes in self-evaluations can be observed. On the one hand a rearranged achievement distribution within the new reference group has as its consequence that former self-evaluations have to be revised in adaptation to the new reality. Beyond these reference group effects the causal relationship between achievement and self-concept seems to be of a transactional character. Neither skill-development nor self-enhancement approaches alone can be favored. To clear this point we have to investigate the micro-processes in the person-environment transaction in more detail (Covington, 1984).

On the other hand self-evaluations are impaired with an increasing strength of self-awareness. Moreover, the perceived learning environment produces changes in self-concept, too. In case of perceiving a personal atmosphere in class without excessive demands combined with an individualizing teacher behavior, these changes are positive. Social feedback and a subjectively threatening class climate are more negative determinants of self-concept development (Levine & Moreland, 1984).

In this sample the critical changes in self-concept development were demonstrated to appear at the beginning of grade six in secondary school. From the students' point of view at this time the new learning environments and social rank positions have become stable. In consequence the self-evaluations adapt themselves to these new circumstances. By this the socialization process reflecting the transition from primary to secondary school reference groups is finished for the time being. Further research has to continue the ongoing socialization process during the following grades in school.

NOTE

The research reported herein was supported by a grant from Volkswagen Foundation to Ralf Schwarzer, Freie Universität Berlin.

The Self in Anxiety, Stress and Depression
R. Schwarzer (Editor)
© Elsevier Science Publishers B.V. (North-Holland), 1984

EMOTIONAL FEEDBACK ON ACHIEVEMENT AND THE PERCEPTION OF OWN ABILITY

Ruth Rustemeyer

University of Paderborn, Paderborn, Federal Republic of Germany

Under certain conditions, emotions displayed during social interaction can be very revealing to the receiver. In a conversation, for example, the person one is talking to may smile approvingly, or frown disagreeably, thus clearly indicating his attitude toward the topic of conversation. We use the emotional feedback by others as a cue to make inferences about others, and about ourselves as well. At the same time, we consciously employ the expression of emotions as a means of attaining certain goals. An individual often knows, or assumes that he knows, what kind of inferences an observer will make from his behaviour. Imagine, e.g., that a poor student has failed a test again, and that the teacher intends to encourage him and to reinforce his self-confidence by expressing the emotion of pity towards him. Moreover, the teacher praises the student extensively upon completion of a very simple task in order to provide him with a feeling of success. But will this teacher actually succeed in strengthening the student's self-esteem, or will he perhaps accomplish just the opposite of what he intended to do ?

Weiner (Weiner, Russell, & Lerman, 1978, 1979; Weiner, 1980) has demonstrated that there is obviously a close relationship between certain emotions and attributional processes. In the context of achievement, for example, the expression of pity is closely associated with the attribution of lack of ability, while anger is linked to lack of effort. The perceived controllability of events plays a decisive role in determining which emotions are exhibited. In a study by Weiner, Graham, & Chandler (1982), subjects imagined that they were playing the role of a teacher whose student has just failed. Eight different causes for the student's failure were manipulated, and the subjects indicated how strongly that teacher would experience pity and/or anger towards the student in each particular case. Anger was felt most strongly when the assumed cause was perceived to be controllable (e.g., lack of effort), whereas pity was indicated when the cause was seen as being uncontrollable (e.g., lack of ability). In a second study, the same authors had children and adolescents recall events from their lives in which they had experienced pity or anger towards others; the association between these two emotions and controllability was clearly confirmed. Whereas uncontrollable situations, such as injuries resulting from an accident or the loss of a loved-one, produced pity, anger occurred as a result of physical aggression or rejection. This connection between emotions and attributions can be detected very early in children and adolescents.

It may be assumed, then, that the inferred causes of an event determine the corresponding emotional reactions, the idea behind which is that we feel like we think. Cognitively oriented psychotherapies, like the Rational-Emotive-Therapy (Ellis & Grieger, 1977) are based on that assumption. An important premise of Ellis's can be traced back to the Stoic philosopher Epiktet (60 B.C.): people are not bothered by things per se, but by the way in which they perceive these things.

If certain emotions like pity or anger are reactions to specific attributions such as lack of ability or lack of effort, then the perception of other's emotions could provide a clue to the thoughts that preceded them. If, for example, a student sees that the teacher shows pity following his failure or surprise following his success then he concludes that the teacher thinks he has low ability. Weiner and coworkers have shown in several studies (Weiner, 1980; Weiner, Graham, Stern, & Lawson, 1982) that the emotions conveyed to a receiver have attributional consequences. They described the following situation to subjects: "A student failed a test, and the teacher became angry. Why did the teacher think the student failed ?" Weiner and coworkers manipulated various emotional responses of the teacher. The subjects were then supposed to indicate to what degree the teacher attributed the student's failure to certain causal factors such as lack of effort, low ability, bad luck, etc. Anger, pity and surprise, along with other emotions, were used in the emotional feedback. The results show that emotions are used to make inferences about causal factors. Table 1 summarizes the most important results of the study.

If a teacher exhibits anger when a student fails, the latter may infer that the teacher is indicating that he did not work hard enough. If, on the other hand, the teacher shows pity, he should consider lack of ability to be the dominant cause of this outcome. Weiner (1980) has shown that bad luck is linked to surprise, whereas Weiner, Graham, Stern & Lawson (1982) found a distinctive relationship between lack of effort and surprise, although both experiments were almost identical in design and procedures. The reported link between surprise and lack of effort is easily explained. Surprise following failure may indicate that the teacher actually expected a much better performance from this student. Surprise, then, may cause the student to conclude that the teacher thinks he has sufficient ability in order to be successful if he only tried hard enough. Weiner's emotion-attribution link between surprise and chance can only refer to a successful performance, (Weiner collected the data using an unsuccessful performance). Surprise following success may indicate to the student that the teacher attributes his good performance to luck rather than ability.

Table 1

Relations Between Teacher's Emotional Reactions and Inferred
Dominant Causes

Teacher's Emotional Reaction	Inferred Dominant Cause
Anger	Insufficient Effort
Pity	Low Ability
Guilt	Teacher/Task
Surprise	Bad Luck (Insufficient Effort)
Sadness	Low Ability

Note: 1) The table is adopted from Weiner (1980).
      2) The relationship enclosed in parentheses has been
         taken from Weiner, Graham, Stern, & Lawson (1982).

Another question with regard to Weiner's study is whether or
not the teacher's assessment as perceived or inferred by the
student via emotional feedback can have an effect on the
latter's self-perception. According to Weiner's results,
emotions are used by a person as cues to draw conclusions
about how he perceived by another individual. What we do not
know, however, is whether the receiver actually uses the
emotional feedback to make inferences about himself.

There are indications that an individual's self-concept is
influenced by the behavior of significant persons with whom he
is interacting. According to Cooley's (1902) Looking-Glass-
Theory, the individual's self is reflected, like in a mirror,
by the remarks, thoughts, actions, etc. of others. The image
the individual assumes other have of him is extremely important to his own self-image. An individual not only reacts to
his actions of others, but he also interprets and ascribes
meaning to them.

The way in which emotional feedback may affect an individual's
self-perception can be illustrated by a model of Meyer (1982).
Employing five different steps, Meyer shows how ability
attributions may be conveyed in a subtle way during interaction, and how they may impinge on an individual's perception
of his ability. This model can be adopted (and somewhat
expanded) to clarify the various attributional and inference
processes.

R. Rustemeyer

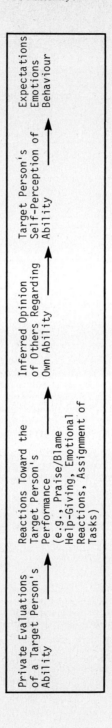

Figure 1. Inferential process and self-perception of ability.

Note. The Figure is adopted from Meyer (1982, 1983).

1. The actor (e.g., the teacher) possesses an idea of an individual's (e.g., the student's) ability. The teacher thus attributes the student's actual performance to certain causal factors according to his evaluation of the student's ability, whether he estimates it to be high or low.

2. If the teacher estimates the student's ability to be rather low, he shows pity when the student fails and surprise when he is successful. If, however, he regards the student's level of ablity to be quite high, he will probably exhibit a neutral reaction following success, whereas anger will be the dominant emotion following failure; Weiner's findings (Weiner, Graham, & Chandler, 1982; Weiner, Graham, Stern, & Lawson, 1982) have proved this latter assumption to be correct.

In addition, we assume that there is a connection between surprise and lack of effort following success.

3. The target person perceives and then employs these emotions. I.e. the student concludes that the teacher obvious-ly attributes his performance to certain causal factors, and he starts to make inferences about how the teacher estimates his ability.

4. The student's inferred opinion of the teacher's evaluation of his ability may influence his self-perception. Graham & Weiner (1983) assume that the student will employ emotional feedback to assess his own ability especially if other attri-butional processes regarding his performance lead to ambiguous results.

5. The perception of one's own ability will be of signifi-cance to the target person's expectations, emotions and behaviour.

Point 2 of Meyer's model deals with various reactions toward a target person's performance. Part of these may be of an emotional nature, and this information, Meyer assumes, is used and processed by the target person for inferential purposes. Meyer and coworkers have shown this with respect to praise and blame (Meyer, Bachmann, Biermann, Hempelmann, Plöger , & Spiller, 1979; Meyer & Plöger, 1979) to aid (Conty, 1980) and to task assignment (Krüger, Möller & Meyer, 1983). Thus, praise following success and aid following the assignment of a simple task may provide the student with the information that his ability is estimated to be low. On the other hand, blame following failure, lack of aid, and the assignment of difficult estimated to be high.

In this study we will examine whether or not emotional feed-back following success and failure actually serves as a cue for the perception of one's own ability. The teacher's emotional feedback will be manipulated as an independent variable, whereas the student's inferences regarding the teacher's evaluation of his (the student's) ability are the main dependent variables. Moreover, whether or not the student's evaluation of his own ability is indeed affected by the teacher's emotional feedback, and whether or not this again modifies the student's expectancy of future success, will be within the scope of the study. In particular, the focus will be on the two questions that follow:

1. In what situations do people actually establish connections between the teacher's emotional feedback and his attributions ?

If the teacher is seen as having valid information regarding the student's general level of ability, his emotional reactions shoud be perceived as resulting from a comparison of the student's actual performance with this information. If, however, the teacher obviously knows nothing about the individual's level of ability, his emotional reactions can easily be attributed to some special disposition of himself, and as such they should not be used as cues to make inferences about underlying attributional processes.

2. Does the teacher's emotional feedback affect the subject's self-perception ?

If the subject is convinced that the teacher is informed of his level of ability and that the teacher conveys this in his emotional feedback, we can expect that following feedback the subject will make attributions about the evaluation of his own ability, and that this has an effect on his self-perception.

METHOD

Overview of the study. The experiment was presented to the subjects as a study of teacher-student interaction. A naive subject and a confederate of the experimenter participated. The naive subject was appointed the role of student, and the confederate the role of teacher. At first the student completed a test, which the teacher pretended to mark, supposedly in order to get an idea of the pupil's ability. In a second experimental condition there was no test-evaluation.

Then the naive subjects were assigned two more tasks of the same type as before. The first was declared as correctly solved by the teacher, whereas he termed the student's result in the second task as incorrect, i.a., failure. Moreover, after every examination of the student's work, the teacher communicated an emotional reaction to him. In one condition, this was "satisfaction" after success and "anger" after failure, in the other condition he showed "surprise" following success and "pity" following failure.

Independent variables. There were two independent variables:

1. evaluation of the initial test (with or without test evalu-
   tion)

2. the teacher's emotional feedback for success and failure, respectively (satisfaction/anger or surprise/pity).

In this 2 x 2 design, 10 subjects participated in every experimental condition.

Dependent variables. The following dependent variables were measured: personal test-performance in comparison to other students, evaluation of one's own test-performance in general, confidence of success with regards to test-tasks to be carried out and the presumed attributions of the teacher.

Subjects. Subjects were 40 male adult university students: the age range was 21 to 35. The subjects were individually approached on the university campus and asked to participate in a short experiment on teacher-student interactions. They received no payment for participation. Psychology students did not take part in the study.

Procedure. The subjects were conducted into a room where both the male experimenter and a second male subject (a confederate of the experimenter) were waiting. Both subjects were informed that the experiment was dealing with the effects of a teacher's emotional reaction to a student's performance, and how these are perceived by a student. Supposedly by chance, the subjects were allocated the roles of student and teacher respectively. In fact, the naive subjects were always allocated the role of student.

At first the student completed a test which allegedly measured certain aspects of visual perception. The 12 test items were taken from Kagan's Matching Familiar Figures test. The subjects were shown a series of slides each displaying a standard figure (e.g., house) and six alternatives, five of which were slightly different from the standard. The one identical figure had to be found, and the corresponding letter (A-F) had to be marked on the answer sheet. 10 seconds were allowed for each test item.

In the condition "without test evaluation" the experimenter put the student's answer sheet on his table without further looking at it. In the condition "with test evaluation" the experimenter handed the answer sheet to the teacher and advised him to mark the test. For this the teacher used a scoring stencil which was at his disposal. Also, the experimenter asked the teacher to develop an idea of the student's general ability for a task of this kind, and to keep this in mind. For this the teacher used a "record table" in front of him.

The following procedure was identical in both the "with" and "without test evaluation" conditions. The student carried out two more tasks which were similar to the test items, and which were said to be quite easy. After every solution the teacher displayed an emotional reaction. He had 8 cards at his disposal with one of the following emotions printed on them:

satisfaction, pity, anger, surprise, disappointment, happiness, sadness and relief. By holding up a card the teacher communicated the corresponding emotional reaction. In all experimental conditions, the student was given success feedback after the first task, and failure feedback after the second. In one condition the teacher displayed satisfaction after success and anger after failure, while in the other condition the student was shown "surprise" following success and "pity" following failure.

The students then filled out a questionnaire. Two questions dealt with the perception of personal abilities, one of a rather general kind ("How do you estimate your ability for tasks like these?"), and the other implying social comparison ("How do you think you have done in this task compared to other students of your age?). Both questions were answered on a 7-point-scale ranging from "very low (1) to "very high" (7).

In the next question the subject was asked to assess his individual probability of success in the future: ("We shall soon ask you to solve several problems of a very similar kind like before, and of a wide range of difficulty. Please indicate how likely you think it is that you will successfully solve the respective problem. Task A (B, C, D, E) is mastered by approximately 20 (30, 50, 70, 90) percent of students of your age.") Indications were required on a 7-point-scale which ranged from "I'll never manage it" (1) to "I'll most certainly manage it" (7).

Another question dealt with a fictitious teacher who was about to allot another problem to this particular student in accordance with his estimated standard of ability: (Good teachers try to assign students tasks in correspondence with their respective standard of ability. The problems should be neither too easy nor too difficult. What kind of a task do you think a good teacher would assign you?"). There was a choice of five tasks with varying degrees of difficulty (10%, 30%, 50%, 70% and 90"). In order to record the subjects' attributions, the student was asked in the last question to specify how he thought the teacher would explain his performance. Three causal factors for success and failure were offered (effort, ability and luck): ("We would like to know what you can guess about the teacher's reasoning with respect to your good or poor performance. How do you think he himself explained you (a) success, (b) failure ?). Questions were once again answered on a 7-point-scale from "not at all" (1) to "most certainly" (7).

After completion of the questionnaire the subjects were debriefed and interviewed by the experimenter, especially with regard to their notion of the study's purpose, the effectiveness of the experimental treatments, etc.

Hypotheses.   In   respect to the associations between emotions
and attributions, we have set up the following hypotheses:

1) Subjects to whom the teacher displays satisfaction
following success, and anger following failure, should
assume that the teacher attributes high ability to them.
Subjects to whom the teacher exhibits surprise after
success, and pity after failure, should conclude that
the teacher does not attribute high ability to them.

2) Subjects to whom the teacher exhibits satisfaction after
success, and anger after failure, will assess their
ability higher than subjects who receive surprise and
pity. Consequently, the former should also show a
higher success expectancy for further tasks than the
latter.

3) In the "without test evaluation" condition, the subject
has no reason to assume that the teacher has any information on his ability. Therefore, the teacher's
emotional feedback should have no effect on the alleged
teacher-attributions, evaluations of own test performance, and success expectancies.

RESULTS

With respect to the number of correct answers in the "visual
examination test", there were no significant differences among
the four groups; averages were between 6.70 and 7.70.

Alleged Teacher Attributions.   In accordance with hypothesis
one, subjects did actually assume different teacher attributions based on the teacher's emotional feedback, as is shown
by two-way analyses of variance with the factors "test
evaluation" (with/without) and "emotions" (satisfaction/anger;
surprise/pity).

For the alleged teacher attribution of ability, there is a
significant interaction between the factors "test evaluation"
and "emotion" ($F(1,36) = 3.74$, $p = .06$).

Further examination by means of a U-test shows that for the
condition "with test evaluation" there is a significant
difference in the dependence on the teacher's emotional
feedback, but not for the condition "without test evaluation"
(see table 2).

Obviously, if the student assumes that the teacher has valid
information on his ability, and he receives satisfaction/anger
feedback, he infers that the teacher attributed his success to
high ability. However, if the teacher responds with
surprise/pity, ability attributions are quite rate. In the
condition "without test evaluation", where the student cannot
assume that the teacher is aware of his level of ability, no
respective differences are found.

Table 2. Mean alleged teacher attributions for ability.

----

	ability		lack of ability	
	with test- evaluation	without test- evaluation	with test- evaluation	without test- evaluation
satisfaction/ anger	3.90	3.50	2.60	3.20
surprise/ pity	2.50	3.90	4.80	4.00

Note. Higher means indicate higher rated attributions. Means within a column provided with the same letter differ signi- ficantly (p at least < .05, according to U-test).

For the alleged teacher attributions of lack of ability the analysis of variance shows a significant main effect of the emotion factor. After a response of surprise/pity, the student more readily assumes that the teacher attributed his failure to lack of ability than after a response of satis- faction/anger, regardless of whether the test was evaluated or not (F(1,36) = 15.11, p < .001). The interaction of "emotion" and "test evaluation" is just below the .05 level of signifi- cance. This would mean that when the teacher seems to know about the student's abilities, and he expresses surprise/pity, the student more readily believes the teacher attributed his failure to lack of ability than if the teacher expresses satisfaction/anger. If the teacher is not thought to be aware of the student's abilities, however, then his emotional responses have almost no influence on the alleged teacher attribution.

Regarding the attribution of effort and luck, neither main effects or interactions were of significance.

Ability assessment as compared with others. In order to examine the second and third hypotheses, a two-way analysis of variance was performed with the factors "test evaluation" (with/without) and "emotion" (satisfaction/anger; surprise/- pity").

Table 3. Mean ability assessment in comparison to other students and without comparison to other students and presumed task assignment by the teacher.

	ability with comparison[1]		ability without comparison[1]		task assignment[2]	
	with test-evaluation	without test-evaluation	with test-evaluation	without test-evaluation	with test-evaluation	without test-evaluation
satisfaction/ anger	4.10[a]	3.20	3.90	4.20	2.70[b]	2.60
surprise/ pity	2.30[a]	3.60	3.00	4.10	3.60[b]	3.10

Note. 1) Higher means indicate higher rated ability. 2) Lower means indicate an assignment of a more difficult task. Means within a column provided with the same letter differ significantly (p at least <.05, according to t-tests).

With regard to the "assessment" of one's own ability there is
no main effect of the 2 factors, whereas their interaction is
significant ($F(1,36) = 10.62$, $p < .005$). In the "without test
evaluation" condition the individual's perception of his own
ability is not affected by either "emotion" condition. In the
"with test evaluation" condition, however, individuals who
receive surprise/pity feedback assess their performance ability lower than individuals who receive satisfaction/anger feedback. As can be seen in Table 3 the interaction refers to the
condition with test evaluation.

General evaluation of ability. Here we see a significant main
effect for the test evaluation factor ($F(1,36) = 4.26$, $p < .05$).
Subjects who think the teacher is not informed about their
ability (without test evaluation) estimate their ability to be
higher than subjects who think the teacher knows their test
results. Obviously, the subjects who think the teacher knows
their ability are in general more cautious about indicating
their own ability. This is especially true of situations in
which the teacher displayed pity/surprise.

Assumed task assignment by the teacher. Emotions also affect
the assumed task assignment. The main effect for the emotions
factor ($F(1,36) = 7.41$, $p < .01$) shows that subjects who received responses of satisfaction/anger assume that the teacher
will assign them difficult tasks, whereas subjects who, on the
other hand, received responses of surprise/pity assume that
the teacher will assign them easier tasks. This applies
regardless of whether the teacher is informed about their
ability or not.

Here we see that subjects who receive emotional feedback (from
the teacher) indicating a high level of ability assume that
the teacher will assign them difficult tasks, whereas when the
emotional feedback indicates a low level of ability subjects
think the teacher will assign them simple tasks.

Success expectancies for future tasks. A three-way analysis
of variance was used with the factors emotions (2) X test
evaluation (2) X task difficulty (5), repeated measurement
being performed on the last factor.

Contrary to expectation the three-way interaction is not
significant. In the condition with test evaluation, there
were supposed to be differences in the success expectancies,
depending on the teacher's emotional feedback, and these
differences were supposed to decrease with the increasing
easiness of the tasks. In the condition without the test
evaluation, this effect was not supposed to occur. The present data show that, as expected, there are major differences
unexpectedly occurred (see Figure 2).

Even when the teacher had no information about the subject's
general ability level his emotional reactions still exerted
some influence on the latter's expectancies for future
success. At least with very difficult tasks subjects with

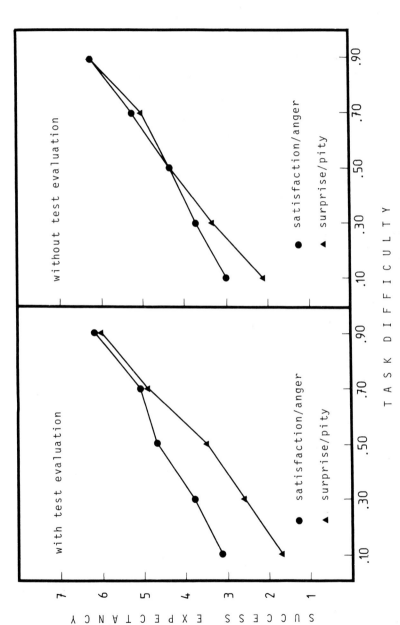

Figure 2.   Mean subjective success expectancies, taking the teacher's emotional feedback, task difficulty, and test evaluation (when used and when not) into account.

"satisfaction" and "anger" still indicated higher expectancies for success than those with "surprise" and "pity", respectively. These findings are probably due to a kind of "transfer" from real life teacher/student interaction by the subjects: these had actually been instructed to take the role of student. In every day school life, however, a teacher is usually well aware of the general ability level of his students, and they themselves are aware of this very fact. So, even in the condition "without test evaluation" some subjects may well have assumed that the teacher, in a way unknown to them, had developed a reasonable idea of their actual ability and, as a consequence, their emotional responses acquired a similar though not as influential meaning, for the subsequent attributional and inferential processes than in the condition "with" test evaluation. For this reason, the further evaluation of the data was carried out separately for the experimental conditions with and without test evaluation.

In the condition with test evaluation the teacher's emotional feedback influenced the student's behaviour ($F(1,18) = 8.87$, $p < .01$). In the condition without, however, it did not ($F(1,18) = 0.89$). That means that if the teacher is informed about the student's ability satisfaction following success and anger following failure lead to noticeably higher success expectancy on the part of the student than do responses of surprise and pity.

If the teacher is thought not to know the student's ability then his emotional feedback has no effect. The main effect of test difficulty for both experimental conditions with test evaluation ($F(4,72) = 92.08$, $p < .001$) and without test evaluation ($F(4,72) = 126.38$, $p < .001$) is due simply to the fact that the success expectancy of the subjects decreases when test difficulty increases. The interaction between the factors emotion and test difficulty is only significant if the teacher is informed about the student's ability ($F(4,72) = 3.77$, $p < .01$). It is not, however, significant if the teacher is uninformed ($F(4,72) = 2.23$). An examination of this interaction by means of a U-test shows a significant difference in the probability of success with very difficult tasks (10%, $p < .05$) and with moderately difficult tasks (50%, $p < .05$) depending on the emotional feedback.

DISCUSSION

The results of this study definitely support the notion that other people's emotions have an effect on one's self perception of ability. A person's (teacher's) emotional feedback causes the receiver (student) to make assumptions about how the teacher assesses his ability level. This was shown by the alleged teacher attributions.

Furthermore, the teacher's emotions actually do have an effect on the subject's self-perception. As expected, after receiving satisfaction/anger feedback and when comparing themselves to others subjects assessed their abilities higher than with surprise and pity feedback. This, however, applies only if the teacher is seen as being aware of the subject's test performance.

The assessment of one's own ability without social comparison clearly follows a similar line. Here, too, self assessment is lowest if the teacher responds with surprise or pity although the respective differences are not significant. This could be due to the fact that the question was understood as not only applying to the perceived ability to solve these specific tasks but also tasks of a similar kind. When interviewed may subjects indicated that, when answering this question, they were reminded of psychological "tests" in magazines. Since such previous experience with similar tasks interferes when subjects answer this question the cues on which their assessment of their own ability is based may be ambiguous or even contradictory. Thus, a person who has had the previous experience of performing well on such "tests" and who then receives feedback indicating poor performance will not make as low an estimate of his ability as somebody who "knows" that he usually does poorly on such tests.

The teacher's emotional reactions also have an effect on predicted task assignments. If subjects receive satisfaction/ anger feedback they expect a "good" teacher to set them more difficult tasks than if they are given surprise/pity feedback. In other words, if the teacher's emotional reactions imply that he considers the student to be quite talented the subjects assume that he will assign this particular student more difficult tasks in the future.

Krüger, Möller & Meyer (1983) have shown that task assignment has an effect on a person's perception of his respective ability. If somebody with valid information about an individual's general ability (e.g., a teacher) sets that person easy or difficult tasks the individual will estimate his own level of ability to be higher if assigned difficult tasks, and lower if assigned quite easy ones.

Similarly, satisfaction following success and anger following failure caused the subjects to establish significantly higher expectancies for success with further tasks than did surprise and pity, respectively. This indicates that the teacher's emotional responses may be of particular significance to the student's achievement related behaviour, and especially to his future efforts.

An interesting result is the statistically significant interaction between the factors "task difficulty" and "emotion" with respect to "expectancy for future success" (cf. Fig.2).

The greater difference between the subjective success expectancies for more difficult tasks than for easy ones should come as no surprise. If the teacher is informed of an individual's abilities, and exhibits satisfaction and anger after that person's success and failure, respectively, the individual will come to believe that the teacher considers him to be quite capable. If, in addition, the person puts enough effort into solving the task he will be more certain of solving even difficult future tasks correctly. In contrast, the emotions surprise/pity have different consequences. They should cause the individual to believe that the teacher does not consider him to be talented at all. Since with low ability even a high degree of effort will not lead to success with difficult tasks the individual is less certain of being able to solve such tasks in the future. For easier tasks, however, there are no differences between the emotional feedback conditions regarding subjective success expectancies since here lack of ability can be compensated for by a very high degree of effort.

Since pairs of emotions were set up for this experiment it is difficult to determine exactly which component, or whether the combination of both, had the greatest impact on the subjects' self-assessment. Pairs of emotions were used because, in real life situations, teachers usually convey their assessment of student's ability by means of multiple cues. Noticeable effects of a teacher's emotional feedback on the students' self-assessment and behaviour should result especially when he uses a variety of cues which, nonetheless, have the same import.

Graham's study (in press) provides further evidence of the influence of emotional feedback on the self-perception of ability. Children repeatedly experienced failure while trying to solve puzzles. The experimenter displayed verbal as well as non-verbal responses of anger and pity or no emotional response at all (control group). Afterwards, the evaluation of perceived competence, of experiment attributions, and of success expectancy was measured.

Graham found that, when pity was exhibited, failure was thought to result from low ability, whereas signs of anger were associated with lack of effort. There was a significant decline in the children's assessment of their own competence from the first to the last trial. The greatest decline was in success expectancy in the condition in which pity was displayed. After the fifth puzzle, the greatest difference in success expectancy between the anger and pity conditions was observed. This indicates that children who receive pity feedback are less confident about solving the next puzzle than children who receive anger or no feedback at all.

Although Graham's study was conducted with children, and a somewhat different procedure was used to demonstrate emotional feedback, the results largely coincide with those of the present experiment.

Interestingly enough, in both studies the two emotions anger and pity seem to acquire meaning contrary to everyday reasoning. As a rule, anger is considered a "negative" emotion whereas in the present context it indicates to the receiver that his ability level is assumed to be high which endows this emotion with a positive meaning. Pity, on the other hand, is generally regarded to be something "positive". In this case, however, it tells the receiver that he is considered to have a low level of ability. As such, it acquires a negative meaning.

In real life situations students will presumably use a teacher's emotional feedback to draw conclusions as to how the latter evaluates them, and these conclusions, under certain conditions, will affect their self-perception and possibly even their self-concept. Even if the teacher tries to conceal his personal opinion (e.g., if he considers a student's abilities to be poor), he nevertheless will reveal it through his emotional reactions, which are not so easily controlled. Even more important, the conclusions drawn by a student from such emotional feedback can hardly be controlled or corrected by the teacher. If, e.g., he displays pity in order to express his concern after a student has failed, the teacher might instead induce feelings of hopelessness and helplessness on the part of the latter.

FOOTNOTE.

Thanks are due to Jens-Jörg Koch for valuable discussions and advice.

The Self in Anxiety, Stress and Depression
R. Schwarzer (Editor)
© Elsevier Science Publishers B.V. (North-Holland), 1984

THE SELF–OTHER DISCREPANCY IN SOCIAL SHYNESS

Warren H. Jones and Stephen R. Briggs

University of Tulsa, Tulsa, Oklahoma, U.S.A.

Shyness is a form of social anxiety that has been characterized as anxious preoccupation with the self in the presence of others (e.g., Crozier, 1979a). Previous writers (e.g., Buss, 1980) have argued that a necessary precondition for experiencing the state emotion of shyness is public self-consciousness, that is, awareness of the self as a social object. Although the importance of self-processes in the experiene of shyness has been generally recognized, the role of the self has not been fully explicated in this regard. We have been conducting an on-going program of research on dispositional shyness, one part of which has focused on an issue of relevance to shyness and the self; namely, the correspondence between perceptions of oneself versus perceptions of others in social situations. Thus, the purpose of this paper is to review previous research on shyness as well as our own recent data with particular emphasis on the discrepancy between self and other perceptions of social behavior.

We begin our essay with an overview of the concept of shyness and its emergence in the psychological literature as a descriptive and theoretical construct. Next, we consider research on shyness including the rate of its occurrence, internal and behavioral correlates, as well as data linking dispositional shyness to limited and problematic social networks. We illustrate our central point with studies demonstrating the discrepancy between self and other perceptions among shy as compared to not shy individuals. Finally we briefly discuss the implications of these findings for a theory of shyness.

Overview of Shyness

Many of the affective and trait dimensions described and studied by psychologists use terms that are common to the nonpsychologist; shyness is a case in point. Shyness typically implies a timid reserve and a shrinking from contact with others. Widespread use of the term in everyday language is hardly surprising because, as is commonly observed, we are by nature social beings. Our lives consist of and are defined by a series of continuing and one-time only social interactions with family, friends, acquaintances, and strangers. Consequently, personal characteristics that either facilitate or impede interpersonal functioning are salient features of our experience and are therefore likely to be perceived and labelled.

Conceptual Issues. The experience of shyness involves attention to the self in social situations and results in timid, inappropriate overt behaviors and internal distress (e.g., anxiety, self-deprecating thoughts, etc.). As a transitory emotional state, shyness is elicited by certain social stimuli and conceivably may be periodically experienced by virtually everyone. Buss (1980) has suggested that the likelihood of shyness increases with novelty (e.g., being at a new school, meeting strangers, job promotions, etc.), the presence of others or one's own conspicuousness -- (e.g., marriage ceremonies, meeting authority figures, being the only man among women), and certain actions of others (e.g., excessive and insufficient attention, intrusiveness, etc.). Recent research has provided confirmation for these speculations. For example, one series of studies (Jones & Russell, 1983) examined situations in which college students report feeling shy, finding that state shyness was greatest when "doing something at which you are incompetent" (average shyness rating of 4.95 on a 7-point scale). Other situations in which shyness is commonly experienced by college students included "being asked personal questions in public" (4.70), "blind dates" (4.36), "first day at a new school" (4.13), "at a party with strangers" (3.99), "meeting a date's parents" (3.89), and so on.

Alternatively, for some individuals shyness is a relatively enduring personality disposition that figures in social behavior across situations and over the life-span. Whereas the origins of the trait of shyness are not yet clear, there is evidence for both genetic (Plomin & Rowe, 1979) as well as developmental and experimental determinants (e.g., Ludwig & Lazarus, 1983). As a trait, shyness is related to a variety of internal and behavioral variables as we will discuss below. At this point, however, it is important to note the status of shyness in the lexicon of trait terms. Considerable research has been directed toward identifying the underlying structure of personality using factor analytic methods in conjunction with item analyses. In such research, social shyness has emerged consistently as one of the major factors underlying personality inventory items (Crozier, 1979b; Howarth, 1980). For example, in a study of 400 items representing 20 putative factors, the social shyness factor (e.g., as reflected in items such as "I usually take the initiative in meeting new friends" which is reverse scored, and "I am likely not to speak to people until they speak to me") accounted for the large percentage of the explained variance (Browne & Howarth, 1977). Shyness, therefore, appears to occupy a well-defined and central position in the universe of trait dimensions.

Finally, it is important to distinguish between shyness and similar constructs. Shyness is not introversion, although statistically and conceptually the two are somewhat related. Shyness does not necessarily involve the inward focus and intellectual orientation of the Jungian introvert, nor should it be confused with the aspects of sociability, impulsivity, and sensation-seeking that characterize Eysenck's dimension of extraversion-introversion. Eysenck (1956) himself distinguishes between introversion and shyness by positing two types of shyness: (1) introverted social shyness (individuals who prefer to be alone but have no difficulty interacting with others when it is necessary or to their advantage to do so) and (2) neurotic social shyness (those who are self-conscious, lonely and feel inadequate with superiors). A similar distinction is made by Cheek & Buss (1981) who differentiate sociability from shyness. Sociability is the preference for being with others rather than alone; thus, from this perspective, a lack of sociability resembles Eysenck's notion of introverted shyness. Shyness is defined as tension and inhibition in the presence of others; thus, shyness may be as closely related to Eysenck's superfactor of Neuroticism as to his Extraversion dimension, which may explain why the item "Do you suddenly feel shy when you want to talk to an attractive stranger ?" is scored on the Neuroticism scale rather than the Extraversion scale of the Eysenck Personality Inventory (Eysenck & Eysenck, 1964).

Shyness is also not synonymous with social anxiety. Buss (1980) argues that social anxiety can be decomposed into four types -- shyness, audience anxiety, embarrassment, and shame -- with shyness and audience anxiety sharing certain causes (novelty, conspicuousness) and reactions (fear, sympathetic arousal), and embarrassment and shame also sharing certain characteristics. In this scheme, then, shyness is simply one type of social anxiety.

From a different perspective, Leary (1982; Schlenker & Leary, 1982) defines social anxiety as anxiety that results from "the prospect or presence of interpersonal evaluation in real or imagined social settings". Leary argues that social anxiety should be defined only in terms of the subjective experience of nervousness and dread and should not include any behavioral referents. Although we agree in principle that it might be useful to distinguish cognitive-affective experiences of anxiety from overt behaviors, in practice there appears to be little empirical support for maintaining this distinction (cf. Pilkonis, 1977; Briggs, Snider & Smith, 1983). Moreover, our lives unfold on a social stage where poor performance yields disapproval and disadvantage. In this context, the remarkable feature of shyness is its commonality despite its consequences. Thus, whereas the anxiety associated with shyness is a significant feature of the shy person's personal experience, nevertheless, "shyness is a social phenomenon, always expressed by behavior and only in relation to other human beings" (Lewinsky, 1941).

Shyness Research. Evidence from surveys suggests that shyness is a relatively common term of self-description. For example, Zimbardo (1977) reported that 44% of a sample of adult respondents in the United States characterized themselves as presently shy. By contrast, the base rate of shyness self-labelled for several culturally diverse groups was as follows: Japanese (57%), Taiwanese (55%), Israelis (31%), and Jewish Americans (24%). Shyness is also common among children and adolescents in America. One study found that about 40% of a sample of grade school children labelled themselves as shy: specifically, 26% of the boys and 49% of the girls (Lazarus, 1982). Thus, although there apparently is some variation in the occurrence of shyness based on cultural, age-related and gender differences, shyness refers to a concept that many people use to describe their own personalities and behavior. Shyness is also, of course, frequently used to characterize the actions and tendencies of others.

As both a trait and a state, shyness frequently involves unpleasant thoughts and emotions. Previous research has indicated that shyness is related to global measures of anxiety, depression, hostility, neurosis, communication apprehension, alienation, and so on (e.g., Jones & Russell, 1982). Similarly, Cavert (1982) reported that dispositional shyness was significantly correlated with the following self-reported reactions during videotaped monologues: blushing, "butterflies" in the stomach, heart pounding, dry mouth, self-consciousness, negative thoughts such as thoughts about the unpleasantness of the situation, being evaluated, one's own shyness, escape, and so on.

It is perhaps not surprising that shyness shows consistent and substantial statistical relationships with other negative affective experiences such as fearfulness. However, shyness is not synonymous with general anxiety or fearfulness. For example, in a recent study we correlated five different self-report measures of shyness with specific fears from a fear survey schedule. The shyness measures correlated on the average .44 with social fears (e.g., meeting strangers, authority figures, etc.) and only .13 with nonsocial fears (e.g., sharp objects, blood, high places, etc.).

As mentioned earlier, shyness has been characterized as anxious preoccupation with the self and acute awareness of oneself as a social object. A number of studies have examined empirically the relationships between shyness and measure of self-attention, for example, public and private self-consciousness (Fenigstein, Scheier & Buss, 1975), and self-monitoring (Snyder, 1974). Consistent with the predictions by Buss (1980), the correlations between public self-consciousness (i.e., attention to the overt aspects of the self) and shyness are stronger and more consistent than the correlations between private self-consciousness (i.e., attention to the covert aspects of the self) and shyness. This suggests that shyness is more closely linked to attentional processes involving aspects of the self that are observable to others and social rather than internal. Shyness scores are only modestly related to total scores on the Self-Monitoring Scale, but these figures are misleading in that the factors known to underlie the Self-Monitoring Scale are strongly related to shyness but in opposite directions, thereby suppressing any overall relationship (cf., Briggs, Cheek & Buss, 1980). For example, in one study we found that the correlation between shyness and total self-monitoring was -.22. On the other hand, the correlations between shyness and the components of the self-monitoring scale were as follows: acting, $r = -.22$; extraversion, $r = -.66$; other directedness, $r = .38$.

Also, shyness scores show sizable covariation with indices of self-evaluation. Global measures of self-esteem consistently correlate with shyness scores in excess of -.50 (Briggs, Snider & Smith, 1983; Cheek & Buss, 1981; Jones & Russell, 1982) although this relationship apparently holds more for the social aspects of self-esteem than for the nonsocial aspects (Cheek, 1981b; Crozier, 1979c).

The practical significance of shyness derives not only from the distress of the shy person in social situations, but also from the impact of shyness on the perceptions and reactions of others (Hogan, Jones & Cheek, in press). The latter issue may be divided into three questions: (1) are there behavioral differences associated with shyness; (2) is shyness detectable by others; and (3) how are the behaviors associated with shyness evaluated by others (e.g., are they seen as positive or negative characteristics)? These questions arise, in part, because of evidence indicating that shy persons believe that their behavior is misperceived by others as disinterest in social interaction, or worse, as "snobbishness". In addition, shy persons report that their shyness may prevent others from recognizing their good qualities and assets.

Although previous research has been somewhat inconsistent in this regard, it would appear that greater shyness is associated with less effective and less responsive conversational styles. For example, several studies have demonstrated that shy as compared to not shy college students talk and smile less, give less eye contact, show fewer facial expressions, and have slower speech latencies in conversations with others (Cheek & Buss, 1981; Daly, 1978; Mandel & Shrauger, 1980; Pilkonis, 1977).

Given behavioral differences between shy and not shy persons, the issue becomes how are these differences perceived by others -- what impressions does the shy person create by his or her self-presentations ? Pilkonis (1977) found that shy persons were rated as less friendly, less assertive, less relaxed and more shy in unstructured dyadic conversations. Similarly, Cheek and Buss (1981) found that raters making impressionistic judgments of videotaped dyadic conversations perceived shy persons as being tense, inhibited, unfriendly, and shy.

In one study (Jones, Cavert & Indart, 1983), thirty college students who had previously completed a measure of shyness were videotaped talking about themselves. Subsequently, a group of six raters, who were unaware of the target's shyness score, rendered impressionistic judgments of each target person on a 16-item rating scale. This scale contained four-item measures of poise, friendliness, and talent, as well as single-item measures of shyness, anxiety, and physical attractiveness. Ratings were averaged across judges and these averages were correlated with target's dispositional shyness scores. The analyses indicated that the shyness of the target was positively correlated with averaged ratings of shyness and anxiety and inversely correlated with poise and talent. The correlations with friendliness and physical attractiveness were not reliable. Thus, the higher the level of self-reported shyness, the more the target was seen as shy, anxious, untalented and lacking in poise. It is important to note that the correlation between average shyness ratings and target's shyness scores was .50, indicating substantial covariation between the two variables. Also, we have recently replicated this finding using multiple measures of shyness.

To summarize, these studies would seem to indicate that shyness involves differences in certain key conversational variables (e.g., eye contact, speech latency, etc.), and that observers making impressionistic judgments identify such behaviors as indicative of shyness with a reasonable degree of accuracy. In addition, however, these studies also suggest that the self-presentations of shy people give rise to gratuitous and negative perceptions on the part of others that to an extent go beyond shyness itself, e.g., perceptions involving lack of talent.

It is reasonable to suppose that the relatively unresponsive and generally ineffective verbal behaviors associated with shyness would lead to clumsy, faulting and dissatisfying interactions with others. Such dissatisfaction might, in turn, restrict the social and interpersonal opportunities of shy people particularly with respect to relationships outside of the family. The idea that shyness and other forms of social anxiety would be expected to inhibit the development of relationships is not new and is a logical extension of the concept. Campbell (1896) argued that morbid shyness in adults results in isolation, self-absorption, loneliness, occupational disadvantage and a lack of companionship.

Several studies have indicated that shyness predicts the frequency of social and heterosexual contact and the number of intimate friendships. For example, shyness has been inversely related to dating frequency, number of dating partners, the number of close friends and the number of close opposite-sexed friends among college students (e.g., Jones & Russell, 1982), and these results closely parallel those involving other forms of social anxiety such as communication apprehension (e.g., McCrosky & Sheahan, 1978). In addition, shyness has been found to be rated to more subjectively assessed indices of relationships. Maroldo (1982) reported inverse correlations between shyness and several measures of love including respect, congeniality, altruism, and physical attractiveness. We have found shyness to be positively related to a measure of jealousy among male college students and inversely related to expressed inclusion and affection in one's relationships as well as acceptance of others.

In a recent study, we compared scores on a measure of shyness with responses to several questions about relationships among college students. Table 1 presents the resulting correlations.

Table 1

Correlations Between Shyness and Relationship Variables

Variable	Combined	Men	Women
Closeness to Parents	−.19	−.19	−.18
Closeness to Siblings	−.11	−.08	−.12
Closeness to Friends	−.22	−.36	−.15
Frequency of Social Activities	−.21	−.18	−.22
Social Satisfaction	−.39	−.57	−.27
Number of Friends	−.30	−.43	−.21
Self-Disclosure to Friends	−.24	−.33	−.20
Dating Frequency	−.24	−.32	−.19
Dating Satisfaction	−.38	−.45	−.33

As is indicated, shyness was inversely and significantly related to all items except for closeness to siblings for which a non-significant trend was observed for men and women combined. It is interesting to note that covariation between shyness and reponses to these questions about relationships were generally stronger for male as compared to female respondents, suggesting that the inhibitory effect for shyness may be greater for men.

The concept of loneliness has received considerable recent attention because of its utility as a way of conceptualizing and measuring dissatisfaction with one's social and intimate relationships (Peplau & Perlman, 1982). Several investigators have reported substantial correlations between shyness and loneliness (e.g., Cheek & Busch, 1981; Jones, Freemon & Goswick, 1981), and theoretical statements of loneliness have emphasized the role of shyness and related constructs in the development of loneliness (cf., Jones, 1982). We have found measures of shyness and loneliness to be correlated among a variety of samples including college students in Puerto Rico, adolescents, convicted felons, disabled adults, elderly widows and so on. Thus, it is clear that the connection between shyness and relational dissatisfaction as reflected in measures of loneliness generalizes beyond the usual college student samples. Also, there are some indications that the interpersonal behavior of lonely individuals may be characterized by the self-focus and lower responsivity typical of shy persons (Jones, Hobbs & Hockenbury, 1982).

In our recent research we have attempted to determine, more specifically, the role of shyness in relational dissatisfaction. For example, in one study a sample of college students completed a measure of shyness and the Differential Loneliness Scale (Schmidt & Sermat, 1983) which assesses feelings of loneliness with respect to different types of relationships including family, romantic, friendship and community relationships. Our results indicated that wheras shyness was significantly correlated with all four types of loneliness, it was most strongly related to loneliness regarding one's community relationships and friendships and less so for romantic and family relationships.

Another approach to assessing relationships and social ties concerns the concept of social support defined as helpful information received from the members of one's social network (such as family members, friends, co-workers, etc.) that leads one to believe that he or she is cared for and involved (Cobb, 1976). The importance of social support derives from evidence suggesting that it may ameliorate the deleterious effects of stress. By implications, factors that interfere with an individual's capacity to develop and maintain supportive social networks, may increase the individual's susceptibility to both medical and psychological disorders. In a recent study we examined the relationship between measures of shyness and various measures of social support. In general, our data indicated modest, but significant inverse correlations between shyness and quantitative measures of social support (e.g., number of persons in the network, network density, etc.) and somewhat higher correlations with qualitative measures (e.g., satisfaction with the degree of support received). Not surprisingly then, shyness was also strongly related to the degree of psychological discomfort reported as indicated by measures of depression and anxiety, for these participants.

Available evidence on dispositional shyness generally suggests therefore that it is a relatively common feature of personality and that it is associated with a variety of unpleasant cognitive and affective states, particularly with respect to social stimuli, including negative self-evaluations. It would appear that shyness involves certain behavioral inadequacies consistent with its definition as anxious preoccupation with the self in the presence of others. Furthermore, these differences are detectable by observers and correctly labelled as shyness. On the other hand, consistent with the beliefs of many shy people, the reticence of shyness also appears to elicit gratuitous attributions from others and specifically the assumption on the part of observers that shy people are disinterested in social interaction, which may or may not be correct. Consequently, shyness is associated further with smaller social networks, fewer friends and especially with dissatisfaction with one's available relationships.

These results go a long way toward identifying the correlates and consequences of shyness, at least among the populations sampled thus far. In addition, these data confirm the expected influence of dispositional shyness on social adjustment and well-being as well as the mechanisms by which such influence occurs. Shyness constrains one's social network and relationships because it interferes with social performances. In part, this interference has to do with the behavioral manifestations of anxiety including the tendency to avoid or withdraw from social situations and decrements in appropriate social behaviors (e.g., silence, gaze aversion, etc.). Also involved, however, is the tendency for observers to attribute negative characteristics to the reticent and inadequate behaviors associated with shyness.

The Self-Other Discrepancy

Another mechanism that might contribute to poor social adjustment and poor interpersonal performance among shy persons -- and one that has yet to be fully explored -- concerns the extent to which the shy person is aware of how he or she is being perceived by others. As with all skilled performances, effective social behavior requires accurate feedback and the ability to appreciate how one is evaluated. Shyness is interesting in this regard because of the possibility that its cognitive and emotional correlates prevent an individual from attending to and discerning subtle social cues. Excessive arousal, fear of negative evaluation, and an intense preoccupation with self may result in attention to personal feelings rather than critical social information. Therefore, it is likely that shy individuals would have difficulty judging how they are being evaluated in social situations.

Several laboratory studies have suggested that shyness involves biases in self-evaluation. For example, one study demonstrated that shy individuals have a more accurate memory for negative feedback about themselves than do those who are not shy, and that they are less likely to recall examples of positive feedback (O'Banion & Arkowitz, 1977). Another study found that when anticipating an imminent interaction with a woman, shy men rated the impending discussion and themselves more negatively than did not shy men, and generated more negative self-statements (Cacioppo, Glass & Merluzzi, 1979). In addition, although shy individuals were equally capable of judging the performance of others in a heterosexual interaction, shy individuals tended to underestimate their own performance, whereas individuals low in shyness overestimated their own performance (Clark & Arkowitz, 1975).

In order to further explore these issues, we conducted a study examining the role of shyness in impression formation among unacquainted college students. Participants completed a measure of shyness and were paired with an opposite sex stranger. Each dyad was instructed to become as well acquainted as possible during a brief conversation. After 15 minutes, participants were directed to separate rooms and asked to rate themselves and their partners on interpersonal dimensions such as friendly, outgoing, warm and talkative. These ratings were made from each of three perspectives: (1) self-ratings; (2) how the participant expected to be rated by his or her partner, termed reflected self-ratings; and (3) ratings of the partner. These latter ratings also comprised ratings by the partner for the other member of the dyad.

The ratings were correlated with participant's shyness scores for each rating dimension. Table 2 presents these analyses for each rating perspective averaged across dimensions. As is indicated, shyness was inversely related to self and reflected self-ratings, particularly for women (e.g., participants scoring higher on the shyness scale rated themselves and expected to be rated as less friendly, less open, less warm, etc.). Shyness was also inversely correlated with ratings of the partner (i.e., higher shyness was associated with rating one's partner as less open, less talkative, etc.). Thus, more shy as compared to less shy persons rated themselves and their partners more negatively and indicated that they expected their partners to rate them more negatively. We also found that shyness was inversely correlated with ratings by the partner, suggesting that the partners of shy participants did in fact view them more negatively.

Table 2

Average Correlations Between Shyness and Ratings

Rating Perspective	Combined	Men	Women
Self-Ratings	-.33	-.40	-.25
Reflected Self-Ratings	-.32	-.42	-.24
Ratings of Partner	-.21	-.26	-.20
Ratings by Partner	-.18	-.24	-.12

Correlations $>.21$ are significant with $p < .05$

Thus, shy participants were viewed differently following actual conversations, and specifically, in ways that would not be conducive to the development of a relationship. However, the data also indicated that greater shyness was associated with anticipating that one would be rated even more negatively by one's partner than was actually the case, in other words, a negativity bias. This was determined by correlating shyness scores with the difference between ratings by the partner and reflected self-ratings.

In another study, unacquainted college students completed a measure of shyness and participated in various activities for 45 minutes in groups of 7 to 10 persons each. Following the activities, each participant rated him or herself and every other member of the group on the same dimensions as above (i.e., friendly, open, etc.). Shyness scores were correlated with ratings from each of four perspectives: (1) self-ratings; (2) reflected self-ratings; (3) mean ratings of the other members of the group, termed ratings of others; and (4) mean ratings of the participant by the members of his or her group called ratings by others. These analyses generally replicated the results of the dyadic study.

In addition, the participants were divided at the median of the distribution of shyness scores into high and low shyness groups. Within each group, dimensions were correlated across rating perspectives (e.g., self-rating for friendly with mean ratings by others for friendly, reflected self-rating for open with mean rating of others for open, etc.). Table 3 contains these analyses averaged across rating dimensions. Several of the results in Table 3 are particularly interesting with respect to self-other discrepancies. For example, although both low and high shyness groups expected to be rated in accordance with their self view (as is evident in the self with reflected self comparisons) the degree of correspondence was greater for the low shyness group. The self with ratings of others comparisons may suggest that high shyness participants "projected" their self-image onto their fellow group members whereas this tendency did not occur among low shyness participants. Also, low shyness participants received ratings more consistent with those they had given than did the high shyness participants as indicated by the ratings of others with ratings by others comparisons.

Table 3

Correlations   Between   Rating   Perspectives   Averaged   Across
Dimensions

Rating Perspectives	Low Shyness	High Shyness
Self/Reflected Self	.61	.49
Self/Ratings of Others	.04	.24
Self/Ratings by Others	.40	.10
Reflected Self/Ratings of Others	.11	.29
Reflected Self/Ratings by Others	.45	.01
Ratings of Others/Ratings by Others	.18	.07

Of particular relevance to our current thesis are the correlations between reflected self-ratings and mean ratings by
others.   These analyses indicated that the low shyness
participants predicted with a reasonable degree of accuracy
the ratings they actually received, whereas the high shyness
participants did not.   This suggests that the difficulty in
discerning how one is being evaluated manifested by shy
persons involves more than just a negativity bias in that
reflected self-ratings systematically lower than those actually received would have resulted in significant correlations.
By contrast, the average correlation for the high shyness
group between the reflected self-ratings and mean ratings by
others was .01.   None of the individual correlations were
reliably different from zero for the high shyness group; for
the low shyness group, all relevant correlations were significant (p < .10).

In our most recent study, college students completed five
separate measures of shyness and rated themselves on a series
of adjectives.   Participants were also asked to provide names
and addresses of several acquaintances who would be asked to
participate in the study.   Subsequently, the acquaintances
were contacted and asked to rate the participant on the same
list of adjectives.   Others' ratings were combined for each
participant and both sets of ratings (i.e., self and other's
ratings) were correlated with each of the participant's five
shyness scores.   Table 4 summarizes these analyses averaged
across shyness measures.

Table 4

Correlations Between Shyness and Self and Other-Reported
Adjectives

Adjectives	Self Ratings	Other Ratings
Talkative	−.53	−.34
Extraverted	−.57	−.32
Sociable	−.51	−.33
Outgoing	−.59	−.44
Flirtatious	−.52	−.27
Likes People	−.46	−.26
Relaxed	−.35	−.14
Cheerful	−.30	−.07
Happy	−.31	−.13
Friendly	−.20	−.16
Rule-Abiding	.00	.17
Conscientious	.05	.18
Dependable	−.06	.16
Cooperative	−.01	.10
Leadership	−.41	−.23
Confident	−.54	−.13
Ambitious	−.04	−.12
Assertive	−.35	−.04
Physically Attractive	−.28	−.03

Correlations > .15 are significant with p<.05

As is evident, shyness was generally more strongly correlated with the adjectives for self as opposed to other's ratings, particularly for adjectives most closely related to shyness (e.g., talkative, extraverted, outgoing, etc.). There are, however, a few exceptions. For adjectives such as conscientious and dependable, other's ratings were modestly correlated whereas the correlations for self-ratings were close to zero.

Shyness, however, is not the only dimension of personality that influences the extent to which self-ratings concur with ratings by others. For instance, self-other agreement also differs as a function of the dispositional tendency to attend to the private aspects of oneself. Individuals high in private self-consciousness are more likely to rate themselves similar to the way others rate them than are those low in private self-consciousness (Cheek, 1981). Thus, several personality dimensions are likely to be involved in self-other agreement, and shyness is probably best regarded as just one element in what is undoubtedly a complex process.

Consistent with this point is a recent study by Franzoi (1983) that simultaneously examined the effects of private self-consciousness and social anxiety on the congruence between self-ratings and ratings by friends. Franzoi selected subjects who were one standard deviation above or below the mean on private self-consciousness and also one standard deviation above or below the mean on a social anxiety scale. Subjects rated themselves and were rated by a friend on adjectives taken from the Adjective Check List (Gough & Heilbrun, 1965). There was substantial agreement between self and other ratings for subjects high in private self-consciousness regardless of the score on social anxiety, although subjects high in social anxiety were rated more negatively by both themselves and their friends. For subjects low in private self-consciousness, however, self-ratings and ratings by friends were discrepant. Subjects high in social anxiety underrated themselves relative to the ratings by their friends, whereas those low in social anxiety overrated themselves. Furthermore, when confronted with the discrepancies between their friend's ratings and their own ratings, subjects high in social anxiety were less likely to accept the accuracy of their friend's positive descriptions than were those low in social anxiety. Thus, shyness and private self-consciousness seem to work together in mediating the degree of congruence between self-ratings and ratings by others.

Conclusion

In this chapter we have outlined research on shyness generally and have presented some of our recent findings on dispositional shyness. In our view, these data substantiate the importance of shyness not only in terms of personal well-being, but also with respect to critical interpersonal processes, specifically, the development and maintenance of mutually satisfying intimate and social relationships. Also, we have argued that extant data reveal several mechanisms by which dispositional shyness may inhibit the development of such relationships including the apparently reduced capacity of shy persons to gather and/or correctly process social feedback.

These data also bring into focus an issue of particular relevance to theories that emphasize the role of the self in social shyness. On the one hand, shyness seems to involve an intense preoccupation with the social aspects of the self when engaged in or confronted with an impending interpersonal encounter. On the other hand, despite this self-focus, (or perhaps because of it or its intensity), shy individuals are less able to judge how they are being perceived by others. Moreover, shy individuals tend to denigrate and belittle their own interpersonal abilities by exaggerating the magnitude and importance of their interaction difficulties. Thus, the social inadequacies that exist for the shy person are compounded by the negative and largely inaccurate perceptions that the shy person has of himself or herself.

The Self in Anxiety, Stress and Depression
R. Schwarzer (Editor)
© Elsevier Science Publishers B.V. (North-Holland), 1984

SHYNESS, EMBARRASSMENT AND SELF-PRESENTATION:
A CONTROL THEORY APPROACH

Jens Asendorpf

Max-Planck-Institute for Psychological Research, München, Federal Republic of Germany

Schlenker and Leary in recent reviews related shyness and embarrassment to self-presentation problems (Leary & Schlenker, 1981; Schlenker & Leary, 1982). They propose that shyness arises when people are motivated to make a favorable impression on others but doubt that they will do so, and that embarrassment arises when an event occurs that appears to repudiate their intended self-presentation. Thus, the amount of shyness or embarrassment experienced will depend on the expected or perceived discrepancy between one's own standard for self-presentation and one's actual self-presentation. Embarrassment can be distinguished from shyness by the factual nature of the discrepancy: shyness arises when a discrepancy is anticipated, embarrassment results when a discrepancy is actually perceived. Both shyness and embarrassment are conceived of as different facets of social anxiety.

This approach appears to help integrate most of the existing literature on social anxiety, shyness, and embarrassment. The purpose of this paper is to further explore the self-presentational nature of social anxiety from a control theory point of view. The starting point of this exploration is the observation that socially anxious behavior is not merely a consequence of self-presentation problems. Rather, it also itself leads to self-presentation problems of its own because in most situations appearing shy or embarrassed is inconsistent with the public image that people intend to convey.

This can be observed most clearly in embarrassment. When a person holds the standard not to appear embarrassed in the presence of others but still reacts with overt embarrassment to some event, this reaction promotes itself via a positive feedback loop: it contradicts the image the person wants to convey, and in so doing it constitutes an additional source of embarrassment. The person begins with being embarrassed about some unintended mistake, for instance, and ends up with being embarrassed about appearing embarrassed.

A similar vicious cycle often emerges in shyness. If Leary and Schlenker (1981) are correct, a necessary condition for shyness is the motivation to impress others in certain ways by conveying a particular public image of oneself. In most situations this image is inconsistent with shy behavior. What happens when the intended image of a person is inconsistent with shy behavior but the person still reacts with some overt shyness in a difficult social situation? The shy behavior will increase the person's uncertainty about successfully conveying the intended public image. This, in turn, will further increase the person's shyness. Again, a vicious cycle is established. Consider, for example, a young adolescent going to his first date with a girl he secretly admires. He will most likely lack the social skills to handle this situation; this will make him shy. The more he wants to convey the image that he is a cool hand at dates, the more his shyness will interfere with his self-presentation: it will promote itself via a positive feedback loop.

Thus, both in embarrassment and in shyness vicious cycles of being embarrassed about appearing embarrassed or of being shy because of appearing shy may develop. There are two necessary conditions for these cycles. One is that the per- son holds the standard not to appear embarrassed or shy. Although it seems obvious in our present western culture that adults usually will try not to appear too shy or embarrassed in public, there are exceptions. Socially anxious behavior can be highly ritualized in the presence of those in authority, for example. And some decades ago it was a common tactic among women to coquet with shyness (cf. Hellpach, 1913).

The second necessary condition for the development of these vicious cycles is that the critical behavior is not sufficien- tly under voluntary control. If you could perfectly control all overt manifestations of social anxiety in situations that potentially make you socially anxious, vicious cycles would not develop. But many of our socially anxious reactions are subject to voluntary control to only a limited degree. For example, autonomic responses such as blushing in embarrassment can hardly be controlled at all. Another example is gaze aversion which appears to be controllable to some degree but not completely. This often leads to an ambivalent looking behavior which Darwin beautifully described as follows:

"An ashamed person can hardly endure to meet the gaze of those present, so that he almost invariably casts down his eyes or looks askant. As there generally exists at the same time a strong wish to avoid the appearance of shame, a vain attempt is made to look directly at the person who causes this feeling; and the antagonism between these opposite tendencies leads to various restless movements in the eyes" (Darwin, 1872, pp. 320-321).

The partial uncontrollability of socially anxious behavior brings us to an interesting phenomenon that may play a major role in more severe social anxiety although so far it seems to be supported only by clinical evidence: paradoxical control effects. If you blush in embarrassment and voluntarily try to suppress your blushing, you may often not only fail in your control attempt but may in fact blush even more. This parado- xical control effect has a counterpart in the psychotherapeu- tic strategy of paradoxical intention developed by Frankl

(1960): One way of handling spontaneously occurring behavioral disorders such as excessive blushing or stuttering is to instruct the patient to voluntarily try to <u>increase</u> the problematic behavior. This often seems to lead to a factual <u>decrease</u> of the problem.

Both paradoxical effects can be explained when we again look at the vicious cycles involved in social anxiety. If you voluntarily try to suppress your socially anxious behavior, this will <u>increase</u> the salience of the standard not to appear anxious. As we have seen before, this, in turn, will intensify your socially anxious behavior insofar as you cannot control it sufficiently. On the other hand, the paradoxical intention to increase your socially anxious behavior should prevent the vicious cycle since this intention will <u>decrease</u> the salience of the standard not to appear anxious.

These vicious cycles nicely illustrate the <u>twofold</u> self-presentational nature of social anxiety: Social anxiety is caused by self-presentation problems, and its activation may lead to additional self-presentation problems of its own. This twofold nature is schematically represented in Figure 1 for the particular case of embarrassment; for shyness, the line of reasoning is essentially similar.

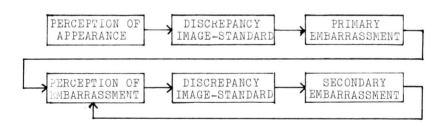

Figure 1: Schema of the vicious cycle involved in embarrassment

Embarrassment begins when you perceive a discrepancy between your public image (i.e., your perception of the impression others have formed about yourself) and a salient standard for this image. The perception of this discrepancy leads to a <u>primary embarrassment reaction</u>. The perception of this primary embarrassment reaction will induce a new discrepancy between image and standard if a standard is salient not to show embarrassment in public. This new discrepancy, in turn, leads to a more intense embarrassment reaction that we may call a <u>secondary embarrassment reaction</u>. The perception of this secondary reaction further increases the image-standard

J. Asendorpf

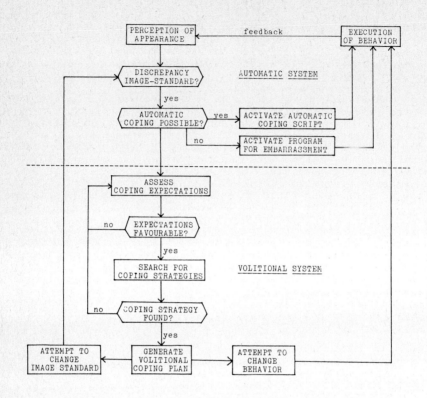

Figure 2: A heuristic process model of embarrassment

discrepancy. Now a positive feedback loop has been established that promotes embarrassment more and more.

You can modify this process, though, by means of coping strategies. Figure 2 shows a more elaborated model of embarrassment that includes coping processes; again, an essentially similar model can be designed for shyness.

The model assumes that it is not the perceived image-standard discrepancy itself that generates embarrassment. Rather it is the perceived inability to cope with this discrepancy which is the critical point. This is consistent with Lazarus's distinction between primary and secondary appraisal (cf. Lazarus, 1966). If primary appraisal de- tects an image-standard discrepancy, this does not necessarily lead to an embarrassment reaction. If there exists an overlearned automatic coping script that can be enacted with minimal conscious involvement (a standard joke, for instance), automatic coping takes place and prevents embarrassment. Only if such an automatic coping script does not exist, a program for a primary embarrassment reaction will be activated.

Note, that until this point of appraisal all processes are assumed to be automatic and preattentive. This is consistent with recent conceptions of emotion that presuppose affective mechanisms functioning on a subliminal level (cf. Zajonc, 1980; Leventhal, 1980).

Whether automatic coping is possible or not, the image-standard discrepancy is amplified for further processing in a volitional coping system. Here, much more extended secondary appraisal processes take place, and new coping plans can be generated which the person has never before executed. Parts of these processes reach conscious awareness.

Volitional coping begins with the assessment of coping expectations. If these expectations are very low the assessment phase will be rehearsed. In this way, the person may become quickly locked in the assessment phase which seriously interferes with effective coping (cf. Carver & Scheier, 1981; Crozier, 1979): people may not even try to search for coping strategies.

If the person sees a chance to cope successfully, a search for an effective coping strategy begins. If this search turns out to be unsuccessful, coping expectations are assessed again. In this way a loop may become established that quickly decreases the coping expectation of the person.

If their search for an effective coping strategy seems subjectively successful, people will generate a volitional coping plan. They will either try to change their image standard (as during the attempted execution of a paradoxical intention) or they will try to change their behavior (as during the attempted suppression of overt embarrassment).

Whether these coping attempts are successful or not will
depend upon the <u>resistance to change</u> in both cases. Changing
one's behavior may be impossible because the critical behavior
is not sufficiently under voluntary control. And changing
one's standard for an actual public image may be incompatible
with higher-level standards for one's social self-concept. In
fact, the control theory perspective assumes that standards at
one particular level of behavioral control can be changed only
by a higher-level system (cf. Powers, 1973; Carver & Scheier,
1981). Thus, image standards can be changed only by a system
on a level higher than image control such as the level of
controlling one's self-concept. In any case, resistance to
change may seriously interfere with the volitional coping
attempt, and the resulting unsuccessful coping will lead to a
less favourable reappraisal of one's coping ability.

This model already accounts for some central features of
social anxiety: vicious cycles involved in shyness and embarrassment, paradoxical effects of attempts to voluntarily
control behavior that is not under voluntary control, and some
aspects of the self-preoccupation found in more intense social
anxiety.

The model still lacks elaboration in at least three respects.
First of all, the self-assessment processes that influence
coping expectations should be elaborated in more detail. In
this connection the model should more explicitly describe the
processes that direct the focus of attention during shyness
and embarrassment. And finally, the model is presently
restricted to just one level of self-regulation: the control
of one's public image. In our discussion of potential resist-
ances to voluntarily changing image standards we have already
pointed out that image standards can be changed only by a
higher-level system, for example by the system controlling
one's self-concept. Future versions of the model should take
this into account more explicitly.

In concluding, a remark on the nature of the model presented
seems necessary. The model is not meant to describe reality in
any one-to-one fashion. I do not assume that the model can be
falsified in a strict sense. It is a <u>heuristic</u> model aiming
(a) to structure the discussion of the various mediating
processes involved in social anxiety, (b) to provide some
guidelines for the operationalization of socially anxious
behavior, and (c) to help to generate new empirically testable
hypotheses.

The Self in Anxiety, Stress and Depression
R. Schwarzer (Editor)
© Elsevier Science Publishers B.V. (North-Holland), 1984

WORRY, INTELLIGENCE AND ACADEMIC BEHAVIOR IN DUTCH SCHOOL CHILDREN

Henk M. van der Ploeg

University of Leiden, The Netherlands

Anxiety generally refers to an unpleasant emotional reaction that results from the perception or appraisal of a particular situation as threatening. The perception of achievement demanding situations as threats to the self generally results in test anxiety, either as a trait (Spielberger, 1980) or as a state (Morris, Franklin, & Ponath, 1983). In essence, test anxiety refers to individual differences in the disposition to experience feelings of apprehension and worry cognitions in academic environments, where the performance of students or pupils is under scrutiny (Schwarzer, Van der Ploeg, & Spielberger, 1982). This conceptualization emphasizes the cognitive determinants of state anxiety reactions in evaluative situations. Test anxiety, defined as a situation-specific personality trait or as a state, contains a cognitive component, worry, and an affective arousal-related component, emotionality. Cognitions about the self appear to be critical precursors in the process of developing test anxiety. These cognitions generally involve negative evaluations about academic ability, self-worth, and one's social standing that make the test anxious person more vulnerable to feeling threatened in evaluative situations (Schwarzer, et al., 1982). The worry component of test anxiety has been defined as cognitive concerns about the consequencces of failure, particularly concerns about poor performance and negative self-evaluations. Worry seems to be responsible for the debilitating effects of test anxiety on performance. The worrying individual directs his/her attention to the self as actor instead of to the task at hand, lacks confidence in his ability, and often feels inadequate and insecure. He thinks that others are much brighter than he is, and consequently perceives himself as more vulnerable to failure (Schwarzer, et al., 1982).

Academic performance is impaired by test anxiety, as is shown in much research. Intelligence, in general, is positively and significantly related to academic grades or academic behavior. Gaudry and Fitzgerald (1971) reported about their research in Australia. Test anxiety as well as intelligence were related to (high) school marks. Their hypothesis was that high anxiety would facilitate the performance of the most able group and lower the performance of the remainder when compared with comparable low-anxious groups. This hypothesis received no support, although their data are generally suggestive of the predicted trends. In some courses (History and Geography) the high anxiety and high intelligence group performed better than

the low anxiety and high intelligence subjects, while high
anxiety was associated with lower performance at the lower
ability levels. In other courses (English, Mathematics,
French, and Science), the pattern of interaction was similar
to that found in History and Geography, with the effect of
anxiety being produced only in the lower ability
(intelligence) groups. High anxiety has a detrimental effect
on performance at the two lowest (of five) and the second
highest level of ability, whereas the direction of the effect
was reversed at the highest level of ability. Inspection
of their tables reveals that this reverse of effect at the
highest ability level could hardly be of any significance.
Unfortunately they did not study the components of test
anxiety and did not look for the impact of the worry
cognitions.

Sharma and Rao (1983) reported about their research in India.
They also studied test anxiety, intelligence and performance
interactions. They found that low test anxious girls scored
consistantly higher than their high test anxious counterparts
on the three courses they studied in their research (English,
Mathematics and General Science). Also high intelligence was
associated with high academic performance. Their interaction
results can be summarized by stating that the low intelligence
groups scored low and at comparable levels irrespective of
their levels of test anxiety. At the high intelligence level
the academic performance (in English and Mathematics) was
significantly debilitated by high test anxiety. They concluded that the debilitating effects of high test anxiety on
performance were nested in the upper range of intelligence,
and that school girls within a lower range of intelligence
achieved less and at comparable levels regardless of their
test anxiety levels. The findings are more or less inconsistent with the ones reported by Gaudry and Fitzgerald (1971).
Unfortunately, Sharma and Rao did not look for the impact of
the worry cognitions, too.

As may be clear from the above, relationships between test
anxiety, intelligence, and performance are complex ones.
Furthermore, we are hardly aware of longitudinal relationships
within the test anxiety and performance interactions.

In order to investigate that above-mentioned relationships,
unfamiliar with the study by Sharma and Rao (1983), in 1980 –
1983 a study was conducted by taking test anxiety, including
both the worry and emotionality components, and intelligence
as independent variables. The dependent variables were
academic performance indices, consisting of the sum of grades
of male and female Dutch children in their first and second
year at secondary school.

METHOD

Sample. We studied a group of secondary school children (57 boys and 97 girls) in their first (aged about 12 years) and in their next or second year (aged about 13 years) at secondary school. They were tested in six groups, containing about 25 children (6 classes) each, approximately three months after the beginning of their first year course, and also in their second year course (approximately 14 months later).

Measures. We administered the Test Anxiety Inventory (Van der Ploeg, 1982, 1983), a Dutch adaptation of the Spielberger Test Anxiety Inventory (Spielberger, 1980). The TAI-D (TAI-Dutch) provides a total score, and two subscores indicating: worry (W) and emotionality (E). The Dutch TAI appears to be an internally consistent, reliable and valid scale for measuring test anxiety in Dutch speaking populations.

The State-Trait-Anxiety Inventory (STAI-DY, Van der Ploeg, Defares, and Spielberger, 1979, 1980; Van der Ploeg, 1981, 1984), a Dutch adaptation of the Spielberger State-Trait Anxiety Inventory, Form Y, (Spielberger, Gorsuch, and Lushene, 1970; Spielberger, 1983) was administered as well. We made use of the trait anxiety (T-Anxiety) score. The STAI-DY can be considered as a reliable and valid scale for measuring anxiety in The Netherlands.

The level of intelligence was based upon two separate indices with regard to the children's abilities upon leaving elementary school. In the sixth year at primary school an independent testing office advised about the level of intelligence and the best level of education at secondary school. In The Netherlands one can choose between several streams. Besides this independent advice we made use of the advice given by the teachers and the head of the primary school about the best secondary stream to be followed. These two advices are highly and significantly correlated (for boys $r = .72$, $p < .001$; for girls $r = .64$, $p < .001$). We combined these two advices and constructed one score indicating the level of intelligence. In the following we shall divide the group into pupils with either high or low level of intelligence, depending on the median of the combined intelligence scores.

Procedure. The anxiety tests were administered to small groups under standard conditions. The intelligence score was obtained following the above described standard rule. Achievement scores were obtained by inspection of the most important report, the one at the end of the course, just before the summer holidays. This report is decisive as to whether or not a pupil will go on to the next (second, or third) form. In the first year the pupils follow seven courses: three languages, Dutch, French, English, and History, Geography, Biology and Mathematics. In the second year two other courses are added: the German language and Physics. In most of our analysis we have summed up the grades obtained at

these summer reports, the total of which at the end of the
first year being the sum of seven, and at the end of the
second year the sum of nine grades.

RESULTS

Correlational Analysis. Test anxiety, measured in their first
year at secondary school, is a better predictor of achievement
than trait anxiety. Within test anxiety worry is a somewhat
better predictor than emotionality, as is reported by many
others.

Test Anxiety (TAI Total). The influence of test anxiety on
the mean sum of grades, in the first and second year at
secondary school is reported in Table 1 (left part), for boys
and girls separately.

For the high test anxious boys as well as girls the performance indices are more or less the same. Low test anxious
boys, however, obtain higher mean sums of grades than their
female counterparts. This may indicate that boys experience
larger performance decrements from being anxious than female
pupils in the same classes.

Table 1:   Mean Sum of Grades, groups divided into below and
             above median TAI Total and median score for
             Intelligence

SUM OF GRADES	TEST ANXIETY		INTELLIGENCE	
	LOW	HIGH	LOW	HIGH
FIRST YEAR				
BOYS	54.2	46.8	47.8	53.6
GIRLS	50.9	46.6	45.7	51.8
SECOND YEAR				
BOYS	67.2	57.4	58.7	67.6
GIRLS	63.2	57.8	57.5	63.7

Intelligence.   Besides   the influence of test anxiety we have
also   studied   the influence of intelligence upon the   sum   of
grades.   As can be seen in Table 1 (right part), in which the
differences   are   about   the same as compared with   the   performance   decrements influenced by test anxiety,   lower levels
of intelligence have detrimental effects upon the mean sum   of
grades.   Whereas,   in   the   male   groups,   these   detrimental
effects   of test anxiety are relatively large,   with regard to
intelligence the picture is less clear.   In the first year   a
somewhat larger diversity is to be seen in the group of girls,
in   the second year the means for boys differ more.   However,
as stated before, the differences are very small.

The   interaction of test anxiety and intelligence.   Both test
anxiety   and   intelligence   are important   variables   for   the
explanation of the achievement of the pupils under study.

Table   2 shows that our groups of pupils were   divided   within
their   own sex-group according to the median scores for   test
anxiety and for intelligence.   Afterwards we computed the mean
sum of grades obtained by the different subgroups of boys   and
girls   in their first,   and in their second year at   secondary
school.

The   highest   means   are   obtained by low   anxious   and   high
intelligent   pupils.   High anxious and low intelligent pupils
are the worst performers.

In   the groups of girls it can be observed that girls   with   a
lower   level   of intelligence are hardly influenced by   higher
levels of test anxiety.   The performances of low   intelligent
girls   are comparable,   to some extent,   irrespective of their
level of test anxiety.

But   in the groups with a higher level of   intelligence,   high
levels of test anxiety produces large performance   decrements.
The   performance   discrepancy is more outspoken for boys   than
for girls.   Also,   in the second year,   these differences are
more outspoken than in the first year.

Table 2:   Mean Sum of Grades, Groups divided into below and above median scores for Test Anxiety (TAI Total) and for Intelligence

---

	BOYS		GIRLS	

FIRST YEAR	INTELLIGENCE		INTELLIGENCE	
TEST ANXIETY	LOW	HIGH	LOW	HIGH
LOW	50.7	56.2	46.9	53.4
HIGH	46.4.	47.6	44.9	48.6
SECOND YEAR				
TEST ANXIETY				
LOW	60.7	71.7	58.5	66.0
HIGH	57.7	57.6	56.7	59.8

The interaction of worry and intelligence. In Table 3 we have summarized the mean sum of grades for the groups of pupils with scores below and above the median for worry and intelligence.

Performance decrements are larger with the high intelligent groups. Furthermore, worry causes more detrimental effects than the total score for test anxiety. In these analyses, girls with a lower level of intelligence seem to be less influenced by worry cognitions than low intelligent boys. Also, high intelligent boys seem to be the ones most influenced by the worry factor, especially in their second year.

Table 3:   Mean Sum of Grades, Groups divided into below and above median scores for Worry and for Intelligence.

	BOYS		GIRLS	

FIRST YEAR	INTELLIGENCE		INTELLIGENCE	
WORRY	LOW	HIGH	LOW	HIGH
LOW	51.7	56.2	48.4	54.2
HIGH	45.7	47.6	44.1	48.7
SECOND YEAR				
WORRY				
LOW	63.6	71.7	59.0	67.6
HIGH	56.3	57.6	56.2	59.5

The interaction of emotionality and intelligence. Finally, we studied the interaction of emotionality and intelligence. Again, emotionality "causes" less performance decrements than worry. Low intelligent girls are hardly influenced by high emotionality. High intelligent boys seem to be the most influenced pupils in these analyses. In the second year at seondary school the discrepancies between low and high levels of emotionality are greater than in the first year.

Further analyses. Several separate analyses of variance (2 x 2 x 2 ANOVA) were carried out. The sum of grades, the grade for the Dutch language (the mother tongue) and the one for Mathematics, in the first as well as in the second year, were the dependent variables. Intelligence, test anxiety (TAI total), and sex were the dependent variables.

A consistent main effect of test anxiety was observed with low test anxious boys or girls scoring higher than their high test anxious counterparts.

Also, a consistent main effect of intelligence was observed with low intelligent boys or girls scoring lower than their more intelligent counterparts.

The main effect for sex turned out to be statistically significant for the sum of grades in the second year and for Mathematics in the first and in the second year, with boys scoring higher.

H.M. van der Ploeg

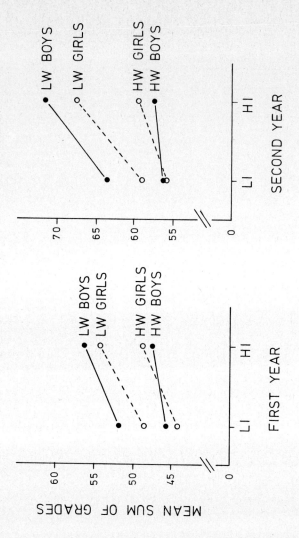

Figure 1: Mean Sum of Grades for Test-Anxious and Non-Anxious Girls and Boys

Significant interactions of test anxiety and intelligence were observed in all cases, except for the grades for the Dutch language in the first year at school.

Finally, there was a rather weak interaction between test anxiety, and sex for Mathematics in the second year.

Thus, we can conclude that the most detrimental effect of test anxiety and especially of the worry component, can be seen in the groups with a higher level of intelligence.

Groups with a lower level of intelligence perform at a lower level and seem to be less influenced by test anxiety and its components.

DISCUSSION

The findings that in the first place test anxiety and intelligence are significantly related to achievement and secondly that high test anxious boys and girls achieve lower than their low anxious counterparts are consistent with the conclusions of previous research.

Furthermore, it was found that the debilitating effects of high test anxiety on performance are nested in the upper range of intelligence. Boys and girls with a lower level of intelligence achieved less and were less influenced by the impairing effects of test anxiety. This finding was found also by Sharma and Rao (1983) for a culturally different group of female pupils in India, and is consistent with the results reported by Gaudry and Fitzgerald (1971) on Australian high school boys and girls.

In the group of low intelligent boys, the introduction of the worry factor produces in our study larger mean performance discrepancies upon comparing low and high test anxious versus low and high worrying boys. Also, for low as well as for high intelligent girls the introduction of the worry component of test anxiety produces somewhat larger differences between low and high test anxious versus low and high worrying girls. Worry, as a self-related cognition, is of great importance for the explanation of performance impairment, more important than the (general) concept of test anxiety. This cognitive component is highly related to the debilitating effects of high test anxiety on the academic behavior of pupils in the upper range of intelligence.

These high intelligent and high anxious pupils/students may improve after getting rid of their anxieties, even if it would be only a slight part of it. Besides the development of programs for the treatment and help of pupils with high levels of worrying, also their study habits, the amount of time spent on their studies, their social standards as well as their vocational aspirations and their perceived parental pressure

to succeed deserve our attention. For some of these relatively young pupils these parental influences must have been
rather stressful, and may have caused a lot of anxiety and
self-related cognitions (Van der Ploeg-Stapert and Van der
Ploeg, 1984).

In our further study of the test anxiety phenomenon, besides
other before mentioned relevant variables, we want to include
these parental pressures. Because it is most probable that in
our (Dutch) culture parents require different achievements
from their sons than they do from their daughters, and because
(test) anxiety may be differentially felt and reported, it is
of great importance to differentiate between boys and girls in
the study of test anxiety.

The Self in Anxiety, Stress and Depression
R. Schwarzer (Editor)
© Elsevier Science Publishers B.V. (North-Holland), 1984

PERFECTIONISM AND THE THREAT TO SELF-ESTEEM IN CLINICAL ANXIETY

Chris J.S. Nekanda-Trepka

Bangour Village Hospital, West Lothian, Scotland

Burns (1980b) has characterised a certain type of patient as perfectionistic. Perfectionism is described as an attitudinal style, the main elements of which may be summarised as follows:

- The maintenance of standards of behaviour, performance or appearance which are extremely high, if not impossible to meet.
- The linking of self-esteem to the attainment of these standards, whereby failure to reach them causes a reduction in self-esteem.
- The tendency to self-evaluate in all-or-nothing terms, such that events are perceived in terms of absolute success or failure rather than varying degrees of achievement.

Burns suggests that the resulting attitude may dispose an individual to develop certain psychiatric problems, including obsessive-compulsive disorder, depression, and social or performance anxiety. Associated problems might include tendencies to procrastinate, 'drop-out' of competive situations, and fear of criticism or rejection, resulting in low self-disclosure. These phenomena result from fear of failing to produce the 'perfect article'. Similarly, over-concern with the quality of performance can impair overall efficiency, since the perfectionist would spend an inordinate amount of time to get small details just right. Burns specu-lates about how this maladaptive cognitive style might origi-nate from a childhood in which parents and teachers have high expectations of the child, making approval and other contin-gent upon outstanding performance.

The present author has recognised many of these features in some patients encountered in routine clinical work. For example, one girl presented with a phobia for examinations which had incapacitated her during some recent exams. Assessment indicated that she also experienced anxiety in many situations not connected with her academic work. The common link between all the situations was her fear that she would not perform at the upper limit of her potential with regard to whatever task she happened to be undertaking. For her, failure to do this represented failure as a person, carrying the implication that she would never get anywhere in life.

Clearly, this patient's approach to life fits the above description of perfectionism. Moreover, her perfectionistic ideas appeared to be triggering her anxiety reactions in a very direct way.

Burns has also outlined principles for modifying perfectionism. These have proved useful in treating patients like this girl. It has been our experience with cases like this that basing a treatment programme on modifying perfectionism can lead to the successful resolution of anxiety problems. What is interesting is that symptomatic improvement appears to occur as a direct result of altering attitudes. Techniques of learning how to cope with anxiety and tolerate exposure to anxiety-producing situations have rarely appeared to be necessary. In contrast, the treatment of non-perfectionistic anxious patients has generally relied heavily on the use of such anxiety management techniques. Subjectively, it appears that the apparently similar anxiety problems presented by perfectionistic and non-perfectionistic patients are most rapidly resolved by very different treatment strategies.

The main part of the paper further investigates the differences between perfectionistic and non-perfectionistic patients. Burns' concept is an interesting one, of apparent clinical relevance, but it lacks any empirical basis. Objective criteria for identifying perfectionism are necessary. Furthermore, it is unclear whether identification of patients as perfectionistic carries any predictive power with regard to other important characteristics of the patients and their psychopathology.

METHOD

Owing to the lack of previous findings about perfectionism, this investigation was necessarily exploratory rather than taking the form of a controlled trial. Nevertheless, all possible steps were taken to avoid bias or other sources of error.

The subjects of the investigation were 22 patients treated by this author from his usual sources of referral. This sample was drawn from 86 caseload records on thhe basis of the presence of a clearly identifiable primary anxiety disorder. So that the group would be relatively homogeneous, patients with complicating factors such as concurrent depression, alcoholism, personality disorder, or psychosomatic illness were not included in the sample. Nor were those patients whose anxiety problems failed to meet the diagnostic criteria in DSM III (American Psychiatric Association, 1980).

Nine of the twenty-two cases thus obtained had previously been identified as perfectionists, during the course of treatment.

These were compared with the remaining thirteen 'non-perfectionists' on the information that was available in caseload records. This information had also been collected by this author as a matter of routine for all patients who were seen. Hence, it had not been obtained or coded specifically for this study.

One of the clinical objectives in the early stages of assessment of this series of patients was to pinpoint the main types of threat perceived by each individual in anxiety-producing situations. Appraisal of danger or threat is considered by cognitive theorists to play a primary role in triggering anxiety reactions (e.g., Beck, 1976). This view is widely accepted in that appraisal of threat is allocated a central place in contemporary models of anxiety, such as that proposed by Lader and Marks (1971). Cognitive-functional analysis (Meichenbaum, 1976) was employed to identify the environmental determinants and consequences of anxiety and analyse accompanying cognitions. Such analysis produced a specification of the major threats which appeared to trigger anxiety in each individual. Thus the two groups could also be compared using the resulting material.

RESULTS

Table   1:   Diagnosis   and   content   of   ideation   of
----------   ' perfectionistic' anxious patients.

DIAGNOSIS	CONTENT OF IDEATION
Obsessive-Compulsive disorder	Carelessness (causing an accident)
Obsessive-Compulsive disorder	Failing to understand = stupid; no self-control
Obsessive-Compulsive disorder	Not doing things right; being a bad mother
Social phobia	Blushing; being seen as weak
Social phobia	Blushing; being seen as incompetent
Phobia (work-related)	Not doing things ' right'
Phobia for exams	Failing to do well
Generalised Anxiety disorder	Failing to cope
Generalised Anxiety disorder	Failing to cope; criticism

The threats identified in cognitive-functional analysis with the perfectionistic patients are listed in table 1. Many of these patients appeared to become anxious when they feared they would not perform well. Others were concerned about

their appearance in social situations, often accompanied by
fears of negative evaluation by others. Subjectively poor
quality of performance often led to the patients applying
disparaging labels to themselves such as stupidity or
weakness. A common link between the fears is that they all
primarily relate to self-esteem. These patients seemed rather
less concerned with any possible external consequences of poor
performance than with the implication poor performance had for
their view of themselves. Thus the exam phobic was not primarily concerned about failing her exams, but about being a
failure as a person. Similarly, an obsessional patient feared
accidentally poisoning her family. Analysis of this fear
revealed that what bothered her about this was not so much the
possibility of causing serious harm to anyone but of confirming to herself that she was a careless, irresponsible person.

Table 2:   Diagnosis and content of ideation of 'nonperfectio-
           nistic' anxious patients

DIAGNOSIS	CONTENT OF IDEATION
Agoraphobia	Suffocation
Agoraphobia	Fainting
Agoraphobia	Fainting; suffocation
Agoraphobia	Uncontrollable vomiting
Agoraphobia	Being attacked, mugged, or raped
Phobia for heights	Falling; going berserk and jumping
Phobia for flying	Plane crashing; going berserk
Phobia for wind	House blowing down; going insane
Phobia for hospitals	Having major surgery and dying under anaesthetic
Phobia for dental treatment	Going berserk; death under anaesthetic
Generalised Anxiety disorder	Going insane; killing or injuring someone
Generalised Anxiety disorder	Sudden death while asleep; suffocation
Panic disorder	Heart attack; suffocation

The content of these fears may be compared with comparable
material elicited from the non-perfectionistic patients. Many
of these individuals feared for their physical well-being,
anticipating death, serious illness or accidents. Several
feared loss of psychological control e.g., going insane or
running amok. The fears of these patients do not primarily
pertain to self-esteem, but to specific adverse physical or
psychological events. Comparison of the two tables suggests
that perfectionism may be identified in an analysis of
anxiety-related ideation by the presence of perceived threats
to self-esteem.

The perfectionists and non-perfectionists also appeared to differ with regard to the relative proportion of sub-categories of anxiety disorder. The non-perfectionist group contained a high proportion of phobic patients. Several were agoraphobic, while others had phobias specific to certain situations such as heights, air travel, and wind. Some of the perfectionists also had phobias, but these were exclusively social or performance phobias. Individuals with obsessive-compulsive disorder were confined to the perfectionistic group. Hence, there appear to be some diagnostic differences between the two groups.

Table 3: Questionnaire scores obtained by perfectionists and non-perfectionists

	PERFECTIONISTS		NON-PERFECTIONISTS			
	MEAN	SD	MEAN	SD	t	p
TRAIT ANXIETY (STAI-T)	52.4	11.0	58.5	10.7	.91	ns
FEAR OF NEGATIVE EVALUATION (FNE)	21.5	6.2	23.0	7.7	.11	ns
MALADAPTIVE ATTITUDES	-6.0	14.4	6.0	11.4	1.39	$<.10$

Table 3 shows mean group scores on three questionnaires completed by the patients just after the initial assessment interview. The two groups did not differ on trait anxiety (Spielberger, Gorsuch & Lushene, 1969) or fear of negative evaluation (Watson & Friend, 1969). However, there appeared to be some difference on a measure of maladaptive attitudes. This measure originates from the Dysfunctional Attitude Scale developed by Weissman and Beck (1978), and is based on the shortened version used by Burns (1980a). The scale is intended to measure perfectionistic tendencies, need for achievement, approval, and love. It has a theoretical mean of zero which would indicate a balance of functional and dysfunctional attitudes. The perfectionist group obtained a lower mean score on this scale, suggesting more maladaptive attitudes.

The perfectionists were significantly higher in socio-economic status (Mann-Whitney U = 26, p $<$ .05). All of them came from

social classes two and three, while the other group contained
some individuals from the lower social classes. A similar
picture is found with educational level. Several of the
perfectionists held higher educational qualifications, while
the majority of the other group had no qualifications at all.
The difference is significant at the .05 level (U = 25.5).

Treatment of the two groups took very different forms.
Treatment of the perfectionists focussed on attitude change,
while anxiety management techniques were emphasised in
treatment of non-perfectionistic patients. However, outcome
was very similar in both groups. 75% of the perfectionists
achieved a satisfactory outcome, and the mean number of
sessions for those treated successfully was 7.8. The
corresponding figures for the other group were 78% and 6.4
sessions.

STUDY TWO

It is, of course, important to establish whether the apparent
differences in cognitive content reported above are
sufficiently distinct to be replicable. Hence, the
reliability of identifying different types of perceived threat
in reported ideation was examined.

Brief details about the content of anxiety-related ideation
for 32 anxious patients are presented by Beck and Emery
(1979). The present author and a colleague independently
classified these patients into two groups as the basis of
these details. The aim of classification was to seperate
those patients whose main fear appeared to concern threats to
physical well-being from those whose main fear related to
self-esteem.

This constituted a rigorous test of whether reliable
classification of anxiety-related ideation was possible. The
classification categories were broad, and Beck and Emery's
data had not been produced for this purpose. Neither judge
had seen any of the patients or had any other information
available about them, and one of the judges had no background
in cognitive theories or treatment, specialising in
psychodynamic work. Nevertheless, the percentage agreement
obtained was 93.75%, giving a Kappa coefficient (Cohen, 1960)
of .875. Notwithstanding any difficulty in operationalising
the contrast of ' perfectionism' per se, such a high level of
agreement indicates that threats to self-esteem can be
identified from reported anxiety-related ideation with
acceptable reliability.

DISCUSSION

This investigation is an exploratory one. Its results cannot be claimed to establish an empirical basis for the concept of perfectionism described earlier. Nevertheless, the findings seem consistent with Burns' (1980b) analysis, and may be of heuristic value.

The patients classed as perfectionists did appear to link their valuations of themselves to events and behaviours. Their anxiety problems could be understood to result from this, whereas those of the other anxious patients could not. Brief therapy emphasising modification of perfectionism seemed to be effective.

The validity of the concept of perfectionism and treatment implications require to be tested by further research. In order to do this, clear objective criteria for identifying perfectionism are necessary. These findings suggest such criteria might include the type of threat perceived in anxiety-producing situations. It remains to be seen whether the presence of perceived threats to self-esteem indicates the presence of a perfectionistic attitudinal style.

Even if this should prove not to be the case, the distinction to different types of threat might yet be of value. This distinction may help us to understand clearly the difference between sub-types of anxiety-disorder. For instance, the present findings suggest the cognitive phenomenology of social and performance phobias is different from that of agoraphobia and some situation-specific phobias. It is conceivable this reflects different areas of evolutionary significance. Perhaps the latter phobias might be understood in terms of physical survival, while the former pertain to the maintenance of one's place in the pecking order.

It would be interesting to compare classification of anxiety disorders based on these cognitive differences with categorisations derived from learning theory, such as that of Seligman (1971), who employed the concept of preparedness. As Marks (1969) has pointed out; the value of any classification depends largely upon the predictive power it provides. Isolation of different types of threat does appear to predict differences in social class and education. Perhaps the fundamental difference is in intelligence. The associations observed need to be confirmed in a controlled study.

Another relevant variable could be onset of the disorder. Beck and Rush (1978) reported that anxiety disorders with slow, insidious onset tend to be associated with fears of criticism, rejection, or interpersonal failure. In contrast, fears concerning physical well-being or loss of control were found in disorders of acute onset. This distinction in the content of anxiety-related ideation appears identical with the one observed here.

The relative effectiveness of various forms of treatment for
anxiety is another variable for which prediction is important.
Comparative research has not identified major differences in
the effectiveness of the main therapies for neurotic
disorders, and it is possible that a clearer picture might be
obtained from the examination of more discrete sub-categories
of disorder (Shapiro 1980; Rachman & Hodgson, 1980). The
present analysis suggests the two types of anxious patients
might be most effectively treated by somewhat different
treatment strategies. Confirmation of this would not only
establish the validity of distinguishing anxiety problems
involving perceived threats to self-esteem, but would further
the cause of comparative research.

Conceptually, this distinction can be made reliably.
Nevertheless, major questions remain. The reliability with
which perceived threats can be elicited from anxious patients
has yet to be studied. Moreover, the relationships observed
with threats to self-esteem still have to be shown to hold
when cases are independently classified into sub-groups.
Until this has been done, no solid conclusions can be drawn.

However, one final point is worth making. Several authors
have emphasised the importance of establishing reliable
procedures for assessing cognitions to the development of
cognitive-behavioural therapies (e.g., Kendall and Korgeski,
1979; Mahoney and Arnkoff, 1978). Such procedures appear
difficult to establish for many reasons, including problems of
accessing cognitive phenomena which are of direct relevance to
psychopathology. This investigation has led to consideration
of the nature of the threat underlying anxiety-related
ideations. The results suggest this area could be a fruitful
one for further examination.

The Self in Anxiety, Stress and Depression
R. Schwarzer (Editor)
© Elsevier Science Publishers B.V. (North-Holland), 1984

TEMPORAL PATTERNS OF ANXIETY:
TOWARDS A PROCESS ANALYSIS OF ANXIETY AND PERFORMANCE

Rainer Wieland

Free University of Berlin, Federal Republic of Germany

In recent years there has been considerable interest in anxiety and its relationship to performance (Krohne, 1980; Krohne & Schaffner, 1980; Albert, 1980; Heinrich & Spielberger, 1982). The conceptual distinction between state and trait anxiety has proved useful in stimulating research on stress and anxiety and its relationship to performance (see Schwarzer et al., 1982). On the basis of this conceptualization it is argued that the degree of anxiety experienced (A-state) is interactively determined by the individual's susceptibility to anxiety (A-trait) and by the amount of stress in the situation. The basic interrelationships between trait anxiety, state anxiety, environmental stressors and performance can be summarized as follows: "State anxiety is determined jointly by environmental stress and trait anxiety, and it is state anxiety rather than trait anxiety which has a direct effect on processing activities" (M. Eysenck, 1982, p. 96).

With respect to performance there is a lot of evidence that this temporary emotional state, as a motivating factor as well as an additional internal demand (see Hamilton, 1975; Schönpflug, 1976, Heckhausen, 1982), leads mostly to performance decrements. Moreover, depending on certain conditions high anxiety may also have performance facilitating effects (e.g. for easy tasks the performance of high-anxious subjects will be superior to that of low-anxious subjects or later in learning, high anxiety will begin to facilitate performance).

But despite the empirical evidence for the hypothesis of a performance debilitating effect of anxiety, we do not feel that it offers a generally satisfactory account of the effects of anxiety on performance. For the purposes of this paper, we will focus on the following problems.

First of all, the hypothesis of a performance debilitating effect of anxiety becomes ambiguous as soon as real-life situations are investigated instead of artificial tasks (see Lazarus & Launier, 1978; Krohne, 1980; Krohne & Schaffner, 1980).

In accordance with Krohne and his co-workers, we believe that anxiety has a different impact on performance in real-life situations than in laboratory experiments or specific test situations. Most of the studies in this area investigated the

influence of anxiety in the actual achievement or testing
situation. Little attention has been paid to those factors in
real-life settings Krohne & Schaffner (1980) described as "the
length of preparation time" and "the opportunity to prepare
for an achievement situation". Furthermore, most studies have
been too narrowly restricted to the kind and range of
activities real-life situation naturally encompass. They
especially neglect the significance and influence of objective
and perceived degrees of freedom on the organization of action
(sequence and time-structure of actions; see Wieland, 1980,
1981). Secondly, there is a lack of distinction between
anxiety-related coping strategies **prior** to a performance
situation and of coping activities **during** confrontation with
achievement-related tasks. Anxiety related coping activities
should be distinguished with respect to their functional role
they play in different stages of the coping process. So, for
instance in the anticipation-period (between task announcement
and task application) avoidant thinking (see Houston, 1977) or
mental withdrawal (see Carver & Scheier, 1982,1984) may be
effective in reducing anxiety and the immediate costs of
effort-expenditure (performance is not required and avoidant
thinking may divert one's attention from stressful aspects of
the situation). However, during task-execution the same
strategy may be 'situation-inadequate' (see Epstein, 1976,
1979) by distracting the attention away from task-relevant
material and thereby preventing the allocation of available
resources to task-requirements (see Kahneman, 1973). Therefore
we concluded that persons, although reporting low pre-test
anxiety may obtain a low performance level. They are able to
control challenging or threatening information being relevant
prior to the performance situation (e.g. announcement of a
performance evaluation). However, if informational control is
a result of information rejection (see Holmes & Houston, 1974;
Niemelä, 1974), it may prevent an adequate preparation for
task-solution, and thereby behavioral control in the course of
a performance situation.

The main concern of this paper is to investigate temporal
patterns of state anxiety in achievement-related stress
situations. In this context, this present chapter is focused
on the following aspects:

(1) The validity of predictions of high or low anxiety states
from high or low scores in trait anxiety.

(2) The relationship between measurements of state anxiety in
different stages of a performance situation and the
performance level and efficiency.

(3) The interrelationship among temporal patterns of state
anxiety, personality, different coping modes and performance.

METHOD

Experimental design and the measurement of state anxiety. In
order to investigate the influence of anxiety on performance,
an experimental paradigm was designed including (1) a
computer-assisted training program (learning under non-stress
conditions), and (2) the testing situation, following the next
day.

FIRST DAY   PSYCHOLOGICAL SIGNIFICANCE
                             OF SITUATIONAL DEMANDS

TRAIT-STATE ANXIETY   UNCERTAINTY. Appraisal of an
  (1. Meas.)   achievement-situation without
                             knowing task-and situational demands.

COMPUTER-ASSISTED-   LEARNING under non-stress
TRAINING PROGRAM   conditions,
                             EVALUATION of task-requirements
                             and -difficulty.

            Opportunity to prepare for task-demands
               (e.g. sensitive or defensive coping)

SECOND DAY

PRE-STATE ANXIETY   THREAT/CHALLENGE. Appraisal of an
  (2. Meas.)   achievement-situation with
                             knowing the tasks, situational demands,
                             and working conditions.

EXECUTION OF TASKS   MODELING (e.g.Redefinition of tasks),
(On-line registration   GOAL-SETTING (e.g. orientation to the
of physiological   conditions   of   the   environment
data, and actions)   and within the data of memory).
                             STRATEGY FORMATION (e.g. designing or
                             reproducing of subgoals and action
                             programs.

POST-STATE ANXIETY   EVALUATION of intended results, ex-
  (3. Meas.)   pected consequences, unintended re-
                             sults, unexpected consequences, and
                             subjective effort/efficiency ratio.

Figure 1:State anxiety measurements and situational demands

Our subjects had the opportunity to prepare for the testing situation, and consequently three measurements of state anxiety were available: Before the training program, before the testing situation, and after the test. Figure 1 shows a simplified version of the experimental procedure used in our study.

Tasks-requirements and experimental conditions. According to the theoretical concept introduced above, the tasks and experimental conditions should be similar to those in real-life settings. Therefore we started with a detailed analysis of working conditions (clerical work) by means of individual interviews in field settings. Based on these interviews experimental tasks and conditions were constructed, which intend to simulate the most important features of the field setting.

Data from our field study documented that the following conditions were typical for clerical workers in carrying out their jobs:

(a) degrees of freedom for individual decision-making and goal setting, e.g. they were allowed to determine time and sequence of tasks-execution,

(b) task-requirements of varying difficulty and content,

(c) degrees of freedom regarding the regulation of work- and recovery-periods.

Based on these typical characteristics of the investigated work place, we tried to establish similar conditions in our experiment. Consequently, our subjects had degrees of freedom with regard to the above mentioned aspects. Corresponding to new technological developments often used in administrative work, our subjects had to perform their tasks using a video screen and keyboard with computer-assisted instructions. By pressing different keys the subjects could request all kinds of information relevant to task-solution. Each task consisted of a problem, four or five alternative decisions (one being considered optimal), and one to twelve pieces of information (e.g. price-lists, specified orders, personal data etc.). Depending on the kind of task (e.g. checking bills, controlling checkes, controlling bills), one to six pieces of information were necessary for task-solution. On the whole, eight blocks of tasks, each consisting of 8 to 15 single tasks of varying difficulty, complexity, and content had to be solved. No time-limits were set for task-solution or duration of recovery periods. The cognitive requirements made on the the subjects and the operations necessary to solve the different tasks can be summarized as follows: Problem-identification, goal-setting, decision-making, and evaluation of results. Our subjects were not restricted with regard to the duration, number or sequence of the operations mentioned above. Our subjects thus had to develop their own strategies.

Sample. The subjects were unemployed clerical workers from a local labour office. Seventy-two persons (50% females, 50% males) participated in the investigation. They were given about three and a half dollars per hour plus an extra gratification if they solved a certain number of tasks within a certain time-limit. Subjects were informed about these conditions.

Procedure. Each subject was tested in an individual session lasting a day and a half. The first day they were asked to respond to various questionaires (STAI; German version by Laux et al., 1979; coping modes, and other personality traits; for detailed information, see below, and Schönpflug & Wieland, 1982) and to take three subtests of an intelligence test (IST-Amthauer, 1971). They were then asked to work on the computer-assisted training program. In order to become familiar with the screen, the keyboard, and the different kinds of tasks which had to be solved in the testing situation, the subjects could go through the training program as often as they wanted to. There were no time-limits set. Pre-test state anxiety was measured the second day (see Figure 1) before the subjects were given the test program instructions. The third measurement of state anxiety was taken after working through the test program lasting on the average three and a half hours. For the duration of the test program, the state of general activation and emotional well-being was measured at the end of each block of tasks. Thus we were able to obtain some relevant information concerning the dynamic processes taking place during task-execution.

RESULTS AND DISCUSSION

Appraisal of the experimental setting. According to Prystav (1982), predictibility and controllability with regard to situational demands and task demands in achievement situations are the most important factors determining whether a person appraises such a situation as threatening or not. He states that achievement-situations being charaterized by temporal predictibility and predictibility with regard to the content and difficulty of the tasks are experienced by most subjects as being less threatening than those having the opposite characteristics on the above mentioned dimensions. According to such a classification, our data correspond well to Prystav's hypothesis. The three measurements of state anxiety indicated that the varying demands as described in Figure 1, do not have a substantial effect on the level of state anxiety (see Table 1).

Table 1: Means and standard deviations for the three
         measurements of state anxiety (N=72)

	Mean	Std Dev
Trait Anxiety	42.0	7.42
State 1 (day before)	37.9	8.12
State 2 (pre-test)	36.9	6.93
State 3 (post-test)	36.2	6.40

Further analysis of the self-report data revealed that most of
the subjects (63%) appraised the testing situation as a
challenge (and not as a threat), and that 69 0f 72 subjects
regarded the challenge of planning individual action-
strategies for tasks-solution as an opportunity, and not as an
additional demand. Furthermore, we apparently succeeded in
realizing an experimental setting similar to real-life
settings: 83.5 % of the subjects answered the question
concerning this aspect positively.

Comparison of low- and high-anxious (trait anxiety) subjects:
Pre- or postdiction? The comparison of high- and low anxious
subjects as shown in Table 2 demonstrated that the Trait-
State- Model as proposed by Spielberger (1972,1976) obviously
cannot be applied to achievement-requirements given subjects
the opportunity to prepare for tasks-demands. As our findings
indicated, high- and low-anxious subjects (A-trait) do not
differ with regard to pre-test state anxiety (the high
correlation between trait anxiety and state anxiety the day
before is not astonishing, since the two scales were taken at
the same time)
On the other hand, there was a significant difference in the
post-test state anxiety level. Obviously, the actual
confrontation with tasks demands and the coping strategies
used for task-solution seemed to be more important for the
interaction between trait anxiety and situational and/or task
demands. We therefore analysed the relationship between
anxiety and performance for further clarification.

According to Schönpflug (1982); Schulz & Schönpflug (1982),

and M. Eysenck (1979, 1982), we calculated two indices of
performance outcome: performance level achieved or correct
solutions   and   time   related efficiency (ratio   between
performance level and effort-expenditure whereby effort-
expenditure is defined as time spent on task solution).

Table 2: Comparison of high- and low-anxious subjects
           (A-Trait)

                        TRAIT ANXIETY

                   Low   High
            (< 40, N = 35) (> 41, N = 37)   p

State 1 (day before)   35.17   40.43   < .01

State 2 (pre-test)   35.18   37.19   < .67

State 3 (post-test)   34.37   37.92   < .03

As can be seen from Table 3 (see below) there were no
substantial correlations between trait anxiety, state anxiety
the day before and performance level. On the other hand, the
negative correlation coefficient of pre- and post-test state
anxiety indicated that high levels of state anxiety were
associated with impairements of information processing and/or
limitations of working memory (see Kahneman, 1973; M. Eysenck,
1979,1982). The difference between the two coefficients (r =
-.21 vs. r = -.34) gave evidence for the assumption that
anxiety,   elicited during task-execution is more closely
related to capacity limitations of working memory and/or
impairements of information processing. In contrast, high
levels of state anxiety at the begining of the test situation
does **not** have an impact on efficiency. It seems to be
reasonable to conclude from these findings that anxiety levels
before and after the test reflect different aspects of the
situational focus involved: After the test, the anxiety level
is primarily indicative of evaluation anxiety (see Wine, 1982)
resulting from the performance level achieved and subsequent
appraisal of coping activities used. The state anxiety level
before the test primarily reflects the ability and/or strategy
to   control challenging or threatening information (e.g.
announcement and/or anticipation of performance evaluation).

Interestingly, the within group changes of the pre- and post-
test   state anxiety levels (see Table 3) did **not** show

significant difference-scores between the two measurements.
Taking into account the discrepancy between the pre- and post-
test correlations of state anxiety and efficiency, we assume
that there were some intraindividual changes in state anxiety
not adequately represented if merely mean-scores of state
anxiety were calculated. Therefore, further analysis of data
has focused on intraindividual changes in state anxiety with
regard to temporal patterns of anxiety deriving either from
'increments' or 'decrements' in anxiety level (pre-post-test
difference-scores) as well as 'no-change'('no-change'
encompasses those subjects varying from + 1 to - 1 points on
the state anxiety scale).

Table   3:   Correlations between trait-state anxiety and
             performance outcome and efficiency (N = 72)

	PERFORMANCE OUTCOME	EFFICIENCY
Trait-Anxiety	.05	.07
State 1 (day before)	.01	.07
State 2 (pre-test)	-.21	-.13
State 3 (post-test)	-.34	-.28

Coefficients above .20 are significant at the .05 level

Individual differences as reflected in temporal patterns of
anxiety. According to the theoretical position taken in the
last section, pre-post-test difference-scores of state anxiety
were computed. The differing patterns in the three groups
(decrements, increments or no-change with respect to pre-post-
test state anxiety) are demonstrated in Figure 2, including
the first measurement of state anxiety the day before.

In accordance with the sensitization-repression
conceptualization (see Krohne, 1978; Krohne & Rogner, 1982;
Otto, 1983), and the elaboration of this theory by Weinberger
et al. (1979), it seems reasonable to interpret the temporal
patterns of state anxiety shown in Figure 2 as follows: Those
in the anxious-sensitive group (AS) obviously prefer a
vigilant coping style. As Krohne & Schaffner (1980) stated, it
is the goal of the sensitive plan to facilitate, by means of

an increased arousal during preparation, the construction of a person-internal coping system which can occur during confrontation. In contrast, the anxious-defensive group (AD), being familiar with task-requirements and -difficulty after finishing the training program, primarily aims at the defense of the perceived arousal and/or disturbing cognitions.

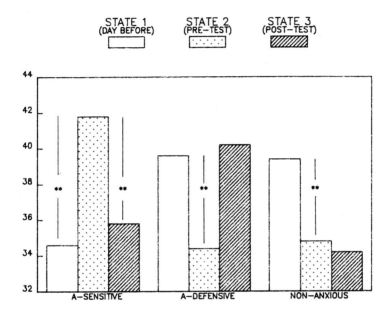

Figure 2: Temporal patterns of state anxiety for anxious-defensive, anxious-sensitive, and non-anxious subjects

But, compared with the AS-Group, the relative efficiency of its coping style as documented in the low pre-test state anxiety level, is accopmanied by a significant increase in state anxiety after the test. Finally, the self-perception of the non-anxious group (NA) seems to be relatively accurate or relistic. Their estimates of their state anxiety level before the test seems to be congruent with the estimates of their capacity available for solving the tasks, since they do not experience any elevations in state anxiety after the test.

The extent to which our interpretation was confirmed by further analyses of relevant data (personality, coping modes, and performance outcome) is documented in the follwing sections. First of all, personality and coping modes, as well as intelligence will be considered.

Intelligence, personality, and coping modes. The ratio between
demands (or difficulties) of problems and capacities (or
abilities) of individuals has been considered as a mediating
factor of stress by many theorists (see Lararus and Cohen,
1977; Lazarus et al., 1982; Nitsch, 1981; Lazarus & Launier,
1978; Schulz & Schönpflug, 1982; Schönpflug, 1983). As can be
seen from Table 4, there were no significant differences
between the three groups with respect to their intelligence or
ability.

Table 4: Means and standard deviations of personality traits
         for anxious-defensive, anxious-sensitive, and non-
         anxious subjects.

	ANXIOUS-DEFENSIVE		ANXIOUS-SENSITIVE		NON-ANXIOUS		
	M	SD	M	SD	M	SD	p
Trait Anxiety	43.8	8.1	39.6	4.9	42.4	7.7	n.sig.
Reactivity	23.3	6.3	24.2	4.8	23.6	5.6	"
Performance de-bilitating and	40.4	9.6	41.9	7.5	42.8	9.1	"
facilitating anxiety	26.6	5.0	29.8	5.4	29.7	5.9	"
Task-irrelevant cognitions	41.8	7.8	43.3	7.4	42.9	6.3	"
Achievement motivation	44.8	7.0	46.6	7.9	49.0	9.1	"
Inventory for emotional well-being:Anxiety	59.8	15.7	62.5	15.1	59.3	17.2	"
Depression	28.1	9.0	29.1	7.8	28.9	10.0	"
Exhaustion	27.5	9.5	29.2	7.7	28.7	9.1	"
Aggression	28.8	8.1	28.1	8.4	29.8	7.3	"
Shyness	29.4	7.5	29.5	8.0	30.8	7.3	"
Loneliness	28.8	6.2	29.0	7.3	28.4	7.5	"
General well-being	61.1	10.6	63.2	7.0	62.2	10.2	"
Intelligence	100.0	7.2	103.4	8.6	103.8	8.2	"

Furthermore, there were no differences in trait anxiety, reactivity (Strelau, 1972), task-irrelevant cognitions (Heckhausen, 1978), habitually emotional states (Inventory for emotional well-being: anxiety, depression, exhaustion, aggression, shyness, loneliness, and general well-being; Ullrich & Ullrich de Muynck, 1978), performance debilitating anxiety, performance facilitating anxiety, and achievement motivation (Brengelmann et al., 1978). There were also no differences in age, and women and men are almost equally distributed in each of the groups.

Yet, despite the homogeneity regarding the personality traits, there were significant differences between the groups with respect to coping modes. In contrast to anxious-sensitive and non-anxious subjects, anxious-defensive subjects reported that they had a stronger tendency to lower their aspiration level ($F(2,69) = 4.46$; $p = .01$) when confronted with different kinds of stressful events (e.g. time-pressure, noise, too many task-requirements).

Furthermore, we distinguish two kinds of coping modes: direct action or external regulation and intrapsychic coping modes or internal regulation (see Lazarus & Launier, 1978; Schönpflug. 1979, 1983).

With regard to these coping modes there were remarkable differences between the groups: anxious-defensive subjects more often used external modes of coping with noise-stress in achievement-related situation than anxious-sensitive and non-anxious subjects ($F(2,69) = 5.01$; $p = .o$) and they show a greater discrepancy between external and internal coping modes (see Table 5). Recently Lantermann (1980,1982) has emphasized the significance of an imbalance between internal- and external-oriented cognitions with respect to their monitoring and governing function in actual task-solving behavior. The present author as well as Otto (1982) were able to demonstrate that an imbalance between internal- and external oriented cognitions is accompanied with performance decrements.

Another remarkable result concerns the disposition with increased effort-expenditure to environmental stressors (e.g. noise). On an scale containing five items, anxious-defensive subjects score significantly higher than the other groups ($F(2,69) = 4.57$; $p = .01$). On the other hand, the subjects in the anxious-defensive group do not differ with respect to the last category in Table 5, namely the disposition to change action-strategy under external load (e.g. noise-stress), which encompasses instrumental problem-solving activities. For example, perfering very simple rules (e.g. logical or mathematical) or rough ratings instead of complex ones, even if they are highly skilled in their use, is considered a strategy representing this disposition.

To summarize the results presented in this section, it seems worthwhile to emphasize that there were no differences between

the three groups with respect to intelligence or ability (see
Table 4). The same holds true for internal demands (performance
debilitating   and   facilitating   anxiety,   task-irrelevant
cognitions). Thus, one can assume that acquired coping modes
are the most crucial factor leading to the different patterns
of state anxiety as presented in Figure 2.

Table 5: Means and standard deviations of coping modes for
         anxious-defensive, anxious-sensitive, and non-
         anxious subjects

	ANXIOUS-DEFENSIVE		ANXIOUS-SENSITIVE		NON-ANXIOUS		
	M	SD	M	SD	M	SD	p

Decrements of aspiration level as a function of external load (noise)	13.6	3.1	17.1	4.2	16.1	4.2	<.01
Disposition to cope with external load (noise): External Regulation:	6.5	2.6	9.0	2.1	9.8	2.6	.00
Internal Regulation:	9.3	3.5	9.5	2.3	9.8	2.6	n.s.
Disposition to react with increments of effort-expenditure under noise-stress	6.9	2.5	9.2	2.4	8.7	2.9	<.01
Disposition to change action-strategy under noise-stress	9.2	2.5	10.5	3.1	10.3	3.7	n.s.

In a next step, we looked at performance data, peceived states
of stress during and after the test, as well as the causes
perceived as most responsible for success or failure.

Performance outcome and efficiency. According to M. Eysenck
(1979) it can predicted that anxious individuals, under
certain   circumstances,   (e.g.   favourable   preparation
conditions; see Krohne & Schaffner, 1980), could reach the
same performance level as non-anxious persons.   Their

efficiency, however, would be inferior since they invest a larger amount of effort for task-solution.

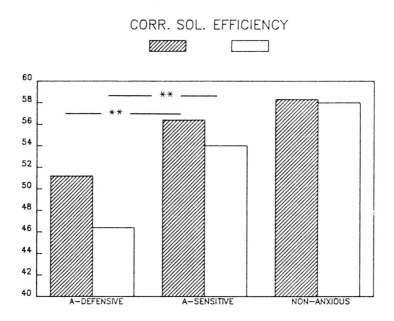

Figure 3: Performance outcome and efficiency-scores for anxious-defensive, anxious-sensitive, and non-anxious subjects

The results confirm, as expected, that anxious persons (high scores in pre-test state anxiety) reached the same performance level as non-anxious subjects (see Figure 3). For anxious-defensive persons, however, the performance level (number of correct solutions) is significantly lower ($F_{(2,69)} = 5.86$; $p = <.01$). On the other hand, both anxious-defensive and anxious-sensitive subjects have lower scores regarding time-related efficiency ($F_{(2,69)} = 8.01$; $p = .01$).
It seems, however, that the discrepancy between performance level and efficiency does not have negative consequences for anxious-sensitive subjects. Contrasting anxious-senitive and

anxious-defensive subjects, the low efficiency-scores (see
Figure 3) are accompanied by different states of emotional
well-being and/or caused by different states of general
activation.

General activation and emotional well-being. As mentioned
above, general activation or energetic arousal and emotional
well-being was measured at the end of each of the eight blocks
of tasks. In order to avoid expectation or carry-over effects
which might have been caused by the repeated measurement of
the checklists after each block, video tapes were made. The
last five minutes of each block were recorded and played back
to the subjects at the end of the experiment. This method has
been proved very useful, because watching the recordings
enabled the subjects to remember their feelings during the
different phases of the experiment quite well. According to
Thayer (1970,1978), general activation was described by the
adjectives 'energetic', 'tired', and 'vigorous' (we applied a
short form of the general activation dimension using only the
most discriminating three adjectives). Emotional well-being
was characterized by the most discriminating six adjectives of
the Inventory of Emotional Well-Being (Ullrich & Ullrich de
Muynck, 1978):'tense', 'quiet', 'satisfied', 'lonely',
'angry', and 'joyful'.

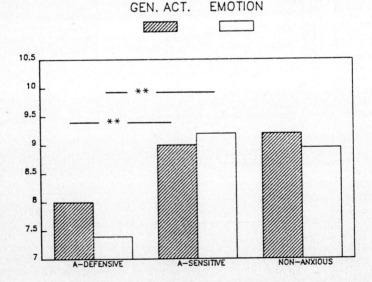

Figure 4: General activation and emotional well-being for
          anxious-defensive, anxious-sensitive, and non-
          anxious subjects

As can be seen from Figure 4, anxious-defensive subjects (AD)
scored significantly lower on the general activation scale
($F(2,69) = 3.75$; $p = .03$). Contrasting these findings with the
reported performance data (see Figure 3) and taking into
account the downward shifts of aspiration level (see Table 5),
we can conclude that the anxious-defensive coping style is
obviously associated with the inability to allocate available
resources to task-requirements (there were no differences
between the groups with respect to intelligence (see Table 4).
Consequently, because of their low performance level **and**
low efficiency-scores, they feel more emotionally stressed or
disturbed than the other groups (low scores represent negative
emotional states). The reported differences between the groups
are significant ($p = .05$) for all eight measures.

We gained further support for our former conclusion
(allocation of available resources) from correlational
analysis. We found a significant positive correlation between
general activation and performance outcome (correct solutions)
in the anxious-defensive group only (AD-Group:$r = .35$; $p = .05$;
AS-Group:$r = -.11$; NA-Group:$r = -.10$). On the other hand, for
both the anxious-sensitive and non-anxious subjects
intelligence and efficiency was positively correlated (AS-
Group:$r = .52$; $p = .01$; NA-Group: $r = .48$; $p = .01$). In
contrast, the anxious-defensive group had a nearly zero
correlation ($r = .06$).

Attribution of failure. In order tp prove our hypothesis that
the performance debilitating effects in the anxious-defensive
group may derive from a discrepancy between resources
available and the resources applied, we investigated the
'attributional process' (see Weiner, 1980, 1982). Following
our argumentation, it seems reasonable to assume that the
anxious-defensive subjects most probably suffer from deficits
with respect to self-regulation of activation, effort, and/or
attention; see Pribram & McGuinness, 1975; Sanders, 1983).
Consequently, we assume that the anxious-defensive coping
style is closely related to internal, unstable causes (e.g.
mood, immediate effort expenditure; see Weiner, 1982).
With regard to questions concerning the 'attributional
process' we used the same procedure as described in the last
section. That is, we obtained eight measures for each
dimension reported below.

Inasfar as the list of conceivable causes of success and
failure is infinite (see Weiner, 1982), ascriptions of
nonattainment of a goal in achievement settings to ability,
task difficulty, and external load (e.g. noise; see
Schönpflug, 1982; Schulz & Schönpflug, 1982) on the one hand,
and self-imposed time-pressure, effort, and deficits in
conscious attention (see Posner, 1978) on the other hand, have
to be considered the most important dimensions. As expected,

with regard to stable causes (ability and task difficulty)
there were no differences between the groups (see Table 6; the
subjective frequencies were rated on a 4-point scale; 1 =
almost always ... 4 = almost never).

Table 6:Internal and external causes of failure: Means and
        standard deviations for anxious-defensive, anxious-
        sensitive, and non-anxious subjects

	ANXIOUS-DEFENSIVE		ANXIOUS-SENSITIVE		NON-ANXIOUS		
	M	SD	M	SD	M	SD	p
Ability	25.1	4.5	25.8	5.2	27.0	5.5	<.38
Task-difficulty	24.0	3.7	25.3	5.7	26.6	5.6	<.16
Self-imposed time-pressure	22.6	6.5	25.8	6.3	26.6	6.1	<.06
Effort	21.8	6.6	19.9	6.0	24.1	4.4	<.04
Conscious attention	19.8	3.6	22.5	2.2	22.5	3.1	<.00
External causes (e.g. exp.- setting)	18.8	7.8	24.3	7.6	22.4	7.0	<.05

But, we found that anxious-defensive subjects attribute
failure to conscious attention, self-imposed time-pressure,
and external causes more frequently than the other groups.
Presumably, as effort and/or conscious attention can be
increased volitionally, ascriptions of nonattainment of a goal
th these dimensions will result in the sustaining hope and
increased persistence toward a goal. On the other hand, since
ability is stable and not subject to volitional control,
ascriptions of nonattainment of a goal to low ability and/or
task-diffculty results in giving up and cessation of goal-
oriented behavior (see Weiner, 1982).

An additional analysis of performance data (e.g. the micro-
structure of actions; see Wieland, in press) supports this
interpretation quite well. With respect to the number of
operations performed (requests for task relevant pieces of
information) anxious-defensive subjects do not differ from the
other groups. Obviously, the reported relation between
internal-unstable and -stable, and external-stable

attributions had been beneficial for anxious-defensive subjects. That is, they did not resign from task demands by reducing calls for relevant pieces of information or time working on each piece of information. Instead, they seem to suffer primarily from impairments of information processing or limitations of working memory. Consistent with this notion was the reported frequency concerning the question:" How often while working on the tasks was your inability to concentrate on task demands responsible for your actual capacity falling behind your normally available competence"? (the subjcetive frequencies were rated on a 4-point scale; 1 = almost always, and 4 = almost never). In contrast to anxious-sensitive and non-anxious subjects, this question was reported more often by anxious-defensive subjects (AD-Group: M = 1.82, SD = .88; AS-Group: M = 2.47, SD = .87; NA-Group: M = 2.55, SD = 1.0; F(2,69) = 4.71; p = .01). On the other hand, anxious-sensitive subjects differ from non-anxious subjects only with regard to effort (see Table 6).

FINAL REMARKS

Taking into account the data reported in this paper, it seems reasonable to conclude that anxious-sensitive and non-anxious subjects represent those being described as low- and high-anxious in the Trait-State-Model. On the other hand, we found no differences between the groups with respect to trait anxiety (see Table 4). In contrast to Spielberger (1972,1976) who stated that trait anxiety refer to individual differences in anxiety-proeness, i.e. the tendency to respond with high A-State in ego-threatening situations, it seems to be that predictibility and/or consistency of behavior appears not to have the generality as supposed in the trait measurement model (see Laux & Vossel, 1981). In accordance to Laux & Vossel (1981), and Zuckermann (1976) who has proposed to define a trait as a sum of states, the three measures of state anxiety (see Figure 1 and 2) can be interpreted as a coherent pattern of behavior representing "test-anxiety" (Sarason, 1975) or "evaluation anxiety" (Wine, 1982).

These patterns of behavior as reflected in the described temporal patterns of state anxiety (see Figure 2) supported as well the hypothesis of Epstein (1979) who noted:"... that when measures of behavior are averaged over an increasing number of events, stability coefficients increase to high levels for all kinds of data, including objective behavior, self-ratings..., and that objective behavior can then be reliably related to self-report measures ..." (Epstein, 1979, p. 1097).

Furthermore, our results gave evidence to assume that the registration of coping modes (in addition to situation-specific trait measures) is useful with respect to the operationalization of anxiety. For example, the diagnosis of a defensive coping style (anxious-defensive persons) as

reflected in decrements in the state anxiety the day before to
pre-test state anxiety (see Figure 2) and downward shifts in
aspiration level (see Table 5) enables a comparison of 'true'
low-anxious subjects with high-anxious subjects. That is,
those describing themselves as low-anxious because of their
defensive coping style but being in fact high-anxious-
defensive subjects could be reliably eliminated from the
analysis.
Finally, the observation that it is not the degree of anxiety
states 'per se' being the most important factor determining
performance outcome, efficiency, and reported states of
stress, but the temporal patterns of state anxiety having the
most powerful predictive validity seems to have important
implications for (a) conceptual reflections with regard to the
interrelationship between trait-state anxiety and performance,
and (b) the development of experimental paradigms in the area
of anxiety research.

NOTE

The research reported in this paper was supported by a grant
from Bundesministerium des Inneren der Bundesrepublik
Deutschland (Umweltbundesamt) to Prof. W. Schönpflug.

The Self in Anxiety, Stress and Depression
R. Schwarzer (Editor)
© Elsevier Science Publishers B.V. (North-Holland), 1984

COMPUTER ANXIETY AND SELF-CONCEPT OF ABILITY

Virginia Blankenship

Oakland University, Rochester, Michigan, U.S.A.

Within the dynamics of action theory (Atkinson and Birch, 1970) anxiety is conceptualized as an inhibitory force which delays initiation of the activity subject to inhibition. When the dynamics of action is applied to achievement motivation, test anxiety (fear of failure) is represented as an inhibitory force which opposes the positive instigating force to engage in achievement activities. In this paper I wish to present the Atkinson and Birch dynamics of action theory, show how it is applied in the achievement domain, tie it to Weiner's using computers to present achievement-orientated stimuli and to measure achievement-dependent variables. This research points to the presence of computer anxiety in subjects playing a computer target-shooting game and suggests that time spent in the achievement task is related to self-concept of ability.

Achievement Motivation. Fineman (1977) has proposed that achievement motivation is multi-dimensional and has encouraged that the measures of individual difference in achievement motivation be task-specific. In tests of the dynamics of action theory of behavior, I have been presenting on a microcomputer achievement tasks (easy, intermediate, and difficult levels of a target-shooting game) and a non-achievement task (watching a color design, Kaleidoscope, develop on the monitor). The computer has the advantage of controlling the difficulty level of the target-shooting game by increasing or decreasing the size of the target in response to the subject's success rate without the subject's knowledge. That is, if the subject's success rate falls below the expected 5 out of 10 successes for the intermediate task, the target is increased in size, thus increasing the subject's success rate subsequently. Because the subjects are only told by how much they missed the target, they cannot directly infer the size of the target. Thus, individual differences in ability are reduced because the computer changes the task difficulty in response to each subject's performance. The computer also collects data on task choices, amount of time spent at the achievement and non-achievement tasks, and success/failure outcomes. Once the subject has been trained on the task and shown how to make choices among the available tasks, he or she is left alone to work on the computer. The computer presentation of tasks has allowed us to remove the experimenter from the room during testing, a highly desirable situation since past research has indicated that social approval and affiliation motives may swamp achievement motives (cf., Horner, 1968).

Dynamics of Action. Within the Atkinson and Birch dynamics of action theory our lives are conceptualized as a stream of behavior in which the sequence of activities is the result of the relative strengths of underlying tendency levels as they change in time. The image of a stream suggests that what occurs "upstream" has an effect on subsequent behavior. In the dynamics of action three principles are mainly responsible for the changes in behavior: instigation to action, inhibition from action, and consummation in action. If an activity is intrinsically satisfying or has been rewarded in the past, the stimulus situation (environment) produces an instigating force which causes an increase in the tendency to perform the rewarded activity. If the activity is painful or has been punished in the past, then the environment produces an inhibitory force which blocks expression of the behavior (Atkinson, 1977). In the achievement realm, if a student has been rewarded for test taking in the past with high grades,then the test-taking situation will create a positive instigating force. If the test-taking situation has been painful in the past (i.e., the student has experienced test anxiety), then the test-taking situation will create a negative inhibiting force. Since most students have experienced both satisfaction and pain in relation to test taking, that activity produces both an instigating and inhibitory force. What is important when performing research on individual differences is to represent the relative strengths of these two forces. When streams of behavior are generated for individuals with high instigation to achieve (high hope of success, HOS) and low inhibition (low fear of failure, FOF) the stream of behavior is quite different from a simulation of behavior with the assumption of low instigation (low HOS) and high inhibition (high FOF) (see Table 1). The negative action tendency which results from inhibition and which opposes (dampens) the positive action tendency becomes stabilized after a time because of the force of resistance. A moderately inhibited behavior will be performed eventually, but initiation of the behavior will be delayed while stabilization of the negative action tendency occurs. In our test-taking example, a person with moderate test anxiety will take the required test, but he/she will delay working on the test for a while. Less inhibited persons will have started the test sooner than the test anxious person. The most salient differences are between the streams of behavior depicting high HOS - low FOF and low HOS - high FOF (lines 1 and 4 in Table 1). For low HOS - high FOF subjects there is a predicted delay in initiation of the achievement task and less overall time spent in the achievement task even following initiation when compared to the stream representing high HOS - low FOF. Distinctions between high HOS - low FOF and high HOS - high FOF (lines 1 and 2) are more difficult to make based on latency and percentage of time spent, as are distinctions between low HOS - low FOF and low HOS - high FOF (lines 3 and 4). It is clear from the simulations, however, that high HOS - high

FOF subjects are expected to behave quite differently from low HOS - low FOF subjects, and that high FOF (test anxiety) results in a slightly greater percentage of time spent once the achievement task has been initiated when HOS is held

Table 1

Hope of Success	Fear of Failure	Latency to Achievement Task	Percentage of Time Spent in Ach. Task (once initiated)
1. High	Low	20	89.2
2. High	High	44	90.6
3. Low	Low	188	46.7
4. Low	High	404	55.1

constant.   These two characteristics,   latency to achievement task and percentage of time spent in achievement tasks provide the   bases for testing the dynamic theory within the   achieve-ment domain.   Independent measures of hope of success and fear of failure are necessary in order to test the dynamic model in the achievement realm.   In the research to be presented,   the Thematic Apperception Test (TAT), Mandler-Sarason Test Anxiety Questionnaire (TAQ),   and the Mehrabian Achieving Scale (1969) were used to obtain these measures.

Attribution   Theory.   Weiner has developed attribution   theory in the achievement domain (cf., Weiner, et al, 1971). Weiner's model emphasizes four causes of success and failure: ability, effort,   task   difficulty,   and luck.   In   my   research,   62 subjects,   31 males and 31 females, worked on the computer and played 21 trials of the target-shooting game.   They were then asked   to   attribute   their   success   and   failure   to   ability, effort,   task difficulty,   and luck by placing their mark on a line   representing their relative attributions to ability   and effort,   for instance.   At one end of the line was the option "I'm always good" and on the other end was the option "I tried very   hard."   Four choices werde made for   success   and   four choices   were   made   for   failure   and in each case   two   causal

attributions werde matched on internality or stability.
Weiner has systematized the four major causal attributions on
the extent to which they are internal or external causes
(ability and effort are internal; task difficulty and luck are
external) and on the extent to which they are stable or
unstable causes (effort and luck are unstable; ability and
task difficulty are stable).   In each of the pairings of
causal attributions, both causes are internal, for instance,
but differ on stability, as is the case of our example,
ability versus effort.   Or the causes are both stable or both
unstable but differ on the internality/externality dimension.
Subjects came in one week and made 21 choices among the easy,
intermediate, and difficult levels of a target-shooting game
presented on a micro-computer.   At that time they attributed
success and failure among Weiner's four causal categories.   A
week later the subject returned and was allowed to freely
choose among the three levels of the target-shooting game and
a non-achievement task, watching a color design develop and
change on the computer monitor.   The situation in the second
session allows the subject to avoid the achievement task by
choosing to watch the color design.   We would expect that
subjects with high situational anxiety related to playing an
achievement game would spend more time at the color design
activity and less time at the achievement task.   In both
cases, as conceptualized within the dynamics of action model,
long latency to the achievement tasks and high percentage time
spent in the non-achievement task would be indicative of high
inhibition or anxiety combined with low motivation to achieve.

METHOD

The study presented here was designed to develop a computer-
based measure of resultant achievement motivation.   In past
research where the computer was used to present achievement-
related tasks, traditional measures of individual differences
in achievement motivation, the TAT and the TAQ, were not
successful in differentiating subjects on time spent on the
computer tasks.   Following Fineman's suggestion, I had decided
to develop a task-specific measure of achievement motivation,
a computer-based measure.   From traditional achievement
motivation theory and its precursor, level of aspiration
theory (Lewin, Dembo, Festinger, and Sears, 1944), I had found
two studies which promised to provide direction in developing
a computer-based measure.   In 1965 Moulton had shown that
males high in resultant achievement motivation, as measured
with the TAT and TAQ, made fewer atypical shifts when
confronted with achievement tasks of varying difficulty.   An
atypical shift is defined as the choice of a more difficult
task following failure or the choice of an easier task
following success.   Moulton's subjects worked on an anagram
task of intermediate difficulty and were then given success or
failure feedback.   When they subsequently were allowed a free
choice between easy and difficult tasks, 11 of 31 subjects

with low resultant achievement motivation made an atypical shift. Only one subject with high resultant achievement motivation made an atypical shift. The second study was by Littig (1963). Littig presented poker dice hands with probabilities of success ranging from 1/10 to 9/10 and with points to be won from 50 points to 240 points. Each subject was presented with 3 sets of 20 combinations of probabilities and points and asked to bid on each hand. Subjects who were low in resultant achievement motivation, based on the TAT minus TAQ measures, responded to the variance of the combinations, a function of the point incentives, and bid more as the points to be won increased. Subjects with high resultant achievement motivation did not respond to the point incentives.

In my experiment subjects during the first session were given 21 trials on which they chose among the easy, intermediate, and difficult levels of the target-shooting game. On half the trials, every second trial, point incentives were given. On the other half no points were offered. The computer kept track of the choices made and the success or failure outcomes, and computed the number of typical and atypical shifts made. Subjects who made fewer atypical shifts were classified, based on Moulton's findings, as high in resultant achievement subject based on the frequencies of choices among the three difficulty levels on incentive versus no-incentive trials. A high chi-square statistic indicated responsiveness to incentives, and those subjects, based on Littig's research, were classified as low in resultant achievement motivation. When the 62 subjects were classified as high and low in resultant achievement motivation based on number of atypical shifts and responsiveness to incentives, 23 were classified as high, 23 were classified as low, and 16 were mixed (that is, above the median on one criterion and below the median on the other).

When subjects returned a week later to play the achievement target-shooting game or to watch a color design develop on the color monitor, they were briefly retrained and then asked to start watching the color design. They were told that at any time they could start playing the target-shooting game at the easy, intermediate, or difficult level, and that they could switch back and forth among the four activities as often as they liked. The experimenter then left the room, and the subject watched the color design, switched to the achievement task whenever he/she liked, and was free to choose from among the four activities for a 15-minute period. The computer kept track of the choices made and the amount of time spent at each activity. Following this session, subjects wrote TAT stories, filled out the TAQ and the Mehrabian Achieving Scale and were thanked for their cooperation, debriefed, and dismissed. (See Blankenship, in prep., for details.)

RESULTS

Subjects who made attributions of failure to lack of ability spent significantly more time on the non-achievement task one week later (see Table 2). For males, high anxiety, as measured

Table 2

| | Percentage of Time Spent in Non-Achievement Task | |
Attribution of Failure	Males	Females
"I'm Never Good"	22.4	15.8
	n=16	n=17
"Task Was Difficult"	10.7	11.2
	n=15	n=14

$$F\ (1,58) = 7.80,\ p = .007$$

by the Mandler-Sarason TAQ, was also related to attributions of failure to lack of effort (r = -.49, N = 31, p = .002). Females who attributed success to task ease and failure to task difficulty avoided the achievement-oriented task and chose the easy level when finally engaging in it. These results are consistent with the Atkinson and Birch dynamic model and the assumption that anxiety results in activity inhibition. Dweck, Davidson, Nelson, and Enna (1978) observed teachers attributing boys' failures to lack of effort more often than they did girls' failures. They also discovered that teachers made negative evaluations that were more indicative of low ability for girls than for boys. This forms a coherent picture of gender differences in attributions and anxiety: Males have a self-protective strategy which involves attributions of failure to lack of effort. Females lack this strategy and make attributions of success to task ease.

There is evidence that a large element of the anxiety reflected in this research is related to mathematics and/or computer anxiety, situation-specific anxiety. The evidence is indirect. Subjects filled out the Mehrabian Achieving Scale following their second session on the computer. A normative sample of 395 subjects filled out the TAT, TAQ, and Mehrabian Scale in a neutral classroom situation. Exploratory factor analyses revealed that five factors underlie the Mehrabian Scale for both samples, and confirmatory factor analyses (Sörbom, 1974; Sörbom and Jöreskog, 1976) demonstrated that the factor structures differed between the computer group and the classroom group. The data for the classroom group resulted in the usual achievement-oriented first factor accounting for a large percentage of the variance and a less important second factor tapping test anxiety or fear of failure. For the computer group four of the five factors tapped fear of failure and the achievement-oriented factor was the fourth factor, accounting for only 15% of the common variance. The factor scores for the computer sample correlated with time measures from the computer activities in a way consistent with the dynamics of inhibition in the Atkinson and Birch model. Subjects with high fear of failure scores (test anxiety) spent more time at the easy game and less time at the difficult game (see Kuhl and Blankenship, 1979).

CONCLUSIONS

The results are consistent with the dynamics of inhibition predictions. The combination of low achievement motivation and high test anxiety results in less time at the inhibited activity. This principle has tremendous long range implications for the anxious person. Because test anxious people spend less time at achievement tasks, especially when they can avoid them by choosing non-achievement tasks, they gain fewer skills and face subsequent achievement tasks with less experience and ability. The effect is cumulative, especially in areas such as math where lack of prerequisites preclude a normal progression through increasingly difficult courses. The common finding that test anxious people spend more time at their tasks is obtained in situations where no avoidance option is available. When the test anxious person cannot physically avoid being in a testing situation, he/she can psychologically avoid by thinking of other things. Worrying about self-worth can be viewed as a consequence of these avoidance thoughts as deadlines approach. Therapy should focus on increasing the time in achievement tasks by shortening latency to initiation.

The Atkinson and Birch dynamics of action theory provides a useful conceptualization of test anxiety. The focus on latency to task and percentage of time spent in tasks subject to anxiety allows the generation of testable hypotheses concerning individual and situation differences. Through the assignment of parameter values representative of these differences, simulated behavioral streams can be generated. Experimental situations can then be designed to test crucial assumptions.

The Self in Anxiety, Stress and Depression
R. Schwarzer (Editor)
© Elsevier Science Publishers B.V. (North-Holland), 1984

INTERACTION OF SELF-CONCEPT AND STATE/TRAIT ANXIETY UNDER DIFFERENT CONDITIONS OF SOCIAL COMPARISON PRESSURE

William D. Crano and Suellen L. Crano

Michigan State University, East Lansing, Michigan, U.S.A.

In this paper, we discuss the relationship between self-concept and state-trait anxiety, and the ways that different levels of social comparison pressure might affect this relationship. The starting point of our discussion is Festinger's (1954) original statement of the theory of social comparison, a position that is generating increasing interest in social and personality psychology today (e.g., see Suls & Miller, 1977). In this theory, Festinger observed that in the absence of objective information, people compare themselves with others in order to judge the correctness of a belief or the extent of a given ability. This comparison process is not viewed as a mere preference; rather, it is thought to have the qualities of a social drive.

The theory further specifies that comparisons will be sought with others of similar attitudes or abilities, since such persons are thought to provide a more accurate comparison point for the actor. In some ways this corollary of Festinger's theory is persuasive, especially in situations involving the comparison of skills or abilities. For example, if a novice chess player were to seek an appraisal of his improvement over six months' time, he would be unwise to match himself against a grand master in an important tournament. The predictable outcome of such an exercise would tell the novice very little about his rate of improvement. However, if he were to match himself against another novice of approximately the same experience in the same, the outcome could, indeed, provide some indication of his development.

While this hypothesized preference for similar others with whom to compare oneself appears plausible in this example, other examples that would appear much less persuasive also could have been drawn. This difficulty plays a role in much of the recent research that has been focused on social comparison theory, and it is a problem to which we will return in developing the theoretical rationale of the research that is to be decribed in this report.

UPWARD VERSUS DOWNWARD COMPARISON

As noted, considerable recent research has been focused on Festinger's (1954) theory. In general, this research has provided support for the basic postulates of the social comparison model, though qualifications, extensions, and modifications of the original theoretical statement are quite common (e.g., Crano, Crano, & Biaggio, 1983; Goethals & Darley, 1977; Jones & Regan, 1974; Reckmann & Goethals, 1973; Suls & Miller, 1977). One area in which considerable refinement to the theory has been made is concerned with the individual's choice of the 'other' with whom to form a comparison.

Generally, in sympathetic discussions of social comparison theory, the positive side of the central postulate of the theory (i.e., that people use the attitudes and/or behaviors of others to judge the rectitude of a belief, or the quality of a behavior or performance) are stressed. In this instance, the comparison process appears to be a socially facilitative mechanism, which would enable the individual to rationalize his or her cognitions, and justify his or her performance. However, it is clear that in some circumstances, the social comparison process could produce information that places the individual performing the comparison in a very negative light, by suggesting, for example, that his/her level of skill or ability on a given task is far below that of the comparison other, or that the attitude or ability in question is extremely deviant from that of a host of valued comparison persons. In these instances, well-established postulates of cognitive consistency (e.g., Aronson, 1968) developed and supported over years of research in social psychology would suggest that people would avoid such information, or, under appropriate circumstances, would devalue or distort it (e.g., Crano & Schroder, 1967). In such cases, the information value of the social comparison data would be reduced appreciably.

Clearly, social comparison can operate as a two-edged sword, either confirming an individual's belief (or ability), or demonstrating its lack of communality with that of a comparison group (or person). As such, at least under some circumstances, the process of social comparison can become an ego-threatening activity. From considerable research, we know that individuals are not likely to enter into such activities voluntarily. Thus, the generality of Festinger's (1954) ideas on the use of social comparison must be questioned.

One area in which such questioning has been common is concerned with "upward" and "downward" comparison (i.e., does the individual compare him/herself with others who are expected to be "better" or "worse" at the particular comparison activity than the actor). The importance of this subarea of investigation is that it (1) allows for a more fine-grained analysis of the parameters of the social comparison process (in that it helps to clarify the likely comparison object in various social comparison situations), and (2) it can provide a means of accomodating social comparison theory with the mass of research that demonstrates people's concern with maintaining a positive self-concept (and hence their tendency to avoid unfavorable comparisons).

While consensus in this area of research has yet to develop, some general trends are in evidence (e.g., see Hakmiller, 1966; Wheeler, 1970). For example, under conditions of high threat or anxiety, downward comparison appears more likely. This seems reasonable, as the anxious individual would appear to be more intent on discovering that he or she was "superior" on the ability (or attitude) in question than the comparison person. Conversely, we might assume (though the data appear less compelling here) that under conditions of low threat or low vested interest (cf. Sivacek & Crano, 1982), upward comparison would be more likely. Obviously, considerations of the self-concept play a role in the development of such expectations.

Situational Factors. Such a possibility has led some theorists to postulate a tendency in people that would tend to counteract the enactment of social comparison behaviors (e.g., see Gruder, 1977; Thornton & Arrowood, 1966; Singer, 1966). This countervailing tendency has been termed "self-enhancement" (vs. Festinger's self-evaluation, or social comparison). The basic assumption of the self-enhancement position is that people have a need to protect or enhance their self-concepts (e.g., Aronson, 1968).

In some circumstances, it is conceivable that the need for accuracy (i.e., self-evaluation) would come into conflict with the need for ego protection or enhancement, and as such, social comparison could be unwise, since the information derived from social comparison activity could threaten the self. In situations of this type, there is a clear theoretical conflict between Festinger's social comparison approach and the ego enhancement position. It is unlikely that one or another of these tendencies is always prepotent, given the lack of closure that characterizes the research literature in this area. We might hypothesize that the nature and importance of the task (or attitude) might dictate the individual's choice of comparison or enhancement strategy. For example, in a situation in which the individual's life would be strongly affected by the outcome of the comparison process, he or she would seem more likely to seek information that would prove useful, rather than merely ego-enhancing. Research by Hillis and Crano (1973) has provided some evidence that is consistent with this reasoning. In situations entirely lacking in vested interest -- i.e., those in which the outcome or attitude has little, or no, hedonic relevance for the actor (Sivacek & Crano, 1982) -- then we would expect that self-enhancement would be stressed. It is also likely in such circumstances that downward comparison would be most common.

Some support for these speculations has been provided by Jones & Regan (1974), who showed that subjects tended to seek social

comparison information when they were attempting to decide
upon the difficulty level of a task in which they were <u>about</u>
<u>to engage</u>. In such a situation, the information provided by
the actions and opinions of others could prove useful, and as
such, was sought out. However, in another condition of the
study, the information-seeking behavior of subjects who had
<u>already chosen</u> the task-difficulty level was assessed, and in
<u>this sitution</u>, Jones and Regan showed that these individuals
were not interested in learning about the choices of others.
Such information not only was useless to them, but could call
into question the wisdom of their own decision. As such, it
was avoided.

<u>Individual difference factors</u>. In addition to situational
factors, there appear to be a number of more individualisti-
cally oriented variables that would appear to be likely
candidates to influence people's choices of information which
could result in self-enhancement, or foster a more accurate
self-appraisal, regardless of the implication of such
information for the self. One of the most obvious of these
variables is the self-concept. It is intuitively obvious,
though far from well-established, that the more secure an
individual in his or her self-concept, the more likely it is
that such a person would be open to information that would
foster accuracy of beliefs or actions; in other words, the
more likely it would be for this person to engage in social
comparison. Likewise, when placed in a situation involving
the possibility of social comparison, the individual with high
self-esteem would be less threatened by this prospect and,
accordingly, would be less anxious than the person whose self-
concept was not as well-established.

On the other hand, an individual who has an insecure self-
concept would be less likely to engage in social comparison,
no matter what the vested interest implication of such action.
In addition, when such a person was placed in a situation that
explicitly involved the possibility of social comparison, he
or she would find the setting more noxious, and thus, more
anxiety-arousing.

The speculations form the basis of the research to be discussed. We expect that as a function of an extensive past
history of unfavorable learning experiences, the individual
with a negative self-concept will find the process of social
comparison to be anxiety-evoking. Accordingly, as a rule,
such people will be prone to avoid situations in which such
actions are fostered. When avoidance is not possible, these
individuals will prove to have appreciably higher levels of
(state) anxiety than those whose self-concepts are more
positive. In the absence of the "threat" of social comparison, there will be no difference in (state) anxiety between
these two types of individuals, but general (trait) anxiety
should still distinguish the groups, with the low self-esteem
individuals demonstrating appreciably higher levels of this
variable.

STATE-TRAIT ANXIETY AND SOCIAL COMPARISON

Research and theory developed by Spielberger and his colleagues tends to lend some support for these expectations. In his work, Spielberger (1972) distinguishes between anxiety as a transitory emotional state and anxiety as a relatively stable personality construct. This distinction is crucial for, as Spielberger (1972, p. 39) notes, "State-anxiety may be conceptualized as a transitory emotional state or condition of the human organism that varies in intensity and fluctuates over time. This condition is characterized by subjectively consciously perceived feelings of tension and apprehension, and the activation of the autonomic nervous system. The level of A-State (state anxiety) should be high in circumstances that are perceived by an individual as threatening, irrespective of the objective danger; A-State intensity should be low in nonstressful situations, or in circumstances in which an existing danger is not perceived as threatening. Trait anxiety proneness, that is, to differences in the disposition to perceive a wide range of stimulus situations as dangerous or threatening ...".

In addition to the central hypothesis (i.e., that subjects of low self-esteem will respond to "enforced" social comparison with higher levels of A-state than will subjects of more positive self-concept, Spielberger's observations also foster the expectation that the general anxiety level (A-Trait) of subjects having negative self-concepts will be greater than that of individuals who have more positive self-concepts, or higher self-esteem (we are using these terms interchangeably here). The research discussed in the paper represents an initial test of these speculations -- an initial attempt, that is, to link the concepts of anxiety, self-concept, and social comparison in a theoretical matrix that takes into account not only research on social comparison, but also the vast literature on A-Trait and A-State, along with considerations of a more social psychological nature, derived from current research on ego defense and enhancement (e.g., Wegner & Vallacher, 1980).

METHOD

Subjects. The sample that was studied in this research consisted of 31 seventh-grade school children, who were enrolled in a university -- affiliated laboratory school in Porto Alegre, Brazil (Universidade Federal, Rio Grande do Sul). There were 14 boys and 17 girls in the sample. All subjects were tested in their homeroom classes.

General Procedure. In their homeroom classrooms, all subjects completed a translation of Eagly's (1967) revision of the Janis-Field (1959) test of self-concept (Crano & Crano, in press). Two weeks later, they were asked to participate in a research project. At this point, the manipulation (discussed

below) was introduced. Some subjects were led to believe that
the results of the test they were about to take would be
compared with those of other respondents; comparison was not
mentioned in the control condition.

Manipulation.   Two different levels of social comparison were
created in this research. In the high social comparison condition, subjects were given a complicated test that pur-
portedly was capable of being used to assess each individual's
level of creativity.   The test was said to be a sensitive and
accurate measure.   Subjects in the high social comparison
condition were told that their performance on the test would
be compared with that of other students from several countries
in North and South America.   Subjects further were told that
the principal reason for the research was to determine if
students who attended campus laboratory schools (as they did)
were more creative than children who attended regular schools.
To lend credence to this manipulation, a native English-
speaker was involved in the test administration in this group.
In addition, subjects were required to sign their names to the
answer sheet of the test.

The low social comparison (or control) condition subjects were
given the identical instrument.   However, they were told that
the test of creativity was new, and still under development.
Further, they were informed that the administrator was not
certain about its accuracy or sensitivity, and that its
validity has not been established.   No mention was made of
comparing scores with other groups or, indeed, of plans to
perform comparisons within the students' group in the control
condition.   In this condition, only the native Portuguese-
speaking experimenter was involved in the test administration.
Subjects were not required to sign their answer sheets,
although for comparison purposes, they were identifiable, and
their responses in this section of the study could be matched
with their earlier responses on the self-concept scale.

The creativity test that was administered was the Barron-Welsh
Art Scale, a pictorial test which was given in its original
English language booklets to emphasize the comparative nature
of the research.   Instructions were presented orally.   The
test was used only to enhance the manipulation; its results
were not of interest for the purposes of the study. Since the
reliability and validity of this scale for Brazilian respondents have not been established, because instructions were
printed in English, and because of the special and unusual
conditions under which this test was administered, the data of
the creativity test were not analyzed.

After the students completed the Art Scale, they were administered a Portuguese translation of Spielberger's State-
Trait Anxiety Inventory (cf Biaggio, Natalicio, & Spielberger,
1976).   The A-State instructions emphasized that subjects
respond in a manner that was consistent with their current
feelings, and special emphasis was placed on current feelings,
given that their Art Scale performance was to be compared with

that of their international counterparts. The A-Trait scale also was given, and the instructions here asked subjects to respond as they generally felt.

The control group, too, was asked to take the Barron-Welsh Art Scale, but the task was introduced as a means of inferring the validity of the instrument for a Brazilian population. The students were told that there was no need to worry about their performance, because psychologists were still attempting to determine whether the test was useful or worthwhile ("valido") before adapting it for use in Brazil. No mention was made of comparison with other groups. Following this task, these subjects completed the Portuguese version of Spielberger's State-Trait Anxiety Inventory (Biaggio et al., 1976). Subjects were given the usual instructions -- respond to A-State items as they felt at the moment, and to the A-Trait as they generally felt. Following these operations, all subjects were debriefed, and the true nature of the experiment was explained to them.

RESULTS

Self-Concept and Experimental Condition. An analysis of variance was performed on subjects' self-concept scores, to determine whether any initial differences existed between the experimental and control groups independent of the manipulaton. This analysis, which was undertaken primarily for control purposes, disclosed no difference in the mean self-concept scores of experimental and control subjects M = 73.0, 70.2, respectively, F (1, 29) = 2.24, ns.

Planned Comparisons of Theoretically Implicated Subgroups. Given this result, the analyses could proceed as planned. Accordingly, subjects within the experimental and control conditions were divided into high and low self-concept subgroups on the basis of a median split of their scores on Crano and Crano's translation of the Eagly self-concept scale. Given the directional hypotheses advanced earlier, the rather restricted sample size, and the somewhat insensitive median split procedure that was, of necessity, employed, an omnibus F test was not indicated (see Crano & Brewer, 1973; Winer, 1971). Rather, a series of planned comparisons, contrasting the mean state and trait anxiety scores of the experimental and control subjects who had been divided on the basis of self-concept scores, were undertaken.

Self-Concept and A-State. The first series of comparisons investigated the effects of treatment condition and self-concept on A-State. The means on which these comparisons are based are presented in Table 1. These comparisons provided strong support for the hypotheses developed earlier in this work. As suggested in Table 1, there was a significant difference in A-State as a function of self-concept among the subjects of the experimental group, who had been exposed to social comparison pressures. The mean state anxiety score of experimental group subjects with positive self-concepts (M = 22.44) was significantly less than that of the subjects who scored below the median on the self-concept measure (M = 35.17; t (13) = 2.15, p < .05, two-tailed). However, no differences in A-State were discovered between high and low self-concept subjects who were not exposed to the pressures of social comparison, t (14) = .51, ns.

Table 1: Mean A-State Scores as a Function of Self-Concept and Experimental Condition

	Self-Concept Score	
	Low	High
Experimental	35.17	28.44
Control	32.43	31.44

Self-Concept and A-Trait. Consistent with expectations, the results of the planned comparisons involving the A-Trait measure were different from those of the A-State analysis. As hypothesized, a significant difference was observed between subjects of high and low self-concept in mean A-Trait score in the untreated control conditions, M = 36.77, 41.76, respectively, t (14) = 2.00, p < .05. However, as illustrated in Table 2, these self-concept related differences were attenuated in the social comparison conditions, M = 37.0, 38.17 for high and low self-concept groups respectively, t (13)) = .39, ns. As the correlational findings will illustrate, however, over all subjects an obvious relationship does exist between anxiety (either state or trait) and self-concept.

Table 2: Mean A-Trait Scores as a Function of Self-Concept and Experimental Condition

	Self-Concept Score	
	Low	High
Experimental	38.17	37.00
Control	41.86	36.78

Correlational Results.   A matrix of correlations summarizing
the relationships observed between experimental conditions,
anxiety, and self-concept measures is presented in Table 3.
While it is not our intention here to overinterpret the data
presented in this table, it is important to note the strong
and significant negative correlations between self-concept and
both anxiety measures.   These correlations suggest that higher
self-concept scores are associated with lower levels of both
A-Trait and A-State.   These results hold even when the effect
of experimental condition are held constant statistically
through techniques of partial correlation.   For example, the
zero-order A-State/self-concept correlation (r = -.42, p < .01)
was diminished only slightly (r = -.41) when the presence or
absence of the experimental treatment was held constant.   This
same pattern held in the case of the A-Trait/self-concept
relationship: the original zero-order correlation (r = -.53,
p < .01)   was only slightly influenced when treatment
presence/absence was "partialled out" of the relationship (r -
-.52).   The significant, but far from perfect correlation
between A-Trait and A-State (r = .46, p < .01) suggests that
the two anxiety measures are not tapping the same underlying
dimension -- that different processes are operative in determining A-State and A-Trait, as hypothesized by Spielberger.

Table 3: Matrix of Intercorrelations of Critical Variables,
         With Means and Standard Deviations (SD) of all
         Measures

	1	2	3	4
1. Condition	1.00			
2. A-State	.07	1.00		
3. A-Trait	.14	.46	1.00	
4. Self-Concept	-.27	-.42	-.53	1.00
Mean	1.52	31.52	38.26	71.94
SD	.51	5.27	5.46	6.85

DISCUSSION

In his original discussion of social comparison theory, Festinger (1954) stressed the drive-like nature of social comparison processes. People needed to validate their opionions and abilities, and in the absence of objective data, this need could be satisfied through the information provided in social comparisons with others. The social comparison process was theorized as a ubiquitous phenomenon, theoretically influencing the behavior of all people. Since such information could help the individual meet the demands of day-to-day existence, social comparison, as originally envisioned, was conceptionalized as a nonthreatening, socially facilitative process.

Later research involving "upward" and "downward" comparison, however, has suggested that the act of social comparison can be a source of negative arousal, or anxiety. These new studies considerably expanded Festinger's orginal conceptualization of social comparison, while, at the same time, setting some limits on the generality of the phenomenon. This modification of Festinger's original conceptualization suggests that social comparison is not necessarily a nonthreatening action and, as such, might not always be engaged in the absence of other forms of (objective) information. In addition, the concepts of upward and downward comparison suggest (1) that situational variables might prove to be strong determinants of the likelihood of the engagement of social comparison processes, (2) that individual differences might have a major impact on people's use (or avoidance) of social comparison information, and (3) that these differences might interact with situational factors.

As discussed earlier, the situational constraints that operate in a setting might have a strong influence on a person's use of social comparison data. For example, in a setting that has little hedonic relevance for the individual, there appears to be rather little motivation for the engagement of social comparison. The failure to engage social comparison processes appears especially likely in situations in which such an action seems likely to provide information that places the actor in a negative light. Thus, it appears realistic to attempt to gauge the hedonic relevance (or vested interest) of an ability or opinion before making predictions regarding the likelihood that the actor would activate the social comparison process in attempting to judge the rectitude of the opinion, or the quality of a skill or ability.

Similarly, even prior to this research, it seemed reasonable to postulate that individual differences could have a major impact upon the likelihood that a person would engage in social comparison processes. If, as hypothesized, social comparison can operate as a two-edged sword, than it appears clearly reasonable to expect that those who are more threatened by the prospect of invidious comparisons would be less likely to employ social comparison in judging the quality of their skills or the validity of their opinions. One such individual difference variable that immediately suggests it-self as of possible relevance, given the validity of this hypothesis, is self-esteem. On the basis of considerable theory in this area (e.g., Suls & Miller, 1977) it seems reasonable to hypothesize that individuals whose self-concept was not well established, or positive, would be more sensitive to the possibility that social comparison information could prove threatening. As such, these individuals would seem to be more prone than those with more positive self-images to avoid social comparison.

Results in accordance with this reasoning were discovered in the research discussed in this report. Consistent with expectations, the experiment demonstrated that respondents of low self-concept were much more anxious (as measured by Spiel-berger's A-State instrument) than high esteem individuals when the possibility of social comparison was stressed. When social comparison was not a salient aspect of the experimental setting, no significant differences in state anxiety were found to exist between subjects of high and low self-concept. It is important to note that these differencees (or lack of difference) operate in terms of A-State. The significant negative correlation between A-Trait and self-concept, regard-less of the social comparison treatment, suggests strongly that low self-concept is associated with higher levels of chronic anxiety (A-Trait). In this instance, presence or absence of social comparison appears to have little influence on the relationship.

The integration of all of the results of this study provides support for the logic that underlies the hypothesized re-lationship between self-concept, anxiety, and social compari-son. Our findings further suggest that Festinger's (1954) original statement on the role of social comparison in behavior be modified to take into consideration the inter-active effect of anxiety and self-concept on the likelihood that an individual will engage in self-evaluation, or self-enhancement, behaviors. While our data do not speak to the conditions under which self-enhancement will be undertaken, they clearly show that social comparison can be anxiety arousing, especially in situations involving individuals of low self-concept; hence, such processes are likely to be avoided. Ego-bolstering actions (self-enhancement) under such circumstances would appear likely.

Obviously, this research cannot (indeed, did not intend to) confirm all of the hypothesized relationships that have been implied throughout this paper. However, the research does provide an initial basis for a model that can be made to integrate the increasingly complex data pattern that has developed in research on social comparison over the years.

The Self in Anxiety, Stress and Depression
R. Schwarzer (Editor)
© Elsevier Science Publishers B.V. (North-Holland), 1984

TEST ANXIETY DEVELOPMENT IN WEST GERMAN SCHOOLS:
A STRUCTURAL EQUATION ANALYSIS

Ralf Schwarzer, Matthias Jerusalem and Joachim Faulhaber

Free University of Berlin, Federal Republic of Germany

Test anxiety is considered here as a situation-specific emotional trait (Spielberger, 1972) which is acquired by experience with threatful environmental demands. The person learns to appraise different situations as threatening to the self and anticipates danger and harm when situational cues announce the advent of that specific kind of demand. For children and students these are mostly academic situations where their performance is scrutinized, tested and evaluated. Then, students are often socially exposed and observed by others which puts them into a state of public self-awareness (see Buss, 1984, Wicklund, 1984). Test anxiety, therefore, is related to social anxiety and self-concept. The person worries about his performance, anticipates negative outcomes, questions his own competence, ruminates about the possible consequences of failure etc. In addition, bodily reactions and feelings of tension occur, which is perceived as an emotional state. Therefore usually a cognitive component (worry) and an emotional component (emotionality) in test anxiety are distinguished - a distinction made at the state as well as at the trait level (Morris, Franklin & Ponath, 1983, Spielberger, 1984). It may be fruitful, however, to search for multiple components of test anxiety (Sarason, 1984, Stephan, Fischer & Stein, 1983).

This paper deals with test anxiety as a situation-specific trait in the school environment. Our aim is to explore the antecedents and concomitants of test anxiety in several West German student samples. The perceived learning environment, as there is achievement pressure or anonymity, is seen as one determinant of anxiety. The actual social context which can be understood as a reference group is another determinant. Self-concept and self-awareness are investigated as further variables of importance.

STUDY I

The West German secondary school system provides three achievement tracks which students enter at the age of 10 after having been mainstreamed for four years in Primary School. Those who have been located at the bottom of the achievement distribution enter the low track (Hauptschule). Those who have

been at the top enter the high track (Gymnasium). Also, there
is a mid track (Realschule). In addition, in some places
comprehensive schools (Gesamtschulen) are established where
all kinds of students are taken together. Reference group
theory predicts that those who enter the low track will feel
better than before while many of those entering the high track
will have a hard time because they will no longer be favored
by social comparison processes (see Levine, 1984, Schwarzer,
Jerusalem & Schwarzer, 1983, Schwarzer & Lange, 1983).

The study to be reported is based on a sample of 622 students
investigated within a longitudinal design. A subsample of 112
students entered grade 5 of the low track, and 107 entered the
high track in September 1980. They were followed up until
March 1982 when attending grade 6. There were 5 measurement
points in time. The subjects responded to the German form of
the Test Anxiety Inventory (TAI; Spielberger, 1980; Hodapp,
Laux & Spielberger, 1982), an instrument designed to assess
both components in test anxiety, worry and emotionality. The
psychometric properties of this version turned out to be
satisfactory (see Schwarzer, 1984).

Figures 1 and 2 show the development of both measures over
time. When leaving Primary School there is a significant
difference between low and high achievers. However, after
having been adapted to the new reference groups both samples
converge with respect to their mean worry and emotionality.
This is in line with reference group theory: The subjective
well-being depends on the social context; students compare
their outcomes and ability with their peers' and establish a
within group rank order where they locate themselves; if their
individual rank is favorable they may experience "relative
gratification", if it is unfavorable they may experience
"relative deprivation" because their scope is limited to the
immediate reference group instead to national or other
standards.

This result is replicated by means of the structural equation
approach (see Hagtvet, 1983, Hodapp & Henneberger, 1983,
Schwarzer, 1983, Schwarzer et al. 1983 for the application of
this method in test anxiety research). The school tracks are
specified as a dummy variable (1=high track, 0=low track).
Test anxiety is specified as a latent variable with two
indicators: worry and emotionality, measured at five points in
time. The structural model was specified as one independent
latent variable (school tracks or reference groups) and five
dependent latent variables (anxiety as a repeated construct).
When LISREL V (Jöreskog & Sörbom 1982) was used the model
could not be fitted by the data because only at the first
point in time a direct impact of school tracks was found. The
respecified model (as in figure 3) obtained a chi-square of
204.33 (40 df) which was significant (rejected). The goodness
of fit index provided by the program was .79, the Tucker-Lewis
coefficient .78, Bentler's delta was .82 and the root mean
square residual was .065. Therefore the fit can be regarded as

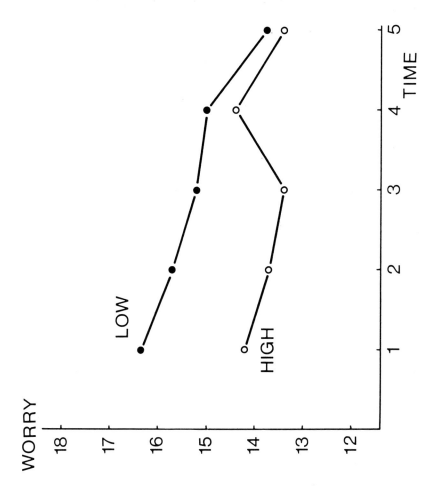

Figure 1: Development of Worry over Time

R. Schwarzer et al.

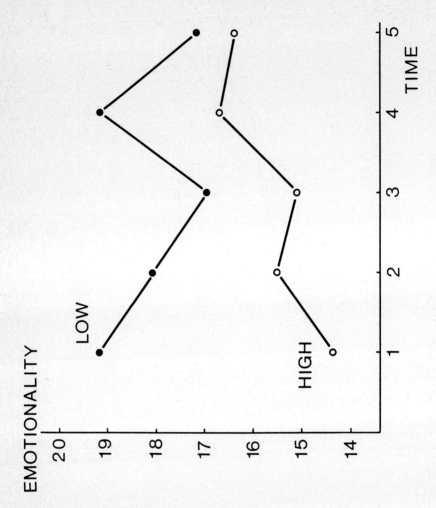

Figure 2: Development of Emotionality over Time

satisfactory. The results (see table 1) show that there is a strong impact of group differences at the first point in time appearing as a direct causal effect (-.45). At later stages of the development there are only indirect effects of -.31, -.28, -.23 and -.18 respectively. This is a descending order of a reference group effect over time. It quantifies the convergence depicted in figures 1 and 2, this time at the level of a latent variable.

Table 1: Parameter estimates for the impact of reference groups on test anxiety development (Standardized LISREL V solution)

LAMBDA Y- Matrix

	ETA 1	ETA 2	ETA 3	ETA 4	ETA 5	ETA 6
Groups	1.00					
Worry 1		.65				
Emo 1		.82				
Worry 2			.74			
Emo 2			.84			
Worry 3				.78		
Emo 3				.79		
Worry 4					.87	
Emo 4					.82	
Worry 5						.79
Emo 5						.67

BETA-Matrix

	ETA 1	ETA 2	ETA 3	ETA 4	ETA 5
EQ. 2	-.45				
EQ. 3		.70			
EQ. 4			.88		
EQ. 5				.82	
EQ. 6					.80

PSI - Matrix

EQ. 1	EQ. 2	EQ. 3	EQ. 4	EQ. 5	EQ. 6
1.00	.80	.51	.23	.32	.37

R. Schwarzer et al.

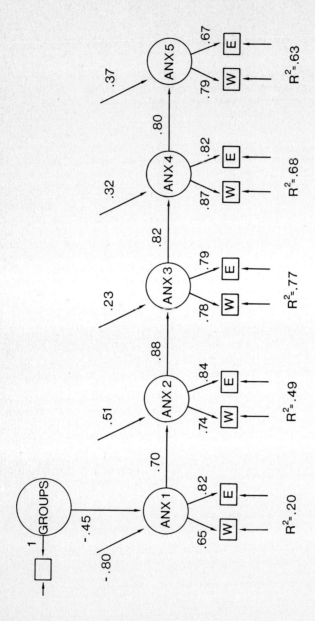

Figure 3: The Influence of Reference Groups on Test Anxiety over Time

STUDY II

While the first result was obtained with the objective school environment, the next one deals with the perceived environment or classroom climate in connection with some self-related cognitions. This study is based on the same sample as before including students in the mid track and in comprehensive schools (N = 287). The question was how test anxiety development is related to self-concept, self-awareness and classroom climate. Self-concept was assessed by a self-esteem scale (German form of the Rosenberg scale, 1965) and by a self-concept of ability scale (Meyer, 1972). Self-awareness as a trait (or "self-consciousness") was assessed by two subscales, private and public self-consciousness (Fenigstein, Scheier & Buss, 1975, preliminary German form by Filipp, unpubl.). Classroom climate was assessed by an achievement pressure scale and an anonymity scale (Fend, unpubl.). Self-concept was measured at the first two points in time, self-awareness at the fourth, and classroom climate at the fifth. A causal model was specified with cross-lagged relationships between self-concept and test anxiety. However, it had to be respecified as depicted in figure 4.

This final model obtained a chi-square of 426.5 (125 df) which was significant (rejected). The goodness of fit index provided by the LISREL V program was .80, the Tucker-Lewis coefficient was .84, Bentler's delta .83 and the root mean square residual 0.14 (Table 2).

This may be satisfactory for some rough interpretations. First, there is no causal relationship between self-concept and test anxiety but only a covariation. Self-awareness has a considerable impact on test anxiety. The more students are aware of themselves the more they perceive themselves as being anxious. However, this is a controversial issue (see Carver & Scheier, 1984). The classroom climate also has a strong impact (.67) on anxiety at the last point in time. Those who perceive a great deal of achievement pressure and anonymity in school tend to be more anxious.

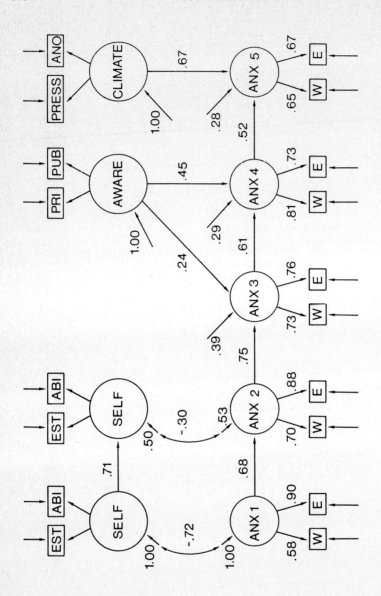

Figure 4: Anxiety Development with Respect to Self-Related Cognition and Classroom Climate

Table 2: Parameter estimates for the second study
         (Standardized LISREL V solution)

LAMBDA Y- Matrix

	ETA1	ETA2	ETA3	ETA4	ETA5	ETA6	ETA7	ETA8	ETA9
Worry1	.58								
Emo1	.90								
Worry2		.70							
Emo2		.88							
Worry3			.73						
Emo3			.76						
Worry4				.81					
Emo4				.73					
Worry5					.65				
Emo5					.67				
Self 1						.89			
Ability 1						.57			
Self 2							.83		
Ability 2							.75		
Private								.88	
Public								.71	
Ach. Pressure									.81
Anonymity									.76

BETA - Matrix

	ETA1	ETA2	ETA3	ETA4	ETA5	ETA6	ETA7	ETA8	ETA9
EQ. 2	.68								
EQ. 3		.75							
EQ. 4			.61				.24		
EQ. 5				.52			.45		
EQ. 6								.67	
EQ. 7						.71			

PSI - Matrix

	ETA1	ETA2	ETA3	ETA4	ETA5	ETA6	ETA7	ETA8	ETA9
EQ. 1	1.00								
EQ. 2		.53							
EQ. 3			.39						
EQ. 4				.29					
EQ. 5					.28				
EQ. 6	-.72					1.00			
EQ. 7		-.30					.50		
EQ. 8								1.00	
EQ. 9									1.00

CONCLUSIONS

These are some first steps in unravelling the complex relationships which exist in the development of trait test anxiety in academic settings. The perspective here is a macro-perspective focusing on quasi-experimental field designs. The present results were partly replicated in other studies (Schwarzer et al. 1983, 1984, Schwarzer & Lange, 1983). Test anxiety is an important indicator of the individual's adaptation to his school environment, his vulnerability towards potentially threatful demands and his belief in competence, self-efficacy and coping resources. It is therefore of high value in school socialization research.

NOTE

The research reported herein was supported by the Volkswagen Foundation.

The Self in Anxiety, Stress and Depression
R. Schwarzer (Editor)
© Elsevier Science Publishers B.V. (North-Holland), 1984

UNDERGOING SURGERY:
THE SELF-REGULATIVE ACTIVITY OF MEDICAL PATIENTS AS A CO-DETERMINANT OF THEIR EMOTIONAL STATES

Stephan Dutke, Angelika-M. Frenzel, Arne Raeithel and Wolfgang Schönpflug

Free University of Berlin, Federal Republic of Germany

The data presented here stem from three field studies in general hospitals with a total of 52 subjects (i.e. patients) who were undergoing surgery for diagnostic or curative purposes. We investigated the patterns of relations between two sets of variables measured before and after the surgical operation: (1) emotional state items in semantic differential format, and (2) indicators for the type of self-regulative activity (e.g. coping style) which we derived from our general theoretical views about the regulation, and the efficiency, of action (see Schönpflug 1983).

SITUATIONS, ACTIONS, AND THE EFFICIENCY OF COPING

From a transactional perspective the situation of being a patient in a hospital is a special relation between persons and their environment (Lazarus and Launier 1978) which is produced in some socially and physically defined behavior setting (Barker 1968) by the actions, and the non-intentional behaviors, of the interacting persons. Among the main constituents of a situation - physical/ecological, social, and subjective/cognitive factors - we are most interested in the latter: The main postulate of cognitive behavior theory or action theory is that persons have anticipations of the future which they use as base for their personal involvement, active intervention or further orientation. These anticipations also play a vital role in emotional reactions to events which must be evaluated, attributed to some type of cause, and with which the person must cope somehow.

Although we would like to study the detailed structure of such anticipations in future research (Schönpflug, in press), in our present study we concentrated on an abstract description of the actions and anticipations. We interviewed medical patients, and used a threefold classification of their actions: direct actions to produce some non-cognitive result, orienting actions to get, process, or structure information, and actions that are necessary to endure the actions of other persons (e.g. submitting oneself to some medical procedure). The intensity and efficiency of each of these three classes of activity should indicate the global type of situation; when orienting actions are frequent, and not very efficient, for instance, we can infer that the actor has problems in finding

a stable anticipation of coming events, and further infer that
his or her emotional state shows signs of anxiety etc.. In
addition to these indirect indicators we assessed directly the
degree of anticipated success of the main task of the
situation: to undergo surgery (short term effect) for the
restoration of physical health (long term consequence).

Since we take the emotional state of the patients as
the dependent variable in this study, and since we see emotional load and stress as stemming mainly from a necessity to
endure short term physical or cognitive stress for some long
term benefit (Schulz 1983), we also assessed the conditions
under which patients came into the hospital, and the degrees
of freedom they had in this choice.

Table 1: Activity-Questionnaire for surgical patients

Preconditions

1)	It was my own decision to go to the hospital	1 2 3 4 5
2)	I was urged to go to the hospital	1 2 3 4 5
3)	I was able to choose the time for my stay here	1 2 3 4 5
4)	I might have chosen some other kind(s) of treatment	1 2 3 4 5
1	What is your main goal in undergoing surgery ?	open answer
5)	There are severe constraints on what I can do today	1 2 3 4 5

Activity and Efficiency

6)	I have been doing a lot this afternoon	1 2 3 4 5
2	With whom or what are you doing this ?	open answer
7)	I think this is useful for the preparation of surgery	1 2 3 4 5
8)	I am very attentive this afternoon	1 2 3 4 5
3	What is your attention directed to ?	open answer
9)	I have got all the information I wanted	1 2 3 4 5
10)	I have to go through a lot this afternoon	1 2 3 4 5
4	Who performs what you have to go through ?	open answer
11)	I suppose that these procedures are useful for the preparation	1 2 3 4 5

Success and Consequences

12a)	I think that the operation will be successful (pre-interview)	1 2 3 4 5
12b)	As far as I can judge the operation was successful (post-interv.)	1 2 3 4 5
13)	In case of success I expect **positive** long-term consequences	1 2 3 4 5
14)	Even in case of success I expect **negative** long-term consequences	1 2 3 4 5
15)	In case of a non-successful operation I expect negative long-term consequences	1 2 3 4 5

(1: "not at all", 5: "very much so")

Based on abstract classifications of activity,
consequences, and preconditions of the central task of the
situation (undergoing surgery) we designed a questionnaire
(Table 1). We used one item only for each of the conceptual
dimensions. This means that there was a possibility of getting
very unreliable scores, but we also felt that our patients

should not be confronted with a longer and more detailed
questionnaire. We report here only on items with fixed
response format, the starred items in Table 1 were used
differently in the three field studies (see above).

EMOTION AS INPUT SIGNALS FOR SELF-REGULATION

Viewed from a general theory of control processes in
living systems (cf. Powers 1973, van Sommers 1974) the regulation of personal activity is "control of input" (Powers 1978),
is the matching of an input signal that represents some essential aspect of the object of action against a reference signal
that represents the goal. If we want to analyze self-regulation as a control process, we have to specify what the input
signal is, for a person can control him- or herself only
insofar as he or she has sensual (or, still better,
conceptual) signals to use in a process of trying to match
them to a salient standard (see Carver and Scheier 1981 for a
more detailed account). We want to propose that emotions make
up an important part of the input signals that are used by
self-regulation, and that persons are able to shift their
focus of emotional awareness to many different levels of
control, each one corresponding to some concrete, spatio-
temporally constrained situation. Different levels can be
induced by "state" and "trait" instructions, and are also
realized by subjects, spontaneously. Thus, to give an example
from one of our field studies - a patient can talk about the
forthcoming operation in a very rational and quiet manner, but
she will burst into tears as soon as the interviewer mentions
her family, because she is worrying about how her elder son
will get along with his step-father.

These shifts in emotional awareness do not only
produce different affects and moods, but also correspond to
shifts in the conceptual elaboration of action plans (i.e.
time-perspective, branching, and concreteness of the
conceptual network change accordingly, Schönpflug, in press),
to shifts in general arousal and preparedness for direct
action, and to shifts in the standards that become salient for
the present private or public self-focus (Carver and Scheier
1981). However, this hypothetical "focus" should not be
conceptualized as a single sharply bounded region on one level
of control. The situation in focal awareness is always
embedded in wider contexts (ecological as well as conceptual
ones) that influence strongly the general mood, and is usually
structured into "cells" of sub-situations (partitions of the
Lewinian (1946) life-space) from where the more affect-like
emotions stem. In our model the quality and intensity of the
felt emotions then must be a complex mixture or woven pattern
of all the emotional input signals from all levels, some
levels being screened out to a certain extent, some others
forming the ground on which the "focal emotions" figure prominently.

In comparison to other theories that link emotions
with cognitions or actions (Weiner, Russell and Lerman 1978,

Lazarus, Kanner and Folkman 1980, Lantermann 1982, Dörner in press) our sketch of a theory shows much less detail, and does not predict specific emotions to be associated with a specific class of appraisals, causal ascriptions, or other cognitive operations. We tried to be as general as possible without becoming vague, because our main concern is to analyze the structure of the task (undergoing operation), and of the coping activities of medical patients with regard to costs and benefits for the overall result.

Accordingly, we used a very broad assessment of the emotional state of our subjects, an instrument developed for the monitoring of behavior therapy (the "EMI-S" of Ullrich and Ullrich de Muynck 1979), which in its original form comprises 70 bi-polar items of strong emotional content. We report here on the emotional state as shown in 24 of these items (see a rough translation in Table 2), because in our third study we

Table 2: Emotional state items and results of factor analyses

Items from EMI-S translated from German		Loadings in PFA of pre-interview						Loadings in PFA of post-interview				
1 2 3	4 5 6	F1	F2	F3	F4	F5	F6	F1	F2	F3	F4	F5
calm	fidgety	**-79**	-22	29				**-77**				
explosive	lazy	73	35		21			66	28			
inhibited	free	65				27	25	**76**		-20	30	
fearful	fearless	60	42	-35				76		-21	30	
clear	blocked	-62	-34		-32			-75				
hectic	quiet	**78**		-30				52	28			
confused	regular	45	78					74	31			
irritable	resistant	53	59	28				28			**70**	
venturesome	exhausted			**84**				-24	**88**			
lively	dead tired		-24	80				-24	80	-26		
passive	active	-37	31	-27	40				**-80**			-30
vigorous	feeble		-47	54		-39	29		28	-68		
drowsy	dynamical			28	-29	64			-27	**84**		
sarcastic	friendly	31			**86**				75			
spiteful	neutral				83			22	**84**			
assured	insecure		34	21		**60**	37	30	62		31	33
cared-for	abandoned						**-96**		-43	41		**54**
helpless	superior					**78**	32	-33	20	-27	52	-41
threatened	secure	40			28	22	60	**83**				
orderly	chaotic	-25	-41	40		24	-30	-40	-62			
loved	rejected			25	-78		-29	-25				70
cheerful	sad		-73	20				-58	-35	27	-31	25
happy	weepy		-75			-24		-71	-28	28	-26	
grieved	winged		78		21			61	51			

| 1 2 3 4 5 6 | Only loadings greater than .19 shown, without |
| -- range of scores -- | decimal points; boldface indicates marker-items. |

had to reduce the questionnaire to gain time for other tests (see next section for details).

To sum up our theoretical exposition: We wanted to inspect the relationship between time perspective, action class, and perceived efficiency on the one hand, and the emotional states of medical patients on the other. We expected to find group differences that could be interpreted as differential effects of various self-regulative strategies. We did not try to do a detailed process-analysis, but rather compared two points in time (pre- and post-operative situations) as represented in the answers of the patients.

METHOD

Samples and procedure. Three samples of patients from three different hospitals in the city of West-Berlin were available for investigations. Since the original emphasis of our project was on effects of architecture on the emotional states of patients, the selection was based on the architectural and organizational structure of hospitals rather than on complaints or personal characteristics of patients. However, the principal task situation (undergoing surgery) was the same for all patients. There was also a common item pool for all the samples. In detail, the patients and the hospital wards can be described as follows:

(1) GYN: 19 female patients in a gynecological ward of a university clinic undergoing minor operations primarily for diagnostic purposes; the pre-interview followed the visit of the anesthesiologist on the day before operation; the post-interview took place on the afternoon of the second day after the operation, when 7 patients were reassured about their non-dangerous diagnosis, while 11 still waited for the diagnostic outcome. The ward was modern, spacious, the social athmosphere was friendly and quiet.
(2) ORTO: 17 patients (12 male, 5 female) in an orthopedical ward of a general hospital undergoing operations on bones and joints for a purely curative purpose; the pre-interview followed the conference of the surgeons on the day before (patients got their pre-operative information there); the post-interview was on the second day after operation, when patients did not suffer from direct after-effects of the surgery. The ward was situated on the 7th floor of an old building waiting for restauration, it was crowded and there was a harsh tone between personnel and patients.
(3) MIX: 16 patients (8 male, 8 female) in four different wards of a recently built, very big general hospital; the operations had mainly curative purpose, and were mixed as to part of body involved; the time schedule for interviews was as in the other two interviews, the pre-interview again following the visit of the anesthesiologist. The wards were open, colourful, sometimes quite turbulent, and populated by many nationalities.

Table 3: Mean scores of pre-interview clusters on activity items (see Tab. 1)

Item Content	REALISM			FAIL?			OPTIMISM		
	Total	LOSS	GAIN	Total	LOSS	GAIN	Total	LOSS	GAIN
1) own decision	2.7	2.1	3.3	4.4	4.1	4.7	3.5	4.6	2.3
2) urged to go	3.6	4.3	2.9	3.9	4.2	3.4	4.8	4.9	4.6
3) time chosen	2.2	1.3	3.1	3.9	4.3	3.4	3.5	3.8	3.2
4) alternative possible	1.3	1.3	1.3	2.1	1.1	3.4	1.0	1.0	1.1
5) constraints	2.2	3.0	1.4	2.5	2.9	2.0	2.7	4.0	1.4
6) action intensity	2.2	2.0	2.4	2.9	3.6	2.0	1.9	1.8	1.9
7) action efficiency	3.2	4.3	2.1	3.9	4.2	3.4	3.8	4.5	3.2
8) orienting intens.	2.6	2.4	2.9	4.4	4.7	4.0	3.9	4.4	3.5
9) orienting effic.	3.7	4.1	3.3	4.7	4.6	4.9	4.8	4.9	4.7
10) enduring intens.	2.4	3.3	1.6	3.2	3.3	3.0	3.5	4.2	2.9
11) enduring effic.	3.6	4.6	2.6	4.6	4.4	4.7	4.9	5.0	4.7
12a) success of surgery	4.2	4.1	4.3	3.9	3.8	4.1	5.0	5.0	4.9
13) pos. cons. success	4.4	4.3	4.6	4.6	4.9	4.3	5.0	5.0	5.0
14) neg. cons. success	2.6	3.6	1.6	2.4	2.9	1.7	1.4	1.5	1.3
15) neg. cons. failure	2.8	2.6	3.0	3.7	3.7	3.7	2.5	2.8	2.1

Table 4: Mean scores of post-interview clusters on activity items (see Tab. 1)

Item Content	DOUBTS	RECOVERY	SUCCESS
1) own decision	4.5	2.3	3.5
2) urged to go	3.9	4.5	4.2
3) time chosen freely	3.2	1.2	4.4
4) alternative was possible	1.3	1.3	1.6
5) severe constraints	3.2	2.2	1.5
6) action intensity	2.2	1.7	3.0
7) action efficiency	3.5	4.3	4.8
8) orienting intensity	3.6	2.5	4.2
9) orienting efficiency	3.6	3.7	4.4
10) enduring intensity	2.5	1.5	2.0
11) enduring efficiency	2.8	2.4	3.8
12b) success of surgery	3.8	4.8	5.0
13) pos. consequ. of success	4.6	4.8	4.7
14) neg. consequ. of success	2.1	2.4	1.9
15) neg. consequ. of failure	3.6	1.7	1.3

Participation was voluntary; only German speaking patients between 18 and 60 years of age were accepted for interviews. The
drop-out rate was 26 %. In both pre- and post-interviews the
questionnaire in Table 1 was given prior to the EMI-S. The
latter test was filled out completely by the patients in study
1 and 2, while only the 24 items in Table 2 were presented in
study 3. The third study also differed in the following
respects: Both interviews were much longer; other tests were
included, and we accompanied most of the patients to the
operation room on the day of surgery (we do not report these
data here).

Exploratory data analysis. Two separate hierarchical cluster
analyses (CLUSTAN II, using Ward's method) were computed, each
based on a principal components representation (5 dimensions,
explained variance around 60 %) of the 14 items in Table 1.
Items 1 to 4 were assessed only once in the pre-interview
(because pre-conditions of the hospital stay did not change),
so these items contribute identical variance in both analyses.
After inspection of the clustering tree and of the marker
items of each clustering level (that indicate homogeneity of
the cluster on the respective dimension) we decided on 6
clusters before, and 3 clusters after surgery. Because this is
just an exploratory study, we did not attempt further
refinements (reclassification, comparison with divisive
method) but settled upon the result of the hierarchical
method.

We also computed two separate principal factor
analyses (SPSS PA2 with Varimax rotation) of the 24 EMI-S
items in Table 2. We thought this to be necessary, because the
standardized 7 sub-scales of this inventory did correlate
significantly with each other in each of study 1 and 2. We
used a preliminary PFA of the data in these two studies to
select the most typical items on the resulting 5 to 6 factors
with eigenvalue greater than one. Table 2 shows the items
selected; the factorial structure was well replicated in the
third study (analyzed separately), in which just these 24
items were used. Table 2 also shows the result of the factor
analyses for all patients (N is reduced to 44 in both cases,
because some patients were not willing to fill out the inventory, 43 patients answered the EMI-S on both interviews). We
labeled each factor with two marker items (their loadings are
printed in boldface in Table 2). To visualize the emotional
states of the clusters, we computed mean scores of all items
of each factor with loadings greater than .50. We used Tukey's
"Box-Plots" to show the distribution in each cluster (Tukey
1977, computed by SPSS MANOVA), and also report the F-ratios
of both multiple and single analyses of variance (we do not
report exact error probablities, since we did not do confirmatory data analysis).

RESULTS

The situation on the day before surgery. As is shown by the
cluster tree in Fig. 1 we found six fairly dense sub-clusters
which could be subsumed under three less homogeneous clusters:
One cluster of 14 patients, who think their direct and
orienting actions to be only medium effective for the preparation of surgery, who are fairly certain of a successful
operation, and not concerned about negative consequences of a
failure (we call the cluster REALISM); a second cluster of 16
patients, who have the lowest mean scores on predicted
success, the highest belief in negative consequences after
failure, and the highest intensities in all three action
classes (called FAIL? here); and the third cluster of 22
patients, who are very positive that the operation will be
successful, and have the highest efficiency ratings for all
three classes of actions (called OPTIMISM). All three clusters
can be divided in two sub-clusters each: One of them labeled
GAIN, as positive consequences of a successful operation are
high, the other labeled LOSS, because negative consequences of
either success or failure of the operation are high also.
Further details of the patterns of these clusters are shown in
Table 3.

        It seems as if the activity clusters can also be ex-
plained by the purpose of the operation: In REALISM we have
predominantly curative purpose (with high need of practice
after orthopedic operations), while in OPTIMISM there are 11
of 18 patients with diagnostic purpose. This pattern, though,
is not as precise as in the post-clusters (see below).

        In the characterization of each cluster we had to mix
three different anticipation-periods: Patients are either
realistic or optimistic about their present efficiency (or in-
between as FAIL?), they either are very sure about success of
the operation on the next day (OPTIMISM), or not so sure
(REALISM and less still FAIL?), and they anticipate some gain
or some loss in the long run (sub-clusters). If we look at the
mean emotional states (Fig. 2), we can see only minor
differences between the clusters: OPTIMISM is somewhat higher
on "calm/ quiet", and FAIL? is a bit lower on "venture-
some/lively" and "cared-for/secure", but the differences might
not reach significance in a confirmative study. The multitude
of outliers shows that clusters are fairly heterogeneous in
emotional state. In the lower part of Fig. 2 we can see how
these clusters of patients changed their emotional states two
days after surgery. They are all high now on "calm/free" and
"neutral/secure", REALISM is low on "active/venturesome", and
OPTIMISM is highest on every score. In this pattern we can see
the usual result of lower anxiety after surgery, and also that
the patients we called realistic do not feel bad after
surgery; these are also the patients who rate themselves
higher on "passive/exhausted".

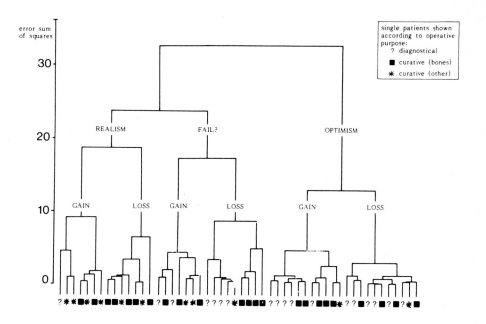

Figure 1: Pre-Interview Clusters of Surgical Patients

Before surgery:
Overall F ≃ 1.1 (p ⌖ .33)

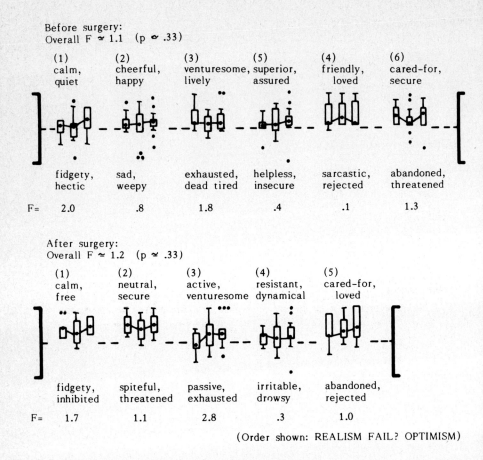

Figure 2: Emotional State of Pre-Interview Clusters

In Fig. 3 we have summed the scores of all three LOSS and GAIN sub-clusters. There are even more outliers in the situation before surgery; therefore it can be concluded that loss and gain mean different things emotionally depending on the kind of anticipation of the result of the operation. After surgery (lower part of Fig. 3) we can see some differential effects: Patients in LOSS feel less "calm/free" and "resistant/dynamical", and more "passive/exhausted" than patients in GAIN.

The situation after surgery: Recovery, success, or doubts. The cluster analysis of the post-interview activity data yielded two dense clusters, and one slightly more heterogenous one (see Fig. 4). The first one (called DOUBTS) comprises 16 patients, who have lowest scores on perceived success, and highest on negative consequences of a probable failure of the operation; they went to hospital on their own decision, but were also urged, they feel severe constraints on their actions this afternoon, and have highest endurance scores (but still under mid point). In the second cluster (called RECOVERY) are 12 patients, which do very little, are not attentive, but think all this to be efficient for regaining health; they had been urged to go to hospital, and now are convinced of success and of mainly positive, but also some (inevitable?) negative consequences of the surgery. The biggest cluster of 22 patients (named SUCCESS) has very positive mean scores: Operation was a succes, consequences will be very positive, they are doing a lot again, are very attentive, and everything is highly effective (these patients could choose most freely when to go to hospital; for more details see Table 4).

All of the patients whith diagnostic purpose who already had been informed about the benign nature of their state are in SUCCESS; 4 of 11 who did not know the result of the diagnosis are in DOUBTS. RECOVERY comprises only patients with severe orthopedical or abdominal operations. If we look at the emotional states of the clusters (Fig. 5), we can easily see that all patients are now higher on "calm/free", "neutral/secure" than on the comparable emotional state factors of the pre-interview; many RECOVERY-patients are now below midpoint on "active/venturesome", while before surgery they were high on "venturesome/ lively", as on every other scale. All patients are above mid on "cared-for/loved". The patients in DOUBTS, though, feel less calm, secure, and cared-for; while the patients in RECOVERY feel more calm, neutral, and exhausted than the others.

So it seems as if the situation after surgery is well explained by purpose of operation, perceived actual success, and therefore by more predictable consequences. The emotional states closely follow the action patterns, but one can also find a difference which must be due to a general precondition: The patients in DOUBT are in hospital on their own decision, and have chosen the time, more often than the patients in RECOVERY. But the latter feel decidedly better, presumably because they place more trust in the medical personnel than

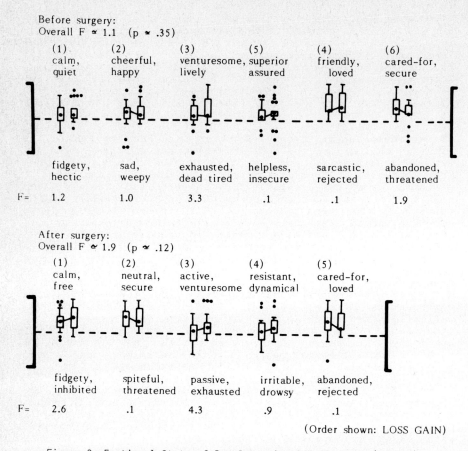

Figure 3: Emotional State of Pre-Interview Sub-Clusters (Summed)

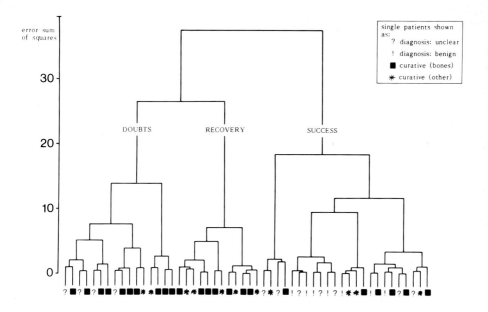

Figure 4: Post-Interview Clusters of Surgical Patients

those in DOUBT (especially before the operation), and
accordingly can relax as reconvalescent patients should do.
According to these data the patient who decides on his or her
own is not likely to feel well after surgery, probably worrying if the decision was the right one.

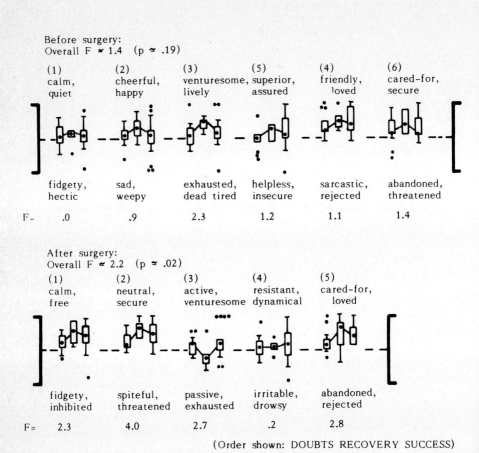

Figure 5: Emotional state of post-interview clusters

DISCUSSION

         We did not find clear patterns of emotional states
before surgery. Fig. 6 shows that we can find an effect of
hospital wards on the emotional states of our patients which
of course is confounded with the effect of the general purpose
of the surgical operation (compare the descriptions above).
The ward effect, though, is much clearer before the surgery
than it is two days later. One can say that patients in MIX
wards feel generally best, most pronounced on "venture-
some/lively", which corresponds nicely with the lively
atmosphere of these wards. The patients in ORTO are very constrained in their judgement on how "friendly/beloved" they
feel before surgery which also agrees with our description of
the ward.

         After surgery we have found that the actual state of
the patients in the process of recovery is more indicative of
their emotional state than the hospital ward. Thus, it seems
that the course of the illness produces different psychological sub-situations in the same ecological and social surroun-
dings, and that the psychological situations determine both
activity patterns, and emotional states.

         We found indications of two different self-regulative
strategies: The patients in FAIL? before surgery were most
attentive and active compared with the patients in REALISM,
who apparently thought the hospital to be trustworthy enough
to relax. The activity patterns of these two clusters can be
interpreted as vigilant and non-vigilant self-regulation with
respect to the anticipation of the success of surgery. We
found two similar clusters after surgery: patients in DOUBTS
again are more attentive and active than patients in RECOVERY,
but at this point in time the surgery has been performed, and
the patients in DOUBTS must cope now with their worries which
are clearly indicated in their emotional state scores, and
which concern mainly the long-term consequences of a probable
failure of the surgery. Thus, we can infer that the focus of
emotional awareness of the patients in the vigilant clusters
is different before and after surgery: Vigilance before
surgery is mainly directed to the surrounding conditions of
the ward, while after surgery it is concentrated on anticipations of long-term consequences.

         One further comment on emotional states: We were
surprised to find that most surgical patients feel quite well,
they had evidently seen the operation as a challenge, or were
very well informed, or at least thought so. But in Figs. 2, 3,
5 and 6 one can also see that about 5 % of the patients do not
describe themselves as feeling well at all (the outliers in
the negative range). Further studies should concentrate on
these patients, but these studies must take into account the
differences between hospital wards, and the different time
courses of surgery. Individual differences in self-regulative
strategy can show up only within the constraints that ecological behavior settings provide, these constraints seem to

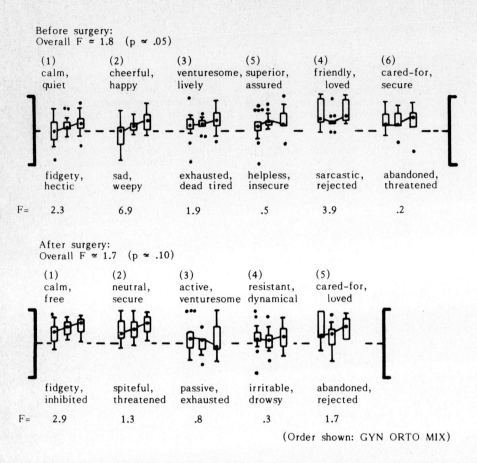

Before surgery:
Overall F ≃ 1.8 (p ≃ .05)

Figure 6: Emotional State of Patients in Different Hospital Wards

influence the emotional state more than the type of activity,
as assessed by our very abstract scales. But our data also
show that behavior settings are modified dynamically by the
patients, the nurses, and the medical doctors: The specific
illness of a patient, together with his or her confidence and
trust in the hospital, make up a concrete sub-situation which
has a constraining power comparable to a behavior setting.

NOTE

This research is part of the project "Angst im
Krankenhaus" which was funded by the Deutsche Forschungs-
Gemeinschaft.

The Self in Anxiety, Stress and Depression
R. Schwarzer (Editor)
© Elsevier Science Publishers B.V. (North-Holland), 1984

EMERGENCY-RELATED ANXIETY AND COPING WITH STRESSFUL EVENTS IN OLD AGE

Anna Maria Asprea and Giulia Villone-Betocchi

University of Naples, Naples, Italy

This article forms part of a research plan intended to study, in a cognitive frame of reference, the reactions to specific stressful events in a community. Its aim is twofold: to study the condition of being old in an emergency situation, and to investigate coping answers in terms of individual-environment interaction processes.

In recent times, research into topics such as stress and anxiety, depression and helplessness, appears to have been increasingly cognitively oriented (Schwarzer, Cherkes-Julkowski, 1982). The cognitive trend has greatly contributed to a widening up of psychological research, both in individual traits and in social interaction processes. The study of cognitive appraisal of both one's competence and the situation is indeed most relevant to the evaluation of stress and of coping with stress. Cognitive appraisal is a necessary process in allowing coping with stressful events. In fact, the anticipation about one's ability to face threatening events as well as behavioral outcomes, are part of one's belief systems and of one's specific competence awareness.

With referene to the terminology of Folkman and Lazarus (Folkman & Lazarus, 1980) this research can be defined as "situation oriented", in that it studies an elderly person's cognitive and behavioral answers to a specific situation, i.e. an earthquake. Thus the study of psychological coping with disaster contingency has been carried out with a "functional" perspective. Cognitive processes of appraisal, together with problem and emotion-focused behavioral strategies, have been taken into account.

As stressed in the literature (Folkman and Lazarus, 1980): "Situation-oriented research on coping tends also to be situation-specific". Within our terms of reference, "coping" is defined as "the cognitive and behavioral efforts made to master, tolerate, or reduce external and internal demands, and conflict among them. Such coping efforts serve two main functions: the management of the alteration of person-environment relationship that is the source of stress (problem-focused coping), and the regulation of stressful emotion (emotion-focused coping)".

The consequences of the 1980 earthquake in Southern Italy were dramatic in that they struck a particularly complex ecological area; its main problem having been for decades migration, marginality of women and old people, and the lack of industrial development. This research was intended to look at those individual psychological needs which stem from an individual historical and ecological background in the conditions of such a natural disaster. Meeting such needs could also imply the possibility of facing and, somehow, relieving the impact of such a catastrophic event. Research carried out in such a conceptual frame of reference allows close connections between theory and practice. Thus, the study of different aspects proves to be related to sociocultural development, present conditions of human living being the necessary object of research.

METHOD

Materials and procedures. This survey was carried out in a small agricultural community in Southern Italy, a year after the earthquake, when the new prefabricated settlements had been completed. The village, which clings to a hill top at the end of a rather narrow road, has been completely evacuated and almost destroyed. In the valley beneath the village there are settlements which have been partially damaged, and there, prefabricated settlements have been located near to the original ones.

The Sample. Out of a total of 288 old people (there were 1,475 inhabitants in the 1981 census) a random sample of 70 subjects (41 women and 29 men) has been taken into consideration. An age limit of 65 was considered a reasonable choice criterion after taking into account the main features of a population which belongs to a rural community.

During the earthquake, 7.5% of the sample suffered the loss of a spouse, 7.5% of one child, 1.5% of grandchildren, and 22.5 % of relatives.
- 65% suffered the total loss of a house, and 35% the partial loss of one.
- 62% live in prefabricated houses set in a valley about 3 miles from their previous housing environment; 38% are still in their same housing environment, although some of them live in prefabricated houses.
- 37.5% are totally capable of self caring; 22.5% are almost self-sufficient; the others are partially dependent.
- Some subjects are capable of some daily activity. Yet the large majority of subjects give evidence of passivity attitudes which they blame on the consequences of the earthquake. The quake is considered both the psychological and the actual source of giving-up attitudes, in terms of

feeling old and demotivated; suffering owing to the change of housing environment; the loss of one's living space and ambience, such as rooms to live in, kitchen garden to take care of; and change for the worse in health and self-sufficiency.

The Interview. A half-structured interview and a clinical interview has been applied individually to each subject. The half-structured interview was designed on the basis of three main topics: old age, the earthquake emergency, and being old in the emergency situation. The main points analysed in the interview were the following:

- Demographic data: age, education, material status, housing and family structure, etc. .

- Interpersonal stability: frequency of interaction (family contacts and communitiy integration) before and after the earthquake.

- Current functioning: self-evaluation of functional self-care capacity. Townsend index in six areas (ability to go outdoors; to use stairs; to get around; to wash; to cut toenails). Description of a typical day, scored to active and passive activity (Lawton, 1980).

- Needs: one's own and other people's, and ways of coping with them, either problem or emotion focused, either suggested or actual. The problem-focused category involves "cognitive problem solving efforts, and behavioral strategies for altering and managing the source of the problem" (actual suggestions, plans and decisions). The emotion-focused category involves "items that describe cognitive and behavioral efforts directed at reducing or managing emotional distress" (Folkman & Lazarus, 1980, pp. 224-225).

- Emotional states. Questions included here assess the reactions to the emergency event in a three dimensional report (during the earthquake, immediately after, and at the time of the survey). Stimuli, in this section, are meant to investigate subjects' feelings about being old in an emergency situation.

- Past experience stresses. In order to better understand reactions to stressful events, an adaptation of Holmes and Rahe's "Social readjustment rating scale" (1967) has been applied. This requires the evaluation of some major life stresses, such as death of a significant other, change for the worse in health and finance, etc. .

- Futurity and death. The meaning of this area stems from the consideration that the emergency has surely caused death anxiety on an actual basis, and has provoked new thinking about one's future. Points analysed were: consciousness of death, frequency of thinking about death and coping strategies. Such variables were particularly relevant being

the catastrophic event of the earthquake an unavoidable source
of death anxiety, and worries about one's future. Actually
the subjects of the research are old, they have been trapped
for hours under collapsed buildings before being rescued; in
many cases they have experienced the death of some dear one.
In considering the future there is the cognitive perspective

of one's future, both as a private and a collective time
dimension.

RESULTS

Since it is not feasible to present all the features taken
into account, we will only give a brief presentation of those
data which are relevant for the study of the coping process.

The impact with disaster. Literature about disaster is
controversial, yet research agrees that in a condition of
shock, the persistence of the stimuli which gave rise to the
shock hampers the structuring of adaptive answers to the
stressful event. As we said before, the village clings to a
hilltop and, though partially destroyed and completely
evacuated, it is being kept in its present state as a
monument. People go there to visit what is left of their
kitchen gardens which can be reached despite the ruins; the
town garden is regularly tidied and cared for by a volunteer
group of workers and gardeners once a week. Even a statue
which broke into two has been preserved without being
repaired. All this probably delays the adaptation to
bereavement, hampering the acceptance of present conditions,
and eliciting at a deeper level, a rejection of the new
situation.

The loss of objects as a result of the disaster. For what
concerns the change in life style, after the event, the
majority of subjects are aware of the change of lifestyle.
Among the few who do not seem to perceive any change are some
who have not sustained any serious loss or damage; others,
most probably, give hints of defensive coping processes.

Table 1: Change in lifestyle after the earthquake

	Women (41)%	Men (29)%	Tot.Ss.(70)%
Total change	29	/	17
No change	8	10	8
Financial losses	19	/	11
Affective losses	12	17	15
Symbolic losses	24	49	35
Decrease in self sufficiency	8	24	14
	100	100	100

A high percentage of subjects impute the change to the loss of their homes, and of the objects in the home, which are necessary symbols for keeping the past alive, for "replaying"

it to allow a sort of validation process which helps to produce life satisfaction. Such losses are clearly distinguishable from financial losses. It is well known in literature how the loss of one's home is loaded with symbolic meaning threatening one's identity. The houses and their contents are the products of social, cultural and psychological processes; they reflect the values incorporated in the structure of society and the lifestyle of the individual.

The process of recovering and helping behavior. Table 2 displays three kinds of coping strategies focused on the energy of life, the received help, the attention to others.

Table 2: Coping strategies: The process of recovering

	Women (41)%	Men (29)%	Tot.Ss. (70)%
One's own will	12	/	7
Being cared by children	/	31	13
Moral duty (struggle for survival)	46	24	37
Duty to help others	12	14	13
Awareness of others' damages	22	31	26
DK answers	8	/	4
	100	100	100

The struggle for survival (the "energy of life") was given as the reason for "pulling themselves together" by the majority of women and a slightly smaller percentage of men. But, among the men's answers are indications of an awareness of their children's care, and in a similar percentage there are answers which acknowledge that "others sustained more damages".

Within the "problem-focused" coping answers such as escaping from ruins, asking for help, etc., it is to be emphasized the process of helping others in the immediate post impact period.

Table 3: Coping strategies: Helping behavior

	Women (41)%	Men (29)%	Tot.Ss. (70)%
Help given to relatives	17	28	22
Help given to neighbours	5	34	17
No help given because trapped or wounded	66	31	51
No help given because emotionally upset	12	7	10
	100	100	100

The experience of disaster; the helpfulness of giving advice.
As we have previously stated, the aim of the survey was to
find out and analyse which were the strategies used to face an
emergency situation. Data concerning advice, if any, given to
others, show evidence of a trend to regard advice as useless.

Table 5: Advice to be given in emergency situations

	Women (41)%	Men (29)%	Tot.Ss. (70)%
Problem-focused advice	24	34	29
Emotion-focused advice	15	21	17
Advice is useless	56	45	51
DK answers	5	/	3
	100	100	100

Subjects who state that advice can help are those who have
sustained more losses. If we break down data along this
variable we can also better understand results concerning
the question of the usefulness of talking about past
experience. Again the positive aspects of talking are pointed
out by those subjects who have sustained more damage. Indeed
it has been frequently emphasized in the literature that a
disaster like this one is not an experience of loneliness, it
is not an alienating one and instead, it may give rise to
different kinds of "prosocial" behavior.

Another interesting point in this area is that more men than
women think that talking about their experiences can be useful
to others and/or to themselves.

Table 5: Usefulness of talking about stressful events

	Women (41)%	Men (29)%	Tot.Ss. (70)%
It is useful	34	65	47
It is useless	61	31	49
DK answers	5	4	4
	100	100	100

An explanation of these results can be found in the cultural variable. The men of the sample who made such statements, had travelled and had long experience of working in other countries and meeting with different sociocultural conditions. Motivations for reticence are mainly defensive; talking is useless, talking is replaying the suffering. On the other hand, motivations for wishing to talk bring in both problem and emotion-focused coping ("can be useful for others", "helps relieve feelings").

The coping processes after the disaster. The majority of subjects give evidence of coping strategies in the immediate post-impact period; women more frequently pray, men try to do something to escape danger or to help, if possible.

Table 6: Immediate post-impact reactions

	Women (41)%	Men (29)%	Tot.Ss. (70)%
Prayers	32	/	21
Active reactions (escape)	48	55	50
Passive reactions (waiting)	20	24	21
DK answers	/	20	8
	100	100	100

The large majority of subjects report having been aware of and frightened by death. Only a few (15%) do not seem to remember the emotions and events of their past experience. Motivated forgetting can explain such a lack of memory, and it appears confirmed when subjects are requested to recall experiences of other earthquakes in the same region, in 1930 and 1962, and which seem to be forgotten at present. When asked what, in a quake emergency, was the most severe damage an aged person had

to sustain, the majority of subjects gave problem- and emotion-focused answers. Physical damage appears to be less important in comparison to feelings of loneliness and lack of future perspective. According to the majority of subjects, the 1980 earthquake was the worst experience of their lives. Such data are consistent with that has been recently emphasized in literature concerning stressful events and environmental changes in life; the earthquake being an environmental experience as well as an individual catastrophic change, it is perceived as an all pervasive stressor. Fear of loneliness and lack of future perspective appear to be understandable depressive reactions in aged subjects.

Looking at long-distance effects, we would like to point out that the activity patterns of the subjects are different according to the sex variable. Men appeared to be less active than women apart from those who still took care of the land. Yet they looked for some mutual company, also with the women; they played cards in the Centre organised by the Red Cross and watched TV programs together. It is substantiated by our findings that the catastrophic experience brought about a change in behavioral interaction patterns in the communitiy.

Table 7 : Interpersonal stability: Means of total scores of the interaction scales before and after the earthquake (N=70)

Interaction with	Before	After	z	p
Family	4.34	3.64	5.98	<.01
Friends	3.51	4.46	6.18	<.01
Opposite Sex	3.43	4.06	6.30	<.01

(Significance testing by Wilcoxon matched-pairs test)

In fact, the main cultural values of the social environment of the subjects are traditionally family-oriented which frequently implies, especially for women, a reduced participation in interaction nets, but kinship. In this respect the emergency has worked as an innovative stimulus.

DISCUSSION

It is possible to say that many subjects reached a good coping level. This assertion is based on a link between the serious damage sustained and coping skills. Although such data are already found in literature about disaster, we want to stress this point because the subjects are old people. In fact if it is difficult for old people to develop skills to cope with prolonged stress of life transitions and oldness crisis, it is striking that the elderly population of the sample learnt how to cope successfully with catastrophic change in the environment. It is known in literature how in the immediate post-impact emergency there can be an increase in prosocial behavior on the part of people who have experienced damage. Such behavior is sustained by the emotion-focused process in coping which works better when the appraisal of the emergency allows an evaluation of one's own and others' losses.

It is due to the new coping skills that some of the subjects gave evidence of having met with big innovations, in comparison with prevailing culture norms and values, such as accepting and attending the Social Centre.

To conclude, it is possible to say that, if functional coping, e.g. specific oriented coping, is taken into account, as it has been in the present situation-oriented research, the reactions of old people are positive, and forward the hypothesis that the emergency event could work as a stimulus for the development of role awareness and consequent role taking.

This seems to confirm the importance of cognitive processes in reducing anxiety, and in organising adaptive answers, even in such particular conditions, those of being old in a severe emergency situation.

The Self in Anxiety, Stress and Depression
R. Schwarzer (Editor)
© Elsevier Science Publishers B.V. (North-Holland), 1984

STRESSFUL LIFE EVENTS AND EMOTIONS IN THE ELDERLY

Christine Schwarzer

University of Düsseldorf, Federal Republic of Germany

The experience of stress is related to anxiety, anger, depression, self-esteem, locus of control, health and other variables. Stress is a special quality of a person-environment transaction. It occurs when an event of subjective relevance is cognitively appraised as challenging, threatening, or harmful (Lazarus & Launier, 1978, Krantz, 1983). Coping with stress requires the availability of personal competence to handle difficult or demanding situations or the availability of situational coping resources like material aid or social support (see Barbara Sarason, 1984). Research on critical life events sheds light on the ways of coping and the experience of stress and emotions in the process of overcoming the event and suffering from it.

Different kinds of life events have to be distinguished from each other. Daily hassles lead to chronic stress or permanent coping processes in the conduct of life. This provides the advantage of building up a set of adaptive reactions to a variety of little stressors in the everyday environment. The person can predict the stressors partly and has the opportunity of preparing a set of actions in order to cope with the demands. However, some individuals are more vulnerable than others and do not feel able to regulate daily hassles. A certain degree of predictability is also common for those critical life events which occur to most persons in certain life periods like marriage, birth of children, death of parents or other close persons, and transitions in the professional career. These life events are called normative. Research on the elderly shows that typical normative events in their life period are diseases and the loss of loved ones. In the pattern of adjustment to these events depression is the most common emotion (Fry, this volume). Non-normative life events, on the other hand, are those which happen unforeseen and only to a limited number of people. Asprea and Villone-Betocchi (this volume) have investigated the emotional reactions to an earthquake by Italian victims. West and Ray (this volume) have investigated the emotions of patients suffering from paraplegia. The present study focusses on normative life events of senior citizen in West Germany.

METHOD

In a cross-sectional study a sample of 133 senior citizen were
questionned with respect to their stressful life events and a
number of psychological variables. It was hypothesized that
those who had experienced a great deal of trouble would suffer
from negative emotions and simultaneously would develop coping
strategies and adaptive beliefs in order to maintain their
self-concept. The elderly attended health seminars and were
made believe that they were questionned from a medical point
of view.

The first part of the questionnaire was a life event scale
including 14 items which were selected to be most adequate for
the sample at hand. Four of these items yielded significant
results in relation to the psyhological variables, and therefore are selected for this report:

    1. Death of a spouse
    2. Disease of a close person
    3. Social conflicts
    4. Eating behavior problems (or obesity)

The items were - of course - retrospective. The subjects were
asked to state which of the events they had experienced within
the last 12 months. Two of the final four events were normative whereas the other two could be classified as daily
hassles.

The second part of the questionnaire consisted of the following scales:

    1. Emotional variables
       - Anxiety
       - Anger
       - Curiosity

    2. Personal control variables
       - Self-efficacy
       - Health Locus of Control

    3. Health Status

The three emotional variables were assessed by a German form
of the State-Trait Personality Inventory (STPI) developed by
Spielberger (1979) and translated by Schwarzer and Schwarzer
(1983). It consists of 10 items for each emotion at the state
and 10 items at the trait level, summing up to a total of 60
items. The two personal control scales were developed by
ourselves with respect to the theory of Bandura (1977, 1983).
Self-efficacy denotes the personal belief to be competent in
face of stressful events ad to be able to use adaptive coping
strategies. Health locus of control denotes being personally
responsible for one's own health (Sandler & Lakey, 1982). The
Health Status was assessed by a 17-item version of the Cornell
Medical Index (CMI). Each item asks for a specific bodily

complaint. All scales were analyzed with respect to internal consistencies. The Cronbach's Alphas turned out to be between 0.70 and 0.90.

Data analyses were performed by use of SPSS procedures and focussed on correlations and parametric group comparisons. For each life event item the number of 'victims' was determined. Then, this group was compared with the rest of the sample according to their level of distress or well-being.

RESULTS

Death of spouse. 27 % of the subjects experienced the death of a spouse within the last twelve months. This group was compared to the rest of the sample. The only significant difference was found for their health status. The 'victims' of this critical life event suffered from a great deal of bodily complaints. The death of a loved one may have more impact in health-related stress than on other psychological variables. However, grieving and depression were not assessed within the framework of the present study. These psychological variables should be dominant ones in such a situation. Table 1 displays the group comparison by a t-test.

Table 1: Health status related to the experience of a spouse's death

		No Loss	Loss	t	p
	N	94	34	2.76	$<.01$
Health	Mean	5.00	7.06		
	S.D.	3.92	3.14		

<u>Disease of a close person.</u>The disease of another person was
associated with a different pattern of emotions. 30 % of the
subjects reported having experienced this during the last
twelve months. For this subsample a higher degree of anxiety
and anger was found. This may be interpreted as existential
anxiety in face of losses. If a close person is very ill this
is appraised as a threat to one's social bounds resulting in
anxiety. The ill person could die and leave the subject alone.
Anger also is a well-understood emotion. The ill person is
responsible for the worries of our subjects and therefore the
target for anger. Attributing harm to another person is a
typical cause for anger (Weincr, 1980, 1982, Averill, 1983).
Table 2 shows the means, standard deviations, and t-values for
both groups and both emotions.

Table 2: Feelings of individuals who have experienced
         the disease of a close person

		No disease	Disease	t	p
	N	95	41		
Anger	Means	15.15	17.46	2.48	<.05
	S.D.	4.99	5.03		
Anxiety	Means	17.85	20.02	2.41	<.05
	S.D.	4.91	4.63		

Anger and anxiety were used in a linear discriminant analysis
separating the two groups of elderly. There was a significant
prediction of group membership by this linear function. The
standardized discriminant coefficients were 0.62 for anger and
0.58 for anxiety indicating that both are merely equally
useful for this statistical purpose.

Social conflicts. 35 % of the subjects suffered from severe social conflicts and arguments with neighbours and relatives within the last twelve months. Using two-tailed t-tests in a conservative way, anger and self-efficacy were nearly significantly related to this daily hassle. From a multivariate perspective, however, there was a significant separation of groups by both variables simultaneously in a discriminant analysis (p µ .03). The standardized coefficients were .74 for self-efficacy and .71 for anger. Elderly people who are involved in social conflicts show more efficacy which could mean more assertiveness. Trying to exert social influence on others leads to more social conflicts. Anger can be a cause or effect of this behavior.

Table 3 : Variables related to the experience of
            social conflicts

		No conflicts	conflicts	t	p
	N	91	49		
Anger	Means	15.25	16.86	1.88	<.10
	S.D.	5.00	4.96		
Efficacy	Means	8.88	9.94	1.82	<.10
	S.D.	3.24	3.06		

<u>Eating behavior problems or obesity.</u> 29 % of the subjects
suffered from eating behavior problems like misregulation of
food intake, or obesity. This problem is associated with
anger, curiosity, and health locus of control.   Suffering
persons show more anger maybe caused by their dissatisfaction
with their misregulation. They show more curiosity maybe indicating their exploratory behavior towards food and other
temptations in life. They show a higher degree of health locus
of control indicating their awareness of problems of this
kind. So far this is the univeriate analysis.

In a discriminant analysis curiosity turned out to be no
longer a predictor of group membership whereas anger and
health locus of control significantly contributed to this
prediction. The standardized coefficients were .71 for locus
and .60 for anger.

Table 4 : Variables related to the experience of
          eating behavior problems or obesity

		No Problems	Problems	t	p
	N	98	40		
Anger	Means	15.27	17.30	2.18	<.05
	S.D.	4.92	5.14		
Curiosity	Means	27.22	29.33	2.09	<.05
	S.D.	5.29	5.49		
Locus of C.	Means	3.82	4.40	2.46	<.05
	S.D.	1.37	.96		

CONCLUSIONS

The experience of four stressful life events by the elderly was related to a set of psychosocial variables indicating distress, emotions, health and beliefs. The events were death of a spouse, disease of a close person, social conflicts, and eating behavior problems. The first two were normative life events, the last two were daily hassles. Death of a spouse was associated with a bad health status, disease of a close person with anger and anxiety, social conflicts with anger and self-efficacy, and eating problems with anger, curiosity, and health locus of control. Depression was not assessed but can be seen as the most dominant phenomenon when appraising events as losses (Fry, this volume, Wertheim & Schwarz, 1983).

The most interesting point in this study was the predominance of 'positive' variables like curiosity, self-efficacy and health locus of control. This may indicate the side effects of coping with stress. Being confronted with a critical life event may lead to an increased state of self-awareness (Filipp, Aymanns & Braukmann, 1984). In this state persons ruminate about themselves asking what kind of people they are and what makes them unique compared to others. They focus on their behavior and their competence to conduct a satisfactory life and search for ways of self-realization. This leads them to observe their feelings ad makes them aware of their most dominant emotional patterns. When responding to a question-naire they report their cognitions and emotions more accurate-ly than before (Wicklund, 1975; Buss, 1980).

Emotional development and personal growth do not occur by stressful life events per se. However, coping with such demands may have a beneficial effect on one's life. Coping competence is developed by the experience of successful coping actions in demanding situations and by attempts to bring aversive or challenging events under control. Therefore, 'stress inoculation training' was proposed. However, there is no clear indication when to train what. It seems to be doubtful if there is a general coping competence valid for all critical life events but a set of specific strategies could be acquired for a defined number of normative events. It would be necessary to identify subpopulations which are at risk for certain stressful events. These subgroups should be trained in adaptive strategies which would be helpful for the adjustment to harm or loss. Prevention should aim at making people less vulnerable (Kobasa & Pucetti, 1983, Murphy & Moriarti, 1976).

The Self in Anxiety, Stress and Depression
R. Schwarzer (Editor)
© Elsevier Science Publishers B.V. (North-Holland), 1984

SOURCES OF STRESS AND WAYS OF COPING IN TEACHING:
TEACHER PERSPECTIVE

Riva Bartell

University of Manitoba, Winnipeg, Canada

Most studies on anxiety in educational settings have tended to focus on aspects of student anxiety. In recent years, however, investigators have begun to turn their attention to the complementary area of teacher anxiety and to the broader phenomenon of teacher stress. Stress in school settings has been increasingly recognized as a major social psychological phenomenon influencing the effectiveness and well-being of teachers, students and their families, school administrators and other personnel (e.g., Phillips, 1978; Kyriacou, 1980; Needle, 1980; Humphrey & Humphrey, 1981; Brenner and Bartell, in press).

The experience of stress is quite pervasive and may be viewed as inherent in the 'human condition' in modern industrialized societies. Three major reasons underscore the need for an improved understanding of teacher stress:
(1) Teachers occupy key positions in the lives of society's young. They are potentially powerful role models entrusted with guiding the course of educational and personal development of their students. During their professional tenure teachers touch the lives of thousands of students through the knowledge they impart, the reinforcements they provide, the classroom climate which they create and the interpersonal relationships they nurture. Given the high intensity, high-frequency nature of teacher-student contacts -- as many as 1,000 a day (Jackson, 1968) -- it is reasonable to expect that teachers' own well-being will affect not only the effectiveness of the teaching-learning process but also the well-being of their students. The significance of the well-being of teachers can hardly be over-stated when one considers the natural opportunities which exist within schools for preventive and interventive mental health work with students (Stickney, 1968).
(2) Teachers as an occupational group are among the high stress-risk occupations (Wahlund & Nerell, 1976; Needle et al., 1980), with an average of 20 to 33 per cent of teachers reporting a high level of stress at any one time (Kyriacou, 1980). These figures, compared with a baseline of about 10 per cent of the working population (Fletcher and Payne, 1980), suggest that teachers as an occupational group merit further study.
(3) If teachers are indeed as stressed as the research suggests, one wonders how they cope with stress.

Very little attention has been given to the way teachers cope
with stress.   In the general field of occupational stress the
research on coping has been "relatively autonomous within the
overall stress paradigm (Payne et al., 1982, p. 141)." It is
conceptually implausible to appraise sources of stress
without relating the cognitive appraisal of one's resources
or vulnerability to the perceived demands of the situation.

Much of the information on teacher stress has been obtained
from close-ended questionnaire surveys (Kyriacou,   1980;
Phillips and Lee,   1980).   The common use of this relatively
low-cost high-access methodology is not surprising given the
descriptive/purposive (Payne et al., 1982) state of the art
of teacher stress.   The research literature to date is
described as "amorphous and ill-defined", and the progress in
understanding the nature, sources and effects of stress on
teachers and their work as "uneven" (Phillips and Lee, 1980).

Kyriacou (1980) cautions (1) that closed-ended questionnaires
tend to overplay the relatively common sources of stress and
thus underplay the possible idiosyncratic, less common sources
of stress;   (2) some sources of stress are more likely to be
"over-reported if they relate to salient aspects of the
teacher's job , commonly attributed sources of stress or which
attribute blame outside the individual (p.   116)." There is a
growing contention in the broader field of occupational stress
that cross-sectional, self-report methodology has altogether
reached a point of satiation in utility (Kasl,   1978; Payne et
al.,   1982).   The "much under-researched" area of the personal
meaning of the situation and phenomenology of stress is also
highlighted as an area requiring more attention (Payne et a.,
1982).

The   need   to   employ more rigorous   research   designs,
notwithstanding,   it appears that information derived from the
'weak' cross-sectional methodology can still be strengthened
by the employment of more robust analytical methodologies (see
for example, Brenner and Bartell, in press) or by combining
research methodologies (Payne, et al., 1982).

The study reported here attempted to complement close-ended
questionnaire data by the use of an open-ended questionnaire
which allowed individual respondents to describe sources of
stress (stressors) and ways of coping with them from the
perspective of their own experience.   It was hoped that such
findings would provide a more accurate picture of the
stressors in teaching and teachers' ways of coping.

Cognizant of the limited validity of verbal reports taken at
one point in time and the dubious independence of two sets of
data derived concurrently from the same subject pool, it was
still felt that the employment of open-ended data could
ameliorate some of the shortcomings of the closed-ended
questionnaire which, a priori, limits the data pool to the
perspective of the researcher.

The present study sought to generate data pertaining to the following:

(1) Psychological stressors will emerge as the most often mentioned stressors by teachers while physical and material stressors will be at least often mentioned.
Teaching involves intense and frequent interpersonal demands and yet it is a relatively solitary activity for the teacher in a self-contained classroom. It involves complex role expectations and a high degree of responsibility yet it carries limited authority and resources and intense public scrutiny. It is reasoned here that the unique psychosocial demands of teaching will figure more prominently as stressors than deficient physical and material resources.

(2) As a corollary of the above, stressors will emerge as essentially chronic in nature rather than acute or episodic.
The interpersonal and pedagogical demands peculiar to the working conditions of teachers are inherently of an ongoing, day-to-day nature, resembling more the stress of daily hassles, suggested Lazarus (1980), than that which emanates from distinct critical events as advocated by Holmes and Rahe (1967).

(3) Situation-specific pattern(s) of coping will characterize teachers as an occupational group.
Although coping strategies tend to vary with individual respondents, common sources of influence -- such as occupational conditions of teaching, belief systems developed during professional socialization, and criteria for selection into professional training -- will have the effect of making teachers, as a group, similar in their ways of coping.

METHOD

Sample. A 10% random sample of the total population of teachers in a central province of Canada was taken in the latter part of the academic year. The sample was considered as fairly representative of Canada socio-economically and ethnically (for more detailed information see Bartell and Brenner, 1982). At approximately 50% return rate, 572 open-ended questionnaires were obtained.

Measuring the variables. A one-page open-ended questionnaire was attached to an extensive closed-ended questionnaire which was then mailed to the teacher sample under the sponsorship of their union, to be filled anonymously. Respondents were asked to describe (1) the most stressful situation in their teaching, and (2) their way(s) of coping with that situation.

Method of analysis.   The open-ended responses were subject to
content analysis by systematically using explicitly formulated
and mutually exclusive categorization rules and   procedures
(Holsti, 1969).

Content analysis is a research technique for the   objective,
systematic and quantitative description of the   manifest
communication (Berelson, 1962, p.18). The analysis was based
on coding   of the manifest content of the   responses.
Subsequently, frequency   counts   within   categories   and
calculation of corresponding percentages were conducted   for
stressors and ways of coping, separately.

Coding was quite straightforward and interjudge reliability
was high (r=.94).

RESULTS

Table 1 displays the overall percentage distribution of
responses to the open-ended questions.   80 percent of the
respondents   described   their most stressful situation in
teaching and how they coped with it. 11 percent of the
responding teachers indicated only what stressed them the most
but not how they coped with the stress, if at all.

TABLE 1

PERCENTAGE DISTRIBUTION OF TEACHERS' RESPONSES
TO 'MOST STRESSFUL SITUATION' AND 'WAYS OF
COPING' QUESTIONS

(n=572)

Response	Percent (%)
Most stressful situation and coping	80.42
Most stressful situation only	11.72
Coping only	1.22
No response	6.64

TABLE 2

PERCENTAGE DISTRIBUTION OF PERCEIVED SOURCES
OF STRESS IN TEACHERS (n=527)

Source of Stress	Percent (%)

Relations with administrators 23.49

	% Subtotal
Lack of support	68.16
Incompetence	15.07
Lack of feedback	8.56
Evaluation	8.21

Relations with students..............................20.59

Discipline, disruption, vandalism, drugs	37.89
Lack of motivation	25.39
Lack of respect	19.14
Lack of co-operation	17.58

Role overload.......................................17.23

Overwork	57.21
Extra-curricular activities	22.14
Class size	20.65

Relations with colleagues 13.12

Conflict	55.83
Lack of Support	22.69
Incompetence	21.48

Flaws in the system..................................8.45
Relations with parents...............................7.34
Lack of support services for students................4.90
Deficient physical-material resources................2.96
Events: Beginning and end of year....................0.96
Personal and other..................................0.96

An examination of Table 2 shows that the predominant categories of stressors included the following: relations with administrators (24%), relations with students (21%), role overload (17%) and relations with colleagues (13%).

The apparent commonality of the first, second and fourth categories is in their interpersonal base. When these categories were combined, and the category of relations with parents (7%) was added as well, it emerged that close to two-thirds (65%) of the stressors were of an interpersonal nature. Stressors related to the physical-material conditions and resources of the school environment appeared to have played an insignificant role (3%), as top priority stressors in this sample of teachers. These findings were consistent with those of the closed-ended data (Bartell and Brenner, 1982) inasmuch as the same categories of stressors emerged in the top five ranks, only in a somewhat modified order, as follows:

Open-ended data stressor	Rank	Closed-ended data stressor	Rank
Relations with administrators	1	Relations with administrators	1
Students	2	Parents	2
Colleagues	3	Role overload	3
Role overload	4	Colleagues	4
Parents	5	Students	5

An examination of these data plus the category of role overload -- totalling 82 percent of the stressors -- together with the qualitative description of the nature of all stressors, indicated very clearly the chronic nature of teachers' stress. Acute, episodic stressful events accounted for hardly 2 percent of all stressors.

Table 3 gives the percentage distribution of the coping strategies reported by the respondents. Major categories of coping included: physical activity (20%), talking with others (19%), recreational activity (15%), treating the symptoms (14%), confronting the problem/situation (5%) and prayer (5%).

TABLE 3

WAYS OF COPING WITH 'MOST STRESSFUL SOURCE OF STRESS'
IN TEACHERS (n=467)

Ways of coping	Percent (%)
Physical activity...................................	19.94
Talking with others................................	18.96

%

Subtotal

Familiy and friends	39.36
Fellow teachers	31.91
Other people	20.21
Superiors	8.51

Recreational activity	14.74
Treating symptoms (drinking, ... eating, drugs)	13.71
Distancing problem situation	9.68
Setting limits to the problem.....................	9.27
Confronting problem/person	4.83
Preparation and planning	4.24
Prayer	4.63

NOTE: Some respondents gave more than one coping response.

The most striking finding was that the majority (90%) of coping responses were of a non-problem-focused nature (Aldwin, et al., 1980). Hardly 10 percent of the responses may be seen as problem-focused ('confronting problem/person', 'preparation and planning').

DISCUSSION AND IMPLICATIONS

Before attempting to discuss the findings reported above, several limitations need to be borne in mind:

(a)   Sample selectivity resulting from a 50% response rate. Was the sample biased by an over-representation of very stressed teachers eager to make their views known, or alternatively by under-stressed teachers who had the presence of mind to respond to the questionnaire? The fact that 20 percent of the sample reported very low levels of occupational stress ('not at all stressed' and 'little stress' on the Likert Scale) as against 28 percent reporting high levels of stress ('very stressed' or 'extreme stress') suggest that the sample was not unduly imbalanced with respect to self-reported stress (Bartell & Brenner, 1982).

(b)   Generalizability of the findings. How representative are teachers from a mid-western province in Canada of teachers in general? If stress emanates largely from the pedagogical and interpersonal communication functions, which are inherent to the teaching profession as such, then there is a reason to expect considerable universality of stressors in teaching. If, however, contextual conditions or 'action constraints' (Cichon & Koff, 1980) predominate (e.g., forced transfer, threat of and actual, violence by students, lack of books and supplies) then a greater situational variability in stressors may result. In view of the absence of a standardized and valid stress measure, it is more probable to attribute inconsistent findings across studies to measurement error rather than to the measured attributes (stressors).
(c)   Self-reported data are subject to ego-defensive distortions. Thus the data may be not taken at face value. However, subjective environmental measures appear to be much better predictors of stress than objective ones (House et al., 1979; 1981 in Payne et al., 1982).
Having said that, several consistent findings seem to emerge across studies.

(1)   Relationship issues and role overload are important potential stressors (Cichon & Koff, 1980; Humphrey & Humphrey, 1981; Bartell & Brenner, 1982). Role overload may reflect the reality of ever increasing demands of the school as a socializer vis-a-vis diminishing resources. Strained relationships with others may contribute to the perception of overload as well as being adversely affected by it.

(2)   Pedagogical concerns are ranked down as potential stressors. Perhaps teachers feel that they have more direct control, and, consequently, experience less stress, over this function, for which they have been trained the most. Or, alternatively, admitting stress in relation to the core area of their competence is too threatening to their self-esteem.

(3)   Perhaps the single most important finding of this study is the very low frequency of problem-focused coping. Hardly any research attention has been given to coping mechanisms utilized by teachers in dealing with occupational stress (Kyriacou, 1980). Non-problem focusing, or palliative strategies, are more likely to be employed in situations which are perceived to be beyond the control of the individual (Aldwin et al., 1980). Is this response pattern reflective of teachers' belief in their powerlessness to modify conditions in their working environment? If so, such a chronic belief, in itself, can become an important stressor.   In a similar study on stressors and coping in school administrators (Bartell & Bartell, 1983), problem-focused coping was found to constitute close to a third of the total coping responses, as compared to only one tenth of teachers' responses. Are teachers selected and socialized to view their working environment as one over which they have litte or no control? It should be borne in mind that the present data did not purport to yield reliable evidence on the effectiveness of the coping nor did it provide any information regarding the performance effectiveness of the respondents.

Several themes emerge for further inquiry::

(1)   If interpersonal relationship issues are indeed central to teachers' stress, then the literature on helping professionals' stress should be examined with a view to expanding the information base of teacher stress.
(2)   Investigation of the differential effects, if any, of chronic, as compared with acute-episodic stress, on the performance, well-being and coping of various occupational groups, could prove conceptually and pragmatically productive.
(3) A longitudinal investigation of stress and coping of pre-service students in teacher training could shed some light on the continuities and discontinuities of the development of coping behavior in the teaching environment.

NOTE

Appreciation is extended to the University of Manitoba Social Sciences and Humanities Research Council Committee for the support which made possible the presentation of this paper at the Free University of Berlin, July 1983.

The Self in Anxiety, Stress and Depression
R. Schwarzer (Editor)
© Elsevier Science Publishers B.V. (North-Holland), 1984

MILITARY STRESS SITUATIONS AND SELF-RELATED COGNITIONS

Wolfgang Royl

University of the Armed Forces of the Federal Republic of Germany

The body of officers of the army is responsible for mastering military stress situations. The officers have to serve as models for their soldiers who are to be trained and guided. Therefore the Ministry of Defense has developed programmatic principles for superiors within the system of leadership and character guidance ('Innere Führung'). Their realization in practice depends on the kinds of stress situations perceived and on the presence of stress-controlling attitudes. The following psychological study deals with questions such as

- how situations in military life are rated as stressors,
- how the evaluated situations group together,
- how dimensions of stress are associated with the ability to control one's actions and with different coping modalities.

The present investigation was theoretically guided by recent research on self-related cognitions. According to Epstein (1973) people develop a self-theory which is organized like a hierarchy of self-referenced statements with highly specific statements at the bottom and highly generalized statements at the top. Descending the hierarchy more and more unstable and situation-specific cognitions are to be located. Military stress situations and corresponding coping beliefs should be found near the bottom of this hierarchy being of immediate behavioral importance. At the same level the expectancies of self-efficacy could be located. This is understood as a set of personal beliefs to be able to control one's environment by successful coping actions (Bandura 1977, 1982, 1983). Four sources serve as cues for the establishment of such cognitions: Performance accomplishments, vicarious experience, verbal persuasion, and emotional arousal. Since the officers anticipate stress with respect to dangerous situations in the future, their perceived self-efficacy has mostly to rely on vicarious experience and verbal persuasion by others or by the literature. Stress situations collected in a paper-and-pencil inventory only can evoke imaginative stress maybe partly related to real life events or anticipated life events. As Cook, Novaco and Sarason (1982) have shown in a study with Marine recruits, such imaginative components make an impact on training outcomes. Behavior is moderated by self-related cognitions, and this is valid in military training, too. Individual differences in self-related cognitions and stress-controlling attitudes lead to differences in military accomplishments and to different qualities of military models. In his theory of action control Kuhl (1980, 1983) assumes that

neither high ability alone or a strong motive alone guarantee
a satisfactory performance. The mediating processes depend on
the person's action control system consisting of two cognitive
factors, namely action-orientation vs. state-orientation.
Action orientation means being performance-centered and
thinking prospectively, whereas state orientation means
reflecting, worrying, and self-related ruminations instead of
acting. Which of both orientations is more adaptive in a
specific coping process is dependent on the situation at hand
but it is likely that in the present context an action-orientation might be favorable. It is an aim of this study to
explore the interrelationship of these orientations with the
perception of military stress situations.

In order to improve military education directed at character
formation as the basis of model function of leaders it seems
to be necessary to learn about stress perception and coping
beliefs of officers.

METHOD

Research Questions. The study was undertaken to serve the
following purposes. (1) To gain information about the perception of stress in situations typical of military service
duties. (2) Clustering perceived stress situations in order to
find significant interpretations for crucial points of
stressors. (3) To explore the relationship between stress
dimensions and cognitive control dimensions such as action-
vs. state-orientation. (4) To explore which coping modes are
preferred by officer-students during a time period when they
have little or no contact with military practice.

Subjects. The data were obtained from a sample of 113 cadets
of the Armed Forces of the Federal Republic of Germany during
their spring term 1983 at the Universities of the Armed Forces
in München and Hamburg. Since 1973 all cadets have to under-
take academic studies in education or commercial or social or
technical sciences for three years in one of these two universities. The academic personel has civilian status and the
examinations are recognized as comparable to civil universities. The officer-students aged between 20 and 25 years are
almost completely unburdened from practical military duties.
This provides free academic study opportunities but, on the
other hand, this is paid for by a lack of experience in military practice. Organizing cadet education this way, doubt-
lessly develops no coping improvement with demanding military
situations by itself. Refelections are necessary how to
compensate for deficits in stress controlling attitudes by
special training units.

Instruments. First, a number of military stress situations
were collected. A final version of 30 items was presented and
responded on a four-point rating scale from 0 to 3. After an
item analysis a reduced version of 19 items was found useful.

Secondly, a questionnaire was constructed in order to assess different coping modes. Each hypothetical situation was followed by five potential self-comments representing alternative self-related cognitions. The subjects rated each coping cognition on a scale from 1 to 6. With respect to face validity five coping modes were identified:

Mode A refers to stimulated self-discipline. Examples:

'There is only one thing I can do: Pull myself together' or 'I have decided to make the official view also my own'.

Mode B refers to former successful coping. Examples:

'This effort stands for many others I have been capable of'. or 'I have tackled such tasks successfully before. So why not this time ?'.

Mode C verbalizes norms of behavior as model reference. Examples: 'The German soldiers at the Russian front had much more to take' or 'Others have been in such dirty holes before me without getting frostbitten'.

Mode D verbalizes the aspiration level of the ideal self. Examples: 'If that is his way of showing me that he thinks I am inferior to him he may just as well forget it because he isn't nearly as smart as I am' or 'I have never had any trouble remaining unimpressed by people trying to make me doubt important decisions concerning my life'.

Mode E consists of a pragmatic self-instruction to act. Examples: 'Anyway, keep a clear head, don't be sentimental - it's do or die now' or 'When I get worried by such thoughts I simply switch off my mind'.

Thirdly, a questionnaire designed to assess state- vs. action-orientation was taken from Kuhl (1980). The short version consisted of 30 items divided into three subscales:

(1) Action- vs. state-orientation after success. Example:
'When I have tried something new and hitherto unknown to me and been successful at it,
  (a) I think about the reason why everything turns out so well for me at the moment
  (b) I soon turn my mind to other things'

(2) Action- vs. state-orientation after failure. Example:
'When I lose something of great value and all searching turns out to have been in vain,
  (a) I have trouble getting over it,
  (b) I don't lose much time worrying about it.'

(3) Degree of prospective thinking and prospective acting.

Example: 'If somebody comes to my mind whom I would like to see again,

(a) I will try right away to set a date when to go visit that person,
(b) I will make a mental note to make that visit sometime or other'.

RESULTS

The inventory of military stress situations was analyzed with respect to mean responses, standard deviations and item-total correlations. Table 1 shows the rank order of perceived situations starting with a 'lack of social support'-item (B. Sarason 1984). The second taps the potential use of nuclear weapons which relates to the current public discussion of this topic. At the bottom of the rank order matters of professional self-assertion are located.

Table 1: Rank order of perceived stress situations (N=113)

	Mean	S.D.	r(it)
1. Not being able to be with my girl friend / wife when posted to a station far away from home	1.90	.95	.41
2. Perhaps having to support the use of nuclear weapons in a war	1.89	1.14	.52
3. Having to cause the death of others in a war.	1.60	1.10	.44
4. Not getting a follow-up assignment at the desired station	1.51	.93	.58
5. To be ordered on guard duty despite being overtired	1.50	.77	49
6. Being worried that someone might commit suicide because of feeling overtaxed	1.45	1.05	.27
7. Having to put in additional duty hours over the weekend	1.35	.91	.45
8. Having to hold out in a field position at below-zero temperatures	1.34	.87	.58
9. To be left all on my own with my unit in war	1.29	1.04	.49
10. Getting utterly bored by the daily grind of military routine	1.27	.96	.51
11. Not being able to get any sleep over a prolonged period in a field exercise	1.26	.76	.48
12. Having to finish a 5000 meter run in 23 minutes	1.10	1.13	.20
13. Being the first to have to stick out my neck for others in war	1.05	.91	.48
14. Marching 19 miles in five hours in a forced march in blazing heat	1.03	.94	.42

15. Being OIC in hand-grenade throwing   .95   .91   .42
    practice
16. Having doubts about whether I chose   .80   .92   .34
    the right job
17. Being cooped up with others in a   .77   .73   .31
    barracks all the time
18. To see someone of equal rank become   .69   .74   .25
    my superior
19. Being responsible for issued equipment   .53   .67   .33
    (compasses etc.)

By cluster analysis and factor analysis four dimensions of
stressful military situations were determined (Table 2). The
first one denotes the conflict between duty and private
interests with an average rating of 1.26. The second is interpreted as responsibility for life and limb with a mean rating
of 1.46 (the highest rating). The third denotes difficulties
in self-assertion, and the fourth stress from serving as a
model. All mean differences are significant at the 5 % level,
except the one between cluster 3 and 4. The factor loading
pattern shows a clear simple structure.

Table 2: Dimensions of perceived stress (N = 113)

                       Cluster / Factor

Item	1	2	3	4
1	.67			
2		.68		
3		.79		
4	.45			
5			.32	
6		.51		
7	.54			
8			.65	
9			.40	
10	.53			
11			.67	
12				.73
13			.54	
14				.57
15				.56
16	.59			
17	.60			
18			.58	
19			.40	

	1	2	3	4
Mean	1.26	1.46	1.09	1.02
S.D.	.60	.77	.53	.76
Alpha	.75	.72	.76	.64

The raw scores based on the extracted clusters were correlated
with the questionnaire data on state vs. action orientation.
Significant negative correlation coefficients were obtained
between clusters 1,2 and 3 and 'prospective thinking and
prospective action' (Table 3). That means that subjects
scoring high on perceived stress situations are more state-
oriented than action-oriented. This result is surprising and
maybe indicates that state-oriented persons worry a lot about
potential sources of stress in the future. The other two
scales in the questionnaire show no correlation at all.

Table 3: Correlations between perceived stress situations and
action-controlling attitudes (N = 111)

Stress cluster	Prospective Thinking	Prospective Action
Duty vs. Privacy	-.23 s	-.18 s
Resp. life and limb	.00	.01
Self-assertion	-.16	-.20 s
Model function	-.28 s	-.19 s

The five coping modes were correlated with the four stress
situation dimensions. It turned out that there were three
significantly negative correlations between stress and the
intensity of coping modes (Table 4). This means that high
rating of demanding situations is associated with a low degree
of specific coping modes. In general there is a neglectable
correspondance between coping modes and stress situation indicating that coping modes are general and not linked to the
occurence of a critical life event. This problem is under
investigation in current projects on stressful life events
(Filipp, Aymanns and Braukmann, 1984). The subjests in the
present study avoid the idea of responding with self-discipline to the conflict between duty and private interests (r = -
-.24) or remembering their own 'ideal self' (r =-.20).

Table 4: Correlations between perceived stress situations and coping modes (N =113)

Coping Modes

Clusters of Stress	A	B	C	D	E
Duty vs. Privacy	-.24 s	-.24 s	-.07	-.20 s	-.02
Resp.life and limb	.02	.05	.05	-.05	.22 s
Self-assertion	-.14	-.16	-.03	-.09	-.05
Model function	-.03	-.08	-.08	-.12	.10

```
Mode A = self-discipline
Mode B = self-reference
Mode C = model-reference
Mode D = self-ideal
Mode E = pragmatism
```

It seems plausible that stress from responsibility for life and limb, especially in case of defense, lies outside of personal experience. The positive correlation between cluster 2 and self-comments of type E (pragmatic self-instruction) appears to be the only way to manage an emergency case of this dimension (r = .22).

DISCUSSION

In this pilot study one of the interesting results is that cadets in the second and third year of their training as officers are mainly stressed by the separation from home and the suspected loss of personal ties. This is in line with recent research on social support (B. Sarason 1984) which serves as a buffer towards the experience of stressful life events (Filipp et al. 1984). It is understandable that the disagreement with some demands of military service can be the logical consequence of endangered personal relationships. The identification with the chosen occupation is put in question. Many cadets may have the impression of too great a discrepancy between their idea of becoming an officer and the reality of military training. This includes the requirement to complete their academic studies within three years.

Character guidance provided with respect to private affairs should be extended to the understanding of the strategic concept of deterrence and the consequences of combat. Endangered by stressors seem to be most of all state-oriented subjects who organize stress control by reflecting situational events which retard the performance-supporting actions. This

implies the question if subjects maybe fail to mature and to
develop an inner-directed stable personality being able to
function as a model for recruits. The necessity of stronger
impulses in character formation seems to be underscored by the
losing option for self-comments in form of self-discipline and
integrated self-postulates of higher abstraction. Further
research is needed in order to clarify the relationship
between cognitive control and coping modes in natural stress
situations within military training. The present study bears
its shortcomings because it has been cross-sectional and does
not assess how officers think and act in the real coping
process. Anyway, the self-related cognitions of officers in
highly responsible positions deserve more attention.

The Self in Anxiety, Stress and Depression
R. Schwarzer (Editor)
© Elsevier Science Publishers B.V. (North-Holland), 1984

SOCIAL SUPPORT AND STRESS:
THEORETICAL PERSPECTIVES AND SELECTED EMPIRICAL FINDINGS

Hans-Henning Quast and Ralf Schwarzer

Free University of Berlin, Federal Republic of Germany

The issue of social support has become a focus of research interests within the last few years. Seen as a central variable in coping with critical life events and everyday-stress as well as a predictor of adjustment and psychological health (Cobb 1976; Caplan 1974; Dean & Lin 1977; Mechanic 1974) a wide range of definitions and conceptions of social support have been proposed. The first optimistic approaches and rather vague conceptualisations of social support were followed by critical demands for precise concepts and theoretical advances and measurements of satisfactory psychometric properties (Heller 1979; Heller & Swindle 1983; Sarason, Levine, Basham & Sarason 1983; Schaefer, Coyne & Lazarus 1982; Wilcox, 1980). These perspectives on "social support" are somehow typical of the emergence and development of a new issue in the psychological research process. People picking up the new idea first tend to come up with their personal idiosynchratic definitions leading them very quickly to the pooling or collection of some items in order to construct a "scale". This is quite convenient for the researcher as there is almost no work done to refer to. After a few years we are faced with considerably varying definitions and "measures" in the area that had been very much promising and supposed to explain some more variance in human behavior. Parallel to the arguments for more precision and clarity we find the trend to go from rather global definitions to detailed analyis of the phenomena in order to reduce redundancy and to detect confounded variables (e.g. Schaefer et al 1982; Marsella & Snyder 1981). Among those who are fighting for more accuracy are people who are suddenly reminded of older, similar or even identical ideas. These ideas and models had obviously been overlooked in the research process due to the fact that they were labeled differently. In this respect Heller (1979) discussed the concept of "social facilitation" brought up by Zajonc (1965) and the idea of "social affiliation" elaborated by Schachter (1959) as precursors and basic parameters of a conception of social support. Right now we have reached a level of conceptual development where we have to get rid of redundant definitions and poorly constructed scales lacking a sound theoretical basis. Heller (1979) and Heller & Swindle (1983) have stressed this task very much. They resume "still, we believe that the main problem in the field is

conceptual, not methodological. If the social support construct could be more clearly defined, crisper measurement
would be more likely to follow" (Heller et al. 1983). Later on
we will come back to their conceptual model when we are
discussing different approaches to social support. In
reviewing the literature on social support we found a wide
range of approaches and studies. This field of research has
been growing very much during the last few years. Unfortunately, the work done is quite heterogeneous. Therefore we
have made the attempt to structure the field by the following
categories. We differentiated between approaches where social
support is seen as a "moderator variable" which is the case
for most of the studies. Under the category "social support as
a predictor" we subsumed those studies in which social support
was used as an independent variable among others to predict
stress, anxiety, depression or self-related cognitions. A
third category was used to deal with studies in which social
support was seen as a" dependent variable" determined by
personality or by ecological factors. Finally we used a
fourth organizing principle that we called "conceptual models
of social support". Studies, primarily directed at the structure of social support will be dealt with under this category.
Recently, substantial work has been done to develop a
differentiated conceptions of social support and to investigate the essential variables involved. The proposed structure
is quite simple, but might help to get an idea of the various
perspectives taken. We have selected a few studies to give
some examples of the basic models used or the underlying
assumptions involved. That is why this paper is not a review
of the literature as we were primarily interested to structure the work done according to certain criteria. We will
proceed in the order of the "categories" mentioned above.
Finally, we will outline our perspective of social
support.

SOCIAL SUPPORT AS A MODERATOR VARIABLE

A sophisticated study was done by Wilcox (1981) who investigated the mediating or buffering effect of social support
against life events and psychological distress. From 500
randomly selected residents of a large community 320 completed
the questionaire handed out. To assess psychological symptoms
he used a 22-item form of the Langner Symptom Checklist
(Langner 1962), the Profile of Mood States-Tension subscale
(Mc Nair, Lorr & Droppelman 1971), a brief version of the Life
Event Scale (Dohrenwend, Krasnoff, Askenasy & Dohrenwend
1978), the Social Support Index and the Social Support
Questionnaire (both developed by Wilcox). According to the
buffering hypothesis social support should protect a person
experiencing high levels of life change from the deleterious
effects of these stressful events. At a low level of life
change there should be no relationship between social support
and psychological distress. In a series of multiple regression

analyses the buffering hypothesis was tested by determining whether the interaction term stressful life events by social support contributed significantly to the prediction of psychological distress measures, or in other words the interaction term was supposed to account for a significant proportion of the variance in the criterion variables. Four regression models were tested. The first multiple regression analysis was made to predict scores of the Langner Symptom Checklist by life events, social support and life events x social support. To be able to see the differential effect of levels of social support people were put in classes of high (1 SD above the mean), medium (average) and low (1 SD below the mean) social support. The regression lines for these three groups of people were compared in all four analyses. The first hypothesis was supported as the interaction term life events x social support accounted for 12% of the variance following the significant contribution of life events (6% of the variance; and social support (11% of the variance) as single predictors. The first analysis showed that for low levels of social support the slope of the regression line was much steeper than for medium or high levels of support. Looking at the unstandardized regression coefficient (B) in his anylysis he found that B was not significant for social support, but the coefficient became significant for life events and social support x life events. This was another evidence that the increase in psychological symptoms is dependent on the interaction of life events with social support. In the second analysis using the Profile Mood Index as a criterion variable he found the same pattern with respect to the regression lines and the B-coefficients. The interaction term life events x social support explained 9% of additional variance in the model. Two more regression analysis were run to see if, the other index of social support (number of supporters) would interact with life events in the same way. Again the same pattern was found with the second index of social support. The interaction terms life events x number of supporters became statistically significant in the regression analysis to predict scores in the Langner Symptom Checklist and scores in the Profile of Mood States-Tension subscale, but explaining far less variance (3%) than in the other models. Wilcox (1981) interpreted the findings as supporting the idea of the buffering effect of social support. Both measures turned out to be valuable indicators of support. The inter-correlation of .58 indicated that both scales overlap to some extent but seem to measure different aspects of social support too (one directed at the quality of a person's supportive network, the other addressing the number of people providing that support). Comparing both indicators it seems to be that "quality of social support" is more important than "quantity of social support" concerning the buffering effect of life events. This is in line with other reported findings. Wilcox pointed out that further research would be needed to focus on the psychometric aspects of assessing social support and to investigate the causal relationships between essential variables in longitudinal designs.

The influences of personality variables on the use and effect of social support was the main focus of a study by Sandler & Lakey (1982). They found that in the literature, social support and characteristics of the person receiving support had not been considered as interdependent aspects of a process. Research on locus of control has provided some evidence that "internals" seem to make use of information in a different way than externals do. Strickland (1978) for instance, found that internals know more about and make better use of information about their disease and treatment. In their own study Sandler & Lakey (1982) wanted to clarify the stress-moderating effects of locus of control beliefs, perceptions of control over negative events and social support. They predicted that internals were less affected by stressors than externals, a result that would replicate previous studies. To analyse the perceived control explanation, they compared the reports of control over recent negative events which had occurred to a group of "internals" with the reports of "externals". Furthermore they looked for differences between "internals" and "externals" concerning the possibility of control of experienced stressful events. 93 college students had to complete the "College Student Life Event Schedule", developed by the first author, the Inventory of Socially Supportive Behaviors (ISSB) developed by Barrera, Sandler & Ramsey (1981) to assess the frequency of helping transactions received during the past month. Psychological disorders were assessed using the Beck Depression Scale (Beck 1967) as well as the State-Trait-Anxiety-Inventory (STAI) by Spielberger, Gorsuch & Lushene (1970). In their data analyses they found that locus of control correlated significantly with the total social support score (r=.21). Externals received more support than internals. There was no significant relationship between locus of control and negative life events, depression and anxiety. Negative life events correlated significantly with depression only (r=.39, p < .01). Measures of stress or symptomatology were not significantly related to social support. To determine the stress-buffering effect of social support for internals versus externals a hierarchical multiple regression analysis was used for both groups separately. Statistically, the stress-buffering effect was tested as the significance added by the interaction term stress by social support to the prediction of anxiety and depression after having partialled out the main effects of stress and support - a procedure described by Cohen & Cohen (1975). Only for the group of internals the interaction term became statistically significant. Afterwards they calculated a regression of negative events on depression and anxiety for internals high versus low in social support (1 SD above versus 1 SD below the mean). In the prediction of anxiety as in the prediction of depression negative life events were not related in the group for internals high in social support. In contrast, negative life events were a significant predictor in the group that had indicated to have low social support. The obtained results support previous findings and underscore that the personality variable locus of control moderates the effects of stress. In addition, coping with stress seems to be different for internals versus externals. Surprisingly another data analysis

showed that the expected differences between internals and
externals concerning their perception of control over negative
life events were not found. Following Lazarus & Launier (1978)
they assume that differences in behavior cannot be explained
by dispositional variables. As mentioned above externals seem
to receive more social support than internals but the stress-
buffering effect of social suppport was found for internals
only. This is in line with several other studies and conceptions considering the quality of social support as the
crucial factor rather than the quantity. It was found, that in
stressful situations internals used information more effectively and were more task-oriented in their coping behaviors
than externals. Further studies should clarify how far internals differ from externals in the development and maintaining
of social support systems and in how far both groups are
different with respect to the kind of support they receive in
stressful situations. This cross-sectional study is limited to
restricted inferences as the majority of the studies done in
the field of social support. Like many of their colleagues,
Sandler & Lakey (1982) establish causal relationships among
their variables as if certain relations were given by nature.
Taking locus of control as an independent variable might seem
reasonable, but the one-shot design does not allow to draw
such kind of conclusions. Although other relationships were
considered too they did not discuss, if for instance, the
experience of different levels of social support through the
life-course of an individual might lead to different ways of
control beliefs. From the developmental point of view we can
assume that a supportive environment during childhood will
have an impact on the development of certain attributional
styles and ways of coping.

Sarason (1980) studied the impact of different levels of
social support on people differing in their test anxiety level. In the experimental condition the subjects had to
solve anagram tasks. In one experimental condition it was
emphasized that the ability to solve anagram tasks had been
found to be related to intelligence and college success. This
was said to characterise the situation as highly evaluative.
The second experimental condition consisted of social support
provided by a freewheeling discussion 20 minutes prior to the
anagram tasks. With respect to the moderator effect of social
support a significant test anxiety by social support interaction was found. Subjects high in test anxiety performed more
poorly in the evaluative situation. Comparing groups of low,
medium and high level of test anxiety it turned out, that
there only was a significant difference between the experimental condition of support versus no support for people high in
test anxiety. In another experiment social support was
provided by having a confederate say something that the other
participants could identify with concerning the perception of
the situation. Again, there was empirical evidence for a
significant statistical interaction between test anxiety and
social support. The performance of the group high in test
anxiety was low under the evaluative instruction, whereas
their performance was equal or even better in support situa-

tions compared with those low in test anxiety. Sarason &
Sarason (1981) interpreted these results, with respect to the
issue of person by situation interaction, as an evidence to
conceptualize social support as a moderator variable varying
with the situation arranged and experienced.

SOCIAL SUPPORT AS A PREDICTOR VARIABLE

On the background of various empirical studies Lieberman
(1983) elaborated the effects of social support on responses
to stress. A central aspect was the role which other people
played in helping a person under stress to cope with the
situation. They asked people who had lost a child to list all
the people they had turned to for help and to indicate who had
been most helpful and who had failed to provide help.
Furthermore the specific activities of the successful helper
was assessed. By measures of mental health and social role
function the relationship among the sources of help, kind of
help as well as their effects were scaled. As an index of
depression and anxiety the Hopkins Symptom Checklist (Derogatis, Lipman & Rickles 1971) was administered and in addition
the Life Satisfaction Index proposed by Neugarten, Havighurst
& Tobin (1961). Their sample consisted of 633 parents, mostly
of women (72%). 96% of the people had turned for help. For
more details see Lieberman (1983, p. 771 ff). Classifying the
respondents according to the main problem they had to face
(psychological well-being, marital problems and parental
concerns) the psychological effects were measured by depression, anxiety and life-satisfaction indicators. A main
significant effect was found between outcomes and sources of
help in the problem areas of mental health and marriage. In
particular the spouse seemed to be the most effective source
of help with regard to psychological problems, followed by
friends as the second most effective group. The next effective
groups consisted of professional helpers on the one hand and
self-help groups on the other. Lieberman (1983) resumed that
"....under extreme stress such as a child loss it is rare to
find individuals without useable social resources. Overall
amount of help provided does not have an impact on the person's marital relationship or well-being; the crucial factor
is who provides the help. The spouse is central" (Lieberman,
1983, p. 771). In a number of other data analyses no evidence
was found that the nature of support was central to stress
reduction but rather the source of any kind of support.

Another example of viewing social support as a causal factor
in personal adjustment and adaptation is a study done by
Holahan & Moos (1982). 267 male and 267 female randomly selected residents of a community participated as subjects in the
project. The following measures were used to assess social
support and aspects of physical and psychological adjustment.
The Negative Life Change Events (NLCE) was used to determine
the number of events experienced by the subjects during the

previous 12-months period. The NLCE was based on the Readjustment Rating Scale developed by Holmes & Rahe (1967). As a
quantitative measure of social support concerning family and
relatives, friends, work and community situation, the QSSI
(Quantitative Social Support Index) was applied. The frequencies index included items as number of visits with relatives,
number of friends etc.. To assess the quality of social relations within the family they used the Family Relationship
Index (FRI), an instrument derived from the Family Environment Scale constructed by Moos (1974). The Work Relationship
Index (WRI) served as an indication of the quality of the
social relationships in the environment of work. This scale
was based on the Work Environment Scale developed by Moos &
Insel (1974). Psychosomatic symptoms and depression were
measured by an index of 17 symptoms experienced as "fairly
often" over the last 12 months (Cronbach's alpha =.75).
Another 7 symptoms referred to depression (Cronbach's alpha
=.71). In a hierarchical multiple regression analyses psychosomatic symptoms and depression were separately examined as
criteria variables. Negative Life Change Events, Quantitative
Social Support Index Family Relationships Index, and the Work
Relationship Index were used as predictor variables. FRI and
WRI were entered into the equation following negative life
events and quantitative social support to determine in as much
additional variance could be explained by the FRI and WRI.
Regression analyses were calculated separately for men and for
women. Negative life change was significantly related to depression for employed men and to psychosomatic symptoms and
depression for employed women. Quantitative social support was
a significant predictor of depression for both groups but was
not significant concerning the prediction of psychosomatic
symptoms. Family relationships explained additional variance
of psychosomatic symptoms for men but not for women and of
depression in both groups. Finally the variable "work relationship" was significant in the equation to predict psychosomatic symptoms as well as depression in the group of employed
men. This predictor was not relevant in the regression equation for women. Results for unemployed men and women turned
out to be slightly different. In general, the results indicate
that the quality of family and work support accounted for
substantial increase in the variance of the dependent measures
for employed women and men. In contrast, quantity of social
support was a far less important predictor of psychosomatic
symptoms and depression. Only in one case the QSSI reached
the level of significance. Holohan & Moos (1982) see their
findings in line with recent work, where distress was greatest
for persons who had experienced a high level of life change
and a low level of social support (Antonowsky 1979; Dean & Lin
1977). Andrews, Tennant, Hewson & Vaillant (1978) suggested to
think of an additive relationship between life change and low
support and not just of a moderating impact of social support
on the effects of life change. Despite of the obtained relationships Holohan & Moos (1982) see the limits of possible
conclusions. They would not exclude the possibility that poor
adjustment might lead to a breakdown of social support. "For
instance, chronic maladjustment may affect long-term social

competencies and habitual patterns of social interaction. In
addition, acute periods of maladjustment may influence an
individual's interest in socializing as well as his or her
social attractiveness to other persons" (Holahan & Moos
1982, p. 412). Like Monroe (1983) they discuss the possibility
of complex interrelationships, where the causal links
remain quite unclear, if simple cross-sectional designs are
used. We agree with this view as we believe, that only experimental or longitudinal analyses might cast some light on
various dependencies in the network of personality and
environmental variables contributing to the "social embeddedness" of an individual. Again, we would like to stress the
necessity to start out with a highly differentiated model of
social support. Such a model could help to avoid working with
redundant variables and mixing up cause and effect in the
complex phenomenon "social support".

The results of a well designed longitudinal study by Henderson, Byrne & Duncan-Jones (1981) are very challenging and
highly stimulating. As psychiatric and epidemiological research has intensively been trying to identify current stressors in the social environment that can be made responsible
for the onset of neurosis and mental illness, their project
focused on a person's field of social relationships and the
support obtained from there. Their main hypotheses were that
(a) lack of social relationships was a causal factor of the
development of neurosis; (b) this causal effect holds whether
the individual is exposed to high or low levels of adversity.
The hypotheses imply that part of the aetiology is due to the
social relationships of a person as well as to his or her
current environment. The following section contains a brief
description of the design and the variables (scales) used.
This is followed by a discussion of their major findings. For
a detailed description of the theoretical background see Henderson et al (1981, p. 11-27). To assess the availability and
adequacy of social relationships Henderson et al. (1981) had
developed the Interview Schedule for Social Interaction
(ISSI). After a series of empirical analyses they could ex-
tract four dimensions that were:

(1) availability of attachment (=AVAT)

(2) perceived adequacy of attachment (=ADAT)

(3) availability of social integration (=AVSI)

(4) perceived adequacy of social integration (=ADSI)

For details see Henderson et al.(1981). At the end of various
analyses and tests they found that their instrument showed
satisfying internal consistency and test-retest reliability.
On the background of quite extensive investigations they resumed that the ISSI was a valid instrument. As a measure of
adversity and psychiatric morbidity they applied a list of
recent straining experiences, based on the widely discussed
concept that life events and changes experienced by a person

would have an impact on his/her personal adjustment and psychological well-being. The general dependent variable of the project was neurosis. More precisely, they wanted to identify non-psychiatric disorders which are mainly characterised by mild to moderate depression as well as the psychological and somatic manifestations of morbid anxiety. The General Health Questionnaire (GHQ) developed by Goldberg (1972) was considered a suitable instrument to assess psychiatric symptoms of neurosis. They adapted the GHQ slightly. Using the Present State Examination (PSE, Wing, Cooper & Satorius 1974), a standardized psychiatric interview, was another way to determine psychiatric disorders. But the GHQ and the PSE do not provide information in terms of classifying people according to diagnostic categories but rather they indicate the prevalence of neurosis at a given level of severity. In order to obtain a specific measure of depression the Zung-Self-Rating Depression Scale was used (Zung, 1965). An additional instrument to detect different clinical symptoms was used : the Delusions-Symptoms-States-Inventory that had proved to be a quite successful self-completion questionnaire (Foulds & Bedford 1975). The whole instrument has 12 sections containing 7 items each and covering a wide range of psychopathological phenomena. Henderson et al. (1981) selected five sections covering depression, anxiety, phobias, compulsive symptoms and ruminations that made 35 items all together. Finally, a variety of sociodemographic variables were gathered too. In the area of personality variables they administered the Eysenck Personality Inventory (EPI) Eysenck & Eysenck (1964), the Mehrabian scale of affiliative tendency and sensitivity to rejection and the Crowne-Marlowe Inventory for measuring social desirability. The field study included four waves of measurements. The whole range of scales and instruments were not administered at all points in time. In a summary table Henderson et al.(1981, p. 102) gave an overview of instruments used in each of the waves. The sample of wave 1 consisted of 953 individuals on the Electoral Role. A subsample of 323 people was drawn and asked to remain in the project for assessments in waves 2, 3, 4 taking place at four months intervals. Finally, 231 subjects completed the instruments on wave 4. The major results of various regression and partial correlation analyses turned out to be:

(1) the measure of affiliative tendency and sensitivity to rejection (Mehrabian scale) were strongly related to extraversion. Sensitivity to rejection was dependent on neuroticism.

(2) the availability of attachment depended to some extent on the "affiliative drive" as indicated by the Mehrabian scales

(3) the "affiliative drive" was an important determinant of availability of social integration.

(4) people high on trait neuroticism tend to experience more adversity, especially when they are sensitive to rejection.

(5) people high in affiliative needs perceive moderately high

availability as inadequate, whereas those with lower level of affiliative needs perceive them as adequate.

(6) adequacy of attachment was determined directly by availability of attachment.

(7) neuroticism and adversity contributed to adequacy of attachment too, but to a lesser degree.

(8) neuroticism explained 69% of the variance in illness. Consequently, it was the dominating predictor in any equation where background variables and personality variables were entered to predict illness. Low affiliative drive and adversity were also relevant predictors of illness in particular when combined with each other.

(9) when personality variables and background variables were controlled in the equations, availability of social relationships turned out to contribute a rather negligible amount of variance to the explanation of illness.

(10) taking personality and background measures as well as availability of social relationships and adversity together, these predictors accounted for 67% of the variance of perceived adequacy of attachment, for 51% of the variance in the perceived adequacy of social integration and for 85% of the variance in illness.

(11) the variables used in the analyses accounted for the whole of the relationship between adaquacy of attachment and illness and nearly all of the relationship between adequacy of social integration and illness. When adequacy of integration was introduced in the equation following all causally prior variables it explained additional 2% of the variance in illness. They considered their findings as an evidence, that "... the incidence of episodes of neurotic illness is to be explained in a very large degree by personality traits, to a significant but lesser extent by the impact of contingent life crises, to a very small extent by the perceived adequacy of, and satisfaction with, social integration, and not at all by other aspects of social relationships", (Henderson et al. 1981, p. 188). This was a result they did not expect, as their main hypotheses, based on plausible theoretical concepts, postulated that social relationships, when deficient of absent, contribute to the cause of neurosis. Instead, they only found a weak relationship between lack of availability of social ties and the subsequent onset of symptoms. In other words: lack of close affectional relations was not found to be linked to greater risk as often argued. The adequacy of social relationships had substantial predictive power but only if distressing events were experienced at the same time too. If the adequacy variable is considered as a characteristic of the person, the predictive value of adequacy in combination with adversity can be called an interactionistic term. Henderson et al (1981) finally conclude, that the obtained results suggest to turn our attention again towards measures of temperament

and other intrapsychic processes after psychiatric research has focused on the social environment as a primary cause of psychiatric disorders for over the last 20 years.

We have taken this study as the findings are contrary to the main stream of concepts and empirical studies in social support research. In general, it is assumed that social support has a direct or at least a moderating effect on the psychological well-being of people and serves as a buffer against various kinds of stressful demands. Taking into account the findings of Henderson et al. (1981) it seems too early to attribute positive health effects in general to the social support available or received. Further research is needed to refine relevant instruments and to test various hypotheses concerning the range of possible linkages among relevant variables.

SOCIAL SUPPORT AS A DEPENDENT VARIABLE

Looking through the literature of social support we found far less studies in which social support was seen as a dependent variable or effect of personality or other variables. Eckenrode (1983) asked for the effect of dispositional variables on the mobilization of social support. He had a sample of 356 randomly selected women. One dispositional measure was the Health Locus of Control, an instrument designed to assess rather specific versus global control expectations. This scale was significantly correlated to Rotter's I-E Scale (Rotter, 1966) in a study done by Wallstone, Wallstone, Kaplan & Maides (1976). The scale had a reliability of alpha = .65. The second personality disposition was measured by the "Efficacy of Help Seeking Scale" that indicates the belief in the benefits versus costs of seeking and accepting help from others. This scale was used in an interview session. The reliability coefficient was 0.61. Social support was measured in two ways by focusing on (a) potential supporters consisting of the number of individuals mentioned by the respondent that she could rely on and turn to in case of need. The measure of support mobilization (b) represented the number of persons, who had actually been supportive in critical life events during the previous year. The correlation analyses showed that there was a strong relationship between the efficacy of help seeking and the number of potential supporters, however the causal relations remain unclear based on such cross-sectional data. Eckenrode (1983) believed that a series of multiple regression analyses could help to determine causal relationships. As he had expected, support mobilization was significantly related to the number of potential supporters. Both dispositional variables independently influenced the mobilization of support. Locus of control did not show a strong relationship to the number of potential supporters. The author interpreted his findings as being consistent with the results obtained by Sandler & Lakey (1982) showing that internals may have less social resources

than externals but using them more efficiently. With respect
to the sociodemographic variables e.g. education, income etc.
he found that the number of social supports, internal locus of
control, and positive help-seeking beliefs influenced the
mobilization of social support to a greater extent among
people with higher education. Similar results were obtained
for other social class indicators. On the background of several interactions between sociodemographic variables and personality variables influencing social support mobilization,
Eckenrode (1983) concluded, that a dipositional variable might
not have the same effect for people with different sociodemographic characteristics. This study brings up the important
issue of the relevance of dispositional variables for the
development and maintaining of social support systems of an
individual. It is very likely that there are crucial dependencies of the kind: personality--social support in comparison
with widely favored concept of social support--personality.
But nonetheless Eckenrode's data do not allow for such conclusions. Barrera & Sandler (1981) looked at this issue from an
environmental point of view. The influence of features of the
community on social support was the topic of their paper.
Their sample consisted of 160 subjects of four communities
randomly chosen by digit dialing. Social support was measured
by a modified version of Brim's Social Relationship Scale
(Brim 1974) containing three dimensions: assistance,
concern, and trust. The mediating variables that were supposed
to influence aspects of social support were social segmenta-
tion, assessed by asking people how frequently they had
encountered neighbours outside of the neighbourhood. The
second mediating variable was the concern about the evaluation by others or in other words, caring what neighbours
think. This attitude was measured by the single item "How
much do you care what your neighbours think of you" ?, with a
four point rating scale. The third mediating variable was
social participation measured by the Social Participation
Scale developed by Phillips (1967). Eight demographic variables were used to characterize the respondents. In their
causal model they hypothezised various relationships e.g.
"caring what neighbours think" was supposed to have the only
direct effect on social support. To determine the degree of
fit between their model and the empirical data a path analytic
approach was used. The hypothezised model did not fit very
well with their data. Direct effects of community size and
network size on social support needed to be introduced into
the model. The path coefficients for the new model calculated
were accepted. But the assumed direct effect of "caring what
neighbours think" on social support was only (p=.14). This
path remained in the model as it's deletion would have reduced
the fit obtained. Social support was also influenced by community size (p=-.17) and network size (p=.20). That means that
smaller social support was linked to larger community size,
smaller network size and less caring what neighbours think.
The multiple correlation of community size, network size and
caring what neighbours think with average social support was
r=.32. Oxley et al. (1981) concluded, that the mediating
variable used did not seem to be important in the relationship

between community size and social support. Community size had a direct influence on social support provided by the network members. The obtained findings underscore that further research is needed to identify and specify the variables that mediate the relationship between community size and social support. However, Oxley et al. (1981) made the attempt to see social support as depending on environmental and community variables. This environmental perspective is supported by findings of Korte (1978) who could show that people living in high-rise apartments developed less social ties or friendships among the coresidents compared with those living in low-rise buildings or single family homes. Increased urbanisation seems to lead to decreasing helpfulness and friendliness toward other people (Michelson, 1970).

The prevention project of Felner, Ginter & Primavera (1982) was subsumed under our headline "support as a dependent variable" too. In their project they wanted to increase the level of social support available and to reduce the degree of flux and complexity in the school environment. The intervention was aimed at those students who entered high school and had to cope with a new social environment. Furthermore, it was intended to increase the instrumental and affective social support from peers and teachers. In this respect social support is seen as a dependent variable that can be modified or influenced by specific manipulations. The subjects were 59 project students and 113 students in the control group randomly selected from 450 students entering a large urban high school. On the backround of theoretical assumptions and various empirical findings they hoped that the program would reduce the vulnerability to the development of academic and emotional difficulties during this transition phase and/or positive perceptions of the school environment could be developed or maintained. We will describe the essentials aspects of the study. First, they restructured the role of the teachers, who participated voluntarily in the project. Their new role included, apart from teaching, everyday-life things they had to care for in and outside the school, eg. administrative, counseling services. The changing of the tasks aimed at (a) increasing the amount of instrumental and affective social support sources in daily school life; (b) increasing students feelings of belonging to certain social systems (class) and (c) to provide better access to important information. The second element of the program was a partial reorganization of the social system the student just had entered. It was intended to reduce the degree of flux and to facilitate the development and maintaining of stable support systems. "Stable" school classes were established to reduce the constant shift of peer groups due to different courses or classes taken by the students. At the midpoint of the academic year and at the end of the school-year three criterion measures were taken to assess the effect of the program: (a) a self-concept scale (b) a measure of students' perception of different aspects of the social climate in school (c) the students' eighth and ninth grade attendance records and grade point averages (GPA's). As a self-concept scale they used the Self-Appraisal

Inventory (SAI) developed by Frith & Narikawa (1972) addressing scholastic, peer, family and general self-concept. As a
measure of school climate the High School Environment Scale
(HES) was used. The HES was a modification of the Classroom
Environment Scale (CES) introduced by Tricket & Moos (1973).
The HES contains several dimensions of the social environment
as (a) a relationship dimension including the involvement,
affiliation and teacher support and (b) a personal development
dimension consisting of task orientation and competition and
finally (c) a system maintenance and system change dimension
concerning order, organization, rule clarity, teacher control
and innovation. Total scores were obtained by summing up the
scores of the subscales. Academic Adjustment Measures were
gathered by the students permanent record. Running various
ANOVA's they found that in the project group self-concept
measures remained quite stable whereas in the control group
the scores decreased over time. Concerning the dependent
variables of the social environment the data analyses revealed
significant main effects for group membership. The students in
the project group reported more positive feelings than
students in the control group with respect to the school
climate and they reported more positively on dimensions
concerning relationships with others.

Looking at this study we found some support for our idea to
view social support not only as causal factor of poor or good
personal adjustment but also as an effect determined by specific variables. Another finding of Felner et al (1982) provided
additional evidence for that. They found that project
students reported higher levels of teachers' support, teacher
affiliation and involvement compared with students of the
control group. In general, the scores of the project students
remained quite stable over time whereas the scores of the
other group decreased. The data of the study suggested that
the project students by and large were more successful in
coping with the transition to the high school than students in
the control group. The academic performance of the experimental group remained stable from the eighth to the ninth grade,
but the students in the control group performed significantly
less well. Despite various limitations of the study (design,
scales) the findings underscore the necessity to look for
potential determinants of social support and to design longitudinal studies in order to understand the development and
change of supportive actions and systems.

As cause and effect relationships are far more complicated
than assumed in the field of social support, Monroe (1983)
tried to "untangle" cause and effect among social support
and disorders variables. This study could be subsumed under
our headline "social support as a predictor" as well as under
our headline "social support as a dependent variable" as
Monroe (1983) demonstrates how we can analyse social support
as a dependent or independent variable. He compared results
from retrospective designs with results from prospective
studies. His main interest was to understand in how far
support-disorders relationships vary as a function of the

research design used, the kind of control variables and the type of disorders studied. 168 subjects working in a cooperation of about 450 employees volunteered to participate in the study. 93 subjects participated in the retrospective design and 75 in the prospective design. To assess psychological symptoms the General Health Questionaire (GHQ) developed by Goldberg (1972) was administered. High scores on the scale indicate strong anxiety in nonpsychotic cases (and disphoric of recent onset). The instrument is regarded as a well-constructed scale with adequate psychometric properties. Physical symptoms were assessed by the Health Review Symptom Checklist developed by Rose, Jenkins & Hurst (1978). An index of social support was obtained by adapting a questionnaire of Rose et al. (1978). Finally, the Psychiatric Epidemiology Research Interview (PERI) Life Events Scale designed by Dohrenwend, Krasnoff, Askenasy & Dohrenwend (1978) was applied to assess indices and frequencies of life events with respect to the previous year. In the follow-up study the materials were distributed at monthly intervals for a period of four months. In the following section we will concentrate on results concerning psychological symptoms and social support. The retrospective data analyses showed a significant relationship between social support and psychological symptoms. This result is quite often obtained and interpreted as indicating that people with relatively low perceived support tend to experience higher levels of psychological symptoms. In comparison to the retrospective analyses, the prospective data analyses revealed that on the one hand support was still a strong predictor of symptoms, when entered alone into the regression equation. On the other hand, it turned out that support was no longer a significant predictor of follow-up symptoms when prior symptoms had been controlled for in the hierarchical regression model, but prior symptoms were significantly associated with the follow-up symptoms measured. Monroe (1983) concluded that support was a significant predictor of symptoms in prospective designs when exclusively used as variable. But when the control variable "symptom status" is introduced social support was no longer an independent predictor. In another analyses the interaction effects of support by prior symptoms and support by life events were tested to determine their predictive value for later symptoms. The data analyses made clear that none of the interaction terms proved to be statistically significant. The received results were seen as a warning against confounding variables in order to untangle cause and effect.

CONCEPTUAL MODELS OF SOCIAL SUPPORT

It was more difficult than expected to find conceptual models of social support. Although the definition and elaboration of a construct or concept of social support should preceed any empirical study, arranged to investigate causal relationships between social support and other variables, just recently

systematic work has been done in this respect. Many   attempts
were based on rather vaguely and unprecisely defined   concepts
constituing   the   phenomena   of   social   suppport   somehow.
Recently,   progress   has   been made in   the development   of   a
theoretical   background   of social support as well as   in   the
construction   of   adequate   scales   (Heller   &   Swindle   1983;
Gottlieb 1983;   Barrera, Sandler & Ramsey 1981; Sarason et al.
1983).   Barrera   et al.   (1981) differentiated their   approach
from others by several aspects. Reviewing several studies they
found,   that some scales centered around the social embeddedness or the nature and structure of peoples' social ties   with
important   others.   It   is assumed that these   important   ties
serve   as a social support resource.   Another way is to assess
peoples' perception of the supportiveness of their significant
social   relationships.   Moos (1979) described these scales   as
measuring   "emotional   support" or aspects   of   "cohesion".   A
third   approach   is to focus on   different   helping   behaviors
provided by others when the individual is in need. In a series
of studies Barrera et al.   (1981) wanted to develop an instrument   to assess help received from natural support sytems   and
to   compare their scales with other measures of social support
used.   Their   behavioral approach was based on   various   ideas
proposed (Gottlieb,   1978).   In several meetings they rewrote
items selected from the literature,   to eliminate   redundancy,
and   to   write   new items that appeared to   address   important
support   functions.   As a result of this process,   a 40   item-
version   was   generated (Barrera et al 1981).   On a 5-point
rating   scale   subjects could indicate the frequency   of   the
helping behavior received.   The Inventory of Social Supportive
Behaviors (ISSB) was completed by 30 male and 41 female undergraduates two times at an interval of 2 days. 25 subjects were
asked   to answer other self-report measures   in   addition.   To
illustrate   the   kind of scale we will give some   examples   of
items: "Gave you over $25"; "Listen to you to talk about your
private feelings";   Taught you how to do something"; Was right
there   with you (physically) in stressful   situations";   "Told
you who you should see for assistance". Adding up the frequency   ratings   of   each item individual total   ISSB-scores   were
calculated.   These scores were correlated r(69) =.89 for   both
sessions.   The   alpha coefficient for internal consistency was
quality of the scales.   To investigate the relationship of the
new scale with other scales assessing other aspects of   social
support   (construct validation) they administered the   Arizona
Social   Support   Interview Schedule (ASSIS) an interview   that
consisted of six questions addressing (a) material aid   ;   (b)
physical assistance;   (c) intimate interaction;   (d) guidance;
(e)   feedback   and (f) positive social   interaction.   Subjects
were asked to indicate which people would provide help of that
kind and who had actually given help.   The authers called that
the"   available network size" and the " actual social   support
network   size".   The   data analyses showed that the ISSB   was
correlated with the available network size , r(43)=.42 and the
actual social support size r(43)=.322; p < .05.   Finally, they
wanted to find out the relationship of the ISSB to the individual's appraisal of the social support. As the Family Environment   Scale   (FES)   had been used in   various   studies   before

(Moos, 1975) they made use of this instrument in another study. The instrument was modified by combining the nine cohesion items of the FES with nine items of the Achievement Orientation Subscale. The instructions of the ISSB were changed in order to make the instrument refer to family members only. It turned out that the FES-Cohesion subscale correlated significantly with the ISSB r(41)=.359). People reporting higher frequencies of socially supportive interactions with family members perceived their family as very cohesive. In their discussion Barrera et al. (1981) underline that the scale was developed to assess a number of support functions across different populations. The items are considered as representative of various kinds of supportive actions discussed in the literature. The limitations of the design concerning data collection and subjects (college students again) were discussed. The reported results concerning the psychometric properties of the scales demonstrate the high quality of the developed instrument.

To validate a newly developed measure of perceived social support Procidano & Heller (1983) ran 3 studies. A major issue was the differentiation between social network and perceived social support. Following Heller & Swindle (1983) the perception of social support is seen as one element in an individual's appraisal process of stressful situation (a concept elaborated by Lazarus & Launier 1983). To measure social support the PSS (=Perceived Social Support Scale) was developed. The instrument is focused on the individual's perception of his/her needs for support, information, and feedback that are fulfilled by friends (PSS-Fr.) and family members (PSS-Fa.). They assumed that a distinction between family and friends support was important as both groups might provide support in different situations in different ways. In their first study an item pool of 84 items was given to 222 college students. Thereafter this pool could be reduced to 35 items and finally to a 20-item version. The final version was varied with respect to family and friends' support. Three groups were given both forms (PSS-Fr. and PSS-Fa.) and different measures concerning life-events, social network, symptomalogy and maladjustment, social desirability as well as scales of interpersonal social competence were administered too. PSS-Fr. and PSS-Fa turned out to be quite homogeneous measures with a Cronbach's alpha of .88 and .90. With respect to the other measures they found that the PSS-Fr. scale and the PSS-Fa. scale were better predictors of symptomalogy than life-events or characteristics of the social networks. But Procidano & Heller (1983) warn to be careful with interpreting the direction of the associations found. In a second study they wanted to find out in how far the situation influences the reports of social support of the subjects. They induced positive and negative mood states by a procedure described by Velten (1968) in two groups. People in the "positive" mood group reported fewer feelings of anxiety and depression and were rather internally than externally oriented but did not respond differently to the PSS-Fr. and the PSS-Fa.. In the group of negative mood induction the subjects reported lower

levels of PSS-Fr. and greater feelings of depression. PSS-Fa.
were not influenced by the treatment. The results were seen as
an evidence of the relative stability of the developed scales
although the PSS-Fr. scale was vulnerable to negative mood
induction. The effects of negative states on the perception of
social support from friends seem to explain the often found
negative association between social support and depression.
This is often interpreted as an indication that low levels of
social support are causal factors of depression. But now, the
other way round seems plausible too: depressed people tend to
perceive and report less support that might be a function of
their negative self-appraisal that might again influence the
development and maintaining of their support systems. A third
study was made to investigate the similarities in the perception of networks, anxiety level, willingness to disclose and
actual disclose levels between friends and sibs. They found
that the subjects perceptions of their friends and family
networks were similar to that of their friends, but less
similar for siblings. The PSS indices were good predictors of
disclosing behavior exhibited with companions. As in study I
PSS-Fr. was related to social competence. Subjects high in
PSS-Fr. had lower levels of anxiety, measured by the State-
Trait-Anxiety Inventory (Spielberger, Gorsuch & Lushene 1970)
and were more eager to talk about themselves to companions
(friends or siblings). People low in PSS-Fr. tend to show
verbal inhibition in the presence of friends, but this effect
was much stronger for people low in PSS-Fa. They interpreted
the results as an indication of the tendency to withdraw from
interactions with family and friends, when those are perceived
as negative concerning support. In the last study PSS-Fr. and
PSS-Fa. were considered to be independent variables. Subjects
were devided into groups of high versus low scoring in these
two measures. Again, the reported findings do not allow to
make any causal inferences regarding the various variables
involved. The developed scales proved to be valuable measures
to assess important aspects of social support. In the following section we will describe a conceptual approach that has
been suggested by Heller & Swindle (1983).

As mentioned in the introductory part of this paper Heller &
Swindle (1983) complained about the vagueness of social
support constructs and the confounding of independent and
dependent measures in a large number of studies. In a model
they have conceptualized various facets of the social support
domain and coping processes involved. This is one of the rare
attempts to develop a theoretical framework that can serve as
a basis for future research. Their model consists of the
following components influencing the "cognitive appraisal of
self, assets, perceived social support and action alternatives":

(a) ecological, community, family and peer influences;

(b) social connections (networks) provided by the environment;

(c) environmental demands and stressful life events;

(d) person characteristics (traits, coping styles and social

skills in assessing and maintaining social interactions

(e) genetic and constitutional predispositions and behaviors

reinforced in early development.

In very many studies the stress buffering effect of social
support was investigated but the results turned out to be
quite equivocal. Heller & Swindle (1983) believe that this is
in part due to a lack of specified and explicated relationships among the determinants of social support. From their
point of view the various facets of social support have to be
seen as non static but developmental in character over time.
One's current support systems are determined by one's biographical support resources as well as by one's momentary life
situation. Support might change under the influence of critical life events and the development of personal maladjustment.
A second important aspect of their model is the idea of a
dynamic system. People play an active role in the development,
selection, maintaining and availability of social support.
Different social skills and competencies are necessary to
aquire a social embeddedness. In general they suggest to view
social support as a potential part of coping processes. Heller
& Swindle (1983) elaborate their model by incorporating several empirical findings that underline the relevance of the
different elements defined. Two concepts make the core of
their social support model: social connections (networks) that
are provided by the environment and person characteristics as
traits, coping styles, and skills in accessing and maintaining
social connections. The first factor is influenced by ecological, community, family and peer influences. They stress the
necessity to distinguish between "social connections" or "social networks" to refer to behaviors provided by the environment and "perceived social support" to describe the impact of
that behavior on the person. Both aspects overlap to some
extent. In several studies the advantages and disadvantages of
close versus less dense social networks have been discussed.
It seems to be the case that closer networks are not always
the better. The specific value of certain networks depends
upon the problem or the task to be solved or performed. Late-
ron we will come back to this point when we discuss the problem of "social control" and social support. With respect to
the ecological and community influences on the development of
social networks there has been some empirical evidence that
some environmental settings are more network-enhancing than
others. Wicker (1979) gave a review of the literature concerning this problem. Increased urbanization, larger institutions
and density in housing areas as high-rise apartments are just
some of the enviromental characteristics that seem to reduce
helpfulness, friendliness and social interaction. On the other
hand we have to take into account specific personality variables that contribute to the perception, development and maintaining of social relationships and support, e.g. sociability

or extraversion, assertiveness, comfort in intimacy, lack of
social anxiety, conversational skills, role-taking skills as
well as social problem-solving skills. To some degree these
personality aspects are stable and unchangeable (extraversion)
whereas others can be modified or shaped as assertiveness,
role-taking ability etc. Trower (1980) could show that the
training of perception in the sense of cue-reading in social
situations is as necessary as training social skills. The
person characteristics mentioned are in turn influenced by
genetic and constitutional predispositions as well as behaviors that have been reinforced in the learning history of the
individual. The central components social connections (networks) and person characteristics are supposed to determine
the cognitive appraisal processes concerning self, assets,
perceived social support and action alternatives. The appraisal concept is borrowed from Lazarus & Launier (1978) that has
proven to be a useful conception in stress research and has
been updated by Averill (1979). Social support can be seen as
a part of the whole cognitive appraisal process in two ways.
Perceived social support resources may be focused on during
the phase of secondary appraisal. The perception of potential
help and assistance will regulate future actions. In a
threatening situation social support may function as a buffer
against a decrease in self-esteem and self-concept in secondary appraisal or will encourage the individual to initiate
supportive actions by members of his or her support networks.
In this way social support becomes an element of behavior
regulation and a mode of coping strategies. This has to be
distinguished from unsolicited actions or information given by
others to support the individual. It has been argued that
information provided by others might not always be helpful to
reduce stress and enhance coping. The crucial point is whether
the individual feels to be in need of additional information
or specific information from certain people. From this point
of view support seeking can be considered a useful coping
strategy. On the other hand we have to ask if support seeking
outside one's normal network or turning for help quite often
in various domains of human life might indicate a lack of
personal adaptation and adjustment. Obviously there has to be
a balance between asking too much for support and too little
for support. We will come back to this issue later. Finally,
Heller & Swindle (1983) discuss various empirical findings
concerning "perceived" social support. As we have already
mentioned some studies dealing with this aspect, we will skip
this part of their model.

We think that the model proposed by Heller & Swindle (1983) is
a very useful conception of social support that will help to
differentiate between a range of relevant personality and
environmental variables involved. A similar model has been
suggested by Gottlieb (1983). He discusses personal resources
(traits, coping styles etc.) and social resources (network) as
mediating variables in the stress process as well as influencing exposure to stressors and health outcomes directly.
According to Gottlieb (1983) it would be too early now to make
any firm conclusions about the actual effects of social sup-

port in the stress process as the definitions proposed and the measurement scales used are quite heterogeneous. He listed several studies in which a stress-buffering effect of social support was found and others where it was not found. Therefore, he suggests a classification of current measurement strategies. He named three approaches differing with respect to the aspect of social support they focus on. In the first approach social support is regarded as a resource arising from peoples' participation and integration in society. In the second approach social support is seen as an expression of the affective intensity of particular intimate relationships. While the first approach is centered around the quantitative aspect of support the second is focused on the qualitative aspect of support. In neither approaches the actual extension of help in social interaction has been considered as well as the structure of the social field and its influence on peoples' access to support. Gottlieb (1983) distinguishes between four kinds of helping transactions that occur naturally: (a) emotional support (b) tangible aid and services (c) cognitive guidance (d) companionship. He conducted an interview study to analyse the specific types of informal aid given by others. Using content analysis he could identify different forms of aid. Finally, he received a classification scheme consisting of four major classes of informal helping behaviors including 26 categories of concrete actions. The first class was called (a) emotionally sustaining behaviors with categories as "listens"," reflects trust", "provides reassurance" etc.; (b) problem solving behaviors with categories as "provides clarification", "provides information about sources of stress" etc; (c) indirect personal influence as "reflects readiness to act" and finally (d) environmental action as "intervenes in the environment to reduce sources of stress"; (for details see the classification scheme in Gottlieb 1983, p.51-58). We have briefly characterised his approach as it is in line with the model of Heller & Swindle (1983) described above and with our own perspective to view social support as a multidimensional construct. The classification scheme of Gottlieb (1983) provides a highly differentiated system of micro helping transactions that are part of the whole support system and process. We are convinced that these detailed analyses in connection with the analysis of social skills involved in supportive transactions are fundamental elements of a conception of social support.

At the end of this section we want to mention some of our ideas regarding a conception of social support. These ideas are mainly based on various conceptions discussed before as well as empirical findings in the field of social support and related areas. As Heller & Swindle (1983), Gottlieb (1983) and other researchers we started out with the basic assumption that a range of environmental variables as well as personality variables constitute the phenomena of social support. We assume a process of interaction between specific variables of both sets of variables. In table 1 we have listed the main facets of social support and a range of relevant personality and environmental variables. The list of variable could be

continued. We did not intend to give a complete list of
relevant aspects of the environmental and the personality
component but to exemplify the range of potential influences
on the "social embeddedness" of an individual.

Table 1: Variables related to social support

environmental variables   **personality variables**

- ecological context   - level of anxiety

  (urban or rural area)   (social anxiety)

- availability of social   - level of depression

  organisations & insti-   - concept of social

  tutions (groups,clubs)   self

- availability of support   - shyness

  services (counseling &   - self-efficacy

  information centers)   - locus of control

- work/school climate   - self-awareness

- family relations   - neuroticism

- friends relations   extraversion/

- etc.   introversion

                                  - social skills

                                  - coping strategies

                                  - etc.

In part these variables have been studied with respect to
their relevance in the domain of social support, others have
been added by us. These added variables seem to be important
on the background of other theoretical considerations. We have
to take into account that the variables overlap to some extent
and are likely to interact within one component or across the
two facets. For instance there is some evidence that level of
social anxiety and social skills are intercorrelated and
interdependent. On the other hand it is plausible to assume a
relationship between social skills and friends relationships.
People with effective social skills are more likely to have

good relationships with friends. But we have to be careful with interpreting directional influences or causal dependencies. We may also assume that having good relationships with friends will shape social skills. In turn, the developed social skills will contribute to the maintaining of positive social relationships. The crucial question to answer is: Which of the variables do interact in which way and contribute to the "social embeddedness of the individual"? As described above the ISSB developed by Barrera et al. (1981) gives an assessment of the frequency of the helping behavior received. This aspect can be seen as a part of family and friends relations. But receiving help from others requires to communicate the need for help somehow. Communicating one's need for help is a kind of social skill. Much more research is needed to understand the complex network and interactions of social support. An experimental approach to investigate the relationship between self-described social support, social behavior, and self-related cognitions has been demonstrated by Sarason (1984). She sees her findings in line with other results indicating that people who are placed in a social situation that arouse worries and preoccupations about self-adequacy show an increase in self-reported cognitive interference and performance. Supportive interactions seem to improve the performance of people who are highly test-anxious and of people who are low in self-described social support. In contrast these interventions obviously do not influence the performance level of people high in self-described social support and of those low in test anxiety. We think that such micro analyses in laboratory settings will enable us to proceed in the development of a differentiated model of social support. Very refined studies on the analysis and training of social skills have been done by Trower, Bryant & Argyle (1978) who based their work on the idea that some kinds of mental disorder are caused by lack of social competence. Training of social skills can alleviate these disorders. They see two possible sequences of events "(1)Failure of social competence is primary, leading to rejection and social isolation, which in turn produces disturbed mental states. (2) Other kinds of mental disturbancies affect all areas of behavior, including social performance; social inadequacy results in rejection and isolation, thus adding to the original sources of stress and leading to deterioration (Trower et al. 1978). The clinical approach of Trower et al. (1978) demonstrates that different disciplines in psychology can contribute to the analysis and understanding of the basic variables involved in social support.

We will end our conceptual discussion by pointing out to a dimension or aspect of social support that has been overlooked and might explain some contradictory findings: the issue of social control and its relationship to social support. The value of close versus less dense networks was discussed by Hammer (1981) and Hirsch (1980). In general, we cannot say that close networks are better than less dense networks. The value of certain network characteristics seems to depend on the kind of problem faced or the tasks to solve. Moreover, we believe that it is important to imagine that social support might turn into" social control". Patients in psychiatric clinics are for instance very much "embedded" in a social support system but on the other hand socially controlled to a high degree. People living in highly controlling environments (clinics, prisons, military camps) probably do not perceive their environment as a positive supportive system. It is rather likely that they feel being "cared for too much" and receiving support they did not ask for. If we call this pole of the social control dimension "total social control" we can name the other end of the continuum "social isolation", a state or situation where nowbody cares about the individual. The social environment is probably perceived as totally indifferent to one's personal life-situation. This phenomenon is often found in places of high population density e.g. highrise buildings. We suggest to speak of a "continuum of social control" and propose a model of the functional relationship between "social control" and "perceived social support". Social support can be seen as dimension ranging from social support asked for by the individual and perceived as positive to support urged upon the person by the environment.

According to the function proposed, we would hypothesize that a "balance area" in the middle between "total social control" and "no control" or "isolation" is related to a high level of "social support perceived as positive". Of course this is not a strict mathematical model but rather an heuristic illustration of possible associations. A satisfying "social embeddedness" requires to be not totally dependent on others and institutions on the one hand and to have made certain commitments to the community on the other hand. This kind of social embeddedness has to be distingushed from a situation in which an individual asks for help constantly and becomes more and more dependent on the helping transactions of the environment.

AN EXPLORATORY STUDY FOR ILLUSTRATIVE PURPOSES

The aim of this study is aimed at the improvement of measures for assessing critical life events and social support. A contribution to construct validity lies in the establishment of a network of hypothetical relations between a set of relevant variables. The hypotheses were:

1. Students who report negative life events show an impaired

   subjective well-being. That is, they feel depressed and

   anxious and are concerned about symptoms.

2. Perceived social support decreases distress caused by

   negative life events.

Method. 602 students who attended their first year at the
University of Washington were given a self-report questionnaire in fall 1978. The complete data sets of 190 students, 77
male and 114 female, were analysed in order to answer the
above mentioned research questions. The following variables
were included in this validation study.

(a) Critical life events. The Life Event Survey (LES) by
Sarason, Johnson & Siegel (1978) was used. The subjects
received a list of 64 life events. They had to select those
which had happened to them within the past year and to rate
them as bad or good and how strongly they were affected by
them. The sums of the intensiveness ratings of negative life
events served as an independent variable in our model.

(b) Social support. To measure the perceived social support
the students filled out the Social Support Questionnaire
(Sarason et al. 1983) which consisted of 27 items. Each of
these items first asks for the persons (parents, siblings,
peers ...) who can be seen as supportive and, second, asks for
the degree of satisfaction with support. Thus two measures are
derived: the number of supportive persons and the satisfaction
with support.

(c) Lack of protection served as a third self-report measure
which indicates the perception of too less protection during
early childhood.

(d) Subjective well-being. The are three measures of subjective well-being: test anxiety, depression and concerns with
symptoms. The Test Anxiety Scale (Sarason 1978) was used as a
measure of individual differences which could be affected by
life events and which could also moderate the more specific
measures of well-being like depression and symptoms concerns.
Depression was measured by the Multiple Affective Checklist
(MAACL) developed by Zuckerman (1968). The model contains
three sets of variables. Negative life events and social
support measures are to be seen as independent variables
whereas subjective well-being is to be seen as dependent on
both. In detail the relationships are complex as can be seen
by the results.

Results and Discussion. The first step of the data analysis is
the matrix of intercorrelation of the 7 variables (cf. table
2).

Table 2: Matrix of intercorrelations

concerns with symtoms	.35					
lack of protection	.24	.37				
test anxiety	.29	.29	.40			
depression	.03	.19	.27	.14		
number of support	-.00	-.06	-.19	-.03	-.30	
satisfaction with support	-.07	-.09	-.15	-.07	-.38	.30
	(1)	(2)	(3)	(4)	(5)	(6)

As expected there is no significant correlation between negative life events and social support. There is only a low
correlation between depression and symptom concerns indicating
that the assumption of a homogeneous set of well-being variables is less fruitful than the assumption of different specific
criterion variables. In a second step the correlation matrix
is reduced to a smaller number of relationships with respect
to the causal hypotheses in order to lead further studies
which should be longitudinal and/or experimental. A path
analysis was conducted and the results are depicted in figure
1.

Negative life events, number of social supports and lack of
protection are treated as exogeneous variables whereas the
other variables are to be seen as endogeneous variables. Most
dependent are symptom concerns and depression. All coefficients in the diagram are significant. All other potential
pathes are near zero or causally irrelevant. To control for
indirect causal influences a decomposition of effects was
calculated (cf.table 3).

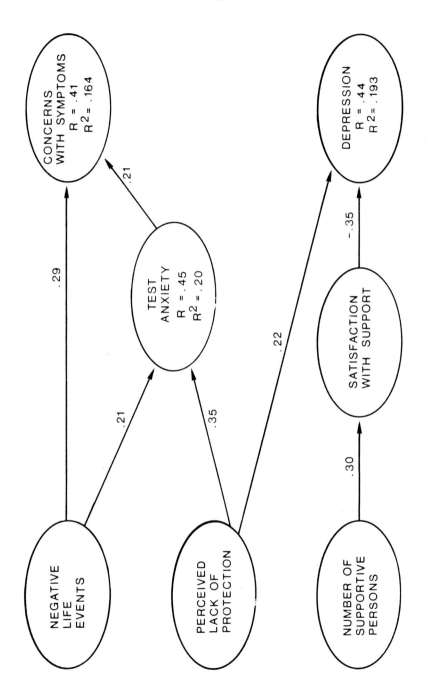

Table 3: Decomposition of effects

Criterion	Predictor	Causal Effects direct	indirect	total	noncausal effects	bivar. corr.
concerns with symptoms	negative life events	.29	.04	.33	.02	.35
	test anxiety	.21	.00	.21	.08	.29
	lack of protection	.00	.07	.07	.30	.37
depression	satisfaction with support	-.35	.00	-.35	-.03	-.38
	lack of protection	.22	.00	.22	.05	.27
	number of supportive persons	.00	-.14	-.14	-.16	-.30
test anxiety	negative life events	.12	.00	.21	.08	.29
	lack of protection	.35	.00	.35	.05	.40

The results can be interpreted in the following way. There is
empirical evidence that critical life events and social
support are not directly connected with each other. The
variance of depression, test anxiety and symptom concerns are
explained to 16% (R =.41), 20% (R =.45) and 19% (R =.44) by a
very small number of interrelated variables. In summary, there
are the following predictions with respect to the column
"total causal effects" in table 3.

(1) Symptom concerns increase when critical life events occur
and when the students have high scores in test anxiety. This

is especially valid if the subjects report lack of protection.

(2) Depression increases when the subjects experiences low satisfaction with social suport and reports high lack of protection. This is especially true if the subject has too few supportive persons in his environment.

(3) Test Anxiety is more reported by persons who feel less protected earlier in their life and who have experienced negative life events during the last year.

NOTE

Most of this paper was written by Hans-Henning Quast. The exploratory study was done by the second author while he was at the University of Washington, Seattle, in Summer 1980. We are grateful to Irwin G. Sarason for the permission to reanalyze his data.

The Self in Anxiety, Stress and Depression
R. Schwarzer (Editor)
© Elsevier Science Publishers B.V. (North-Holland), 1984

JOB DEMANDS RELATED COGNITIONS AND PSYCHOSOMATIC AILMENTS

Shimon Dolan

School of Industrial Relations, University of Montreal, Canada

and

Andre Arsenault

Institut de Recherche en Santé et Securité du Travail du Quebec (IRSST), Canada

The relationship between extrinsic and intrinsic sources of stress and selected psychosomatic manifestations has been empirically examined, while controlling for differences in personality, occupational and cultural variables. Data was obtained from about twelve hundred hospital workers who were administered an occupational stress questionnaire.

The multivariate statistical analyses indicate that both sources of stress increase all somatic complaints on the system studied: digestive, cardiovascular, visual and musculo-skeletal. Nonetheless, when personality is introduced as a grouping factor, the results become vividly contrasting. For example, the "Hot Cat" type will react to extrinsic job stress through cardio-vascular and visual symptoms, while remaining tolerant to intrinsic job stress; the "Cool Dog" type is also tolerant to intrinsic job stress but complaints on all systems in response to extrinsic job stress; the "Hot Dog" type manifests digestive cardiovascular and muskulo-skeletal symptoms under intrinsic stress as opposed to visual and cardiovascular symptoms under extrinsic stress; finally, the "Cool Cat" type reacts to extrinsic stress with digestive symptoms and to intrinsic stress through digestive and cardiovascular symptoms.

A descriptive analysis also reports on the relationships between the four personality types and occupational categories as well as cultural variables. The inhibition and exhibition of psycho-somatic complaints are discussed in terms of a contingency theory of occupational stress and in terms of intervention strategies.

The concept of stress at work is becoming increasingly prominent in behavioral science research. A number of reasons could explain this trend: (1) Stress at work has been recently related to the etiology of a number of physical diseases such as coronary heart disease (House, 1974; Caplan, 1972; Ivancevich and Matteson, 1979) peptic ulcers, hypertension and

diabetes (Cobb and Rose, 1973; Kasl, 1978). Stress has also
been related to psychiatric ailments (Jenkins, 1976; Kasl,
1973 and 1974). (2) Stress at work has been recognized as a
factor which potentially hinders organizational effectiveness
by contributing to lower employee performance (McGrath, 1976)
and the employee withdrawal behavior such as absenteeism,
tardiness, turnover, etc. (Hrebeniak and Alutto, 1972; Porter
and Steers, 1973; Lyons, 1971). (3) The indirect outcomes of
occupational stress in terms of the financial impact and
worker's compensation are also suggested in a recent report to
be a factor in the increased importance of the stress phenomenon for students of organizations (Beehr and Schuler, 1980).

While many scholars agree with the generic concept of stress,
it is noted that the literature is characterized by great
conceptual diversity. Some use the term stress in reference
to an "objective stimuli condition" (Weitz, 1970); others use
the term interchangeably with a variety of responses (Sells,
1970; Selye, 1974); yet others use the term in reference to a
complete cycle of events representing both the stressors (stimuli conditions) and the organism reaction to them (Lazarus,
1966; French et al., 1974). A recent report concludes that in
the domain of organizational stress many varied and often
conflicting conceptual definitions are employed (Shirom,
1982).

At present, the concept of stress, which seems to dominate
behavioral science research is that which infers stress from a
recurring number of signs and symptoms (Schuler, 1982). The
signs could be physiological or behavioral in nature, and the
symptoms, psychological or somatic. They all supposedly
indicate the individual's inability to cope effectively with
various job demands (French, 1976). Because of hypothesized
interactions between personal characteristics and the job
environment, occupational stress can be said to arise from a
misfit between the individual and his work demands. Many
recent reviews of the literature conclude that this definition
is among the most readily adopted by social science
researchers (Blau, 1981).

A conceptual gap is the prime cause of serious methodological
problems in stress research. A common design in organizational stress research is to select an organization and adminis-
ter questionnaires to gather individuals' perceptions of both
organizational conditions and individual responses. The
stress responses are generally individuals' subjective
feelings such as job dissatisfaction, anxiety, etc. (Beehr and
Schuler, 1980). Recently, several strong criticisms were made
against such designs (Payne et al., 1982). Only a limited
number of studies have included objective measures of stress
responses, be they physiological (i.e. Frankenhaeuser and
Gardell, 1976; Caplan et al., 1979) or behavioral in nature
(Gupta and Beehr, 1979; Arsenault and Dolan, 1983b).

Another criticism relates to the failure to account for
moderating factors in understanding the etiology of the stress

manifestations (Beehr and Newman, 1978). We also believe that
the inconsistencies emerging from many occupational stress
studies   are partially due to the disregard of relationships
between perceived stress and other intervening variables that
might concomitantly influence stress outcomes (Cummings and
Cooper, 1979; Van Sell et al., 1981; Arsenault and Dolan,
1983b).   Specifically, this study is an empirical assessment
of the predictive value of perceived stressors on somatic
complaints while controlling for moderating effects   of
differences in personality.   Moreover, the associated effects
of occupational and cultural variables is examined indirectly
through their relationships with the different personality
types.

THE WORKING MODEL

The conceptual model which guided the authors' larger study is
detailed elsewhere (Dolan and Arsenault, 1979 and 1980;
Arsenault and Dolan, 1983a).   The principal elements in the
model are: (1) Major working conditions (potential stressors)
are cognitively identifiable.   They are peculiar to each
occupation and organization; (2) Conditions at work become
stressors only if they are perceived by the individual as
representing a threat which is contingent on several individual characteristics such as personality, cultural and genetic
background;   (3) The interaction between "stressors" and
individual characteristics results in either "fit" or "misfit"
which could be measured by the exhibition or inhibition of
various signs and symptoms of strain.

Two measures of personality, widely referred to in stress
research, were selected because they reflect individual needs
and values and may influence perceptions of threat as well as
symptomatology: Type A and Locus of Control.   Type A
behavior, first described in the late 50's (Friedman and
Rosenman, 1959), is characterized by intense ambition,
competitiveness, constant struggle against time, achievement
orientation and a strong sense of urgency (Friedman and
Rosenman, 1974; Friedman et al., 1975).   Type B is largely
considered as the relatively absence of these characteristics.
Locus of Control is a personality construct derived from
Rotter's social learning theory (Rotter, 1966).   Individuals,
according to him, may have a generalized expectancy about
whether or not environmental outcomes are controlled by themselves (internal locus) or by luck and fate (external locus).

The signs and symptoms have been classified as physiological
(i.e.:   blood pressure,   cholesterol,   serum uric acid, etc.);
psychological (i.e.: depression, anxiety, job dissatisfaction,
etc.);   and behavioral (i.e.: performance, sexual problems,
drinking, excessive eating, etc.).   In the long run, recurrent
appearances of such signs and symptoms might be conducive to
the development of irreversible physical diseases (i.e.:
cardiovascular heart disease, ulcers, hypertension) and/or
mental illnesses at the individual level.   The organization

might also be affected by high levels of absenteeism, high
turnover, more accidents, etc. In this paper, however, only
part of the above mentioned model is presented. It is schematically represented in Figure 1.

Figure 1
Schematic Framework for studying
Occupational Stress and Psychosomatic Complaints
amongst
Hospital Employees

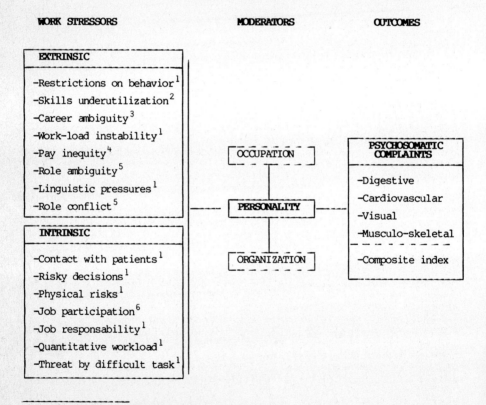

* For operational definitions, see:
[1]Dolan and Arsenault,1981; [2]Taylor and Bowers, 1972;
[3]Quinn and Shepard, 1974; [4]Caplan et al, 1975;
[5]Kahn et al, 1964; [6]Likert, 1961.

METHODS

<u>Sample</u>. About 1200 hospital employees, from eight Quebec
hospitals, representing a wide range of occupations, age
groups, educational levels, etc. were included. All subjects
volunteered for this study. Admission criteria included minimal seniority on present job (6 months) and a minimum of 25
hours of work per week. These were considered critical
control measures for a study of chronic and recurring occupational stress. Data was collected by questionnaires. All
attitudinal data was ascertained by employing Likert type
scales.

<u>Predictors</u>. While many different psycho-social work stressors
are suggested in the literature (see Cooper and Marshall,
1976; Beehr and Newman, 1978), in this study, we retained only
those which are pertinent to hospital work environments;
linguistic pressures, characteristic of Quebec work environ-'
ment was added. A complete listing of these stressors is
given in Figure 1. Two major categories served to classify
the stressors: those which represent the work context
(extrinsic job stressors), and those pertaining to the work
content (intrinsic job stressors).

Predictors were treated in two stages. First, work stressors
were constructed into multi-item scales (linear addition). A
full description of all scales employed, including their
central tendency characteristics was reported elsewhere (Dolan
et al., 1981; Arsenault and Dolan, 1983), yet internal
reliabilities are given in Table 1. Their separation into the
categories of intrinsic and extrinsic sources was based
primarily on conceptualization derived from previous re-
search(e.g. Caplan et al., 1975; House 1974) but have been
adapted in content and wording to the present study population. This classification matrix of all the scales in each
category is also shown in Table 1.

At the second stage, it has been decided to combine the
various scales into two summary indices rather than treating
them throughout the analysis on a single one-by-one basis (for
psychometric justification, see: Ghiselli et al., 1981). The
logic for this strategy is twofold: (1) Most of the research
in this field tends to treat the various role-stressors on a
single basis and despite the many attempts to identify a
universal stressor, it seems that results were confounded with
population, jobs and special circumstances, etc. which prevents one from drawing general conclusions (Cooper and
Marshall, 1976; Kasl, 1978; Van Sell et al., 1981). (2) Even
though it is acknowledged that much information on particular
stressors is lost when a combined approach is used, it seems
to be the direction towards new theories in the domain of
occupational stress. Consequently, two summary indices were
constructed.

Table 1
Internal Reliability and Correlation Coefficients
of Extrinsic and Intrinsic Job Stress Indices.

SCALE	(RELIABILITY)							
EXTRINSIC	(alpha)	1	2	3	4	5	6	7
1. Restrictions on behavior	(.77)							
2. Skills underutilization	(.84)	.37						
3. Career ambiguity	(.67)	.19	.29					
4. Work-load instability	(.80)	-.02	-.11	.08				
5. Pay inequity	(.82)	.06	.02	.08	.08			
6. Role ambiguity	(.85)	-.01	.23	.23	.07	.02		
7. Linguistic pressures	(.80)	.10	.04	.12	.10	.09	-.01	
8. Role conflict	(.77)	.08	.17	.20	.18	.12	.29	.16

INTRINSIC		9	10	11	12	13	14
9. Contact with patients	(.81)						
10. Urgent decisions	(n.a.)*	.37					
11. Physical risks	(n.a.)*	.44	.26				
12. Job participation	(.79)	.07	.14	-.07			
13. Job responsability	(.78)	.16	.24	.09	.24		
14. Quantitative workload	(.77)	.11	.16	.10	.10	.23	
15. Threat by task difficulty	(n.a.)*	.05	.17	.13	.04	.14	.11

*: scales with 2 items only.

The Extrinsic Stress Index was derived from linear addition of responses to the eight extrinsic stressors listed in Table 1. This scale ranges from 1 (low) to 5 (high); the observed range was from 1.1 to 3.3, with a mean score of 1.9 and a standard error of 0.4.

The Intrinsic Stress Index was derived from linear addition of responses to the seven intrinsic stressors listed in Table 1. This scale ranges from 1 (low) to 5 (high): the observed range was from 1.1 to 3.5 with a mean of 2.4 and a standard error of o.4.

The zero order correlation between these two indices is 0.27.

Personality as a key grouping variable. At the personality level, two measures were employed. "Striver-Achiever" is a nine item index based on the work done by the Michigan group (Caplan et al., 1975). A person who is high "Striver-Achiever" has many similar characteristics to the Friedman and Rosenman Type A personality (Friedman and Rosenman, 1959, 1974 and 1975); and vice-versa, a person who scores low on the "Striver-Achiever" scale, resembles type B personality. The internal reliability coefficient for this scale is .67 (alpha). While the measure ranges from 9 (low-type B) to 63 (high-type A), the observed range was 10 to 63 with a mean of 43 and a standard error of 9. Locus of control was measured by Rotter's instrument (Rotter, 1966). The reliability for this measure which was constructed by linear addition of twenty-three items each representing a possible score of one or zero, is .76 (alpha). It ranges from 0 (low-internal locus of control) to 23 (high-external locus of control); the observed range was from 1 to 23 with a mean of 11 and a standard error of 4.

The "Striver-Achiever" scale captures primarily an individual's typical behavior, and Locus of Control captures primarily beliefs, attitudes, and values; moreover the empirical correlation found for these two measures is low ($r = -.15$). It thus appears that a combined index of the two measures might better represent a holistic definition of "personality". Therefore, a median split method was employed on each scale to identify subjects was scored relatively high or relatively low; each subject was thus categorized on two dimensions. This method led to the identification of four distinct categories of personality which were labelled as follows: a) the high "striver-achiever" and high external locus of control - was named "Hot Dog"; b) the high "striver-achiever" and high internal locus of control was named "Hot Cat"; c) the low "striver-achiever" and high external locus of control was named "Cool Dog"; d) the low "striver-achiever" and high internal locus of control was named "Cool Cat".

Occupation and organization. At the occupational level, the sample was divided into the following four categories:

- Executives   and   Professionals   (including   middle
  managers)(TOP-EX)
- Registered nurses (RN)
- Semi-professionals (technicians,   secretaries, etc.)
  (TEC)
- Blue collar workers (including nurses'-aides) (BLU)

At the organizational level, the sample was classified as
follows for subsequent analysis based on the type of the
hospital (predominantly francophone vs. anglophone) and its
location (Montreal vs. non Montreal):

- Montreal Anglophones   (3 hospitals) (ENG)
- Montreal Francophones   (3 hospitals) (FRE)
- Non Montreal Francophones (2 hospitals) (OTH)

Criteria.   Four sub-scales of somatic complaints were derived
through factor analysis.   Their psychometric characteristics
are as follows: the Cardiovascular scale is computed from five
questions by linear addition and its internal reliability
coefficient (alpha) is .79; the Digestive scale is made up of
three questions with a coefficient of .85; the Visual scale of
three questions with a coefficient of .78 and the Muscolo-
skeletal scale with three questions, has an alpha value of.63.
A composite somatic index (CSI) has also been computed by
linear addition of the above four sub-scales plus 18 other
non-specific symptoms; this index has an internal reliability
coefficient of .84.   All the scales follow a normal distribution.

RESULTS

Table 2 presents the results of the multiple regression of
each scale of somatic complaints and of the composite index
(CSI) on extrinsic and intrinsic job stress.   With the
exception of the visual scale, which is not significantly
influenced by intrinsic stress, both sources of stress have a
significant impact at all levels of symptomatology, including
the CSI.

The predictive value of extrinsic stress is much higher than
intrinsic stress.   The variance ratios (F values) are higher
by a factor of 7:1 for the CSI, 6:1 for cardiovascular
symptoms, 2:1 for digestive and about equal to one for the
musculo-skeletal scale.   Extrinsic stress has a very highly
significant prediction on the visual scale whereas the
prediction of intrinsic stress is not significant on this
scale.

The effect of personality as a grouping variable is presented
in Table 3.   The multiple regressions, done in groups, show
the typical somatic profile of each of the four personality
types and is followed by a comparison between the groups. The
results of the analyses of all the individuals considered as a

TABLE 2

**Multiple Regression of Somatic Complaints
on Intrinsic and Extrinsic Job Stress**

Somatic Complaints Scales	Intrinsic Stress			Extrinsic Stress			R^2
	Beta	F	p	Beta	F	p	
Digestive	0.12	10.0	.002	0.18	22.5	10^{-4}	.06
Cardio-vascular	0.11	8.0	.005	0.28	52.3	10^{-4}	.10
Musculo-skeletal	0.09	5.3	.02	0.08	4.5	.03	.02
Visual	0.06	2.2	.14	0.23	33.7	10^{-4}	.06

Composite Somatic Index	0.10	6.7	.01	0.28	48.0	10^{-5}	.10

single group, equivalent to Table 2, are repeated for convenience.

The intercept values refer to the base level of each somatic complaint estimated in the absence of both intrinsic and extrinsic stress. The standardized slopes (beta weights) can be interpreted as the degree of reactivity to each source of stress, without considering possible interactions between intrinsic and extrinsic stress. The between groups test can be influenced by either differences in base level symptomatology or in reactivity to stress.

Table 3A illustrates the moderating effect of personality on the composite somatic index. The difference in base level symptomatology is not statistically significant from one personality type to another. However, the "Hot Dog" type appears to be equally responsive to intrinsic and extrinsic stress; the "Cool Cats" to neither; the "Hot Cats" and the "Cool Dogs" only to extrinsic stress. The significance of the intergroup F value is most probably due to the response pattern (beta) rather than to the base-level differences.

Table 3B reports the response pattern along the digestive scale. The base level symptoms of the "Hot Cats" is the only one that is significantly different from zero while they are

TABLE 3
Multiple Regressions in Groups of Somatic Complaints on Intrinsic and Extrinsic Job Stressors Moderated by Personality

A

COMPOSITE SOMATIC INDEX					
Intercept		Intrinsic Stress		Extrinsic Stress	
PERSONALITY	p	Beta	p	Beta	p
SINGLE GROUP	0.78 10^{-5}	0.10	.01	0.28	10^{-5}
HOT CATS	1.22 10^{-4}	-0.07	.38	0.27	.002
HOT DOGS	0.61 .05	0.22	.01	0.20	.02
COOL CATS	0.89 10^{-4}	0.19	.06	0.15	.13
COOL DOGS	0.97 10^{-4}	0.01	.90	0.31	10^{-4}
BETWEEN GROUP	F = 5.2			p = 10^{-6}	

B

DIGESTIVE SCALE					
Intercept		Intrinsic Stress		Extrinsic Stress	
PERSONALITY	p	Beta	p	Beta	p
SINGLE GROUP	0.4 —	0.12	.002	0.18	10^{-4}
HOT CATS	1.2 .05	0.06	.43	0.06	.27
HOT DOGS	0.2 —	0.20	.01	0.13	.11
COOL CATS	-0.3 —	0.22	.02	0.24	.01
COOL DOGS	0.5 —	-0.01	.93	0.28	10^{-4}
BETWEEN GROUP	F = 2.4			p = .01	

C

CARDIO-VASCULAR SCALE					
Intercept		Intrinsic Stress		Extrinsic Stress	
PERSONALITY	p	Beta	p	Beta	p
SINGLE GROUP	0.6 10^{-4}	0.11	.005	0.28	10^{-4}
HOT CATS	0.7 .01	0.05	.53	0.32	10^{-4}
HOT DOGS	0.4 —	0.19	.02	0.22	.006
COOL CATS	0.7 .001	0.24	.01	0.15	.11
COOL DOGS	1.0 .01	-0.02	.77	0.23	.003
BETWEEN GROUP	F = 2.6			p = .006	

D

VISUAL SCALE					
Intercept		Intrinsic Stress		Extrinsic Stress	
PERSONALITY	p	Beta	p	Beta	p
SINGLE GROUP	0.4 .05	0.06	.14	0.23	10^{-4}
HOT CATS	0.4 —	0.03	.66	0.24	.003
HOT DOGS	0.2 —	0.08	.32	0.27	.001
COOL CATS	1.3 .01	0.03	.76	0.02	.86
COOL DOGS	0.3 —	0.04	.56	0.24	.001
BETWEEN GROUP	F = 1.0			p = .40	

E

MUSCULO-SKELETAL SCALE					
Intercept		Intrinsic Stress		Extrinsic Stress	
PERSONALITY	p	Beta	p	Beta	p
SINGLE GROUP	1.0 10^{-4}	0.09	.02	0.08	.03
HOT CATS	2.1 10^{-4}	-0.00	.97	-0.09	.28
HOT DOGS	0.6	0.17	.04	0.12	.15
COOL CATS	1.2 .01	0.03	.74	0.06	.52
COOL DOGS	0.8 —	0.09	.27	0.15	.05
BETWEEN GROUP	F = 1.9			p = .04	

— Not significant

not responsive to either source of stress: they would tend to have significantly more digestive symptoms even in the absence of stress. In contrast, the "Cool Cats" have a minimal base level but their symptoms increase significantly in response to both sources of stress. The "Hot Dogs" react selectively to intrinsic stress and the "Cool Dogs" to extrinsic stress.

Table 3C reports the response pattern along the cardiovascular scale. From comparable base levels, the personality types respond as follows: the "Hot Dogs" react to both sources of stress, the "Cool Cats" only to intrinsic stress, while both the "Hot Cats" and the "Cool Dogs" respond to extrinsic stress.

Table 3D reports the response pattern on the visual scale. In this case, the base level symptomatology of the "Cool Cats" is the only one that is significantly different from zero and they do not respond to either source of stress: they would tend to have significantly more visual symptoms even in the absence of stress. On the other hand, no significant reactivity to intrinsic stress is detected, the reaction to extrinsic stress being significant for all the other personality types but the "Cool Cats".

Finally, Table 3E shows a tendency for the "Cats", "Hot" and "Cool", to exhibit a higher base level symptomatology of the musculo-skeletal form without significant reactivity to either sources of stress. The "Hot Dogs" react selectively to intrinsic stress, and the "Cool Dogs", to extrinsic stress.

TABLE 4

Stress, Personality and Somatic Manifestations

Somatic Scale	BASE LEVEL				INTRINSIC				EXTRINSIC			
	HC	HD	CC	CD	HC	HD	CC	CD	HC	HD	CC	CD
Digestive	+	.	.	.	.	+	+	.	.	.	+	+
Cardiovascular	.	.	.	.	.	+	+	.	+	+	.	+
Musculo-skeletal	+	.	+	.	.	+	.	.	.	.	.	+
Visual	.	.	+	.	.	.	.	.	+	+	.	+

	BASE LEVEL				INTRINSIC				EXTRINSIC			
Composite Index	.	.	.	.	.	+	.	.	+	+	.	+

Comparing the response patterns (Table 4), one can see several general tendencies:

(a) the "Cool Dogs" have a base level of complaints that is close to the general mean on all scales, do not react to intrinsic stress but show an exquisite and diffuse reaction to extrinsic stress on all the scales.
(b) the "Hot Dogs" share with the "Cool Dogs" a low base level on all scales, but do respond to intrinsic stress on all scales but the visual one; they also react to extrinsic stress, but only on the cardiovascular and visual scales.
(c) the "Hot Cats" have a significantly higher base level of digestive and musculo-skeletal symptoms than the others and do not exhibit any significant further increase of these two scales in response to stress but rather on the other two, cardiovascular and digestive, and only when confronted with extrinsic stress; they are hypo-reactive to intrinsic stress
(d) the "Cool Cats" have a high base level of musculo-skeletal and visual symptoms, react to intrinsic stress with cardio-vascular and digestive symptoms and minimally to extrinsic stress on the digestive scale only.
(e) the "Dogs" share a low base level of symptoms.
(f) the "Cats" share a high base level of musculo-skeletal problems.
(g) the "Hot" types are both reactive to extrinsic stress.
(h) the "Cool" types are generally less reactive than the "Hot" types.

Figure 2 represents the relationships of the four occupational categories and the three hospital groups with the two dimensions of personality. The vertical axis gives the position of the group mean along the Type A scale above and below a general mean of 43.2 (x). The horizontal axis gives the position of the group means along the Locus of Control scale to the left (more internal) and to the right (more external) of a general mean of 10.6 (y). The means (centroids) of each category is recognized by assigning a * for occupations and a # for hospital groups. These respresent only aggregated data and should be referred as such.

There appears to be a distinctive relationship between the type of personality and the aggregated type of both occupation and hospital groups. The former approximating differences in role and the latter differences in culture. The centroids have the general tendency to fall along a diagonal line leading from the "Hot Cat" quadrant to the "Cool Dog" quadrant: the "Hot Dogs" and the "Cool Cats" would be uniformly distributed across roles (job categories) and culture (hospitals).

The executive and professional employees are significantly more internal and "Hot" than the registered nurses; they in turn are significantly more "Hot" than the technicians but marginally more internal; the technicians are not significantly more internal than the blue collars but they are much more "Hot". From the "Hot Cat" pole to the "Cool Dog" pole, there appears to be a dual gradient between the occupational

FIGURE 2

CENTROIDS OF OCCUPATIONS AND HOSPITAL CATEGORIES
ALONG THE TWO DIMENSIONS OF PERSONALITY

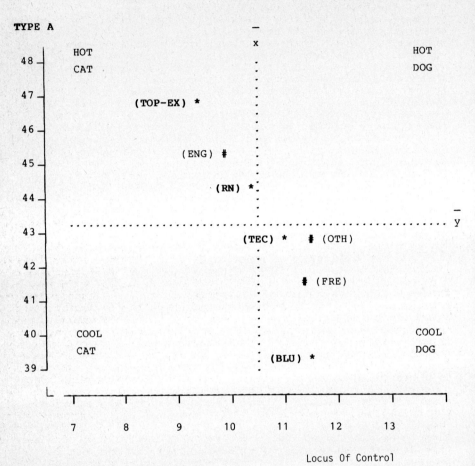

Locus Of Control

roles in terms of the individuals' capacity to internalize control and compete in action.

The differences between hospital groups clearly and significantly separate the French hospitals (FRE and OTH) from the English ones. The hospitals appear to exhibit some sort of "personality", the French being less competitive and more external ("Cool Dog") and the English appearing more competitive and more internal ("Hot Cat").

DISCUSSION AND CONCLUSIONS

The fact that job stress is significantly related to most of the somatic complaints studied here (Table 2) is not surprising. One plausible explanation which can be advanced to explain this finding is the mere fact that both measurements (self-reported perceived stress and self-reported somatic complaints), are within the realm of individuals' subjectivity and thus reflects internal cohesiveness of perceptions of one's both stimuli condition and attitudinal response pattern (see also: House et al., 1979; Posner and Randolph, 1980). By contrast, the introduction of personality and other aggregating variables brings much more clarity to the etiology of these patterns as will be discussed hereafter.

The second general finding relates to the differential effect of extrinsic and intrinsic job stressors on the outcomes studied here. It is noteworthy that (1) the predictive value of extrinsic stress is much more apparent according to the variance ratios reported here (Table 2) and (2) intrinsic stress has no predictive value on visual type of complaints.

Additional insight is gained when the stressor-outcome relationships are aggregated by personality type: there is a significant interaction between personality and patterns of reactivity, certain types showing base level traits that are present even in the absence of stress such as the digestive symptoms of the "Hot Cats" or the visual symptoms of the "Cool Cats". Moreover, there is no universal scale along which all personality types react to either sources of stress. In other words, the stressor-outcome relationship is characterized by prefered axes of somatic expression related to a confounded complex of personality, role and cultural dimensions. The results emphasize the dangers of reaching general conclusions when one does not take into account the concommitant effects of this moderating complex.

Further, when separate consideration is given to either Type A or Locus of Control as moderators of the stress-somatic complaints responses, previous research failed to show consistent findings (Posner and Randolph, 1980; Keenan and McBain, 1979; Batlis, 1980). Whereas the combined taxonomy reported here clarifies our understanding of the stress-somatic manifestations relationship. More particularly, the differential reactivity to the two sources of stress in terms of different somatic complaints deserves further elaboration.

It is proposed that in order to understand the etiology of the
somatic manifestations, one needs to refer to the intent
differences between personality types in terms of the way
people perceive a stimulus as a threat in the work environment
as well as in terms of the admissible overt reactions to these
perceptions.

An interesting anology can be borrowed from the exact sciences
where any signal can be filtered, amplified and modulated at
the input (stimulus) as well as the output (response) of a
processor. In this regard, it is suggested that different
personality types are predisposed to filter or amplify both
stimuli and responses. This "processing complex" would be a
mixture of genetic tendencies interwoven with culturally
acquired modulators which apply colour and contrast to different values and roles in society.

The "Hot Dog", for example, seems to have a low threshold to
both sources of stress and to amplify the stimulus; they would
also tend to amplify the somatic manifestations at all levels.
Such explanation considers the simultaneous presence of a
competitive hard driving trait along with an external locus of
control: any job content challenge (intrinsic stress) is a
distress to their relatively low capacity to exert control
over events and job context difficulties interfere with their
fast doer trait. All this leads to exhibition of many somatic
manifestations that are minimally filtered at the output:
their dionysiac self image is compatible with the overt admission of loss of control.

The "Hot Cat", on the other hand, can be described as amplify-
ing extrinsic stress and filtering intrinsic stress; they
complain mostly on the cardiovascular and visual axes. Their
apparent absolute control over intrinsic job challenge goes
along with their internal locus of control: admitting coping
problems because of job complexity would be detrimental to
their self-image. On the other hand, extrinsic interference
with the rapid execution of tasks leads them to exhibit an
hyper-adreno-energetic preparation to fight, a typical Type A
attitude. On the other hand, their chronic, stress-indepen-
dent, digestive and musculo-skeletal symptomatology would be a
symbolic representation of the perceived power invested in
their herculean self-image.

By contrast, the "Cool Dog" tends to filter both sources of
stress, yet in the presence of limited extrinsic stress,
exhibits an exquisite variety of symptoms of distress. Their
relative lack of competitivity and their external locus trans-
forms them into helpless passive flight prone individuals who
have a hard time to oppose the decree of the Gods. Their
self-image is creonian.

Finally, the "Cool Cats" tend to filter both stimuli and
responses. Their internal locus coupled with their lack of

competitiveness would make them react to intrinsic stress on a parasympathetic digestive axis, a symbolic representation of their relative incapacity to externalize control through action: they would tend to ruminate somatically and perhaps psychologically, becoming informal leaders of artistic tendency. Their self-image would be appollonian.

The extent to which personality moderates the effects of stress on somatic manifestations would also depend on the type of support system in which it operates. Cultural and peer support are suggested as associated key variables. Two proxi measures of such support systems were used in this study. There is of course controversy over the question of self-selection into occupation and/or type of organization. Nonetheless, the results reported here demonstrate a systematic relationship between the types of personality and the occupational distributions as well as the organizations studied. There is a clinical evidence, however, that self-selection into a role is sometimes replaced by forced promotions into occupations through bureaucratic and/or collectively bargained selection criteria. For a typical "Hot Cat", a lateral promotion into a staff position, the shelving process, can be very stressful. For a typical "Cool Dog", a vertical promotion into a line responsibility, the "you can do it" syndrome, can be very detrimental. Similarly, intercultural migration can be a stress or a relief. A French very "Hot Cat" would tend to lose cultural support and be rejected as an adjusted formal leader; immigration into an English "Hot Cat" hospital might go along with better cultural support and an adjusted formal leadership.

These findings may bear practical implications for diagnostic and remedial intervention strategies aimed at reducing somatic symptoms and increasing subjective well-being. It appears that certain individals need to be encouraged in order to solicit their real feelings and problems (the "Cool" types) while others should be put into more appropriate perspective when somatic complaints are exhibited (the "Dog" types). It also bears implications for studying social and cultural support which might be very heterogeneously felt within a given culture between personality types and within a personality type between different cultures.

In summary, our study points out that the logical and empirical testing of occupational stress theories depends on several considerations which are not mutually exclusive: first, what is the focal outcome, is it single or multiple, is one going to study them separately or concurrently ? Second, what the moderating variables to be chosen as mediating the stressor-outcome relationships and what is their relative role ? And thirdly, is one going to choose and examine the work stressors on a one by one basis or in composite summary classifications? This study was designed to show that a more parsimonious approach might be more useful in developing models and theories in the domain of occupational stress. We suggest that a great deal of information is revealed when the outcomes

are studied in contrasted parallels, when the moderators are
carefully selected and the sources of stress are classified
using summary scales. This may bring us closer to the development of a theory of relativity applied to the domain of
occupational stress.

NOTES

1.Financial support was granted by the Institut de Recherce en
  Sante et en Securite du Travail du Quebec (IRSST).

2. The authors have equally contributed to this paper.

The Self in Anxiety, Stress and Depression
R. Schwarzer (Editor)
© Elsevier Science Publishers B.V. (North-Holland), 1984

BEHAVIORAL FACTORS, STRESSFUL LIFE CHANGES AND DEPRESSION IN HEART PATIENTS:
SOME RESULTS FROM THE SOUTH-LIMBURG LIFE HISTORY AND MYOCARDIAL INFARCTION STUDY

Paul R.J. Falger

State University of Limburg School of Medicine, Department of Medical Psychology
Maastricht, The Netherlands

In current behavioral medicine research it is recognized that there exist several psychological and social determinants in the etiology of coronary heart disease (CHD). First it was established that a behavioral disposition - the Type A coronary-prone behavior pattern - constitutes an independent psychosocial risk indicator in the pathogenesis of myocardial infarction (MI). The adult coronary-prone person is characterized by a habitual manner of acting in an alert, hasty, overly responsive and aggressive manner, by a chronic sense of time urgency, by an utterly competitive involvement in work, or - in short - by an exaggerated need for personal recognition through achievement (Friedman & Rosenman, 1974). This psychosocial risk indicator for CHD, extensivelly studied over the last two decades, holds true for employed, middle-aged men and women in the USA (Waldron et al., 1977; Brand, 1978; Haynes & Feinleib, 1982), and - with a similar degree of assocation - in employed, middle-aged man in Western- and Eastern Europe (Zyzanski et al., 1979., 1979; Kornitzer et al., 1981; Appels et al., 1982). It was demonstrated further that social psychological factors like an unprecedented exposure to stressful life changes (LC) in the last years prior to MI may be of particular significance. These findings hold true in European studies (Rahe & Romo, 1974; Siegrist et al., 1980; Theorell, 1980), as well as in American and Australian investigations (Thiel et al., 1973; Byrne & Whyte, 1980). It was also established that MI-cases assess such events in a peculiar cognitive manner, i.e. they perceive these changes as causing much more upsettingness or emotional distress than (healthy) referents do (Byrne, 1980; Siegrist et al., 1982), or as requiring more psychological and social adjustment to (Lundberg & Theorell, 1975; Lundberg et al., 1976). Still another aspect of adult social life, i.e. one's occupational status is considered a specific risk indicator for CHD. While a few decades ago only the highest occupational strata in Western society were afflicted with CHD, nowadays this picture is almost completely reversed. I.e. it is the unskilled, poorly educated laborer in contemporary industry who is suffering most from MI, and with the least chance of survival (Marmot, 1982).

The picture with respect to psychosocial determinants in the development of premature MI is not all drab, however. In several studies it has been demonstrated that social support, when embedded in a network of meaningful social relations, may serve as a most powerful moderator of life stress with regard to subsequent development of illness in general, and the incidence of CHD and MI in particular (Cobb, 1976; Berkman, 1982).

Impressive as these studies have been in providing us with discerning insight into the complex intertwinings of behavioral, psychosocial and cultural factors in the pathogenesis of MI, yet they have almóst completely neglected an equally intriguing question, namely, how those factors may have come about to play such a decisive role in the lives of MI-patients.

Stated differently, what specific developmental trajectories did those patients take during their life course that ultimately destined them to suffer from premature MI, or even sudden cardiac death ? To what extent have coronary cases been able to exert control over their own lifes ? I.e. could they have encountered some LC of particular ideosyncratic relevance that changed their lives inexorably ? In what peculiar manner might the Type A coronary-prone behavior pattern interact with the occurrence and subsequent coping with life changes (LC) in different developmental domains ? Would there be a rather universal ontogenetic pattern leading to premature MI in middle adulthood ? Or, on the contrary, would specific cohort effects that account for unique historical-environmental constellations provide a much better explanation ? And, to address finally a crucial issue that was not brought up yet, to what extent do heart patients suffer from manifestations of vital exhaustion and depression in the last months before infarction as a final common pathway toward breakdown in psychosocial adaptation, as is suggested by the literature on psychic factors in sudden cardiac death ? (Kuller et al., 1972; Alonzo et al., 1975; Kuller, 1978; Rissanen et al., 1978).

THE SOUTH-LIMBURG LIFE HISTORY AND MYOCARDIAL INFARCTION STUDY

In order to address some of the developmental issues, we undertook the South-Limburg Life History and Myocardial Infarction Study. In this retrospective investigation, we are interested first in the question whether the life course of heart patients is characterized by an appreciable exposure to LC in different developmental domains, and whether there may be discernable cohort effects in this respect. Second, the particular manner in which MI-patients may assess those LC, i.e. whether in the perception of the patients under study each reported event has contributed in any positive sense to his psychologial and social development, or on the contrary, has proven detrimental, is of importance to us, as is the extent of social support that is associated with each LC.

Third, we are interested in the differences in cohort-specific prevalence of the Type A behavior pattern in our coronary patients. Fourth we would like to corroborate previous findings of ours, namely that manifestations of vital exhaustion and depression may destine a patient's emotional constitution in the last months prior to infarction (Appels, 1980; Falger & Appels, 1982; Falger, 1983a).

METHOD

The exposure to 51 life changes (LC) in three developmental domains, i.e. (a) childhood, youth and adolescence, (b) work and career, and (c) family and social life, as well as the psychological perceptions, coping strategies, and social support with respect to each reported event, are assessed by means of a structured interview scheme, the Life History and Coping Strategies Interview. This interview scheme was constructed on the basis of extensive interviews with some 35 MI-patients, and the results from a pilot-study on 136 healthy, middle-aged men (Falger & Appels, 1982). Then, at the end of the interview session, each participant is categorized as either Type A (coronary-prone), or Type B, according to the original Structured Interview assessment (Rosenman, 1978). Further, all participants complete the Maastricht Questionnaire (MQ) that was developed earlier to measure prodromal manifestation of vital exhaustion and depression. The MQ has been used in a number of retrospective and prospective studies on MI-patients and several control groups. The MQ pertains to the last half year prior to MI, or interviewing. (For a review, see Falger, 1983a).

An average interview session will last some 2.5 hours.

Subjects. In this case-referent study, three groups of subjects are involved, i.e. MI-patients, healthy neighbourhood referents and hospital referents.

A MI-patient is defined as a male person, between 35-70 years of age, hospitalized with first MI that is clinically documented by ECG and serum enzyme max classifications. All patients come from the two largest hospitals in the South-Limburg Region, and are visited personally by us in the hospital within a few days after admission. Participating patients complete the MQ in the hospital and are interviewed at home some one/two month(s) after their release. After completion of a Life History and Coping Strategies Interview, a healthy neighborhood referent is sought.

A healthy neighborhood referent is defined as a male person, between 35-70 years of age, without documented MI (self-report), living in the immediate vicinity of a MI-Patient from our study. All neighborhood referents are selected by means of a complete list from the telephone directory, containing

all persons in the street where the MI-patient is living.
Then, those referents are asked, by means of a standard
letter, in a random order, and one at the time, to participate
in this study if they comply with our definition. The
neighborhood referent then also is interviewed at home.

In this manner, the life histories of MI-patients can be
compared - in a valid manner - with an equal number of healthy
neighbourhood referents, controlled for socioeconomic status
(Miettinen, 1982).

A hospital referent is defined as a male person, between 35-70
years of age, without documented MI (hospital record), hospitalized with non-stress related ailment (e.g. haemorrhoids,
prostate hypertrophia, inguinal hernia, cataract, etc.) All
patients come from the same hospitals as the MI-patients do.
All hospital referents are asked, by means of the same
standard letter that applies to healthy neighbourhood
referents, to participate in this study if they comply with
our definition. All hospital referents are interviewed at
home, about one/two month(s) after their release.

Including this second referent group allows for further clarification of the crucial question whether the life-span
developmental patterns in MI-patients are identifiable by
a singular structure with respect to exposure to particular LC
during the life course, regarding ideosyncratic coping
strategies, or with respect to social support associated with
each LC (Miettinen, 1982).

Design. The design of this study is such that all MI-patients
and both referent groups are assigned equally to seven age
groups of five years each, spanning the age range from 35-70.
I.e. 15 MI-patients, 15 healthy neighbourhood referents, and
30 hospital referents of 35-39 years of age, 40-44 years of
age, etc.

In this manner, specific cohort influences in the developmental patterns of cases and referents could be identified
(Baltes et al., 1978). Also, in employing this particular
design that covers the largest part of the human life
trajectory, some inherent restrictions of a cross-sectional
approach could be alleviated (Schaie, 1973).

RESULTS

The South Limburg Life History and Myocardial Infarction Study
was begun in December 1980; it most probably will be completed
by the end of 1983. Therefore, the results that are presented
here still bear a preliminary character.

Early in the course of this investigation it became apparent
that older heart patients would be much easier sampled than
younger ones, for the obvious reason of vast differences in

cardiovascular morbidity rates. Since we wanted to comply with our design in order to study cohort effects, we allowed for more than 15 MI-patients to be included within each cohort (with a maximum of 25), and subsequently a like number of same-aged neighbourhood referents.

We will now regard briefly the evidence pertaining to the differences in prevalence of the Type A coronary-prone behavior pattern, and of the prodrome of vital exhaustion and depression prior to infarction, in cases and neighbourhood referent subjects. Then we will proceed to an exemplary examination of the occurence of LC and particular coping strategies in the life trajectories of heart patients, aged 50-59.

The Type A Coronary-Prone Behavior Pattern. By definition, about half of an adult, male, healthy population in contempo-rary industrialized society can be categorized as exhibiting the Type A behavior pattern, and the other half as Type B (Rosenman, 1978). However, in middle aged MI-patients the incidence rates of the Type A pattern are (at least) twice as large compared to Type B cases (Brand, 1978; Zyzanski, 1978; Haynes & Feinleib, 1982).

The prevalence rates of Type A and Type B behavior in MI-patients and healthy neighbourhood referents, depicted as the actual ratio of Type A to Type B behavior for both groups separately, are presented in Figure 1.

It is obvious that the Type A coronary-prone behavior pattern constitutes a considerable psychosocial risk factor in the two youngest cohorts of cases (i.e. age 35-44), but also that this association is diminishing with increasing age, in particular after age 60. However, in all cohorts of MI-patients the Type A behavior pattern prevails over Type B behavior. In refe-rents, on the other hand, the reverse trend can be observed, in particular after age 55.

The Prodrome of Vital Exhaustion and Depression. In all case-referent studies in which the MQ on vital exhaustion and de-pression was employed, it was demonstrated that MI-patients of different ages in general suffer from appreciable manifesta-tions of vital exhaustion and depression prior to premature infarction (Falger, 1983a). In the present study, the mean MQ scores of all cases and neighbourhood referents are 90.2, and 68.9 respectively (t = 6.74, p .001, one-tailed). These results should be read as indicating: The higher the score on the MQ, the more clear-cut is the prodrome of vital exhaustion and depression. When calculated separately for each cohort of cases and controls, the same degree of differences in mean scores are obtained.

Now, in an earlier study on the interaction between the Type A behavior pattern and the prodrome of vital exhaustion and depression in middle-aged healthy subjects, it was found that Type A subjects scored significantly higher on the MQ than

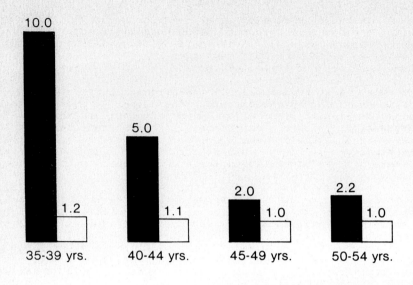

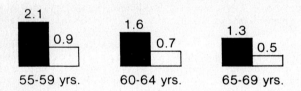

Ratio of Type A to Type B Coronary-Prone Behavior Pattern
in Seven Cohorts of Male Myocardial Infarction Patients
(■N = 121) and Male Neighbourhood Controls (□N = 108)

FIGURE 1

Type B subjects did (Falger & Appels, 1982). A similar pattern was found in the healthy neighbourhood referents in the present study. I.e. the mean MQ score for all Type A referents was 74.4, the mean MQ in Type B referents was 63.6 (t = 2.91; p<.005, one-tailed).

In summary, a majority of MI-patients report a specific constellation of emotions, that we have termed the prodrome of vital exhaustion and depression, in the months prior to their first coronary event. According to us, this prodrome may indicate a final breakdown in resources to cope with the psychological and social burden in their lives (Appels, 1980; Falger, 1983a). To a lesser degree a similar tendency can be observed in healthy, same-aged neighbourhood referents exhibiting the Type A behavior pattern. This finding suggests that healthy Type A subjects may be more vulnerable emotionally than the self-assured outward apparition, corresponding with this overt behavior pattern (Rosenman, 1978), at first sight implies.

In the remainder of this paper, we will examine whether this general breakdown in psychosocial adaptation before premature infarction could possibly have emerged from particular life history patterns.

Stressful Life Changes and Coping Strategies in the Life Course. The results in this section are presented in a different manner than in the previous ones. I.e., the data pertain to one combined cohort: 50-59 years of age. In this cohort, the differences in lifespan developmental patterns are most outspoken; a detailed analysis of differences in all cohorts would be beyond the limited length of this paper. Also, the total number of referents is larger than in the earlier analysis. This is obtained through combining the healthy neighbourhood referents with the hospital referents that have been interviewed so far for this age group, after we analyzed possible differences with respect to the occurence of LC in both referent groups.

Further the results are presented either in the form of chi-squares, corrected for 2 x 2 contingency tables, or as odds ratios 2.0. The odds ratio is an epidemiological measure, indicating the degree of association of a specific parameter with the illness in cases under scrutiny, as compared with referents (Miettinen, 1982). An odds ratio of 1.0 implies that there is no difference in degree of association. All corresponding chi-squares, corrected for 2 x 2 contingency tables, are significant at the .05 level, or less, one-sided (not shown here).

This cohort included 41 MI-patients, and 54 referents. As will be shown, the events in this age group provide us with a detailed image of the particular developmental course that may be conducive of MI in middle adulthood.

Exposure to Stressful Life Changes. In Table 1 the odds ratios are presented - with regard to exposure to LC in the

Table 1: Occurrence of Stressful Life Changes in Myocardial Infarction Patients, Aged 50-59.

A) Infancy, Youth, Adolescence

Event:	Odds Ratio:
Prolongued/Serious Conflicts in Family	2.21
Prolongued Unemployment of Head of Family	2.67
Prolongued Financial Problems in Family	2.02
Subject Having to Work while in School	2.31

B) Work & Career

Event:	Odds Ratio:
Prolongued Period(s) of Unemployment	3.59
Work Place(s) Closed Down	3.54
Prolongued/Serious Conflicts with Supervisor	2.72
Prolongued/Serious Conflicts with Subordinates	2.76

C) Family & Social Life

Event:	Odds Ratio:
Death/Divorce First Spouse	4.18
Getting Child(ren)	2.52
Prolongued/Serious Illness in Child(ren)	3.45
Death Child(ren)	2.60
Prolongued/Serious Educational Problems with Child(ren)	13.50
Prolongued/Serious Conflicts with Child(ren) (in Law), Living on Their Own	15.39
Prolongued/Serious Marital Conflicts	3.35
Prolongued/Serious Illness of Subject	3.03
Prolongued/Serious Conflicts with Family Member(s)	3.72
Prolongued/Serious Financial Problems	3.80

Number of MI-Patients: 41
Number of Referents: 54 (Neighbourhood and Hospital Combined)

developmental domains of (a) infancy, youth, andadolescence, of (b) work and career, and of (c) family and social life, respectively. It should be noted here that the first domain contains 12 events, the second one 16, and the last one 23.

In summary, we observe some particular developmental impediments when being a child or adolescent. Further, a pattern of probably chronic interactional problems with one's children is recognizable here, with additional threat- or loss-related events, like serious illness, or death of children. The rather problematic character of married life in MI-cases also appears to be obvious. With respect to working life it is apparent that unemployment and the closing down of the work place may constitute unequivocal developmental 'breaks' in psychosocial development. It should also be noted that a pattern of possibly chronic conflicts with colleagues may characterize the working life of patients.

Now, it should be noticed here that all results in the present section on particular developmental structures as yet cannot provide an insight into the temporal sequencing of LC over the life course. Also we cannot assess yet to what extent the reported events may be modified by Type A behavior.

These findings suggest, however, that a possible self-evoked, chronic struggling with conflictuous situations in family and working life may form a quintessential aspect of the life of middle-aged (Type A) heart patients.

Evaluation of Stressful Life Changes. Table 2 provides a different picture concerning the role of LC in the lives of MI-patients. Here all significant differences are presented in the manner of evaluating the reported events in the three developmental domains. More specifically, those figures pertain to the fact that cases have evaluated these events as predominantly of ambivalent character with respect to their psychosocial development, either shortly after event occurred (S), or as regarded from the different perspective of the time of inteviewing (L). It should be noted here that these re-sults on the ambivalence of experience are presented regard-less of the fact, whether the LC under study occurs more frequently in the life course of cases, or not.

As can be seen, the former suggestion of self-evoked, chronic struggling with life's chores is strongly reinforced by the findings on the ambivalent nature of specific LC. I.e. events that constitute novel aspects in youth, work, and family and social life, like e.g. coping with the exigencies of school life, or of beginning to work, with increased responsibility at work, with getting children, and later, with children leaving home, among other events, are invariably met with ambivalent emotional feelings, sometimes both shortly after the event occurred, as well as in retrospect. In the discus-sion section we will argue that such findings could be inter-preted as congruent with the notion that MI-patients perceive their personal environment as predominantly uncontrollable, in

Table 2: Ambivalence of Experience of Stressful Life Changes in Myocardial Infarction Patients, Aged 50-59.

A) Infancy, Youth, Adolescence

Event:	Chi-Square/p:	
Hospital Admission(s) of Subject (S)	4.80	.045
Coping with School Period of Subject (L)	5.74	.028

B) Work & Career

Event:	Chi-Square/p:	
Coping with Work Beginning (L)	4.71	.047
Searching after Other Job(s) of Own Accord (S)	5.69	.029
Compelled to Look for Other Job(s) (L)	5.90	.026
Increased Responsibility at Work (S)	7.61	.011

C) Family & Social Life

Event:	Chi-Square/p:	
Getting Child(ren) (S)	6.16	.023
Getting Child(ren) (L)	12.66	.000
Child(ren) Leaving Home (S)	8.31	.008
Child(ren) Leaving Home (L)	21.63	.000
Prolongued/Serious Illness of Subject (L)	5.96	.025
Prolongued Illness/Death of Family Member(s) (In Last 5 Yrs.) (S)	3.68	.027
Prolongued Illness/Death of Family Member(s) (In Last 5 Yrs.) (L)	4.43	.017
Moving (S)	4.05	.044
Spouse Having a Job (S)	13.96	.000
Effected Considerable Loan (L)	5.23	.037

Number of MI-Patients: 41
Number of Referents: 54 (Neighbourhood and Hospital Combined)

spite of their sometimes vigorous efforts, or in other words, that they habitually may experience a considerable discrepancy between their invested efforts in life and ensuing results.

When we summarize all findings concerning the life course of MI-patients, two aspects appear to be important. First, cases have been exposed to more LC in the course of their lives than same-aged referents. The differences in exposure between cohorts are substantial, however. That is, the largest discrepancies occur in the middle cohort, aged 50-59, where no less than 18 out of 51 events are reported more often by cases than by referents. Most of these LC are associated with developmental 'breaks', i.e. with events that may signify disruptions in the normative developmental pattern within a particular cohort. Also, most events appear only in this particular cohort.

In our opinion, these findings argue in favour of a rather unique life structure in different cohorts of MI-patients. In other words, we do not find here some universal psychosocial pathway conducive of MI, as is found in most (methodologically less sophisticated) retrospective investigations of this type (Rahe & Romo, 1974; Theorell, 1980).

A second aspect appears to be even more important to us. I.e. we do not only find that some LC, to which cases have been exposed significantly more frequent than referents, are also the ones that are evaluated as predominantly ambivalent. Rather, we observe that about half of the remaining non-discriminating events are evaluated as predominantly ambivalent with respect to subsequent psychosocial development in MI-patients. It should be noted here that events like attending school, beginning to work, or getting children, hardly can be expected to yield different prevalence rates in cases and referents. However, these events that usually mark the beginning of new psychosocial developmental sequences are nevertheless experienced rather different with respect to their emotional impact.

All these ambivalently evaluated LC can be said to deal with either novel, but rather expected events in psychosocial development (e.g. coping with school, with work beginning, with getting children, with children leaving home), or with rather unexpected changes that may induce profound adjustment with respect to psychosocial development (e.g. moving, unemployment, effecting a considerable loan, death of relatives or friends).

In this manner, then, the effects of these particular LC constitute an additional psychosocial burden in the lives of MI-patients.

As we observed before, such an overburdened life course in most instances is associated with manifestations of vital exhaustion and depression as a final common pathway in the months prior to infarction.

In the discussion section we will present briefly a concise
ontogenetic theoretical framework that will focus upon
perceived control over one's own life, as a central concept to
guide further interpretation of those findings.

DISCUSSION

The preliminary results from our study suggest that there
exists a synergistic interaction pattern between the Type A
coronary-prone behavior pattern, the occurrence and ambivalent
evaluation of LC over the life course, and the prodrome of
vital exhaustion and depression. This synergistic interaction
pattern that could result in dysfunctional behavior as such
may considerably enhance the risk for the development of
premature MI since it already has been demonstrated, that the
former constellations are associated, independently from each
other, with the onset of MI, and other manifestation of CHD
(Falger, 183b; Falger, Appels & Lulofs, 1983).

A highly relevant notion in this respect that may link dysfunctional behavior with respect to coping with LC to the
development of depression, is provided by the general concept
of learned helplessness (Abramson et al., 1978), and by the
further specifications for adult coronary-prone subjects
(Glass & Carver, 1980). As we discussed elsewhere (Falger &
Appels, 1982), the former concept states that depression is
the outcome of specific learning processes in interpersonal
development that are characterized by a considerable discrepancy between invested efforts and ensuing results. One of the
core aspects of the Type A coronary-prone behavior pattern,
i.e. the dimension of situationally determined, perceived
controllability is particular relevant in this respect
(Matthews, 1982).

From the laboratory experiments by Glass (1977) it can be
concluded that a learned and probably lasting inability to
respond properly to a personal environment that is perceived
as predominantly uncontrollable may account for this peculiar
feature. According to these experiments, a subject exhibiting
the Type A coronary-prone behavior pattern will be striving
hard for control over his personal environment. Challenging
exigencies from this environment, in particular when these
incentives provide an opportunity for competition, or for
enchancing control, will initially be met with a hyperreactive
response pattern that is anchored in psychological arousal,
that could set highly complex regulatory systems in motions
that are conducive to cardiac malfunctioning (Eliot, 1977;
Sterling & Eyer, 1981). However, when such efforts fail
eventually, in spite of prolonged striving for control, a
hyporeactive phase may emerge. In this peculiarly vulnerable
state, that also can be described as such from a psychophysiological and neurohormonal regulatory point of view (Sterling &
Eyer, 1981), a subject may no longer be capable of performing
adequately, and may hence begin to develop manifestations of

vital exhaustion and depression. It is conceivable, now, that the ambivalent evaluation with respect to noveL LC, and to LC that may require profound adaptation, that were demonstrated unequivocally in the life courses of the MI-patients under study, could considerably enhance the emergence of a cyclic sequence of hyperreactivity, in order to grasp control over novel situations induced by LC, and hyporeactivity, when efforts to control are failing, sometimes after extensive trying (cf. the chronic character of many reported events).

Another line of reasoning, linking the occurrence of LC to learned helplessness and depression, should be mentioned here to reinforce the previous arguing. As we demonstrated in some studies on cognitive characteristics of LC and subsequent depression (Fairbank & Houh, 1979; Silver & Wortman, 1980; Hamen & Mayol, 1982), it is particularly LC that are perceived as relatively controllable, internally caused, intended, and likely to reoccur that appear to be most conducive to depression. This tendency is clearly apparent in the LC from the family and social life domain, that receives most emphasis in MI-patients. In could be argued, now, that MI-patients, who lack emotional support in their daily familial environment (Cobb, 1976; Berkman, 1982), for which lack they feel to be held responsible themselves, cannot cope adequately any more with the additional stressful burden of working life, when LC associated with this domain may constitute a severe disruption in psychosocial development, as we observed in our coronary cases. This peculiar constellation of lack of emotional support, and overburdening by events that are perceived as controllable, but occur to be uncontrollable could lead, then, to vital exhaustion and depression, and finally to premature MI (or sudden cardiac death).

NOTE

All data were compiled, and all statistics were programmed (SPSS) and computed by Jos Bekkers, student-assistent to this research project.

SELF-AWARENESS AND COPING STYLE:
DIFFERENTIAL EFFECTS OF MILD PHYSICAL EXERCISE

Jürgen Otto

Johannes Gutenberg-University, Mainz, Federal Republic of Germany

It is generally acknowledged in the major conceptualizations of coping that in dealing with a stressful situation the individual is confronted by a dual-task. The person has to deal with the external demand and has to take instrumental actions and at the same time s/he has to deal with the motivations and different emotions that occur during this transaction. Examing the most prominent self-report techniques for the assessment of mood, arousal, and somatic perception (Mackay, 1980), it is obvious that a general activation factor is predominant in the naive or subjective conceptualizations of internal states. Activation seems to be both an empirical physiological concept as well as a phenomenological concept in which the physiological processes are integrated into feeling states like alertness, exertion, energy, enthusiasm and so on. Mood seems to emcompass a much broader realm of behavior and is not so easy to manipulate experimentally as activation. Somatic perception is a too narrow concept to use in any investigation with relevance to goal-directed behavior. Using activation concepts as a first approach to the study of self-awareness one has to select between the various one-, two-, or multidimensional models offered. At least a two-dimensional model like the one developed by Thayer (1978) out of Nowlis's pioneering research allows to think of discrepancies between the different levels of behavior (self-report level, physiological level) not only as measurement artifacts but as valid diagnostic information. In Thayer's multidimensional activation model which is based on second-order factor analytic techniques two separate but interdependent activation dimensions were postulated: Energetic arousal and tension arousal (also activation dimension A and B). Energetic arousal consists out of the two first-order factors 'general activation' and 'deactivation-sleep'. Tension arousal groups the first-order factors 'high activation' and 'general deactivation' together. He summarized his theory: "Therefore, at present it appears that four seperate activation factors may be identified, and that these factors generally, but not always, act as two reciprocal pairs". (Thayer, 1978, p.6).

In general an elaborated theory about the transaction of physiological processes with the self-report level of behavior is missing. Such a theory must capture topics like organismic

sensitivity, learning experiences, cognitive schemes, transfer
into linguistic concepts, social factors influencing the

report like social desirability, idiosyncratic meaning of
expressions and so on. The reported experiment can only be a
first, simple attempt to follow these lines of thought. Due
to the relevance of the self-report of activation for other
behaviors and experiences it seems worthwhile to start with an
experimental manipulation of this important psychological
factor. Continuing recent research of Thayer on the
Activation-Deactivation Adjective Check List (AD ACL) exercise
on a treadmill (ergometer) seems to be a suitable mean to
manipulate the activation/arousal factor which has shown
intriguing results.

Typically he used not the traditional single-occasion
nomothetic laboratory design but a short-term longitudinal
experiment, involving repeated measurements (Thayer, in press
b). Multiple measurements seem to be a good example of the
principle that aggregation of data increases the stability of
summed scores because it averages out error sources present in
any one measurement (Rushton et al., 1983). Using this
approach (Thayer, in press b) the effects of a 10-minute rapid
walk are perhaps the most striking of this whole experiment.
This relatively small amount of moderate exercise led to
significantly increased energy and decreased tension for as
long as two hours after the activity. Other research (e.g.
Morgan et al., 1971) in this area which has shown no effects
of physical exercise had typically used unusual high exertion,
inappropriate psychometric instruments and only single-
occasion measurement.

At the same time it was attempted to supplement this general
approach with a differential perspective, i.e. the assessment
of personality variables relevant to coping styles. It is
expected that people differ greatly in their sensitivity to
bodily changes and their willingness to become aware and
conscious of these changes. Due to the different meaning of
this internal information for individuals these should develop
habits to rely on this information or disregard it in their
normal course of action and consequently report more or less
of it if asked to do so. They have a different self-awareness
(Carver & Scheier, 1981). Especially so called sensitizers
are known to overestimate these internal changes whereas on
the other extreme repressers are known to deny these processes
and not to speak about them (Weinberger et al., 1979).
Therefore the purposes of our study were to:

(1)   Investigate the effects of exercise on the self-report
      of energetic and tension arousal (Thayer, in press a).
(2)   Use a treadmill as a naturalistic equivalence to
      everyday walking to manipulate the amount of exercise
      (DeVries, 1980).
(3)   Conduct a longitudinal assessment of the effects (10
      times every 10 minutes) with a short-form of the AD ACL
      following ipsative-normative approaches (Lazarus &

DeLongis, 1983).
(4)   Keep a differential perspective by taking into account
        coping styles, which were identified by the combined use

        of the classic State-Trait Anxiety Inventory
        (Spielberger et al., 1970) and the Marlowe-Crowne Scale
        (Crowne & Marlowe, 1964) (cp. Asendorpf et al., 1983;
        Weinberger et al., 1979).
(5)   To assess - besides the self-report level - other levels
        of behavior. Physiological measures were taken in the
        cardiovascular and electrodermal system, different
        behavior orientations like Averill et al. (1977) were
        offered and special concern was given to the attention
        deployment (Monat 1976).

METHOD

<u>Procedure</u>. 40 subjects (Mean age: 21, SD = 5.78) were
recruited from introductory psychology classes in spring 1983
and received two credit hours which they needed as part of the
course requirements. They were assigned to a 2 x 10 experimental plan. The between subject factor included the experimental and control condition; the within subject factor consisted of the 10 repeated measurements of the self-report and
physiological variables. Measurements were conducted every 10
minutes. From the first four measurements the base-line
values were taken. The personality questionnaires were
answered during the first 20 minutes of the experiment after
the initial instructions. Only the Attention-Deployment Scale
was administered at the end of the experiment after two hours.

To control for base-line effects and the expectations which
might have been caused by an initial assignment to the control
or experimental group the following instructions and
assignment procedure were used.

INSTRUCTIONS

Thank you for coming and serving as an experimental
subject. You will participate now in a
psychophysiological experiment which will last two
hours. At the end you will receive two credit slips.

Psychophysiology is concerned with the interaction of
physiological systems and the conscious level of
behavior. Therefore, it is essential for our experiment
to measure both the physiological level of behavior and
the conscious or self-report level of behavior during
the next two hours.

The physiological level is assessed by these electrodes.
This one has a special light bulb in it. This light is
absorbed by the blood in your fingertip. With every

heartbeat the blood in the fingertip changes.   So using
the different absorption I can monitor your heartbeat on
a polygraph in the next room.   These other ones measure

the   electrical   properties of your   skin.   These
properties change when the nerves in the skin become
innervated.   In   this way I can monitor your nervous
activity.   Both electrodes are designed in such a way
that no electrical shock can occur to you.   They go on
your nonwriting hand, which you should rest in a
comfortable manner on this foam rubber pad, and move as
little as possible during the whole experiment.

For the self-report level we have designed this short
checklist.   You have to answer it 10 times during the
next two hours.   The checklists are numbered and I will
announce the number to be taken over the intercom to
you.   These checklists can pick up even subtle mood
changes and are to be answered quickly, but very
carefully every time.   The large number of checklists is
necessary to calculate reliable correlations with the
physiological measures.   So we must get a minimal number
of measurements.

Also to compare different persons on their   psychophysiological measures it is necessary to establish comparable baselines for our subjects. People who had done
different things before should come to the same resting
levels in order to compare their measures.   In fact,
these baselines will determine if you will be assigned
to the control or the experimental group.   Even I do
not know now to which group you will be assigned. If you
happen to be in the experimental group we will ask you
to take an exercise on this treadmill.   Therefore
please read this attached release sheet and sign it.

To start now I will attach the electrodes and go to the
adjacent room to monitor the equipment. If you have any
questions just talk to me, I can hear you over the
intercom.   You can read these instructions again or
start with answering these questionnaires which assess
habits or attitudes that are known to be relevant to the
field   of   psychophysiological   and   self-report
correlation.   When you have finished the questionnaires
I will bring you some textbooks, newspapers, and audio
cassettes with lectures or music which you can enjoy so
that the situation is not too monotoneous for you.
After 30 minutes we will have measures of the base-line
and I will come in and tell you to which experimental
group you have been assigned.

Do   you have any procedural questions at this point
concerning the experiment?

Experimental condition only:

Due to your base-line you are assigned to the experimental group just because the subject before you who was in the category was a control. So we will ask you to walk on this treadmill at a rapid and brisk pace. Because all people have different leg length the right speed is somewhere between 2.5 and 3.5 mph. Please help us to set the right speed. When you step on here put both your hands on the railing. Later you can use one hand or no hand at all. I will speed the tread-mill up to a speed which is a brisk walk for you. After 3 minutes I will return and we can make another adjustment if necessary. This clock runs for ten minutes and it will show you how much time you have to go.

Control condition only:

Due to your base-line you are assigned to the control group just because the subject before you who was in this category was an experimental. We ask you to go on with the activities that you are doing for the rest of the experiment. Answer the checklist every time it is announced over the intercom.

The subjects were informed about the importance of comparing equal base-lines in psychophysiological research and all had to sign the release sheet for the exercise in the beginning to equalize the expectations. Then their assignment depended on the actual values reached during the base-line period. In order to control for different self-report base-lines of energetic arousal in addition to time and gender the following logic was employed: We used four base-line categories taking the mean of measurement three and four on this variable: (The control of base-line effects became first priority before the balancing of gender influences, followed by the time of day.) The first subject is an experimental one in any category. The second subject in the same category is a control subject as is the second subject in a new category. The third subject is another one than the last entry or an experimental one and so on.

To find a real equivalent for a brisk and rapid walk for the subjects, each subject's speed of walking was determined indi-vidually within a certain general range of 2.5 to 3.5 mph. As it is reflected in the instructions for the experimental group in the beginning the speed was set at 2.5 mph and after three minutes the subject was asked for his personal adjustment and cooperation to achieve a quick and rapid walk. The mean speed chosen was 2.8 mph (SD = 0.37).To cancel suggestion effects the adjectives of the checklist were never used to describe the desired walking speed. The experiments took place in two adjacent laboratory rooms in March and April of 1983 (Fig.1).

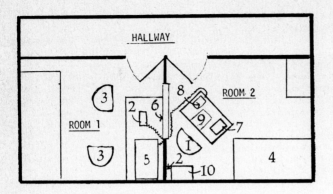

1 Subject
2 Intercom
3 Experimenter
4 Treadmill
5 Polygraph
6 One-way mirror
7 Tape recorder
8 Foam pad
9 Instructions
10 Books, tapes, newspaper

Figure 1: Scheme of laboratory rooms

Instructions and questionnaires.   The initial instructions stressed the importance of the repetitive self-report measurements and made the subject familiar with the physiological recording.

After that a self-constructed survey of morning behavior and exercise practice attempted to scan such topics as sleep, food, medication, sports, and stress to provide some information about possible erroneous influences. Then the trait form of the State-Trait Anxiety Inventory (Spielberger et al., 1970) (STAI) (alpha coefficients from .90 - .89) and the Marlowe-Crowne Social-Desirability Scale (Crowne & Marlowe, 1964)(M-C S-DS) (Internal consistency coefficient = .88) were administered, both well established, valid questionnaires. After that the first Activation-Deactivation Adjective Check List (AD ACL) is applied. For numerous repetitive measurements we used a short-form of the AD ACL containing only the most discriminating eight adjectives: Energetic arousal is described by the adjectives "energetic", "drowsy", "tired", and "vigorous". In this way we used the proposed dimensionality of the seperate activation dimensions of "General Activation" and "Deactivation-Sleep" (Thayer, 1978). Tension arousal is represented by "quiet", "still", "tense", and "jittery".   Only the two latter adjectives were scored for this dimension. The 10 AD ACLs for each subject were numbered, the number to be filled in was announced to the subject over the intercom.

At the end of the whole experiment cognitive coping was measured with an Attention-Deployment Scale (A-DS) (containing six statements) which asked subjects the amount of time (from "not at all" (1) to "very frequently" (5)) they devoted to thinking about the experiment and its implications ("vigilance") or other events, such as exams or dates ("avoidance"). A composite attention-deployment score for each one-third of the experiment was obtained by subtracting the mean rating of time spent on the three vigilant thoughts. The final scores could range from -4 (relatively more time in avoidant thoughts) to +4 (relatively more time in vigilant thoughts) (Monat 1976).

Instrumentation. The treadmill was manufactured by "MD Electronics" (Burbank, CA.) and was used with zero per cent incline. The walkband was 50 inches by 14 inches wide. A railing, a clock, and a speedometer were in front of the subject. The speed was set at 2.5 mph (or 4 km/h) as an equivalent for a brisk walk (DeVries, 1980).

The physiological reactions of the subject were recorded on a four-channel Beckman R511A polygraph which was in the adjacent room. The rooms were lighted, air-conditioned and provided a constant temperature of 72 F (or 23 C). The non-writing hand of the subject was rested on a foam rubber pad on the desk in a way that the main hand was supported and that the fingers were free and not touching the table with any electrode. The electrodes and the phototransducer were taken off during the exercise.

The measurements of the physiological reactions were taken during the last 30 seconds before any AD ACL was announced over the intercom (Thayer, 1971). The physiological measures immediately after the completion of a checklist were sampled but not further analyzed. The mean of the first four measurements served as a base-line score. The pulse volume amplitude (PVA) and the heart rate (HR) were measured using a photocell on the third fingertip connected to a Beckman type 9853A coupler. The mean deflection of a 30 second interval was used as basic data. Since no comparisons of absolute values are possible on this measure the mean of the first three measurements was used as the common reference - or 100%-level. Longer or shorter reference levels show no different results. From the same recording heart rate (HR) was derived on a real time base (Martin & Venables, 1980). For each 30 second interval the number of R-spikes were counted and used as basic data. Using the distal phalanx of the second and fourth finger the skin conductance level (SCL) was measured in a constant voltage mode (0.5 v) using a Beckman type 9842 coupler. Before the area electrodes (Lafayette No. 76602 with adjustable elastic bands) were applied the skin was cleaned with isopropyl alcohol and treated with Beckman conductive electrolyte. The mean of each 30 second interval in S was used as raw data. The data showed polarization effects and were disregarded in further analyses.

Behavior observation. Following the approach from Averill et

al. (1977) any interest in available textbooks or the taped
lectures provided was scored as "vigilant orientation" whereas
reading the newspaper or listening to music tapes was scored
as "nonvigilant orientation". As a composite score the
dominant orientation was sampled for each subject.

To counteract an activating contrast effect of doing nothing
during a base-line period and the activities allowed,
especially for the control group which would have had to wait
10 minutes longer than the experimental group, all subjects
were allowed to engage in the activities immediately after
they finished the questionnaires. Therefore no "pure" base-
line was used but instead the various activities were used as
a background against which the exercise effect was compared.

RESULTS

All physiological and self-report data were checked for the
law of initial values. Also this "law" is disputable (Levey,
1980, p. 617/618). In no case was the correlation
sufficiently large enough to warrant covariance or other more
complex modes of analysis.

General effects. For the self-report of energetic arousal
there was an elevation for the experimental group up to 10
maybe 30 minutes after the exercise whereas during the base-
line period the values for the experimental and control group
were not significantly different. The between factor of an
ANOVA for repeated measures was not significant, the within
factor (for measurements five to 10) was significant, $F(5/38)$
= 4.48, $p < .01$ as well as the interaction, $F(5/38) = 4.38$,
$p < .01$. Single t-tests for the data immediately after the
exercise, $t(38) = 3.44$, $p < .001$ (all one-tailed) and after 10
minutes, $t(38) = 1.94$, $p < .05$ as well as after 30 minutes,
$t(38) = 1.44$, $p < .10$ showed the effect of mild exercise as it
is depicted in figure 2. The a priori assumption of
independence was questionable in these t-tests and similar
groups of t-tests described below. In these cases, the
analyses were of points on what is essentially a continuous
cognitive or physiological process. If these comparisons were
independent an adjusted alpha level should be used. In any
way, curve fitting seemed to be a more suitable statistical
method. Using linear and quadratic components the regression
equation for the experimental group was $y = 14.5 - 1.73x +
0.113x^2$ and for the control group $y = 10.4 - 0.0575x + 0.0054x^2$
for measurement 5 to 10 after the exercise. The different
level of the curves as well as the practical and statistical
importance of the negative linear component for the
experimental group $(t(3) = -3.69$, $p < .05)$ became obvious.
95.5% of variance was explained by this fit. This fit mirrors
the decay (trend) of energetic activation after the treatment.

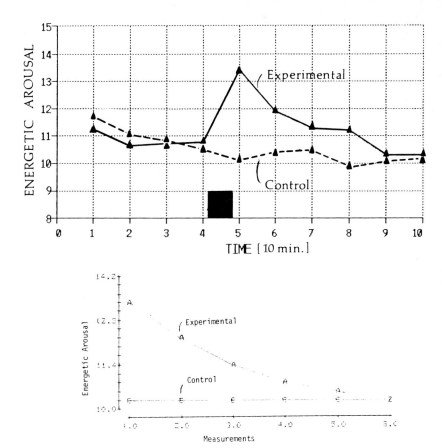

Figure 2: Self-report of energetic arousal
            (Upper graph: Actual Means;
            Lower graph: Predicted Means)

J. Otto

For the self-report of tension arousal there was a significant difference between the experimental and control group on the last measurement, $t(38) = 2.18$, $p < 0.5$ (two-tailed). At the end of the experiment the control group showed more tension.

The heart rate data showed no significant difference between the groups. Also there was a steady decline over the two hours of the experiment from 73.1 bpm (SD = 11) to 68 bpm (SD = 10). This was reflected in a significant within factor, $F(5/38) = 3.51$, $p < .05$. The pulse volume amplitude was significantly higher for the experimental group up to 40 minutes after the exercise whereas on the fourth measurement the values for the experimental and control group were not significantly different. The between factor, $F(1/38) = 4.45$, $p < .05$ as well as the within factor, $F(5/38) = 3.62$, $p < .01$ became significant. Single t-tests for the data immediately after the exercise, $t(38) = 1.67$, $p < .10$ (all one-tailed), after 10 minutes, $t(38) = 2.57$, $p < .01$, after 20 minutes, $t(38) = 1.79$, $p < .05$, after 30 minutes, $t(38) = 1.53$, $p < .10$, and after 40 minutes, $t(38) = 1.75$, $p < .05$ showed the exercise effect as it is depicted in Figure 3. The regression equation for the experimental group was $y = 104 + 10.5x - 2.35x^2$ ($R^2 = 91.8\%$) and for the control group $y = 84.8 - 0.12x - 0.562x^2$ ($R^2 = 96.3\%$). The higher level of the experimental group was evident as well as the practical and statistical importance of the negative quadratic component ($t(3) = -2.91$, $p < .10$) which reflected the decrease of the finger pulse amplitude after the exercise.

Differential Effects. Using the classical State-Trait Anxiety Inventory and the Marlowe-Crowne Scale sensitizers were defined as above the median on the anxiety scale and below the median on the social desirability scale. Repressers were defined according to these questionnaires as below the median on the anxiety scale and above it on the social desirability scale (Asendorpf et al., 1983; Weinberger et al., 1979). Whereas there were no differential effects (i.e. comparing the experimental or control group for either repressers or sensitizers) for heart rate, pulse volume amplitude, or the self-report of tension arousal there was a differential effect for the self-report of energetic arousal. Figure 4 showed this effect for the groups of subjects according to the classic personality tests. As a reference level the scores of the "normal" group (low on anxiety and social desirability) are also shown.

Only for the sensitizers there was a significant effect immediately after the exercise, $t(10) = 3.8$, $p < .01$ (all tests two-tailed), after 10 minutes, $t(10) = 4.02$, $p < .01$, and after 20 minutes, $t(10) = 2.4$, $p < .05$. The regression equation for the repressers was $y = 15.5 - 2.67x + 0.313x^2$ ($R^2 = 88\%$), for the sensitizers $y = 14.6 - 0.387x - 0.786x^2$ ($R^2 = 96.7\%$) and for the nonspecific defenders $y = 14.4 - 1.58x + 0.143x^2$ ($R^2 = 95.6\%$). All groups had nearly the same level whereas the curves were strikingly different. The group of nonspecific defenders showed a significant negative linear

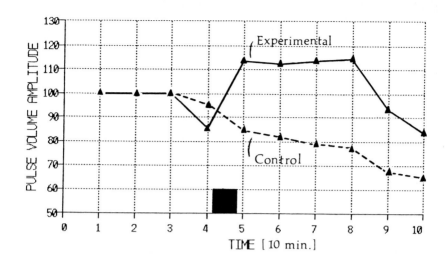

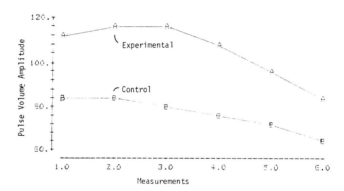

Figure 3: Pulse Volume Amplitude
(Upper graph: Actual Means;
Lower graph: Predicted Means)

J. Otto

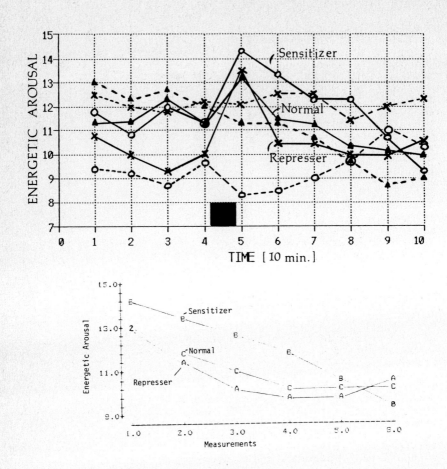

Figure 4: Coping Style and Self-Report
(Upper graph: Actual Means;
Lower graph: Predicted Means)

component (t(3) = -4.23, p < .05) similar to the general exercise effect which became obvious in this negative trend and decay of energetic arousal. No coefficient was of statistical significance or practical importance for the sensitizers. Their self-report showed no trend. They maintained the same undifferentiated high level throughout the experiment. The repressers instead showed not only a significant negative linear component (t(3) = -3.84, p < .05) which was similar in direction to the one by the nonspecific defenders, but statistically different from it (t(7) = 2.85, p < .05), but additionally a significant quadratic component, (t(3) = 3.21, p < .05) which indicated a change in the downward linear trend: Another factor's influence which is responsible for the rapid decay immediately after the exercise.

Also there are as less as five subjects in the different groups no systematic influence of gender, time of day, energetic arousal base-line, attention deployment, behavioral orientation or actual walking speed was obvious.

DISCUSSION

The effect of mild exercise (10 minute brisk walk) found in this study showed itself in a reported increase in feelings of energetic arousal up to 30 minutes later which was paralleled by pulse volume changes which also started to decay after 30 minutes. The absence of any effect on heart rate or tension arousal due to exercise might have been due to the mild, nonthreatening kind of exercise and the dominantly thermoregulatory functions of the peripheral blood flow involved as it was reported in Bevegard & Shepherd, 1967 (p. 181); Obrist, 1976, 1981(p. 32). Perhaps a feeling of warmth, readiness and relaxation was the connecting link in self-awareness between the physiological and psychological effect of mild exercise as it is a central part of Jacobsen's relaxation technique employed in systematic desensitization in Behavior Therapy. This effect of increased vigor and less tension and fatigue can last as it was reported by Blumenthal et al. (1982) for a group of healthy middle-aged adults after a 10-week program of regular walking-jogging. The finding of a constant heart rate could have been a measurement artifact. The fifth measurement took place 2-3 minutes after the exercise since the subjects had to step off the treadmill, get hooked up on the electrodes again and had to be instructed again. It might have been that the cardiovascular system, which is highly overregulated, responded too fast to the treadmill exercise, so that this variable showed no longer an effect after 2-3 minutes.

The concept of demand might be another possible competing explanation for the reported results. But in our experience with studies in which large numbers of AD ACLs were completed over time, each test completion soon became a more or less automatic activity in which little thought is given to the overall purpose of the experiment. In an excellent analysis of this possible error, Berkowitz & Donnerstein (1982) have made the point that there is relatively little evidence of a consistent expectation effect. Moreover, they argue logically and with empirical data that even if subjects are aware of the purpose of an experiment there is no reason to believe that they would necessarily provide confirmatory results.

Although the general effect of this experiment was uncontroversial its differential outlook was quite intriguing. As a differential variable coping style was identified. The general elevation of the self-report of energetic arousal is actually the "mean" of a wide continuum of experiences from total neglect to nearly oversensitivity. Both seem to be a purely psychological effect, since not any physiological changes measured in this experiment could be the base for these individual differences. Also it could not be the usual correlation one has to expect between different paper and pencil tests (method variance) since for repressers it was missing. Cognitive expectancies and appraisals seemed to be predominant. Different levels of self-awareness were involved (Carver & Scheier, 1981). For extreme cases of coping styles in a situation in which there is a certain degree of ambiguity of its impact for the individual, the great variety of subjective experiences corresponding to these coping styles were shown: From virtual neglect of any feeling at all to an oversensitive monitoring of "changes" up to 20 minutes. Probable reasons for the repressers not to report energetic arousal might have been the denial or trivialization of the experimental impact itself as it was clearly shown in a semester trend. In this way the results of the Attention-Deployment Scale were discerning. The relatively high self-report of energetic arousal of the repressers in the control condition might have been due to their heightened attention deployment to the probable purpose of the experiment compared to their experimental counterparts, $t(10) = 2.6$, $p < .05$. Or the repressing of conflicting motivation might have been the cause for their denial: After the exercise many subjects reported feelings of energy and the wish "to act it out" which was opposing the demand to remain seated during the rest of the experiment. Since an experimental situation is often non repetitive for the subject and a direct action is seldomly possible the benefits of denial may outweigh its cost in this case (Lazarus, 1983).

While an objective classification of experimental tasks is missing (Hackman, 1970) the introduction of some activities as a background to compare the experimental task with had certain advantages over a control group doing "nothing". But the control was still more tense at the end of the experiment. And certain activities seemed not to include the circle of anticipation- preparation- confrontation- feedback- relaxation that is associated with a real task. So a faked task would have been preferrable to just some activities. Using a faked task the control group would have been no longer distracted by interfering thoughts about the purpose of the experiment with which they had to cope, especially when they were repressers.

SUMMARY

Using a multidimensional model of activation (arousal) (Thayer, 1978, in press a) the long term effect of mild exercise (10 minute treadmill walk) was investigated. Additionally the habitual coping style and self-awareness of the subjects were assessed using a questionnaire technique. N = 40 male and female introductory psychology students served as subjects. The session for each subject lasted two hours with measures taken every 10 minutes on the self-report dimensions of the Activation-Deactivation Adjective Check-List and physiological indicators such as heart rate, pulse volume amplitude, and skin conductance level. The results showed a general exercise effect for a time period up to 30 minutes after the exercise: The self-report of energetic arousal as well as the pulse volume amplitude were significantly elevated for the experimental group. A differential analysis provided further insight into this phenomenon: Also there were no differences on the physiological level of arousal repressers and sensitizers displayed significant different verbal reports stressing the importance of the underlying self-awareness and cognitive appraisals. Whereas extreme repressers spoke of no feelings at all, sensitizers reported an "effect" for 20 minutes.

NOTE

I like to thank Bob Thayer for his support and helpful comments during this research.

The Self in Anxiety, Stress and Depression
R. Schwarzer (Editor)
© Elsevier Science Publishers B.V. (North-Holland), 1984

THEMATIC CONTENTS OF DEPRESSIVE COGNITIONS IN THE ELDERLY

Prem S. Fry

The University of Calgary, Calgary, Alberta, Canada

As noted by Hollan (1981), cognitive mechanisms of change are those cognitive processes presumed to be central to the change process. Hollan concludes that relevant cognitive mechanisms are specified by a given cognitive theory; for example the goal of an intervention inspired by Seligman's learned helplessness theory (1975) might be to alter the cognitions of noncontingency; the goal of Bandura's self-efficacy approach (Bandura 1977) would be to alter cognitions of negative self-evaluations and to improve expectations of self-efficacy through imagery treatment; and the goal of Lewinsohn's approach (Lewinsohn, 1974) might be to increase the rate of response-contingent reinforcement. In any of these instances, the ultimate goal involves reduction in depression in the elderly, and this latter goal can be viewed as the major outcome of interest in this chapter. Each of the many cognitive mechanisms implicated for therapy involves conveying a new perspective to the client which will lead to a new conceptualization of the problem and which will become a reminder to use the coping skills that (s)he has learned and thus to enhance a sense of personal control. The essential question always is as to whether cognitive manipulations are able to alter cognitive processes which must precede any change in depression. As noted by Hollan (1981) and Bandura (1977) any efforts to evaluate the efficacy of specific cognitive processes in reducing depression are frequently confounded by the overlap between various cognitive mechanisms and procedures used to produce change. Description of cognitive strategies to produce change in unadaptive cognitions involve multiple self-referent and management procedures. The lack of evidence for which set of negative cognitions, negative self-referent statements, or negative perspectives about the present or future would produce the greatest depression (and therefore ought to be brought under greater personal control) has led many authors (see Crits-Christoph & Singer, 1981; Fry, in press; Fry & Trifiletti, in press; Hollan 1981; Zeiss, Lewinsohn, & Munoz, 1979) to conclude that depression is the product of nonspecific cognitive processes. To what extent can the various cognitive or cognitive-behavioral mechanisms or processes be said to be effective in the amelioration of depression in the elderly ? This chapter examines the research and application of various cognitive-behavioral manipulations which have been found to be conceptually important in the reduction of depression in subclinical samples of the elderly. Particular attention will be directed towards attempts to integrate these cognitive approaches with major classes of cognitive theory based on (a) Beck's (1976) model of the cognitive triad in depression; (b) Seligman's (1981) reformulated model of learned helplessness in depression; and (c) Bandura's (1977) model of self-efficacy as related to depression management.

While it is not clear that such efforts at integration have been hitherto achieved by investigators who have been employing cognitive approaches in the treatment of depression in the depressed elderly, there is some small evidence, at least, that the work has already begun. For purposes of this chapter, the present discussion will focus on the elderly's cognitions of hopelessness, self-blame, guilt and helplessness, their cognitive appraisals of life stress and their perceptions of cognitive failure. An attempt will subsequently be made to show how all these factors are rooted in a cognitive theory and therapy of depression in the elderly, as differentiated from psychodynamic behavioral theories of depression.

As noted by several authors (e.g., Dessonville, Gallagher, Thompson, Finell, & Lewinsohn, 1981; Gallagher & Thompson, 1982; Gallagher & Thompson, 1983; Steuer & Hammen, 1983) the decade has seen a sharp increase in the number of published articles describing cognitive-behavioral interventions in the treatment of depression in the elderly. The impetus for the present chapter arose partially in response to this enormous interest to examine the elderly's depressive cognitions and to see how their cognitive appraisals, attributions and cognitive failures correlate with environmental and personality factors to serve as mediators of depression in the elderly. As noted by Beck (1976) the study of cognitive factors in depression has led to the belief that the etiology and maintenance of the clinical syndrome are, at least in part, a consequence of maladaptive thinking styles and negative self-statements. Investigations of thinking styles and personal constructs are beginning to focus increasingly on specifications of thinking distortions, and irrationality in self-referent statements (Kendall & Korgeski, 1979). However, as the small number of assessment measures reported in the gerontological literature indicates, assessment of cognitive variables and cognitive mechanisms underlying change is not well advanced, and evidence for this is sparce (Gallagher & Thompson, 1983).

The study of these cognitive variables with respect to depression in the elderly has also made an impact on therapy and treatment of depression. In therapy there is a renewed emphasis on teaching the elderly strategies for acquiring cognitive control and positive self-evaluations. Some previous studies of the present author (see Fry, 1982; Fry, 1983 (a); (b); Fry, in press; Fry & Grover, 1982; Fry & Leahey, in press; Fry & Trifiletti, in press) have demonstrated that the elderly's cognitions of hopelessness, external control, dependency, self-blame, and self-criticism are clearly implicated in the elderly's cognitions of depression. Following a brief review of the methodology and results of these studies there will be a further discussion of these variables which are assumed to be mediators of depression in the elderly. At first, however, it is important to examine the meaning of these various categories of cognitions and the related cognitive distortions which may occur to impair the person-environment interactions of the elderly. While evidence is accumulating to support the need for restoring efficacy, independence and self-concept, the data base for the cognitive formulations is surprisingly limited (Sutton-Simon & Goldfried, 1979, pp. 193-194). The corollary assumption that mediational problems lead to maladaptive cognitive and behavioral responses in the elderly has been examined from a variety of perspectives in my own exploratory research (e.g., Fry, 1983 (a); Fry, in press; Fry & Grover, 1982; Fry & Trifiletti, in press).

ISSUES ADDRESSED IN THE RESEARCH

A number of important conceptual and methodological questions have been addressed in some of the present author's studies with the depressed elderly. Chief among these are sample homogeneity and thematic contents of the depressive cognitions of the elderly, with some explanations of methodology used and interpretation of results obtained in the specific classes of cognitions examined.

SAMPLE HOMOGENEITY

While the present author's studies provide only beginning indications of the relationship between faulty thinking patterns and maladaptive emotional reactions or affects in the elderly, they have a definite application for larger samples of the elderly in that the data were based on nonpsychiatric populations drawn from community settings, rather than small populations typically encountered in institutionalized and/or clinical settings. Thus, descriptions of both functional and dysfunctional cognitions in the elderly were based upon interviews conducted with non-psychiatric, subclinical subjects unselected for the severity of depression and cognitive distortions. In a majority of cases, subjects were between the ages of 65 and 78 years and were living independently, or with their families. In order to be included in these investigations of cognitive assessment, subjects were required to have little evidence of acute confusional states, uncontrolled seizure disorders, uncontrolled cardiac difficulties or dementia. All subjects had to be willing participants in the different studies and were not under any observable pressure of family or friends to become involved. Thus, the objective in assessing cognitions of these particular nonclinical samples was twofold. First, to study the

presence or absence of faulty thinking and beliefs in unadap-
tively coping individuals, and secondly to suggest treatment
procedures or guidelines that could alter the faulty cognitions. Specifically, these exploratory studies have sought to
determine the extent to which faulty thinking patterns or
cognitive distortions are differentially associated with two
forms of depression assessments: depression as assessed by
geriatric depression scales (see, for example, Brink,
Yesavage, Lum, Heerseema, Adey & Rose, 1982; Geriatric Scale
of Depression) and by ratings of behavioral depression conducted by family members, and friends of the depressed elderly.

THEMATIC CONTENTS OF COGNITIONS IN THE ELDERLY

The types of cognitions studied are outlined below and were
reported by the depressed elderly to occur under a number of
general conditions.   Consistent with Beck's (1963) formulations, the term cognition, as used in this chapter, refers to
specific thoughts and interpretations including statements of
self-command, self-criticism, self-appraisals and cognitive
failure.   The contents of depressive cognitions in which the
elderly were asked to respond to particular types of stimulus
situations and subjects were expected to respond within the
context of certain thematic contents.   Secondly, typical
depressive cognitions were also observed in client's ruminations and reminiscences (see e.g., Fry, 1983(a)) when the
subjects were engaging in free association and reacting to
general environmental stimuli. Thus the research reported here
deals not mereley with the elderly's episodic cognitions of
hopelessness, self-criticism and self-blame, self-appraisals
and self-commands.   These cognitions were assessed   in
situations where the clients had no logical or plausible bases
for harbouring such cognitions or self-ratings but were
showing "schema-based" or relatively stable response patterns
in a variety of situations (Beck, & Rush, 1978; Beck, Rush,
Shaw, & Emery, 1979). Thus, for purposes of this chapter, it
is proposed that the studies reported here include both
classes of elderly depressives, those who showed schema-based
responding and those who were responding more veridically to
environmental information.   Specific classes of cognitions
examined for thematic contents were as follows:

1. Cognitions of Hopelessness in the Elderly. The relationship between hopelessness and depression has been the focus of
several studies in adults (Beck, 1972; Melges & Bowlby, 1969;
Beck, Weissman, Lester, & Trexler, 1974) but any systematic
attempt to assess cognitive themes or patterns of hopelessness
in geriatric samples is not evident in the existing gerontological literature or research. Recently, however, an increasing concern has been expressed about the elderly's attributions and/or cognitions of hopelessness and the effects that
these cognitions might have on the mental well-being and
adaptive functioning of the elderly.   Statements such as "I
have nothing to look forward to".or "There is no sense in my
doing anything new for I will soon be dead" are commonly made

by the elderly (Blazer, 1982) and assumed to reflect the elderly's cognitions of enduring pessimism and futility. Intervention studies with the depressed elderly (e.g., Fry, 1982; Fry, 1983 (a); Fry, in press; Gallagher & Thompson 1982; Gallagher & Thompson, 1983) have provided sufficient evidence that the elderly's covert self-statements of warranted or unwarranted pessimism about the present, the future and the self are powerful mediators of their depressions. Hopelessness, has been defined by Stotland (1969) as negative expectations toward oneself and the future. In the view of Kovacz and Beck (1978, p. 527) it is understandable that if the temporal experience is a depressive condition, the future loses its meaning and becomes a singular state of pessismism and despair rather than a multiplicity of experience and opportunities. Thus, with regard to the elderly, it was reasoned that old age offers such shortened time perspective for restitution that many elderly may perceive it pointless to nurture any faith or optimism in regard to future goals or outcomes, to the extent that they may spontaneously experience or/emit cognitions of sheer hopelessness.

Method. In order to identify the covert self-statements of hopelessness reported by the elderly, Fry (in press) developed and validated a geriatric scale of hopelessness modeled after a version of the adult scale of hopelessness (Beck et al., 1974). The expectation was that this 30-item-scale of hopelessness would reflect attitudes of pessimism and futility which the elderly hold but rarely think about, at least not in terms of specific themes of hopelessness or categories of hopelessness cognitions. This 30-item-inventory that identified cognitions of hopelessness (reported as being present in association with mild to severe depression) proved to be very useful both in terms of being an independent self-reporting measure of the level of hopelessness experienced by both depressed and nondepressed elderly, and also provided insights into the specific kinds of perceptual and cognitive self-statements of hopelessness that underlie the cognitions of depression in the elderly.

Results. Comparison of the depressed and nondepressed elderly showed that the depressed elderly had higher scores on self-report items such as: (1) What's the point of trying ! I don't think I can ever get back my energy and strength; (2) I will always be old and useless; (3) I don't think God will ever forgive me for my useless life on earth; (4) All I can see ahead of me is more grief and sadness; (5) All I fear is God's punishment for my sins; and (6) I see no reason why anybody would notice me.

A principal components factor analysis which was performed on the interview responses of 178 elderly subjects yielded 4 major factors, each factor representing major hopelessness themes in the cognitions of the elderly (See Table 1):

Factor 1: Hopelessness about recovering declining
physical and cognitive energies. The factor, accounting
for 22% of the total variance, represented the elderly's
anxiety cognitions about physical feebleness, physical
and mental fatigue, and declining ability to enjoy
activities.

Factor 2: Hopelessness about personal and interpersonal
worth and attractiveness. This factor, accounting for
21% of the variance, represented the elderly's feelings
of uselessness, lack of self-worth and absence of
personal attractiveness.

Factor 3: Hopelessness about receiving spiritual faith
and grace. This factor, accounting for 13% of the
variance, represented the elderly's hopelessness
cognitions concerning God's forgiveness; God's love and
uselessness of offering prayers to God.

Factor 4: Hopelessness about deserving other's nurturance, respect or remembrance. This factor, accounting
for 11% of the variance, represented anxiety cognitions
concerning personal worth in terms of receiving others'
love, respect, remembrance and care.

Thus this recently developed geriatric scale of hopelessness,
used in conjunction with the findings of the four factors
represents major themes of hopelessness or recurrent schemas
of thinking associated with depression. Thus, a principal
task for the geriatric therapist would be to reduce depression
by systematically altering these negative beliefs. Of course,
further study of the hopelessness themes would be needed to
determine if the measure is sensitive to change as a result of
therapeutic intervention. A closely related issue concerns
the ubiquitousness of hopelessness cognitions across subtypes
of unipolar and bipolar depressed elderly. However, it would
not be unreasonable to maintain that the geriatric
hopelessness scale would be a promising tool for assessing
hopelessness cognitions among subclinical depressives.

Table 1:   Factor Analysis of Hopelessness Data

Factors	Factor Loading

Factor 1: A sense of hopelessness about recovering
          lost physical and cognitive abilities.

Poor concentration	.71
Feeble physical state	.70
Increasing physical fatigue	.72
Increasing mental fatigue	.69
Decreasing ability to enjoy anything	.75

          (Cronbach's Alpha   .72)
          (Armor's Theta   .76)

Factor 2: A sense of hopelessness about recovering
          lost   personal   and   interpersonal   worth   and
          attractiveness.

Increasing feeling of uselessness	.72
Increasing feeling of aloofness	.68
Increasing feeling of physical unattractiveness	.70
Increasing feeling of being dull	.73
Increasing feeling of worthlessness	.68

          (Cronbach's Alpha   .74)
          (Armor's Theta   .72)

Factor 3: A sense of hopelessness about regaining
          spiritual faith and grace.

Feeling undeserving of God's forgiveness	.66
Feeling that prayer is useless	.67
Feeling hopeless about God's love	.68

          (Cronbach's Alpha   .68)
          (Armor's Theta   .70)

Factor 4: A sense of hopelessness about receiving
          nurturance, respect or remembrance

Feeling unworthy of remembrance after death	.72
Feeling nobody cares or will care	.72
Feeling unworthy of love	.68
Feeling unworthy of respect	.74

          (Cronbach's Alpha   .74)
          (Armor's Theta   .76)

2. Cognitions of Self-Criticism, Dependency and Inefficacy in the Elderly. As noted by Blatt, Quinlan, Chevron, McDonald and Zuroff (1982), it is vital for clinical research and practice that meaningful differentiations be made among the complex and heterogeneous clusters of cognitive beliefs, cognitive processes and cognitive errors that are associated with depressive states. In an empirical study of psychological experiences associated with depression, Blatt, D'Affliati and Quinlan (1976) noted two highly stable factors - Dependency and Self-Criticism which where significantly correlated with independent measures of depression in several samples of male and female students. Our own reseach (Fry & Trifiletti, in press) also recently found that factors similar to self-criticism and dependency differentiated depressed and non-depressed nonclinical samples of elderly subjects.

Method. In distinguishing concepts of self-criticism and low self-evaluations we specified that cognitions of self-criticism represented only those rebukes which the elderly leveled against themselves in reference to behaviors or attributes which they themselves highly valued, as distinct from low self-evaluations in which they expressed cognitions of inferiority, guilt, social rejection and worthlessness relative to comparison groups and other-referenced criteria. Our subjects' pretest self-reports on the Depressive Experiences Questionnaire (Blatt, 1974) revealed very high positive loadings in items of (1) dependency (e.g., I often think about the danger of losing someone close to me; I worry a lot about offending or hurting someone close to me); (2) self-criticism (e.g., Often I feel I have disappointed myself; I often find that I don't live up to my own standards or ideals); and (3) inefficacy (e.g., negative loading on items such as: I have many inner resources; what I do or say has an impact on those around me).

Results. As a formal extension of Blatt's (1974) conceptualizations, Fry and Trifiletti (in press) assessed cognitions of dependency, self-criticism and inefficacy in an extended sample of nonclinical elderly subjects and identified a useful set of self-referent cognitions in the depressed elderly. For example, the depressed elderly in our sample revealed in their cognitions a dominant need for nurturance and support and clingingness, passivity and avoidance of anger. These findings are congruent with Arieti and Bemporad's (1980) formulations of the "dominant other" type of depression. Additionally, these cognitions appear quite consistent with the tendency of depressives to attribute failure, disappointment etc. to internal cognitions of inferiority (Abramson, Seligman, & Teasdale, 1978).

Overall, our identification of Dependency, Self-criticism, and Inefficacy as empirically derived factors in depression in the elderly, is consistent with (a) the cognitive formulations of Seligman (1975) who discusses cognitions of helplessness or dependency as a central issue in depression; (b) the cognitive-behavioral conceptualizations of Blatt (1974) and

Arieti and Bemporad (1980) who discuss the depressed subjects'
intense feelings of helplessness and weakness. According to
these researchers, themes of dependency and self-criticism are
manifested in cognitions of fear of being abandoned, wishes to
be cared for, loved, and protected; and intense feelings of
inferiority and guilt; and (c) Bandura's (1977) conceptualizations of the self-efficacy model in which he hypothesizes that
self-perceptions of inefficacy, loss of personal controls and
incompetence would be important antecedents of the occurrence
of depression. For purposes of treatment of depressives,
Bandura advocates a social learning perspective in which the
techniques of self-monitoring of cognitions, cognitive
rehearsals and practice of success-oriented fantasies would be
particularly direct ways of strengthening self-efficacy
expectations. Thus Bandura's concept of self-efficacy cuts
across many types of cognitive mechanisms and may require the
subject to bring under control various cognitions of self-
criticism, dependency and hopelessness (Crits-Christoph &
Singer, 1981).

3. Cognitive Appraisals of Life-Stress. Although analysis of
the cognitive appraisals of stressful events have demonstrated
some ability in distinguishing depressed and nondepressed
responses in adult samples (e.g., see Hammen, 1978; Kuiper,
1978; Rizley, 1978; Seligman, Abramson, Semmel, & Von Baeyer,
1979), it is argued that the relationship between causal
ascriptions and depression are by no means invariant or
uniform across age groups. Therefore, in an effort to
determine whether cognitive appraisals of stressful events are
different in the elderly population (as compared to younger
adults) and lead to varying degrees of measured and perceived
depression, Fry & Grover (1982) conducted an exploratory study
of 304 Asian and Caucasian elderly. The objective in this
study was to examine attributions and causality appraisals
related to the occurrence of stressful events.

Method.   Subjects were asked to respond to questions designed
to assess various cognitions of control and functioning:

-Personal Control (Do you think you could have prevented   or
avoided the stressful events ?)
-Self-responsibility (Did this stressful event occur because
you got nervous, angry, confused ?)
-Self-evaluation (Did this event occur because you lacked
ability, effort etc. to cope with it ?)
-Globality (to what extent to you feel this event has or will
affect other areas of your life ?); and
-Self-confidence in future coping (Do you feel more self-
confident about coping with a similar event if it were to
happen again ?)

Results. The results of this study offered substantial
support for the cognitive mediational hypothesis of depression
in that the cognitions of the depressed and nondepressed
elderly subjects were significantly different in terms of
personal control, self-responsibility and self-evaluation in
relation to coping with future stressful events.   The results
suggested a strong relationship between depression and
cognitions of self-blame, lack of personal control and lack of
self-confidence in handling stressful events, fear of
recurrence of similar stressful events and fear of inability
to handle such events.

These data, examining the causality attributions of the
appraisals of the elderly, support the hypotheses of locus of
control and helplessness postulated by Cohen, Rothbart and
Phillips (1976) and DeVellis, DeVellis and McCauley (1978) for
adults.   The identification of uncertainty, fear of
recurrence, and self-blame and self-criticism cognitions is
consistent with Brown and Harris' (1978) hypothesis of
depression as related to cognitions of loss of control.

The concept of depression which best relates to the elderly's
cognitive appraisals of life stresses (see Fry & Grover, 1982)
is that of Seligman's (1975) learned helplessness which is
clearly associated with a perceived loss of control over life
situations. Depressive mood especially in the elderly, can be
usefully viewed from this perspective in that a number of
factors would seem to lead to a potential loss of perceived
control in this group; for example, compulsory retirement,
failing physical health, loss and bereavement, loss of social
support, and diminished finances to mention but a few.   This
in terms of adaptive functioning and future coping it is quite
understandable how learned helplessness, especially in the
elderly, would lead to cognitions of further loss of controls
and effectance.   With increasing age it is to be expected,
that certain negative beliefs would become realistically reinforced in the elderly, beliefs (a) that their skills are no
longer effective for reaching their goals; and (b) that they
have failed and may continue to fail due to personal incompetence and the increasing need to rely on others for decision-
making and cognitive effort.

Whether these negative beliefs are warranted or unwarranted, from Beck's point of view (Beck et al., 1974) they will predispose the elderly to distort their experiences and to substitute cognitions of pessimism, futility and hopelessness for more positive cognitions of optimism and self-confidence concerning the present, future and the self. Thus the data from Fry and Grover's (1982) study of cognitive appraisals of the elderly are consistent with Beck's (1976) exposition of the negative cognitive triad. The elderly's negative expectations, that stressful events will reoccure and that they personally lack the competence or confidence to cope with the future reoccurence of stressful events, equal the <u>negative view of the future</u> as postulated in Beck's negative cognitive triad. The elderly's negative attitudes toward themselves (as seen in their self-perceptions of inadequacy, and hopelessness about restitution and improvement in the future) equals <u>the negative view of self</u> in Beck's negative cognitive triad.

From Beck's point of view therefore, what would be necessary for depression reduction would be: (a) to provide the depressed clients a set of "environmental enrichment" which would reduce aversive outcomes (e.g., poor housing conditions, lack of social support, poor medical facilities) and thus to boost their general morale; (b) teach them to monitor their negative cognitions of failure, incompetence and lack of control and help them to recognize the connections between their negative cognitions, negative affects of depression and their negative coping behaviors; and (c) to identify and alter the dysfunctional beliefs of personal incompetence, hopelessness and lack of control that predispose them to depressive cognitions.

Conceptualized from the reformulated learned helplessness point of view (Abramson, Seligman, & Teasdale, 1978; Seligman, 1981), what the elderly subjects need to be taught is how to make (a) particular internal, global and stable attributions of causality for positive and pleasant events; and (b) particular external attributions for negative events. Thus Seligman's (1981) suggested tactic for helping the depressed elderly clients to recognize the connection between negative events and negative self-attributions would include both (1) <u>personal control training</u> i.e., tactics that will help the client to make more positive expectations of future outcomes and less negative expectations of personal abilities and competence to cope with future outcomes; and (2) <u>resignation training</u> which would require making expected uncontrollable aversive outcomes less aversive, and making desirable, but unattainable outcomes, less desirable.

The use of both personal control training and resignation training with the elderly poses some practical problems. Seen in the context of Erikson's (1950) explanation of depression and negative attributions, a certain level of internal negative attributions and loss of control in the elderly may, perhaps, be essential to their integration of the final stage

of life. In the view of many researchers (e.g., Blazer, 1982)
declining personal competence and declining personal controls
may, in fact, be an objective and accurate account of the life
situation of millions of elderly in North America.   When the
elderly look to the future, they may <u>realistically</u> assess that
the negative things that are now happening to them will
continue unabated and that this continuance may <u>logically</u>
result from their personal deficits.   It may be that the
personal rejection which the elderly experience, and the
resulting negative self-assessments they make, are based on an
<u>objective</u> and <u>accurate</u> account of their interactions with
their environment and their inability to cope.   In support of
this position Blazer (1982) notes that in the perceptions of
both depressed and nondepressed elderly, old age offers such a
shortened time for restitution and improvement that indeed,
objectively speaking, there may not be enough time to alter
the negative attributions of the elderly or to restore in them
a sense of personal controls.   Therefore, it may be that
Seligman's suggested tactic of "resignation training"
(Seligman, 1981, p. 126) as opposed to control training may
have a greater appeal to the more practically minded gerontologist using cognitive-behavioral strategies.   Lest I be
misunderstood, let me emphasize that I think personal control
training as <u>preventative technique</u> would be extremely
effective in offsetting future negative self-attributions in
the elderly.   But resignation training, as explained in the
context of learned helplessness, provides a more well-defined,
parsmonious and reality-oriented framework for the cognitive
treatment of depression in the elderly.   In   essence,
resignation training would assist the elderly: (a) in the
renunciation and relinquishment of unattainable goals; (b)
provide more realistic goals and norms within which short-term
gratification and reinforcement may be achieved; and (c)
assist in the reevaluation of unattainable goals and the
formulation of more short-term and attainable goals.

As noted by Seligman (1981), resignation seems to be a natural
process. Resignation training may be particularly useful in
working with the distorted cognitions of the elderly
especially in the wake of bereavement and loss.   As noted by
Barraclough, Bunch,Nelson and Sainsbury (1974), helplessness
cognitions are particularly dominant in the elderly following
bereavement and loss ("He's gone and there is nothing I could
do about it"), and failure to work through the helplessness
results in subsequent depression (Ramsay, 1977).   Elderly
clients may not have motivation or energy to acquire new
skills of communication or behavioral responses of personal
controls.   Thus, as deduced from Seligman's (1981) premises,
resignation training and environmental enrichment strategies
may have <u>more</u> far-reaching implications for work with the
depressed elderly than would personal control training.   Put
in a nutshell, <u>less</u> depression will occur if the elderly,
objectively speaking, are trained to resign themselves to the
fact that with increasing age there is a greater likelihood of
some negative events (e.g., bereavement and loss of social
support, and declining ability for personal autonomy and

control). Consequently, the elderly may be <u>more</u> encouraged to view the negative state of affairs as not necessarily resulting from internal, stable and global factors but more from external events of an episodic nature.

<u>4. Self-Reportings of Cognitive Failure</u>. During the past few years a considerable amount of concern has developed in the assessment of the elderly's self-reported failures in perceptual, and cognitive functioning. The concern is perhaps due to the work of Lazarus (1966) and Broadbent, Cooper Fitzgerald and Parkes (1982) who have discussed a variety of cognitive failures (e.g., absent-mindedness, forgetfulness, negative self-appraisals of inability to concentrate, preoccupation, clumsiness, disorganization and lack of observational skills). These authors have hypothesized that cognitive failures are associated with persons who have poor self-image, poor mental health or are on the verge of clinical stress. In this regard, Crown and Crisp (1966) also noted a significant correlation between cognitive failure and the stress features of the environment and postulated, along with Broadbent et al. (1982), that cognitive failure may be an early indication of clinical difficulties and negative affective symptoms of depression.

From the perspectives of the elderly, the most plausible hypothesis that needed to be tested is that the experience of repeated cognitive failures is associated with self-criticism, self-blame and depression. In order to explore the elderly's perceptions of cognitive failure, Fry (1983 (b)) attempted to get some assessment of the elderly's self-reports of cognitive failure and to compare these with the reports given about the same elderly person by another friend or family member who knows them well.

<u>Method.</u> Twenty-five cognitive failure items, half of which were adapted from Broadbent et al.'s (1982) cognitive failures questionnaire, were assembled from events which the elderly had frequently experienced and reported. Each of the individual respondents was asked to indicate on a five-point rating scale (1=never; 5=very often) the frequency with which (s)he makes such mistakes. Responses were required with reference to the last six-month period. Thus, for example, the elderly subjects were asked: Do you forget whether you turned off the light or locked the door ?; Do you forget how much money you had in your wallet ?; Do you forget where you put away something that is very important to you ?; Do you find you can't think of anything to say ?; Do you find you are unable to remember the important things at the right time ?; Do you find you forget why you went from one part of the house to the other ?; Do you find you forget people's names ?; Do you find you forget which way to turn on a road you know well but rarely use?; Do you have trouble identifying familiar faces ?; Do you have trouble concentrating on what people are saying to you ?; Do you have trouble remembering something you recently read ?

The cognitive failure questionnaire, as given to the elderly, was also given to other respondents who were friends or family members of the subjects. These respondents were asked to report on the elderly's subject's tendencies for absent mindedness, forgetfulness, clumsiness, difficulty in making up his (her) mind and other similar cognitive failures.

Results. Several suggestive findings emerged from this study (Fry, 1983 (b)). First, the findings showed a close correspondence between the subject's own reportings of cognitive failure and those of others rating them (r=.69; p < .01). Second, there was a significant positive correlation between the incidence of cognitive failures and incidence of depressive moods (r=.67; p .01). Third, there is some evidence that high scores on cognitive failures corresponded to an accurate behavioral liability to make such failures. Fifth, in a majority of subjects, subjects' scores remained relatively unchanged over a 24 week test-retest period providing some evidence that the scores on cognitive failures remained relatively constant.

In an attempt to explore whether the high rate of cognitive failure in most subjects may be associated with other perceptual or emotional variables, Fry (1983(b)) interviewed the elderly subjects individually in order to get at the elderly's causal attributions for their cognitive failures. Several suggestive findings of a correlational nature emerged. Appraisals of loneliless, social rejection and psychological weakness seemed often obscured in client's thinking about their present and anticipated future experiences. The high loneliness and high rejection scores were significantly correlated with high cognitive failure scores (r=.47, p<.05). One of the most plausible interpretations of these finding is that clients may often find it difficult to acknowledge that they feel sad or that they feel interpersonally needy; and therefore instead of cognitively assessing their situation as being one socially lonely, they may obscure any real feelings of loneliness in perceptions of cognitive failure. It may also be that high cognitive failure is a vulnerability factor making the elderly individuals less able, cognitively, to evaluate any real feelings of isolation or loneliness which they might have experienced.

Comparison of the social behavior ratings of high and low cognitive failure subjects showed that high cognitive failure elderly were perceived to be: (a) less self-assured; (b) less fluent in speech; c) less humorous; (d) less warm; (e) less assertive; (f) less friendly; (g) less open and self-disclosing and (h) more depressed in the group interactions. These items for ratings were assumed to measure social skills and to reflect thoughts and attitudes of the elderly that were interpersonally observable. An additional important finding was a greater discrepancy between self-ratings and observer ratings for elderly subjects with high cognitive failure scores than for low cognitive failure scores. This finding suggests that more cognitive distortion concerning interpersonal functioning is associated with cognitive failures.

All these data provide some tentative evidence that a high cognitive failure state increase the elderly's vulnerability to social situations requiring the use of social competence skills. This interpretation helps to explain why greater stress in social situations would be experienced by those who fear cognitive failure. While it leaves obscure the origins of the liability to cognitive failure itself (Broadbent et al., 1982), the Fry (1983(b)) study provides some clues that would facilitate the work of cognitive therapists in guiding the attentional processes of high cognitive failure subjects. Future work examining the possible mechanisms such as fear, anxiety, fatigue underlying the cognitive failures of the elderly would be very useful.

SUMMARY

This chapter has discussed cognitions of hopelessness, self-criticism, dependency and inefficacy in the depressed elderly and attempted to relate these to the premises of the reformulated learned helplessness theory of depression (Seligman, 1981), Beck's (1976) theory of the negative cognition triad in depression, and Bandura's (1977) model of self-efficacy. An attempt has been made to draw out various cognitive strategies of treatment that may be deduced from the premises of Beck's and Seligman's theories and to discuss some of the practical problems related to using personal control training in the treatment of depression in the elderly. It has been argued that environmental enrichment and resignation training provide a more well-defined and parsimonious framework for the cognitive treatment of depression in the elderly. Finally, the premises of cognitive failure in the elderly have been examined; followed by a discussion of the behavioral, affective and perceptual correlates of cognitive failure in the elderly and the resulting implications and applications of cognitive failure perceptions for the general mental health of the elderly.

NOTE

Preparation of the chapter was supported, in part, by a 1981-82 grant from the Department of National Health and Welfare, Ottawa, Canada.
Requests for reprints of the chapter may be sent to P.S. Fry, Department of Educational Psychology, The University of Calgary, Alberta, Canada, T2N 1N4.

The Self in Anxiety, Stress and Depression
R. Schwarzer (Editor)
© Elsevier Science Publishers B.V. (North-Holland), 1984

THE SUITABILITY OF COGNITIVE THERAPY FOR DEPRESSION:
SOCIAL ANXIETY AND SELF-RELATED COGNITIONS AS KEY VARIABLES

William Jeyam Alagaratnam

*Department of Psychology, University of London Goldsmiths' College, New Cross
London, Great Britain*

In recent years notions of the self and aspects of the self such as self-referent thought and self-focused attention have made a strong impact on social, clinicial and personality psychology. In the field of depression, psychoanalytic and phenomenological theories have focused on the self as central to the experience of depression. Recently, for example, Mollon & Parry (in press) have proposed an empirically testable concept of 'the fragile self' in which they describe the narcissistic disturbance and protective function of depression.

However, cognitive-behavioral theories of depression have focused on such limited concepts as negative self-evaluation and self-reinforcement. This chapter will therefore necessarily be limited to such concepts since the purpose is to suggest a strategy for assessing the suitability of cognitive therapy for depression. According to the research and clinical literature, social anxiety and self-related cognitions would seem to be key constructs in any such strategy.

The first part of this chapter reviews the premorbid personality associated with unipolar nonpsychotic depression. Evidence from mood-induction studies, the studies of the correlates of 'normal' and clinically depressed mood is presented. Beck's (1983) characterization of the personality dimension of 'social dependency' and its relationships to "anxious depression" are touched upon. Then, the cognitive characteristics of those predisposed to depression is discussed with reference to the concepts of self-reinforcement and cognitive control. Next, aspects of negative self-evaluation are considered in terms of sex differences, secondary gain and the functional meaning of depressive statements. Finally, aspects of poor social competence are discussed in terms of the depressed state, premorbid personality and maladaptive cognitions.

In a recent critique of Beck's cognitive theory of depression the present author (Alagaratnam, 1983 a) notes that Beck has not suggested any experimentally based or clinically derived strategies for assessing the suitability of patients in relation to treatment outcome either in terms of premorbid personality or cognitive characteristics or subtype(s) of 'neurotic' depressions.

As Rush & Giles (1982) note:

> As yet there are no predictors for patients best suited to cognitive therapy alone, medication alone, or the combination. Further studies are needed to identify the specific indications for cognitive therapy or the combined approach. p. 169.

In this paper, a tentative strategy for assessing the suitability of cognitive therapy is proposed by identifying the 'premorbid' personality correlates of susceptibility to depressed mood based on preliminary findings, the theoretical rationale of Beck's theory of depression and the research literature.

This proposal is made as a heuristic for clinical research. It is not being claimed that depressed mood is synonymous to clinical depression. Screening students for depression with the Beck Depression Inventory (BDI) remains a controversial issue. However, as Oliver & Burkham (1979) point out, the validity of the BDI in a university population (Bumberry, Oliver & McClure, 1978), however, suggests that such depression in students bears some resemblance to clinical depression.

PERSONALITY AND DEPRESSED MOOD

In a prospective study, Alagaratnam (1983 b) used Velten's mood-induction procedure (MIP) in an attempt to identify the 'premorbid' personality correlates of susceptibility to depressed mood in seventy undergraduates (32 males, 38 females).

Interestingly, although a number of personality variables correlated with initial (pre-induction) mood, none correlated with the final (post-induction) mood in the male sample. However, in the female sample, ego strength, tenseness, anxiety (as measured by Cattell's 16 PF Questionnaire, Cattell, Eber & Tatsuoka, 1970) and guilt (as measured by the Buss-Durkee Inventory, Buss & Durkee, 1957) correlated with both 'normal' (initial) mood and post-induction mood.

Of particular interest to the present discussion is that the presence of guilt and (to a lesser extent) anxiety were correlated with the degree of mood change, but again only for the female sample.

Table　1:　　Personality correlates of normal and induced
　　　　　　　depressed mood.

	Hostility	Guilt	Ego Strength	Tense	Extra-version	Anxiety
BDI 1 (initial mood)	14 (18)	52 (29)	-32 (-21)	41 (35)	14 (43)	32 (42)
BDI 2 (induced mood)	14 (20)	62 (21)	-34 (09)	32 (02)	-01 (17)	38 (04)

Note: Verbal hostility and Guilt scores are from Buss-Durkee
　　　　Inventory.　Other　dimensions　are　from　Cattell's
　　　　16PF.　Correlations for males are in parentheses.

(Pearson's r: decimal points omitted)

For males　　(n=32) $p < 0.01(r > 0.409)$

For females (n=38) $p < 0.01(r > 0.381)$

(MIPs　have been criticized as being solely due to the effects
of demand characteristics or suggestibility.　However, recent
reviews　(e.g.　Clark,　in press;　Goodwin & Williams,　1982)
support　MIPs as being valid analogue of　clinical　depression
since　the　effects　have been observed to　affect　clinically
relevant　variables　across　affective,　cognitive,　somatic,
behavioral　and　physiological　dimensions　and　are　rather
difficult to fake.)

Thus one may speculate that perhaps cognitive therapy would be
maximally　effective　for　females with　depression　in　which
anxiety and guilt are prominent.　This hypothesis is currently
being　tested in a longitudinal study of clinically　depressed
in-patients meeting Research Diagnostic Criteria (Alagaratnam,
1983　c).　In　passing,　it　is interesting to　note　that　in
Wetzel,　Cloninger,　Hong & Reich's (1980) study,　several　of
Cattell's 16 PF variables including ego strength and tenseness
were　significantly　correlated in depressed　(unipolar)　probands.　These personality variables were not only significantly different from test norms but also from control probands.

Table 2:   Intercorrelations of personality variables for males
           and females.
           (males n=32; females n=38)

Males	Hostility	Guilt	Ego Strength	Tense	Extra-version	Anxiety

Females

Males / Females	Hostility	Guilt	Ego Strength	Tense	Extra-version	Anxiety
Hostility	1.00	-.18	-.34	.41	-.16	.32
Guilt	.21	1.00	-.20	-.10	-.23	.23
Ego Strength	-.26	-.34	1.00	-.46	.17	-.57
Tense	.27	.30	-.54	1.00	-.08	.81
Extraversion	.10	-.22	.31	-.30	1.00	-.18
Anxiety	.25	.38	-.83	.77	-.37	1.00

Note: Verbal Hostility and Guilt scores are from Buss-Durkee
        Inventory. Other dimensions are from Cattell's 16 PF.

In another study designed by the present author and conducted
by a research assistant (Alagaratnam & O'Connor, 1983) an
attempt was made to identify the social skill and cognitive
correlates of experimentally-induced depressed mood.   Thirty-
two undergraduates (16 males, 16 females) were randomly
assigned to either an experimental or control group.   A taped
depressing story and a control tape (Williams, p.c.) was used.
The Gambrill & Richey (1975) Assertion Inventory (a measure of
social anxiety and assertiveness); The Sidney Modification of
the Betts Visual Imagery Questionnaire (Sutcliffe, 1962) were
administered as pre-test measures. The short form of the Beck
Depression Inventory (Beck & Beck, 1972) and a Visual Analogue
Scale were administered both as pre- and post- test measures
of depressed mood.

A factor analysis of the questionnaires using the Principal
Factor Format followed by varimax rotation generated three
factors which accounted between them for 86.8% of the total
variance.   On the basis of inspection it was decided that the
factors were sufficiently orthogonal to each other and tightly
knit within each other to warrant distinguishing between them
and naming them.

Of direct relevance to the present discussion is Factor I:
"Personality set vulnerable to mood manipulation" (high social
anxiety, low assertiveness, high imagery). This accounted for
42.3% of the total variance.   However, in view of the rather
small sample (n=32), this finding is presented here tentative-

ly and merely as suggestive of the potential use of personality variables in predicting mood change.

Table 3: The Correlates of Mood Manipulation
Principal Factor Analysis (Varimax Rotation)

Variables	Factor I	Factor II	Factor III	Communality
Sex	0.04	-0.06	0.05	0.55
Mood Manipulation	0.33	0.74	0.01	0.66
Mood Change (Beck)	-.17	0.58	0.08	0.37
Mood Change (Visual Analogue Scale)	0.01	0.78	-.018	0.65
Social Anxiety	0.84	-0.03	-0.19	0.77
Assertiveness	0.53	0.02	0.16	0.31
Mental Imagery	0.33	0.03	-0.37	0.35
Post-Induction Mood (Beck)	0.64	0.03	0.27	0.54
Pre-Induction Mood (Beck)	0.26	-0.27	0.92	0.99
Pre-Induction Mood (Visual Analogue Scale)	0.03	0.06	0.41	0.17

% of explained variance	34%	33.1%	19.7%	

Factor I: "Personality set vulnerable to mood manipulation"

Factor II: "The effect of the taped mood induction
             (transient mood)"

Factor III: "Permanent depression"

PERSONALITY   DIMENSIONS   AND   THE   SUBJECTIVE   EXPERIENCE   OF
DEPRESSION

Let us now consider clinical findings.   Altman & Wittenborn
(1980)   tested   the hypothesis that formerly depressed women
(patients) now in remission would describe certain features of
their personality in a manner different from that of women who
have   never   been depressed.   They factor-analyzed discriminating items.   Five interpretable factors emerged:

        Factor I   : Low Self-Esteem
        Factor II   : Preoccupation with Failure (Helplessness)
        Factor III: Unhappy Pessimistic Outlook
        Factor IV   : Narcissistic Vulnerability
        Factor V   : Confidence and a General Sense of Competence

What is interesting is that the first four factors,   at least,
are   entirely   consistent   with   Beck's   descriptions   of   the
depression-prone personality and several of the   items   that
relate to these factors are the concerns of cognitive therapy.

Altman & Wittenborn note that Blatt, D'Affitti & Quinlan
(1979) identified self-criticism (cf.   Factor I) and   efficacy
(cf.   Factor   V) as associated with depressive qualities among
college students.   Altman & Wittenborn suggest that the   fact
that   work with patients corresponds in its implications with
studies   conducted with students attests to the pertinence of
personality   in   depression.   However,   they caution that   the
depressive predisposition does not appear to be a monolithic
quality.   Their   data suggest that more than one kind of personality may distinguish those who have been   depressed.   This
is   consistent   with Beck's (1983) formulation of depressive
personalities.

More   recently,   Blatt,   Quinlan,   Chevron,   McDonald & Zuroff
(1982)   in their study of clinically depressed patients confirmed their previous findings in college students and provide
evidence   suggesting   that the subjective   experiences   around
which an individual's depression focuses are a valid basis for
differentiating among types of depression.

Recently,   Seligman   (1981) has subsumed,   rather ingeniously,
the   cognitive   theory   and therapy of depression under   the
learned   helplessness   paradigm.   It is therefore argued   on
theoretical   grounds   that depressed patients displaying   the
depressive attributional style should be ideal candidates   for
cognitive therapy,   assuming, of course, that the aetiological
mechanisms of cognitive theory and/or the procedures deemed to
be effective components of cognitive therapy are valid.

Most recently,   Beck (1983,   see also Beck, Epstein & Harrison
(1983)   has   elaborated his cognitive model in terms of personality   dimensions.   Beck has identified two such major
personality   characteristics   associated with   differential

patterns of depressive aetiology , symptomatology, and treatment response, namely, <u>autonomy</u> and <u>social dependence</u>.

Of relevance here is social dependence. Beck (1983) has
suggested that this <u>dependent type</u> is more likely to have
"anxious depression". Interestingly, this can be related
particularly to Wolpe's (1979) Type II classification of so-
called reactive depressions which he implicates as being due
to anxiety based on erroneous, self-devaluative cognitions.

Social anxiety seems to be related to maladaptive cognitions
and is a key feature of social inadequacy. It is speculated
on the basis of clinical experience that social anxiety may be
a key mediatiating factor in social dependency, maladaptive
cognitions and clinical depression.

SELF-REINFORCEMENT AND COGNITIVE CONTROL

Now to consider the cognitive constructs of self-reinforcement
and cognitive control.

A different approach toward the prediction of mood change has
been proposed by Heiby (1983). She tested the hypothesis that
depressed mood may be predicted from the effects of a
response defined variable, frequency of self-reinforcement,
and the rate of environmentally controlled reinforcement in an
analogue study of eighty undergraduates. Heiby points out
that although a reduction in environmeental reinforcement has
been correlated with depression, not all individuals who
experience a reduction in the environmentally controlled
reinforcement become depressed. She found that subjects
exhibiting a low frequency of self-reinforcement reported a
greater increase in depressed mood following a decrease in
environmental reinforcement than individuals exhibiting a high
frequency of self-reinforcement. However, the specificity of
these variables to depression has not been demonstrated as
yet.

Recently, there has been renewed interest in cognitive processes in depression. For example, Weingartner, Cohen,
Murphy, Martello & Gerdt (1981) pointed out that some of the
cognitive processes that have been shown to be disrupted in
the depressed include aspects of attention, perception, speed
of cognitive response and problem-solving, as well as memory
and learning. They concluded that the processes underlying
cognitive changes are discrete and important in clinical depression.

More recently, Cohen, Weingartner, Smallberg, Pickar & Murphy
(1982) examined motor performance and cognitive function in
depressed patients and controls. They found that increasing
severity of depression was strongly associated with decrements
in performance in both motor and memory tasks. Greatest
impairment was found on those cognitive and motor tasks that
required substained effort. They concluded that their

findings raise considerable doubt as to the reasonableness of
hypothesizing specific memory deficits in depression separable
from the general deficits of motivation, drive and attention.

Similarly, Lazarus, Coyne & Folkman (1982) stress that
depressive symptomatology can be viewed from a behavioral,
emotional, or motivational perspective in addition to a cognitive one. Their contention is that depressive behavior,
negative mood, low motivation, failure, and loss occur together as fused aspects of the same psychological event.

A somewhat related point is made by Broadbent, Cooper,
Fitzgerald & Parkes (1982). They note that traditionally
affective components of clinical problems have been emphasized. They suggest that many such problems also involve
disorders of attention, of memory, and of the control of
thought or action. They suggest that everyday failures may be
sensitive to changes which are not revealed in the laboratory.

They therefore devised a Cognitive Failure Questionnaire (CFQ)
-- a self-report measure of failures in perception, memory and
motor function. Their findings suggest that cognitive failure
is an indicator of general disturbance of control, and perhaps
of vulnerability to stress. They report that the cognitive
failures seem to occur in the same person rather than separating into perceptual, memory and motor failures.
Furthermore, the tendency to report them is not equivalent to
neuroticism, social desirability or low intelligence. The
scores have a stable trait-like quality and correlate with
ratings of the respondent by his or her spouse.

They suggest that high CFQ is a vulnerability factor making
the individual less able to resist the effects of stress.
They recall Lazarus's (1966) suggestion that the initial
impact of a stressful situation is to produce an attempt at
cognitive appraisal and from this a strategy of coping can be
developed. Only if coping is unsuccessful does the person
develop symptoms. In other words, those who cannot cope
cognitively are most vulnerable to stress.

This view is particularly compatible to the model of depression postulated by Trautmann (1983, this conference) in
which 'there seems to be a cognitive "final common pathway"
which a person has to arrive at in order to experience depression, namely the primary appraisal of a situation as
harm/loss and the secondary appraisal of the person's coping
strategies as insufficient.'

Broadbent, Cooper, Fitzgerald & Parkes cite evidence
suggesting that people with high cognitive failure are also
likely to report a high incidence of more conventional
affective symptoms. It is therefore encouraging that
inspection of data of depressed in-patients (currently too
small for analysis) meeting Research Diagnostic Criteria
participating in the present author's current research
(Alagaratnam, c) thus far consistently score higher relative

to nondepressed psychiatric controls on <u>both</u> the CFQ and the Cognitive Style Test (Wilkinson & Blackburn's specific measure of Beck's cognitive triad, revised scale). However, the specificity and stability of CFQ scores in depression has yet to be demonstrated and is currently being examined.

In view of the underlying rationale and features of the CFQ, it is tentatively proposed that it may be useful in helping identity depressed subjects who may respond optimally to cognitive therapy.

SEX DIFFERENCES IN NEGATIVE SELF-EVALUATION AND COGNITIVE STYLE

Let us now consider aspects of negative self-evaluation which may be related to outcome in cognitive therapy. Sex differences in vulnerability to depression and conflicting findings of negative self-evaluation (central to Beck's cognitive triad) in one sex and not the other suggest that the efficacy of cognitive therapy may vary as a function of sex.

For example, Davis (1979) only found partial support for negative self-evaluation in that it was present in depressed males only. However, Hammen and Krantz (1976) found negative self-evaluation for females and only in those who were more depressed.

Several authors have linked negative self-evaluation with the depressive attributional style (e.g. Abramson & Martin, 1981; Seligman, 1981). The depressive attributional style literature suggest distinct sex differences. Abramson & Martin link this difference to sex differences in vulnerability to depression. If indeed negative self-evaluation is a function of sex and/or of severity of depression, then this may have implications for the development of sex-specific strategies for cognitive therapy of depression. The findings of two studies also seem to point in this direction.

Firstly, Hammen & Padesky (1977) have shown that in college samples although men and women did not differ in total depression scores, there were patterns of differential symptom expression. They may have implications for both diagnosis and evaluation of outcome for men and women.

Secondly, Funabiki, Bologna, Pepping & Fitzgerald (1980) in a large study of college students found that men and women showed distinct differences in the nature of their interpersonal behaviors as well as in cognitive styles of coping with depression. It seems that, at present, cognitive therapy is deemed to apply equally to males and females and irrespective of whether the depression is mild or severe. One possible reason for null findings in relation to this issue in most outcome studies of cognitive therapy may be the size and composition of sample and the selection procedures.

In passing it is worth mentioning that Teasdale (in press) has proposed a reciprocal cognitive model of depression in which individual differences in response, for example, to criticism may account for the differential expression of symptoms. For example, a response to criticism with hostility may not result in depression whereas a response with depressed mood may.

A DEPRESSIVE LIFE-STYLE ?

Some authors (e.g. Lazarus, Coyne & Folkman, 1982) have argued that secondary gain may be important in some cases of depression.   Beck's theory of depression and recent elaboration (Beck, 1983) emphasize a predominant mode of functioning and implicate two types of depressive personality, one of which he relates to the so-called reactive depression. In other words, these are the people who have a particular cognitive style and rigid interpersonal behaviors.   It therefore seems that the depression-prone personality which Beck describes is the ideal candidate who is very likely to use a depressive lifestyle to satisfy needs.   In other words, secondary gain may be primary for such depressives. This view is even more convincing if we consider Bonime's contention that:

> ... depression is not simply a group of symptoms that make a periodic illness, but that it is a <u>practice</u>, an everyday mode of interacting ...

> (Cited in Arieti & Bemporad, 1978, p.41).

It is therefore speculated that if a subset of these depressives are identified by a functional analysis (of their personal relationships and the responses they evoke), cognitive therapy as currently proposed would not seem to be the treatment of choice.

It seems that some cognitive therapists are rather eager to elicit cognitive distortions and thereby justify the suitability of the therapy. When a depressed patient reports: "I can't do such and such" it is assumed that this person needs to be given performance feedback in an attempt to demonstrate the irrationality or maladaptiveness of that belief. There is some evidence to suggest that this assumption may be incorrect.

For example, Horowitz, French, Lapid & Weckler (1982) have applied the concept of a prototype to depression. They describe some of the different meanings of "I can't" in interpersonal problems and suggest that we need to understand the intended meaning of the problem statement if we are to formulate appropriate treatment strategies. In other words, it is important to distinguish between a lack of competence (I don't know how to) and an inhibition (I can't bring myself to). It may also be that some depressives mean "won't" when they say "can't".

The point being made here is that a functional analysis of the intended meaning of depressives self-statements seem necessary otherwise cognitive therapy is likely to be inappropriate although such patients may incorrectly be described as having cognitive distortions.

PREMORBID SOCIAL SKILL: PERFORMANCE OR COMPETENCE ?

Poor premorbid social competence has generally been regarded as indicating poor outcome in psychotherapy. However, there may be reason to believe that a subset of depressed patients with poor premorbid social competence may be particularly suitable for cognitive therapy. For example, Wells, Hersen, Bellack, Himmelhoch (1979) argued that their results indicate that social skills training holds promise as a treatment approach for depressed individuals and particularly for those whose premorbid personalities are frequently anxious, shy, and socially deficient.

Recent research (see for example, Alagaratnam, 1982; Curran & Monti, 1982) suggests that a multidimensional conceptualization of social skills is more appropriate. It seems reasonable to suggest, on the basis of the theoretical rationale of cognitive theory, that depressed patients who have poor social skills mainly due to a fear of negative evaluation, distorted cognitions or faulty discrimination may respond well to cognitive therapy. Here cognitive therapy may improve both their social functioning and lift their depression. In passing, it is worth mentioning that recently Fennell (1983) has proposed that the mechanism of change in cognitive therapy may be due to improved cognitive coping skills rather than modification of maladaptive congintive structures. The assessment of premorbid social competence is difficult. There are, of course, serious difficulties in assessing social competence in depressed patients. For example, depression, by definition, implies poor social performance. Maladaptive cognitions may also result in poor social performance. On the other hand, poor social competence may have been a consistent feature of the premorbid personality of the depressive. This may be what Liberman (1982) had in mind when he postulated a modular approach to behavior therapy for depression. He cautioned that only when a patient continues to show cognitive distortions and remains depressed and in need of further therapy would the cognitive approach be strongly indicated.

Thus far this paper has assumed a rather global notion of cognitive therapy as if all components of cognitive therapy are necessary and sufficient for successful outcome. However, outcome research may more profitable follow the suggestion made by Barrett in response to Beck (reported in Beck, 1983):

"... You described a method of matching particular types of interventions, a way of behaving with a particular patient which fits with that patient's need ... to focus

on what sorts of psychotherapeutic techniques are going
to be accepted and are going to work for what types of
people." (p.287).

CONCLUSIONS

In conclusion then, it was tentatively proposed that aspects
of premorbid personality, cognitive characteristics such as
negative self-evaluation, self-reinforcement and cognitive
failures may be useful predictors of successful outcome with
cognitive therapy.   The relationship between premorbid social
competence and current social performance in relation to
depression needs to be functionally assessed.   The meaning of
self-statements implying negative cognitive distortions need
to be explored thoroughly to prevent inappropriate application
of cognitive therapy.   It was speculated that social anxiety
and self-related cognitions may be the key constructs that
cognitive therapists would need to focus on in devising a
strategy for assessing the suitability of cognitive therapy
for depression.   Clinical research testing some of these pro-
posals is in progress.   It is also hoped that clinicians and
researchers would address themselves to some of the issues
raised here to help predict cognitive therapy would be maximally effective.

NOTE

The author thanks the following people: Sihaya Sameena Ahmed,
Valerie Barden, Aaron Beck, Peter Coles, Vanda Dunford,
Shirley Matthews, Marie Montague, Sharon O'Connor, David Rose
& Rolf-Dieter Trautmann. Special thanks are due to the
Department of Psychology Goldsmith's College and the Loring
Memorial Benevolent Fund (GCA).

The Self in Anxiety, Stress and Depression
R. Schwarzer (Editor)
© Elsevier Science Publishers B.V. (North-Holland), 1984

THE TEMPORAL ORDER OF DEPRESSION AND ANXIETY

Mary Ann MacDougall and Robert S. Brown

University of Virginia, Charlottesville, Virginia, U.S.A.

Costello (1976) notes that the mid-twentieth century is called "the Age of Anxiety", but that one hears more and more mention of it as "the Age of Depression". Thus he suggests that contemporary life is being conducted against backdrop of both unhappy states.

Certain it is that the popular notion of good health is concerned more with physical efficiency than it is with mental state, and the primacy of the goal of physical well-being is in accord with the primacy of the goal of physical well-being is in accord with the development of medical science and modern technology. The care of the sick has over time been chiefly directed toward the correction of physical malfunction or organic impairment.

We have come to appreciate, however, that the way an individual reacts to experiences in life -- what he feels about them, and how they cause him to act -- may greatly affect his physical state and, indeed, induce illness. Organic symptoms may, in fact, represent a late stage in an individual's dysfunction, in which case the treatment provided for his physical difficulty may be little more than the treatment of his symptoms; his mental (psychological) problem then tends to be neglected. Totman (1979) has challenged the prevailing notions of illness and health by pointing to social causes of illness.

By the 1970's a considerable body of literature connecting emotional problems with physical illness had been published. Evidence of emotional factors in the causation of rheumatoid arthritis, migraine, hypertension, peptic ulcer, and ulcerative colitis was cited (Alexander, 1950; Grinker and Robbins, 1954). On the other side of the coin appears the evidence of symptomatic improvement from the use of placebos by patients demonstrably suffering from degenerative conditions, as many as 40 different disease entities being identified in the study (Haas, 1963, Totman, 1979).

The sequence proceeding from a mental event to the onset of physical symptoms has yet to be demonstrated, but the

relationship of stress or mental disorder to bodily manifestations -- as well as the difficulty of adapting to bodily
reactions -- has been studied for more than 50 years. Selye
was among the first to bring psychosomatic effects to popular
attention; he spoke of the General Adaptation syndrome in
which he found that the adrenal glands produced chemicals in
the body in excessive amounts during stress. His revised
edition, The Stress of Life, published in 1976 updated contemporary views of stress. Gallagher et al. (1982), Loreto
(1982), Uytdenhoef et al. (1982), Friedman and Jaffe(1983),
Conklin et al. (1983), among others, have also linked
depression and anxiety to physical symptoms.

We seek to explain depression and anxiety as they appear in
our contemporary scene, and we hold that if we are to determine the antecedence and consequences of mental illness, we
must conceptualize their relation to psychosocial and personal
factors and to the relation between depression and anxiety.
We anticipate that our theoretical formulation, derived from
several theories of anxiety and depression, as well as the
empirical results of our study of the temporal order of
anxiety and depression, will provide a basis for 1) identifying what depression and anxiety have in common, and where
they differ; 2) interpreting the phenomena of anxiety and
depression as they relate to psychosocial and personal factors; and 3) integrating the theories of anxiety and
depression (Brown and MacDougall, 1981, 1982).

Anxiety and depression are two neurotic entities, neurosis
itself usually being diagnosed when anxiety and fears, bodily
complaints and physical symptoms without organic cause, and
persistently unsettling and uncontrollable thoughts and acts
are reported, (Mischel and Mischel, 1977).   Anxiety is
described as "pervasive apprehension without obvious specific
cause, vague expectations of impending disaster and specific
fears of losing control of the self." To be sure, certain
situations such as taking an examination or making a public
address bring anxiety, but the anxious neurotic's apprehension
is not merely specific to such situations, but is generalized
and not a temporary state.

McReynolds (1975) has summarized the ways in which anxiety has
been regarded throughout history, offering two theoretical
concepts; "cognitive orientation" and "conditioning orientation". The former stresses experiences in which there is some
conflict among internal stimuli; the latter considers anxiety
the result of a fortuitous temporal association with mentally
traumatic events. He suggests that the two perspectives are
not contradictory, believing that cognitive theories refer to
primary anxiety, while conditioning theories suggest secondary
anxiety (p. 24). The distinction between anxiety as momentary state and as a more permanent characteristic has been
explicated for about 30 years (Nowlis, 1970; Cattell and
Scheier, 1967, Lazarus, 1966).   Spielberger (1966a, 1966b)
formalized these developments in a trait-state-theory of

anxiety. State anxiety (A-State) is described as a transitory, emotional state; trait anxiety (A-Trait) referred to as relatively stable individual differences in anxiety proneness; the conceptual difference between state and trait anxiety has been generally accepted and the consequences of anxiety are usually debilitating.

The characteristics of depression, which some consider less common than anxiety, include "exaggerated sadness toward some failure, frustration, or loss, such as the death of a loved one." Mood analysis discloses its central theme, whether it be described as a psychological or psychopathological state. As a psychological construct mood is defined as intermediate between emotion (lower) and temperament (higher) (Nowlis, 1970; Becker, 1974). Jacobson's clinical analysis of mood contrasts the normal with the pathological; she regards moods as being pervasive in all aspects of personality function and physiological processes, i.e., a "barometer of ego state". Not all enduring mental states are moods; such character traits as pessimism or optimism should be seen as more pervasive and enduring than moods, for example (Weinshel, 1979).

Some investigators of depression doubt that anxiety is the more prevalent mental disorder of our time, since depression is said to afflict at some time in their lives about half of all who live in North America or Western Europe. The National Institute of Mental Health has reported that 15 percent of such adults (some 20 million) may be suffering from serious depressive disorder in any given year (Gallant and Simpson, 1975). Mental health professionals are accordingly eager to explain it; some see it generated by weakness or tension, anxiety or shame -- or as being a meaningless search in the dark nights of the soul (White, 1982). It may take the form of aggression turned inward, and it may come after a break with a loved one, loss of self-esteem, or the adoption of some negative cognitive set. Psychoanalysis, with its emphasis on intrapsychic factors, is ever alert for a diagnosis of depression generated by intrapsychic conflict whereas the behaviorists or sociologically oriented investigators point to external factors, and depend heavily on reinforcement as a treatment modality. Although there are diverse theories about the causes of depression, all subscribe to the fact that people can be helped to overcome feelings of learned helplessness; hopelessness; loss of meaning; and suicidal intent.

In spite of such studies, some continue to believe that depression and anxiety can be classified together simply as affective states, while others advocate categorical differentiation between the two. The Newcastle Group (Roth, 1972) supports both positions seeing observable differences as well as similarities. Roth (1972) stresses differences. A major focus of our research is to resolve this question, to the answer of which an investigation of the temporal order in which the two states occur should bring elucidation. We also hope to conceptualize the operations of anxiety and depression

in our society. Toward this end we offer a model in which the
antecedents and consequences of both states are related to
psychosocial factors.   Our intent is to synthesize the
psychosocial formulations generated by research, particularly
those with psychological, social and biological foci.

THE PSYCHOLOGICAL MODEL

The model shows functional relationships among psychological
components, mental disorders, and healthful and health-damaging behaviors.   It is theoretical, incorporating prominent
features of established theories of depression and anxiety,
but it does not purport to describe the specifics of any one
position.   It is intended to be of general application, independent of any one school's notion of genesis, symptomology,
or treatment.

A central theme of our Psychosocial Model of Adherence (Figure
1) is stress and its cognitive and affective influence on the
individual's motivation to maintain optimal health.   One
recognizes that stress is inevitable in the "average expect-
able environment".   Studies of psychological reactions to
stress indicate the following pattern in its development:
first comes an event or events, usually external, which may be
threatening or simply demanding; second, an intrapsychic
process starts up in response to the event; third, an emotional discharge from the process results; and, finally, psychic
consequences of the event, of the process, and of the
discharge (Rangell, 1967) manifest themselves.   The trauma or
stressful event is absorbed during the intrapsychic process,
setting off a chain of reactions in the mind which can be
expected to result in emotional discharge.   The consequences
of the traumatic event consist of changes in behavior which
may be either temporary or permanent, or of psychological
symptoms (Arieti, 1974).

The degree of stress depends on the meaning of the traumatic
experience to the person in question, the way he relates to
the environment, effects of past experience recalled in response to the current trauma,   and the process of
reconstruction (Arieti, 1974).   The confidence in their
invulnerability most people have before an experience with
trauma may be replaced by feelings of helplessness, particularly in the case of chronic stress of the sort associated
with as physical illness such as diabetes.   Serious concern
over possible deterioration of social vocation, and family
roles may be associated with the loss of physical strength and
control.   The psychological passivity produced by a chronic
illness can be particularly stressful.

The recovery phase of response to stress, whether acute or
chronic, involves psychological reorganization.   Its accomplishment will depend on the strength of the relationships the
individual in question has with other people significant to
him.   According to Titchener and Ross (1974):

"Meaningful communications with other humans restores structure and redefines the self. The connection between fragmented parts of the self is restored in the renewal of social relations, and functions of adaptation are revitalized by the warmth, assurance, and orienting power of personal interchange" (p. 47).

Stress may have the effect of isolating the individual and separating him from crucial relationships.

"Physical illness is a definite and common psychic stress leading, especially in psychologically defensive stages, to a much enhanced and regressive investment in the self, concomitant with less or a different investment in relation with others" (p. 50).

The deepest psychological problems after trauma are associated with "feelings of self-doubt and with doubt or lack of trust of others" (Titchener and Ross, 1975, p. 55). Depression and disappointment may arise from the sense of loss in chronic illness, and anxiety and fear that contribute to the despair of loneliness and isolation may ensue. Eating and sleeping habits may be adversely affected, and the individual may feel little interest in sound health practices.

Figure 1 shows the prominence of cognition and stress in causing anxiety. The assessment of a life event by the person involved may evoke negative or positive emotions which either favor or militate against healthful behaviors. Seen as a complex process, anxiety includes stress, threat, and state and trait anxiety (Spielberger, 1966a). Figure 1 demonstrates that trait anxiety results in such health-damaging behaviors as denial, repression, or even suicide. Although state anxiety may bring dysfunction to a person without pathological levels of fear and anxiety. One may also note from Figure 1 that internal and external factors, life events, personal assessment, and depression are antecedents of trait anxiety. After explicating our model we present empirical results that support the position that depression is an important intervening variable of cause of trait anxiety.

Some patients with chronic illness may avoid depression and anxiety, maintain psychological homeostasis, and yet fail to follow treatment directives responsibly. According to Festinger (1957), this may be due to cognitive dissonance; the act of committing oneself to something that may turn out to be unpleasant or dangerous has specific consequences, and once the decision to do so has been made the individual tends to justify it. "More exactly, he becomes the subject of a psychological state -- a kind of tension known as cognitive dissonance, which he seeks to reduce by finding or concocting reasons for what he did" (Totman, 1979). The inclination to justify one's actions to others and to oneself goes very deep, and if one feels one's lines of defense to be tenuous, and experiences guilt, one will over-justify an action with a number of weak excuses. Unconscious mechanisms such as those

Figure 1

Psychosocial Model of Fitness and Illness

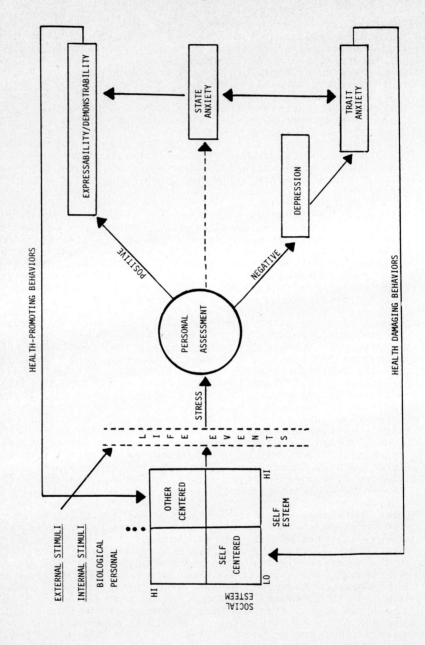

that can be activated by arousal or cognitive dissonance are the hardest for the individual to recognize. Cognitive dissonance may explain the rationalizations of smokers, dieters, drinkers, or anyone elso who fails in regimens designed to promote health. It may also explain the success of those who make a commitment and adhere to it. Patients actively involved in their treatment feel personally committed to it, and experience negative feelings or cognitive dissonance when they deviate from the regimen to which they have made a commitment (Festinger, 1957).

Our model may be used to provide a theoretical rationale for the testing of the theory of cognitive dissonance. Beck's (1967) cognitive model of depression, evolved from clinical observation and experimentation, provides another example of how mental illness relates functionally to psychosocial factors. If one draws an imaginary line from the low self/social (self-centered) quadrant in Figure 1 to the personal assessment component, and follows the negative outcomes, such as depression and anxiety, leading to unhealthful behaviors, one has simulated a cognitive triad to depression in which the subject regards himself, his future, and his experiences in idiosyncratic and negative ways (Beck, 1983).

Intrapsychic process -- our what goes on in the mind -- is essential to both examples of cognitive dissonance and cognitive therapy. We do not disregard those theories that depend heavily on external factors although we focus chiefly on personal assessment in our model; for example, the sociologically and behaviorally oriented schools of thought emphasize reinforcement. Rewards and punishment may take the form of social approval and social sanctions, or they may alter the individual's personality. Our model is intended to incorporate the personal and social phenomena in the individual's life by including concepts of self and social esteem, and life events that result in either beneficial or debilitating behaviors. Our Psychosocial Model of fitness and illness shows health associated with high self-esteem and high social esteem (or concern for others). Not only do life events affect the sense of self, but the response to such events is in turn influenced by the pre-existent sense of self. When psychological resources are already taxed by intrapsychic or interpersonal demands, life events may bring considerable damage. The personal assessment of such events, whether consciously or unconsciously arrived at, may tend to be negative or positive, and in the former case, negative emotional states such as depression and anxiety are generated. They are often experienced psychologically but not expressed, and when they are held in they may endure and affect behavior in many ways; the individual may tend to deny his condition, withdraw, become increasingly self-centered, and poorly motivated to carry out prescribed treatment. Such a construct is consistent with Beck's (1983) relating autonomy and social dependence to the absence or presence of depression.

The individual with intact self-esteem has adequate
psychological reserves to cope with stress in positive and
constructive ways; and the emotions evoked by the events in
his life are expressed normally. He assumes responsibility
for his .behavior, and tries to reorganize himself and re-
structure his environment with self-determination and activity, adapting to circumstances within a reasonable length of
time. His self-esteem is enhanced by his ability to cope in a
responsible way, and his concern for others is maintained.
The psychosocial conditions in his case are ideal for a
healthful lifestyle.

Our model can be viewed as marking a continuous series of
idiosyncratic self-assessments that have a cumulative effect
on the personal and social experience of the individual.
Specific assumptions of our mode are:

> 1. Psychogenic disorders are thought disorders (Beck,
> 1967). Idiosyncratic self-assessments are cognitive
> structures that mediate between stimulus inputs (internal
> or external) and personality responses (Harvey, Hunt, and
> Schroder, 1961, Miller, Galanter, and Pribam, 1960).
> 2. Depression is an outgrowth of self-assessment (Beck,
> 1967), and a predisposing factor for <u>trait anxiety</u>.
> 3. Persons with high A-trait are self-deprecatory, and
> afraid of failure (Atkinson, 1964, Sarason, 1960).
> 4. The person with high A-trait is likely to adopt
> defense mechanisms that result in maladaptive or psycho-
> pathological behaviors (Kroeber, 1963, Haan, 1977).

The purpose of our empirical investigation is to test whether
depression is a predisposing factor for trait anxiety. Our
view is, contrary to popular opinion, that depression, pervasive and relatively stable, may in fact induce, influence, or
contribute to trait anxiety (Beck, 1967, Archibald and
Tuddenhow, 1977). Trait anxiety is episodic rather than
chronic, but one classified as anxious is one who experiences
it frequently.

Suggested antecedents for the serious condition of trait
anxiety include heredity and childhood experiences (Spielberger, 1966 b). If, however, depression contributes to the
establishment of trait anxiety, it may be the more serious
condition, one that poses a graver threat to life-long
personality function. In turn, trait anxiety contributes to
state anxiety, depression being an indirect or secondary
effect. Thus this perspective is both theoretical and clinical. Theoretically, depression (a relatively observable
variable) precedes trait anxiety (a relatively unobservable
construct); thus the clinical perspective should lead to the
treatment of depression to combat <u>both</u> neurotic disorders.

METHOD

Four valid and reliable psychological tests for depression and anxiety, Beck Depression, (Beck & Beamesdorfer, 1974); CES Depression, (Weismann, 1980); Spielberger State Anxiety and Spielberger Trait Anxiety scales, (1970), were given to approximately 250 college students above freshmen in a class in Mental Health at the University of Virginia. They were part of a required battery of psychological tests given at the beginning and end of the academic semester; all data were collected and recorded for consideration of student grades. The analysis compared correlation coefficients of pre- and post-semester test variables, with the use of the cross-lagged panel correlation method (Cook and Campbell, 1979). It is argued (Lazarsfeld, 1938) that the repeated measurement of the same two variables should yield information about the direction of any causal asymmetries between them.

RESULTS

Correlations of pre-semester depression and late semester trait anxiety scores were significantly higher than early trait anxiety and late-depression scores (Figure 2). Early Beck Depression and CES Depression scales correlated with Spielberger Trait Anxiety by .6227 and .6137 respectively. Correlating pretest trait anxiety with the later administration of the depression scales yielded results in the order of .44. Statistically significant differences were established between the cross lag, depression to anxiety vs. the cross lag, anxiety to depression (Ferguson, 1976). Thus the analyses supported the position that depression appears to contribute to anxiety.

Statistics supporting our position are also observed in Figure 2 (c and d). The horizontal axes show reliability between scores for pre-post depression and trait anxiety to be about .50 or above. The vertical axes reveal observed construct validity between both depression scales and trait anxiety to above .60. We theorized that depression would not be shown to be a causal factor of state anxiety, and this was supported by the non-significant difference in the cross lags (Figure 2a and 2b).

DISCUSSION

Our model supports the notion that cognition is essential in the genesis of depression and anxiety. We have empirically demonstrated that depression may well be a critical intervening variable between self-assessment and trait anxiety, the sequence being: self-assessment, depression, trait anxiety. Problems of discriminating between anxiety and depression may

Figure 2

The Temporal order of Depression and Anxiety: A Cross Lagged Panel Analysis

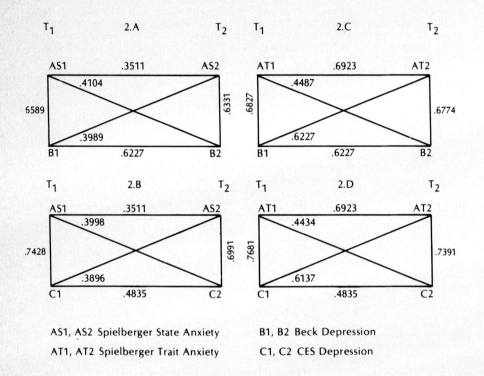

AS1, AS2 Spielberger State Anxiety   B1, B2 Beck Depression

AT1, AT2 Spielberger Trait Anxiety   C1, C2 CES Depression

be exacerbated by confusion in the temporal order of the appearance of depression and anxiety. Often, outcomes of depression are masked by symptoms of anxiety; and the causes of anxiety masked by consequences of depression. It is our contention that if one accepts anxiety as a sequel to depression, the symptoms of anxiety and depression can be more readily identified, and diagnosis and treatment can then be accomplished wth greater accuracy.

If one is to accept the pervasive nature of depression that triggers trait anxiety, one must conclude that both forms of neurosis are prevalent. The ways in which anxiety and depression function in a psychosocial context may well emphasize the seriousness of both mental disturbances (Warren, McEachern, 1983, Wilmotte and Mendlewitz, 1982). It is anticipated that the formulation of socially-based hypotheses and the synthesis of research findings from psychological, sociological, biological, and cultural perspectives will be more widely acknowledged if theoretically-based modes facilitate the recognition of depression and anxiety syndromes.

The Self in Anxiety, Stress and Depression
R. Schwarzer (Editor)
© Elsevier Science Publishers B.V. (North-Holland), 1984

STATE-ORIENTATION AND DEPRESSION IN RELATION TO ANXIETY AND SELF-AWARENESS

Daniele Kammer

University of Bielefeld, Federal Republic of Germany

This paper explores the validity of Kuhl's action control model of depression. The question is raised, whether state-orientation relates to depression and whether it is more typical for depression than for test anxiety, social anxiety, or self-awareness. The following results were obtained from a study with student subjects. (1) Subjects who were action-oriented following failure showed less overall depressed mood than state-oriented subjects and changed their mood positively following completion of a series of discrimination problems. (2) When thinking aloud while working on the discrimination problems, relatively depressed students who were as action-oriented as relatively nondepressed students during an initial baseline block, started to be more state-oriented during a subsequent failure block, and clearly reacted in a more state-oriented way following the failure manipulation. (3) A factor analysis performed on trait measures of depression, action control, test anxiety, social anxiety, and private and public self-consciousness revealed that both state-orientation following failure and state-orientation in prospective planning overlap with all of the remaining concepts, yet seem to be most typical for depression.

Extending Seligman's (1975) (motivational) helplessness model of depression, Kuhl (1981) has introduced the concept of functional helplessness. According to Kuhl, an individual may become helpless due to deficiencies in his/her action control rather than due to decreased expectancies of controllability. The individual is said to be action-oriented when his/her attention is evenly distributed over (a) the present state of affairs, (b) the intended goal, (c) the discrepancy between present state and intended goal, and (d) an action alternative with which to transfer the present state into the intended future one (Kuhl, 1983 a,b). Whenever one or more of these elements are missing, the individual's intention degenerates, and the individual is called state-oriented. Examples for state-oriented activities may be extended information processing about a preceding event, a focussing in one's emotional state, increased focussing on the goal, or indecisiveness as to which action alternative to engage in. Kuhl (1981) has shown that state-orientation following failure may lead to helplessness deficits, and he argues that state-orientation following failure may represent a (secondary) cause for the development (the maintenance) of depression.

Action control, with its extremes state- versus action-
orientation, may be situationally induced or conceptualized as
a trait. To measure individual differences in action control,
Kuhl (Note 1) has proposed the Action Control Scale HAKEMP,
with the following three subscales: HOE (Handlungs-
Orientierung nach Erfolg) to measure action control following
success; HOM (Handlungs-Orientierung nach Mißerfolg) to
measure action control following failure; and HOP (Handlungs-
Orientierung im prospektiven Planen) to measure action control
in prospective planning. Each of the three subscales is again
subdivided into two subscales, measuring behavioral (Handeln)
versus cognitive (Denken) aspects of the respective concept
(subscales HOHE, HODE, HOHM, HODM, HOHP, HODP; e.g. HOM = HOHM
+ HODM etc.). Concerning the validity of the above scales,
Kuhl (Note 1, 1983 a,b) provides evidence that HOM predicts
helplessness deficits whereas HOP mediates the realization of
intentions.

The aim of the present paper is to explore the validity of
Kuhl's concept of action control as a depression model. It is
hypothesized that state-orientation following failure relates
to severity of depression. The hypothesis is tested in three
ways: (1) via correlations between trait measures of action
control and depression, (2) by predicting depressed mood and
mood shifts during a laboratory study from initial action
control scores, and (3) by comparing the verbalizations of
relatively depressed versus relatively nondepressed subjects
during work on a series of discrimination problems where
failure is induced.

Finally, action control seems to be a worthwhile explanatory
construct for the development/maintenance of depression to the
extent that it is more typical for depression than it is for
other related concepts. Here, two constructs come to mind in
which attentional processes play a prominent role.

For the construct of test anxiety it has been shown that
anxious individuals' task performances are hampered by the
fact that their thoughts are centered around task-irrelevant
self-related contents. A subdivision of test anxiety into two
components (worry, emotionality) has proven useful (Liebert &
Morris, 1967). Both components seem to tap aspects of Kuhl's
concept of state-orientation, namely self-referent thought
(worry) and the perception of one's emotional arousal
(emotionality).

On the other hand, attentional processes are central to the
concept of self-awareness (Duval & Wicklund, 1972). Self-
awareness has been further subdivided into the aspects of
private and public self-consciousness and social anxiety
(Fenigstein, Scheier, & Buss, 1975). Again, focussing one's
attention on private versus public aspects of the self or
being concerned with the appraisal of one's behavior by others
may be viewed as different facets of state-orientation. To
summarize, it is hypothesized that the concept of action

control relates more clearly to depression than it does to the
concepts of test anxiety or self-awareness.

METHOD

Subjects. 105 students from the University of Bielefeld (56
male and 49 female) participated in the first part of the
study. 44 of these subjects volunteered for the second part
of the study. Subjects were paid a small amount of money,
seperately for each session.

Overview. The study was conducted in two parts. The first
part consisted of small group sessions in which subjects
completed four personality inventories, measuring depth of
depression, action control, test anxiety, and self-
consciousness, in that order. The second part of the study
was run during the following two weeks. In individual
sessions, subjects worked on three blocks of Levine (1966)
discrimination problems, a mixed block, a failure block, and a
success block, in that order. Subjects were instructed to
think aloud while working on the tasks, and their thoughts
were tape-recorded. Subjects' self-related mood was assessed
twice, at the beginning and at the end of each individual
session.

Material and Procedure. Personality inventories. Severity of
depression was assessed by a German version of the Beck
Depression Inventory (BDI; Kammer, 1983); test anxiety by the
German Test Anxiety Inventory (TAID; Hodapp, Laux, &
Spielberger, 1982); private and public self-consciousness and
social anxiety by the German Self-Consciousness Scale
(Heinemann, 1978); and action control by Kuhl's (Note 1)
Action Control Scale HAKEMP, short form, including the six
subscales HOHE, HODE, HOHM, HODM, HOHP, HODP (action control
following success: behavioral, cognitive; following failure:
behavioral, cognitive; in prospective planning: behavioral,
cognitive). High scores on the action control scales indicate
action-orientation whereas low scores indicate state-
orientation. Evidence for the reliability and validity of the
personality measures can be found in the above references.

Measure of Depressed Mood. Depressed mood was assessed with
the aid of von Zerssen's (1976) Befindlichkeitsskala, parallel
form Bf-S'. Containing 28 adjectives, this check list is
easily administered and highly reliable and valid, as reported
in the manual. Departing from the original scoring, the
present scoring is reversed, i.e. low scores indicate
depressed mood (Results are not affected by this change).

Type of Discrimination Problem. Nine four dimensional Levine
(1966) type discrimination problems were used as tasks, each
consisting of a set of 8 consecutive cards (trials). Each
card, in its left versus right half, contained a combination
of figures which differed with respect to the four dimensions

form (circle, triangle), size (big, small), position (square above, square below), and color (black, white). The problem has one predefined solution (among the eight possible solutions circle, triangle, big, small, above, below, black, and white). The subject's task is to find this solution by presenting a solution hypothesis on each trial and receiving feedback (correct, false) from the experimenter. Blind trials (trials without feedback) were not used. At the end of the 8 trials, the subject names his/her final solution.

Success/Failure Manipulation. Failure was manipulated on a discrimination problem via noncontingent feedback (50% "correct", 50% "false") during the 8 trials, and feedback "false" upon the subject's naming of the final solution. In contrast, success was induced via contingent feedback during the 8 trials, and the final feedback "correct".

Instruction and Treatment. Subjects were instructed about the discrimination problems and told to think aloud while working on the tasks. It was stressed that they should not hesitate to communicate any of their thoughts of feelings since these communications were an essential part of the investigation. Subjects then worked on two sample problems to ensure that they had understood the instructions.

For all subjects the treatment consisted of a series of 9 discrimination problems, arranged in three consecutive blocks of three problems each (S = success, F = failure):
1. mixed block   S F S
2. failure block   F F F
3. success block   S S S
Subjects worked on the problems while thinking aloud, and their reports were tape-recorded.

RESULTS

Relations among the Personality Variables. Pearson correlations between the BDI depression scores and the action control subscales are shown in Table 1 (Due to missing values, the sample size is reduced to N = 81):

Table 1
Pearson Correlations between Action Control
and Depression Scores (N = 81)

	BDI	HOHP	HODP	HOHM	HODM	HOHE
HODE	-.22	.31	.14	.16	.27	.47
HOHE	.09	-.06	.05	.04	.07	
HODM	-.25	.41	.38	.40		
HOHM	-.33	.45	.48			
HODP	-.34	.57				
HOHP	-.40					

(Coefficients above .29 are significant at the 1% level)

HODE   HOHE   HODM   HOHM   HODP   HOHP   Action   Control
      success (cognitive, behavioral), following failure
      (cognitive, behavioral), in prospective planning
      (cognitive, behavioral) (Kuhl, Note 1)
BDI   Beck Depression Inventory (Kammer, 1983)

As expected, high depression scores relate to action-orientation following failure, especially in behavior. Unexpectedly, high depression scores are also related to higher state-orientation in prospective planning. No relationship exists between depression scores and action control following success. For each of the action control subscales, high correlations are found between the cognitive and the behavioral alternative. Whereas action control following failure and action control in prospective planning show substantial overlap, action control following success seems to tap a different aspect, especially for the behavioral alternative.

Next, action control scores were correlated with the remaining personality variables (Table 2).

Table 2
Pearson Correlations among the
Personality Variables (N = 81)

	BDI	EMOT	WORRY	SOCANX	PUBLSC	PRIVSC
HODE	-.22	-.11	-.21	-.13	-.27	-.08
HOHE	.09	-.08	-.21	-.01	-.19	.01
HODM	-.25	-.36	-.32	-.31	-.37	-.18
HOHM	-.33	-.40	-.37	-.47	-.27	-.13
HODP	-.34	-.43	-.36	-.37	-.24	-.02
HOHP	-.40	-.34	-.21	-.37	-.15	-.14
PRIVSC	.30	.03	.17	-.08	.41	
PUBLSC	.23	.27	.46	.31		
SOCANX	.31	.48	.28			
WORRY	.30	.66				
EMOT	.27					

(Coefficients above .29 are significant at the 1% level)

HODE   HOHE   HODM   HOHM   HODP   HOHP   Action Control
        following success (cognitive, behavioral), following
        failure (cognitive, behavioral), in prospective
        planning (cognitive, behavioral) (Kuhl, Note 1)
PRIVSC PUBLSC SOCANX Private and Public Self-Consciousness
        and Social Anxiety (Heinemann, 1978)
WORRY   EMOT Worry and Emotionality components of Test
        Anxiety (Hodapp et al., 1982)
BDI   Beck Depression Inventory (Kammer, 1983)

The results show that state-orientation in prospective
planning and following failure are equally related to both
the emotionality and the worry component of anxiety as well as
to social anxiety and public self-consciousness. The
respective correlations are as high as those obtained with

the BDI depression scores. A factor analysis (iterated
principal factoring with subsequent varimax rotation)
performed on the intercorrelation matrix yielded four
orthogonal factors with eigenvalues greater than 1, explaining
67% of the total variance. From the varimax rotated factor
matrix (Table 3),

Table 3
Varimax Rotated Factor Matrix of
the Personality Variables (N = 81)

	Factor 1	Factor 2	Factor 3	Factor 4
BDI	-.48	.15	.28	.00
EMOT	-.38	.72	-.03	-.01
WORRY	-.20	.75	.18	-.18
PUBLSC	-.18	.40	.43	-.25
PRIVSC	-.06	.01	.91	.01
SOCANX	-.50	.37	-.08	-.01
HODE	.28	.01	-.10	.77
HOHE	-.11	-.16	.03	.65
HODP	.64	-.29	.01	.04
HOHP	.82	.00	-.07	.07
HODM	.46	-.26	-.18	.16
HOHM	.58	-.33	-.09	.03

BDI to HOHM cf. Table 2

these factors can be labeled: a bipolar factor Depression/Action Control Prospectively and following Failure (Factor 1) and three unipolar factors: Test Anxiety (Factor 2), Private Self-Consciousness (Factor 3), and Action Control following Success (Factor 4). Two of the personality variables were not uniquely determined by any one of the factors: Social Anxiety showed substantial loadings on both the Depression and the Test Anxiety factors, whereas Public

Self-Consciousness substantially loaded on both the Test Anxiety and the Private Self-Consciousness factors.

To summarize, the foregoing analysis has substantiated the postulated link between state-orientation following failure and depression. However, a similar link was found between state-orientation in prospective planning and depression. On the other hand, the two action control variables (prospectively and following failure) also had substantial overlap with the remaining personality variables, especially with social anxiety.

Prediction of Depressed Mood from Action Control Scores. Participants in the second part of the study were divided by a median split into groups scoring high versus low in action control following failure (HOM scale). The HOM scale was used as the criterion since the two subscales HOHM and HODM had shown substantial overlap. A two-way HOM (high, low) x Time (before tasks, after tasks) analysis of variance with repeated measures on the Time factor was performed on the mood ratings. The resulting HOM main effect, $F (1,42) = 6.47$, $p < .05$, revealed higher overall depressed mood for the state-oriented subjects (see Figure 1).

Moreover, the tendentially significant HOM x Time interaction, $F (1,42) = 3.23$, $p < .08$, indicated no change of mood for the state-oriented subjects, $t (25) = .52$, ns., yet a positive mood shift for their state-oriented peers, $t (17) = 2.56$, $p < .05$.

Verbalizations of Depressed versus Nondepressed Subjects. Among the participants in the second part of the study, extreme groups of depressed (N=14) versus nondepressed (N=15) students scoring high (BDI 9) versus low (BDI 3) on the BDI were identified. The BDI score of 9 was taken as the cut point for depression, in line with prior research on psychological aspects of depression (see Tabachnik, Crocker, & Alloy, 1983, for a review).

Subjects' tape-recorded verbalizations during work on the three blocks of discrimination problems were categorized by pairs of trained independent raters who were blind to the subjects' depression scores. Interrater agreement was obtained in an iterative way by means of independent categorizations, discussion of eventual disagreement, and subsequent agreement on one solution (mean interrater agreement above 85%).

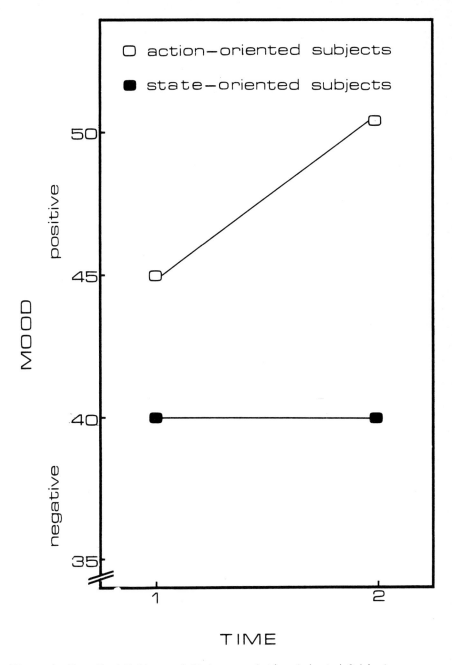

Figure 1: Mean Mood Ratings of State- vs. Action-Oriented Subjects

Three categories were used: Action-Orientation (AO),   State-
Orientation   (SO),   and   a   Remainder   Category   (R).   AO
encompassed   task   strategies,   analysing   the   task,   self-
instructions,   self-reinforcements,   statements   of   positive
affect,   self-assertiveness,   positive   prognoses,   positive
expectancies, and assertive statements about the unsolvability
of the failure tasks.   In contrast, LO consisted of statements
of   negative   affect,   negative   prognoses,   self-depreciating
statements,   attributions   for   failure,   unassertiveness,
statements   of   surprise,   self-monitoring,   repetitions of the
feedback   provided   by   the   experimenter.   The   R   category
contained statements which could not be subsumed under either
LO   or   HO   as   well   as   statements   on   whose LO vs.   HO
classification the two raters disagreed.   Since both types of
statements were rare,   the R category was not incorporated in
the further analysis.

For each subject, a seperate LO/HO quotient was calculated for
each of the three blocks of discrimination problems. For each
block,   the   LO/HO   quotient   equals   the   subject's   number   of
state-oriented   verbalizations   divided   by his/her   number   of
action-oriented   verbalizations,   and   thus   represents   the
subject's   relative   amount   of   state-orientation   during   that
block.   For the present analysis, this quotient was preferred
to   the absolute number of state-oriented verbalizations since
the   overall   frequency   of   statements   greatly   varied   between
individuals.

To   compare   depressed   versus   nondepressed   individuals'
verbalizations   during work on the three blocks   of   tasks,   a
two-way Depression   (high, low)   x   Block   (1,2,3)   analysis of
variance   with   repeated   measures   on the   Block   factor   was
performed   on the LO/HO quotients.   Further analysis   of   the
significant Depression x Block interaction, F (2,54) = 3.21,
p < .05, revealed the following pattern (see Figure 2):

Depressed and nondepressed individuals did not differ in their
relative   amount of state-orientation during the initial mixed
block,   t (27) = .79, ns.   .   During the subsequent   failure
block,   depressed individuals,   on average,   seemed to be more
state-oriented   than   nondepressed   individuals,   yet   the
difference between the LO/HO means did not reach significance,
due   to   the   high   variance within   the   group   of   depressed
subjects   (SD = 1.45) ,   t (27) = 1.67.,   ns.   .   During   the
final block,   i.e.   following the failure treatment, depressed
individuals   are   clearly more state-oriented than their   nondepressed peers, t (27) = 2.49, p < .01.

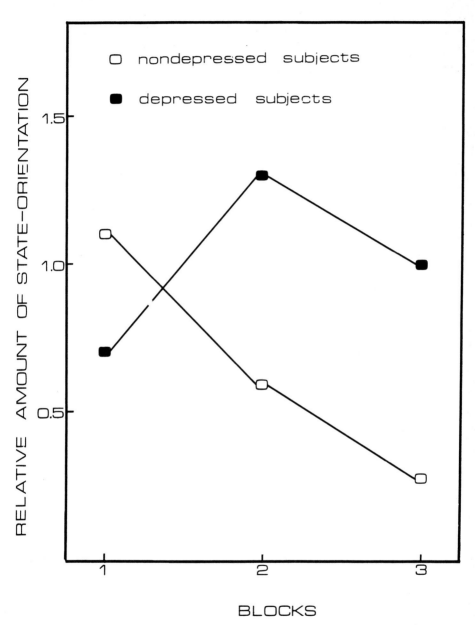

Figure 2: Mean Relative of State-Orientation for Depr. vs. Nondepressed

DISCUSSION

In the present paper, the question has been tackled, whether state-orientation is a viable construct to explain the development (the maintenance) of depression. Correlational evidence has been presented which points to a link between depression and state-orientation on a more than situation-specific level (Strictly speaking of a trait level would be inadequate since depression dissipates in time and the stability of action control scores is yet to be explored). Two limitations have emerged in this context. First, two aspects of action control - action control prospectively and following failure - were closely linked to each other and identically connected to the remaining variables. Thus, there is a need for a clearer operational distinction of these two aspects. Second, even though prospective action control and action control following failure clearly loaded on the Depression factor, they were not totally seperated from the remaining variables, especially not from social anxiety. Thus the question must be further persued whether state-orientation warrants to be discussed as a typical causal agent in depression.

Two results have been obtained which demonstrate the interplay of personal and situational factors and seem to nicely complement each other. On the one hand, action control following failure has been shown to mediate subjects' mood changes during the experiment. Initially, state-oriented and action-oriented subjects did not differ in their moods. However, action-oriented subjects felt significantly better after their completion of the tasks, whereas state-oriented subjects seem to profit from their work on a series of achievement tasks where failure is involved but success is obtained at last; state-oriented subjects do not. On the other hand, the analysis of the verbal protocols has revealed differential reactions to failure in the groups of relatively depressed versus nondepressed individuals. Whereas during the initial block of discriminiation problems the two groups did not differ, depressed individuals started to react in a more state-oriented way during the block of failure trials. Following the whole failure block, the depressed individuals were clearly more state-oriented than their nondepressed peers. Thus, the depressed individuals are more vulnerable to state-orientation following failure than the nondepressed subjects.

In sum, nondepressed individuals tend to remain action-oriented following failure, and action-oriented individuals have ways to profit from their mood regulation in an achievement situation. Depressed subjects, in contrast, are vulnerable to state-orientation where they have no profitable mood regulation.

NOTE

Financial support for this study was obtained from the University of Bielefeld (grant OZ 2774). Thanks go to Karola Bettmer and Thomas Feld who conducted the experimental sessions and helped in the preparation of the data and drawings, to the participants of the depression seminar who volunteered as raters for the tapes, and to Friedrich Försterling and Jonathan Harrow for helpful comments on an earlier version of this paper.

Address all correspondence to Daniele Kammer, Fakultät Psychologie und Sport, Universität Bielefeld, Postfach 8640, D-48 Bielefeld, West Germany.

REFERENCES

Abramson, L.Y. & Martin, D.J. (1981). Depression and the causal inference process. In Harvey, J.H., Ickes, W. & Kidd, R.E. (Eds.), New Directions in Attribution Research (Vol. 3). Hillsdale: Erlbaum.

Abramson, L.Y. & Sackeim,H.A.A. (1977). A paradox in depression: Uncontrollability and self-blame. Psychological Bulletin, 84, 838-851.

Abramson, L.Y., Seligman,M.E.P. & Teasdale,J. (1978). Learned helplessness in humans: Critique and reformulation. Journal of Abnormal Psychology, 87, 49-74.

Alagaratnam, W.J. (1982). New directions in the assessment and training of social skills. Paper presented to the Conference of the BPS. London: Institute of Education.

Alagaratnam, W.J. (1983). A longitudinal study of clinically depressed patients and psychiatric controls. Research in progressc.

Alagaratnam, W.J. (1983). Distortions in Beck's cognitive theory of depression. Paper presented to the Annual Conference of the BPS in Yorka.

Alagaratnam, W.J. (1983). Personality: A predictor of depressed mood. Unpublished manuscriptb.

Alagaratnam, W.J. & O'Connor, S. (1983). The social skill and cognitive correlates of mood manipulation. Unpublished manuscript.

Albert, S. (1977). Temporal comparison theory. Psychological Review, 84, 485-503.

Albert,D. (1980). Anxiety and learning-performance. Archiv für Psychologie,132, 139-163.

Alexander, F. (1950). Psychosomatic Medicine. New York: W.W. Norton and Co., Inc..

Alloy, L.B., Abramson, L.Y. & Viscusi, D. (1981). Induced mood and the illusion of control. Journal of Personality and Social Psychology, 41, 1129-1140.

Alloy,L.B. & Abramson,L.Y. (1979). Judgment of contingency in depressed and nondepressed students: Sadder but wiser ? Journal of Experimental Psychology,108, 441-485.

Alonzo, A., Simon, A. & Feinleib, M. (1975). Prodromata of

myocardial infarction and sudden death. Circulation, 52, 1056-1062.

Altman, J.H. & Wittenborn, J.R. (1980). Depression-prone personality in women. Journal of Abnormal Psychology, 89, 303-308.

American Psychiatric Association (Ed.) (1980). Diagnostic and statistical manual of mental disorders, 3rd ed.. Washington: A.P.A..

Ames, C. (1983). Achievement attributions and self-instructions under competitive and individualistic goal structures. unpublished.

Ames, C. (1984). Competitive, cooperative, and individualistic goal structures: A motivational analysis. In Ames, R. & Ames, C. (Eds.), Research on Motivation in Education: Student Motivation (Vol. 1). New York: Academic Press.

Ames, C. (1984). Conceptions of motivation within different goal structures. In R. Schwarzer (Ed.), Self-Related Cognitions in Anxiety and Motivation. Hillsdale: Erlbaum.

Ames, C. & Ames, R. (1981). Competitive versus individualistic goal structures: The salience of past performance information for causal attributions and affect. Journal of Educational Psychology, 73, 411-418.

Amthauer, R. (1971). Intelligenz-Struktur-Test. Göttigen: Hogrefe.

Anderson, C.A., Horowitz, L.M. & French, R. D. (1983). Attributional style of lonely and depressed people. Journal of Personality and Social Psychology, 45, 127-136.

Andrews, G., Tennant, C., Hewson, D.M. & Vaillant, G.E. (1978). Life events, stress, social support, coping style and risk of psychological impairment. Journal of Nervous and Mental Disease,166, 307-316.

Aneshensel, C.S., Clark, V.A. & Frerichs, R.R. (1983). Race, ethnicity, and depression: A confirmatory analysis. Journal of Personality and Social Psychology, 44, 385-398.

Antonovsky, A. (1979). Health, stress and coping. San Francisco: Jossey-Bass.

Appels, A. (1980). Psychological prodromata of myocardial infarction and sudden death. Psychotherapy & Psychosomatics, 34, 187-195.

Appels, A., Jenkins, D. & Rosenman, R. (1982).
Coronary-prone behavior in the Netherlands: A
cross-cultural validation study. Journal of Behavioral
Medicine, 5, 83-90.

Archibald, P.W. & Tuddenhow, R.D. (1977). Essentials of
Psychology. In W. Mischel & H. Mischel (Eds.), New
York: Random House.

Arieti, S. (1959). Manic-depressive psychosis. In S.
Arieti (Ed.), American Handbook of Psychiatry. New
York: Basic Books.

Arieti, S. & Bemporad, J. (1980). Severe and mild
depression. London: Tavistock.

Arieti, S. & Bemporad, J.R. (1980). The psychological
organization of depression. American Journal of
Psychiatry,137, 1360-1365.

Arkin,R.M., Appelman,A.J. & Burger,J.M. (1980). Social
anxiety,self-presentation and the self-serving bias in
causal attribution. Journal of Personality and Social
Psychology 38, 23-35.

Arlin, M. & Webster, J. (1983). Time costs of mastery
learning. Journal of Educational Psychology, 75,
187-196.

Aronson, E. (1968). Dissonance theory: Progress and
problems. In R.P. Abelson, E. Aronson, W.J. McGuire, et
al. (Eds.), Theories of cognitive consistency.
Chicago: Rand McNally.

Arsenault, A. & Dolan, S. (in press). The role of
personality, occupation and organization in
understanding the relationship between job stress,
performance and absenteeism. Journal of Occupational
Psychology, b.

Arsenault, A., Dolan, S. (1983). Le stress au travail et
ses effets sur l'individu et l'organisation. Final Rep.
to Inst. de Recherche en Sante et Securite du Travail du
Quebec. Quebec: , a.

Asendorpf, D.A., Wallot, G. & Scherer, K.R. (1983). Der
verflixte Repressor: Eine empirisch begründeter
Vorschlage zu einer zweidimensionalen
Operationalisierung von Repression-Sensitization.
Zeitschrift für Differentielle und Pädagogische
Psychologie, 4.

Asendorpf, J. (1984). Shyness, embarrassment, and
self-presentation: A control theory approach. In
Schwarzer, R. (Ed.), The self in anxiety, stress, and

__depression__. Amsterdam: North Holland Publ. Co..

Asendorpf, J.B., Wallbott, H.G. & Scherer, K.R. (1983).
    Der verflixte Repressor: Ein empirisch begründeter
    Vorschlag zu einer zweidimensionalen Operationalisierung
    von Repression-Sensitization. __Zeitschrift für__
    __Differentielle__ und __Diagnostische Psychologie__, __4__,
    113-128.

Atkinson, J. W. (1977). Motivation for achievement. In T.
    Blass (Ed.), __Personality variables in social behavior__.
    Hillsdale, N.Y.: Erlbaum.

Atkinson, J.W. (1964). __An introduction to motivation__.
    Princeton, N.J.: Van Nostrand.

Atkinson, J.W. & Birch, D. (1970). __The dynamics of__
    __action__. New York: Wiley.

Auerbach, S.M., Martelli, M.F. & Mercuri, L.G. (1983).
    Anxiety, information, interpersonal impacts, and
    adjustment to a stressful health care situation.
    __Journal of Personality and Social Psychology__, __44__,
    1284-1296.

Averill, J.R. (1979). A selective review of cognitive and
    behavioral factors involved in the regulation of stress.
    In R.A. Depue (Ed.), __The psychobiology of depression__
    __disorders: Implications for the effects of stress__. New
    York: Academic Press.

Averill, J.R. (1983). Studies on anger and aggression:
    Implications for theories of emotion. __American__
    __Psychologist__, __38__, 1145-1160.

Averill, J.R., OBrien, L. & DeWitt, G.W. (1977). The
    influence of response effectiveness on the preference
    for warning and on psychophysiological stress reactions.
    __Journal of Personality__, __45__, 395-418.

Baltes, P., Cornelius, S. & Nesselroade, J. (1978). Cohort
    effects in behavioral development: Theoretical and
    methodological perspectives. In H. Collins (Ed.),
    __Minnesota Symposia on Child Psychology__ (Vol. 11) (pp.
    1-63). Hillsdale, N.Y.: Erlbaum.

Bandura,A. (1977). Self-efficacy: Toward a unifying theory
    of behavioral change. __Psychological Review__, __84__,
    191-215.

Bandura,A. (1981). Self-referent thought: A developmental
    analysis of self-efficacy. In Flavell,J. & Ross,L.
    (Eds.), __Cognitive social development__. New York:
    Cambridge University Press.

Bandura,A. (1982). The self and mechanisms of agency. In Suls,J. (Ed.), Social psychological perspectives on the self. Hillsdale,N.J.: Erlbaum.

Bandura, A. (1980). Self-referent thought: The development of self-efficacy. In J.H. Flavell & L.D. Ross (Eds.), Development of Social Cognition.

Bandura, A. (1983). Self-efficacy determinants of anticipated fears and calamities. Journal of Personality and Social Psychology, 45, 464-469.

Bandura, A. & Cervone, D. (1983). Self-evaluative and self-efficacy mechanisms governing the motivational effects of goal systems. Journal of Personality and Social Psychology, 45, 1017-1028.

Bandura, A. & Mischel, W. (1965). Modification of self-imposed delay of reward through exposure to live and symbolic models. Journal of Personality and Social Psycholgy, 2, 698-705.

Bandura,A. & Schunk,D.H. (1981). Cultivating competence, self-efficacy and intrinsic interest through proximal self-motivation. Journal of Personality and Social Psychology, 41, 586-598.

Barker, R.G. (1968). Ecological Psychology. Concepts and methods for studying the environment of human behavior. Stanford: Stanford University Press.

Barraclough, B., Bunch, J., Nelson, B. & Sainsbury, P. (1974). A hundred cases of suicide: Clinical aspects. British Journal of Psychiatry,125, 335-373.

Barrera, M., Sandler, I.N. & Ramsay, T.B. (1981). Preliminary development of a scale of social support: Studies on college students. American Journal of Community Psychology, 9, 435-447.

Batlis, N.C. (1980). Job involvement and locus of control as moderators of role perception/individual-outcome relationships. Psychological Reports, 46, 111-119.

Beck, A.T. (1963). Thinking and depression: I. Idiosyncratic content and cognitive distortions. Archives of General Psychiatry, 9, 324-334.

Beck, A.T. (1967). Depression: Clinical, experimental and theoretical aspects. New York: Harper and Row.

Beck, A.T. (1972). Depression: Causes and treatment. Philadelphia: University of Pennsylvania Press.

Beck, A.T. (1976). Cognitive therapy and the emotional
    disorders. New York: International Universities
    Press.

Beck, A.T. (1983). Cognitive Therapy of Depression: New
    Perspectives. In P.J. Clayton & J.E. Barrett (Eds.),
    Treatment of Depression: Old Controversies and New
    Approaches. New York: Raven Press.

Beck, A.T. & Beamesderfer, A. (1974). Assessment of
    depression: The depression inventory. In P. Pichot & R.
    Olivier-Martin (Eds.), Psychological Measurements in
    Psychopharmacology. Basel: Karger.

Beck, A.T. & Beck, R.W. (1972). Screening depressed
    patients in family practice: A rapid technique.
    Postgraduate Medicine, 52, 81-85.

Beck, A.T. & Emery, G. (1979). Cognitive therapy of
    anxiety and phobic disorders. Philadelphia: Centre for
    Cognitive Therapy.

Beck, A.T. & Rush, A.J. (1975). A cognitive model of
    anxiety formation and anxiety resolution. In I.D.
    Sarason & C.D. Spielberger (Eds.), Stress and anxiety
    (Vol. 2). Washington: Hemisphere.

Beck, A.T. & Rush, A.J. (1978). Cognitive approaches to
    depression and suicide. In G. Serban (Ed.), Cognitive
    defects in the development of mental illness (pp.
    235-257). New York: Brunner/ Mazel.

Beck, A.T., Epstein, N. & Harrison, R. (1983). Cognitions,
    attitudes and personality dimensions in depression.
    British Journal of Cognitive Psychotherapy, 1,
    1-16.

Beck, A.T., Rush, A.J., Shaw, B.F. & Emery, G. (1979).
    Cognitive therapy of depression: A treatment manual.
    New York: Guilford Press.

Beck, A.T., Weissman, A., Lester, D., & Trexler, P. (1974).
    The measurement of pessimism: The hopelessness scale.
    Journal of Consulting and Clinical Psychology, 42,
    861-865.

Becker, J. (1974). Depression: Theory and research.
    Washington: V.H. Winston and Sons.

Becker, P. (1982). Towards a process analysis of test
    anxiety: Some theoretical and methodological
    observations. In R. Schwarzer, H.M. van der Ploeg &
    C.D. Spielberger (Eds.), Advances in test anxiety
    research (Vol. 1) (pp. 11-17). Lisse/ Hillsdale,
    N.Y.: Swets & Zeitlinger/ Erlbaum.

Becker, P. (1983). Test anxiety, examination stress, and achievement: Methodological remarks and some results of longitudinal study. In R. Schwarzer, H.M. van der Ploeg & C.D. Spielberger (Eds.), Advances in test anxiety research (Vol. 2) (pp. 129-146). Lisse/ Hillsdale, N.Y.: Swets & Zeitlinger/ Erlbaum.

Beehr, T.A. & Newman, J.E. (1978). Job stress, employee health and organizational effectiveness: A facet analysis model and literature review. Personnel Psychology, 31, 665-669.

Beehr, T.A. & Schuler, R.S. (1980). Current and future perspectives on stress in organizations. Working paper #WPS80-35. Ohio: Adm. Sc. Coll., Ohio State Univ..

Bentler,P.M. (1980). Multivariate analysis with latent variables. Causal modeling.. Annual Review of Psychology, 31, 419-456.

Berkman, L. (1982). Social network analysis and coronary heart disease. Advances in Cardiology, 29, 37-49.

Berkowitz, L. & Donnerstein, E. (1982). External validity is more than skeep deep: Some answers to critisms of laboratory experiments. American Psychologist, 37, 245-257.

Bevegard, B.S. & Shepherd, J.T. (1967). Regulation of the circulation during exercise in man. Physiological Review, 47, 178-213.

Biaggio, A.M.,Natalicio, L. & Spielberger, C.D. (1976). The development and validation of an experimental Portugese form of the State-Trait Anxiety Inventory. In C.D. Spielberger & R. Diaz-Guerrero (Eds.), Cross-cultural anxiety. Washington: Hemisphere.

Blalock,H.M. (1982). Conceptualization and measurement in the social sciences. Beverley Hills: Sage.

Blankenship, V. (in press). Toward a computer-based measure of resultant achievement motivation. .

Blatt, S.J. (1974). Levels of object representation in analytic and introjective depression. Psychoanalytic Study of Child, 29, 107-157.

Blatt, S.J., DÅfflitti, J.P. & Quinlan, D.M. (1976). Experiences of depression in normal young adults. Journal of Abnormal Psychology, 85, 383-389.

Blatt, S.J., Quinlan, D.M., Chevron, E.S., McDonald, C. & Zuroff, D. (1982). Dependency and self-criticism: Psychological dimensions of depression. Journal of

Consulting and Clinical Psychology, 50, 113-124.

Blau, G. (1981). An empirical investigation of job-stress, social support, service length, and job strain. The Organizational Behavior and Human Performance, 27, 279-302.

Blazer, D.G. (1982). Depression in late life. St. Louis: C.V. Mosby.

Blumenthal, J.A., Williams, R.S., Needels, T.L. & Wallace, A.G. (1982). Psychological changes accompany aerobic exercise in healthy middle-aged adults. Psychometric Medicine, 44, 529-536.

Bochner, S. & David, K.H. (1968). Delay of gratification, age and intelligence in an Aboriginal culture. International Journal of Psychology, 3, 167-174.

Boggiano, A.K. & Ruble, D. (1984). Children's responses to evaluative feedback. In R. Schwarzer (Ed.), Self-Related Cognitions in Anxiety and Motivation. Hillsdale: Erlbaum.

Bohrnstedt, G.W. & Felson, R.B. (1983). Explaining the relations among children's actual and perceived performances and self-esteem: A comparison of several causal models. Journal of Personality and Social Psychology, 45, 43-56.

Bossong, B. (1983). Wahrgenommene Sympathie des Lehrers und Selbsteinschätzung des Schülers. Unterrichtswissenschaft, 11, 285-293.

Bower, G.H. & Gilligan, S.G. (1979). Remembering information related to one's self. Journal of Research in Personality, 13, 420-432.

Bowler, R. (1982). A brief review of test anxiety in West German schools. In R. Schwarzer, H.M. van der Ploeg & C.D. Spielberger (Eds.), Advances in test anxiety research (Vol. 1) (pp. 85-94). Lisse/ Hillsdale, N.Y.: Swets & Zeitlinger/ Erlbaum.

Brackhane, R. (1982). Psychologie der sportlichen Betätigung. In A. Thomas (Ed.), Sportpsychologie - Ein Handbuch in Schlüsselbegriffen (pp. 13-25). München: Urban & Schwarzenberg.

Bradley, G.W. (1978). Self-serving biases in the attribution process: A reexamination of the fact or fiction question. Journal of Personality and Social Psychology, 36, 56-71.

Brand, R. (1978). Coronary-prone behavior as an independent risk factor for coronary heart disease. In

H. Dembroski, S. Weiss, F. Shields et al. (Eds.), Coronary-prone behavior (pp. 11-24). New York: Springer.

Brengelmann, J.C., Ullrich de Muynck, R. & Ullrich, R. (1978). Item- und Faktorenanalyse des Leistungsmotivations- und Leistungsangst- Fragebogens (LMA) bei leistungsgestörten Patienten. In R. Ullrich & R. Ullrich de Muynck (Eds.), Soziale Kompetenz. München: Pfeifer.

Briggs, S.R., Cheek, J.M. & Buss, A.H. (1980). An analysis of the Self-Monitoring Scale. Journal of Personality and Social Psychology, 38, 679-686.

Briggs, S.R., Snider, R. & Smith, T.G. (1983). The assessment of shyness: A comparison of measures. In J.M. Cheek (Ed.), Progress in research on shyness. Anaheim, Ca.: Symposium at meeting APA, Anah..

Brim, J.A. (1974). Social network correlates of avowed happiness. Journal of Nervous and Mental Disease,158, 432-439.

Brink, T.L., Yesavage, J.A., Lum, O., Heerseema, P., Adey, M. & Rose, T.L. (1982). Screening tests for geriatric depression. Clinical Gerontologist, 1, 37-43.

Broadbrent, D.E., Cooper, P.F., Fitzgerald, P. & Parkes, K.R. (1982). The Cognitive Failures Questionnaire (CFQ) and its correlates. British Journal of Clinical Psychology, 21, 1-16.

Brockner, J. (1979). Self-esteem, self-consciousness, and task performance: Replications, extensions, and possible explanations. Journal of Personality and Social Psychology, 37, 447-461.

Brockner, J., Gardner, M.,Bierman, J., Mahan, T., Thomas, B., Weiss, W., Winters, L. & Mit(1983). The roles of self-esteem and self-consciousness in the Wortman-Brehm model of reactance and learned helplessness. Journal of Personality and Social Psychology, 45, 199-209.

Brophy, J., Rohrkemper, M., Rashid, H. & Goldberger, M. (1983). Relationships between teachers' presentations of classroom tasks and students' engagement in those tasks. Journal of Educational Psychology, 75, 544-552.

Brophy, J.E. (1983). Research on the self-fulfilling prophecy and teacher expectations. Journal of Educational Psychology, 75, 631-661.

Brown, G. & Harris, T. (1978). Social origins of

depression: A study of psychiatric disorders in women. New York: Free Press.

Brown, R. & MacDougall, M.A. (1981). Assessment of psychosomatic fitness. Paper presented at the Int. Conf. of the American Personnel and Guidance Association, Munich, Germany, Oct.. .

Brown, R. & MacDougall, M.A. (1982). Psychomatic fitness. Christian Medical Journal, 13, 11-13.

Browne, J.A. & Howarth, E. (1977). A comprehensive factor analysis of personality questionnaire items: Atest of twenty putative factor hypotheses. Multivariate Behavioral Research, 12, 399-427.

Brumback, R.A. & Staton, R.D. (1982). An hypothesis regarding the communality of right-hemisphere involvement in learning disability, attentional disorder, and depressive disorder. Perceptual & Motor Skills, 55, 1091-1097.

Brunke, Ch. & Hörmann, H.J. (in press). Veränderungen des Selbstkonzepts bei Jugendlichen nach Abschluß der Gymnasialen Oberstufe. In A. Stiksrud (Ed.), Jugend und Werte Aspekte einer politischen Psychologie des Jugendalters. Weinheim: Beltz.

Bumberry, W., Oliver, J.M. & McClure, J.N. (1978). Validation of the Beck Depression Inventory in a university population using psychiatric estimates as the criterion. Journal of Consulting and Clinical Psychology, 46, 150-155.

Burns, D.D. (1980). Feeling good. New York: Morrow, (a).

Burns, D.D. (1980). The perfectionist's script for self-defeat. Psychology Today Nov., 34-52(b).

Burns,R.B. (1979). The self-concept. London: Longman.

Buss, A.H. (1980). Self-consciousness and social anxiety. San Francisco: Freeman.

Buss, A.H. (1983). Social rewards and personality. Journal of Personality and Social Psychology, 44, 553-564.

Buss, A. (1984). Two kinds of shyness. In R. Schwarzer (Ed.), Self-Related Cognitions in Anxiety and Motivation. Hillsdale: Erlbaum.

Buss, A.H. & Durkee, A. (1957). An inventory for assessing different kinds of hostility. Journal of Consulting Psychology, 21, 343-349.

Byrne, D. (1980). Attributed responsibility for life events in survivors of myocardial infarction. Psychotherapy & Psychosomatics, 33, 7-13.

Byrne, D. & Whyte, H. (1980). Life events and myocardial infarction revisited: The role of measure of individual impact. Psychosomatic Medicine, 42, 1-10.

Byrne,B.M. & Carlson,J.E. (1982). Self-concept and academic achievement: A causal modeling approach to construct validation using a multiple-indicator structural equation model. Paper presented at the annual meeting of the American Educational Research Assoc., New York. New York: .

Cacioppo, J.T., Glass, C.R. & Merluzzi, T.V. (1979). Self-statements and self-evaluations: A cognitive-response analysis of social anxiety. Cognitive Therapy and Research, 3, 249-262.

Campbell, H. (1896). Morbid shyness. The British Medical Journal, 2, 805-807.

Caplan, G. (1974). Supportive systems and community mental health: Lectures on concept development. New York: Behavioral Publications.

Caplan, R.D. (1972). Organizational stress and indiv. strain: A soc. psych. study of risk factors in cor. heart disease: Administrators, engin., scient. Ph. D. diss.. Ann Arbor: University of Michigan.

Caplan, R.D., Cobb, S. & French, R.P. Jr. (1979). White collar work load and cortisol: Disruption of a circadian rhythmby job stresses. Journal of Psychosomatic Research, 23, 181-192.

Caplan, R.D., Cobb, S., French, R.P. Jr., Van Harrison, R. & Pinneau, S.R., Jr. (1975). Job demand and worker health. NIOSH Report. Washington, D.C.: , 75-160.

Carver, C.S. & Glass, D.C. (1976). The self-consciousness scale: A discriminant validity study. Journal of Personality Assessment, 40, 169-172.

Carver, C.S. & Scheier, M.F. (1981). Attention and self-regulation. New York: Springer.

Carver, C.S. & Scheier, M.F. (1981). Attention and self-regulation: A control-theory approach to human behavior. New York: Springer.

Carver, C.S. & Scheier, M.F. (1984). Functional and dysfunctional responses to anxiety: The interaction between expectancies and self-focused attention. In R.

Schwarzer (Ed.), Self-Related Cognitions in Anxiety and Motivation. Hillsdale: Erlbaum.

Cattell, R.B. (1957). Personality and motivation structure and measurement. New York: Harcour, Brace & World.

Cattell, R.B. (1982). The nature and genesis of mood states: A theoretical model with experimental measurem. conc. anxiety, depression, arousal and other mood states. In C.D. Spielberger (Ed.), Anxiety: Current trends in theory and research (Vol. 1) (pp. 115-183). New York: Academic Press.

Cattell, R.B. & Scheier, I.H. (1958). The nature of anxiety: A review of thirteen multivariate analyses composing 814 variybles. Psychological Reporter Monograph Supplement.

Cattell, R.B., Eber, H.W. & Tatsuoka, M.G. (1970). Handbook of the Sixteen Personality Factors Questionnaire (16PF). Champaign: Institute for Personality.

Cavert, C.W. (1982). A trait-situation analysis of shyness. Unpublished masters thesis. Tulsa, Ok.: University of Tulsa, OK..

Center for Human Resource Research (1981). The national longitudinal surveys handbook. Columbus: Ohio State University.

Cheek, J.M. (1982). Aggregation, moderator variables, and the validity of personality tests: A peer rating study. Journal of Personality and Social Psychology, 43, 1254-1269a.

Cheek, J.M. (1982). Shyness and self-esteem: A personological perspective. In M. Leary (Ed.), Recent research in social anxiety: Social, personality, and clinical perspectives. (pp. b). Toronto, Can.: Symposium at APA meeting, Toron..

Cheek, J.M. & Busch, C.M. (1981). The influence of shyness on loneliness in a new situation. Personality and Social Psychology Bulletin, 7, 572-577.

Cheek, J.M. & Buss, A.H. (1981). Shyness and sociability. Journal of Personality and Social Psychology, 41, 330-339.

Cherkes-Julkowski, M., Groebel, J. & Kuffner, H. (1982). Social comparison and emotional reactions in the classroom. In R. Schwarzer, H.M. van der Ploeg & C.D. Spielberger (Eds.), Advances in test anxiety research (Vol. 1) (pp. 105-114). Lisse/ Hillsdale, N.Y.: Swets

& Zeitlinger/ Erlbaum.

Cherkes-Julkowski,M., Groebel,J. & Kuffner,H. (1982).
Social comparison and emotional reactions in the
classroom. In Schwarzer,R., van der Ploeg,H. &
Spielberger,C.D. (Eds.), Advances in test anxiety
research.Vol.1 (pp. 105-114). Lisse: Swets &
Zeitlinger.

Claar, A., Boehnke, K. & Silbereisen, R.K. (in press). Zur
Entwicklung von Motiven prosozialen Handelns bei 12- bis
18jährigen deutschen und polnischen Schülern. In A.
Stiksrud (Ed.), Jugend und Werte. Aspekte einer
politischen Psychologie des Jugendalters. Weinheim:
Beltz.

Clark, D.M. (in press). On the induction of depressed mood
in the laboratory: Evaluation and comparison of the
Velten and Musical procedures. Advances in Behavior,
Research and Therapy.

Clark, J.V. & Arkowitz, H. (1975). Social anxiety and
self-evaluation of interpersonal performance.
Psychological Reports, 36, 211-221.

Cobb, S. (1976). Social support as a moderator of life
stress. Psychosomatic Medicine, 38, 300-314.

Cobb, S. & Rose, R.M. (1973). Hypertension, peptic ulcer
and diabetes in air traffic controllers. Journal of
the American Medical Association,224, 489-492.

Cohen, J. & Cohen P. (1975). Applied multiple regression/
correlation analysis for the behavioral sciences.
Hillsdale, N.Y.: Erlbaum.

Cohen, J.A. (1960). A coefficient of agreement for nominal
scales. Educational and Psychological Measurement,
20, 37-46.

Cohen, R. (1983). Verhaltenstherapie zu Beginn der
achtziger Jahre. Psychologische Rundschau, 35,
1-9.

Cohen, R.M., Weingartner, H., Smallberg, S.A., Pickar, D. &
Murphy, D.L. (1982). Effort and cognition. Archives
of General Psychiatry, 39, 593-597.

Cohen, S., Rothbart, M. & Phillips, S. (1976). Locus of
control and the generality of learned helplessness.
Journal of Personality and Social Psycology, 34,
1049-1056.

Coleman, J.C. (1978). Current contradictions in adolescent
theory. Journal of Youth and Adolescence, 7,
1-11.

Conklin, R., Sturgeon, D. & Leff, J. (1983). The
    relationship between auditory hullucinations and
    spontaneous fluctuations of skin conductance in
    schizophrenia. British Journal of Psychiatry,142,
    47-52.

Conty, M. (1980). Kognitive und affekive Konsequenzen von
    Hilfeleistungen für den Empfänger von Hilfe.
    Unveröffentlichte Diplom-Arbeit. Bielefeld:
    Universität Bielefeld, Abt. Psy..

Cook, T.D. & Campbell, D.T. (1979).
    Quasi-experimentation: Design and analysis issues for
    field settings. Chicago: Rand McNally College
    Publishing.

Cooley, Ch. H. (1902). Human nature and the social
    order. New York: Scribner.

Cooper, C.L. & Marshall, J. (1976). Occupational sources
    of stress: A review of the literature relating to
    coronary heart disease and mental health. Journal of
    Occupational Psychology, 49, 11-28.

Costello, C.G. (1976). Anxiety and Depression: The
    Adaptive Emotions. Montreal: McGill-Queens University
    Press.

Costello,C.G. (1982). Loss as a source of stress in
    psychopathology. In R.W.J.Neufeld (Ed.), Psychological
    Stress and Psychopathology (pp. 93-125). New York:
    McGraw-Hill.

Covington, M. (1983). Anxiety, task difficulty and
    childhood problemsolving: A selfworth interpretation.
    In R. Schwarzer, H.M. van der Ploeg & C.D. Spielberger
    (Eds.), Advances in test anxiety research (Vol. 2)
    (pp. 101-109). Lisse/ Hillsdale, N.Y.: Swets &
    Zeitlinger/ Erlbaum.

Covington, M. & Omelich, C.L. (1982). Achievement anxiety,
    performance and behavioral instruction: A cost/benefits
    analysis. In R. Schwarzer, H.M. van der Ploeg & C.D.
    Spielberger (Eds.), Advances in test anxiety research
    (Vol. 1) (pp. 139-154). Lisse/ Hillsdale, N.Y.: Swets
    & Zeitlinger/ Erlbaum.

Covington, M.V. (1984). Anatomy of failure-induced
    anxiety: The role of cognitive mediators. In R.
    Schwarzer (Ed.), Self-Related Cognitions in Anxiety and
    Motivation. Hillsdale: Erlbaum.

Cowen, E.L. (1983). Primary prevention in mental health:
    Past, present and future. In R.D.Felner, L.A.Jason,
    J.N.Moritsugu & S.S.Farber (Eds.), Preventive

Psychology: Theory, Research and Practice (pp. 11-30). New York: Pergamon Press.

Craik, F.I.M. & Tulving, E. (1975). Depth of processing and the retention of words in episodic memory. Journal of Experimental Psychology: General,104, 268-294.

Crano, S.L. & Crano, W.D. (in press). Development of Portugese- and Spanish-language measures of self-concept. Interamerican Journal of Psychology.

Crano, W.D. & Brewer, M.B. (1973). Principles of research in social psychology. New York: McGraw-Hill.

Crano, W.D. & Schroeder, H.M. (1967). Complexity of attitude structure and processes of conflict reduction. Journal of Personality and Social Psychology, 5, 110-114.

Crano, W.D., Crano, S.L. & Biaggio, A.M. (1983). Relationship between self-concept and state-trait anxiety under different conditions of social comparison. Paper pres. Ann. Conv. of APA, Div. 8. Anaheim, California: .

Crits-Christoph, P. & Singer, J.L. (1981). Imagery in cognitive-behavior therapy: Research and application. Clinical Psychology Review, 1, 19-32.

Crown, S. & Crisp, A.H. (1966). A short clinical diagnostic self-rating scale for psychoneurotic patients. British Journal of Psychiatry,112, 917-123.

Crowne, D.P. & Marlowe, D. (1964). The approval motive. Studies in evaluative dependence. New York: Wiley.

Crozier, R. (1979). Shyness as anxious self-preoccupation. Psychological Reports, 44, 959-962a.

Crozier, W.R. (1979). Shyness as a dimension of personality. British Journal of Social and Clinical Psychology, 18, 121-128b.

Crozier, W.R. (1979). Theories of social shyness. Paper presented at the Annual Conference of the BPS Social Psychology Section at University of Surrey, Guildford. .

Cummings, T.G., Cooer, C.L. (1979). A cybernetic framework for studying occupational stress. Human Relations, 32, 393-418.

Curran, J.P. & Monti, P.M. (1982). Social skills training: A practical handbook for assessment and training. New York: Guildford Press.

Daly, S.   . (1978). Behavioral correlates of social
    anxiety. British Journal of Social and Clinical
    Psychology, 18, 121-128.

Danish,S.J., Galambos,N.L., Laquatra,I. (1983). Life
    development intervention:Skill training for personal
    competence. In R.D.Felner, L.A.Jason, J.N.Moritsugu,
    S.S.Farber (Ed.), Preventive Psychology: Theory,
    Research & Practice (pp. 49-67). New York: Pergamon
    Press.

Davis, G.A. (1966). Current status of research and theory
    in human problem solving. Psychological Bulletin,
    66, 36-54.

Davis, H, (1979). The self-schema and subjective
    organization of personal information in depression.
    Cognitive Therapy and Research, 3, 415-425b.

Davis, H. (1979). Self-reference and the encoding of
    personal information in depression. Cognitive Therapy
    and Research, 1, 97-110a.

Davis, H. & Unruh, W.H. (1981). The development of the
    self-schema in adult depression. Journal of Abnormal
    Psychology, 90, 125-133.

De Loore, K. (1982). Zelfschema's en depressie. Een
    experimenteel onderzoek. Unpublished M.A. thesis.
    University of Leuven.

DeVellis, R.F., DeVellis, B.M. & McCauley, C. (1978).
    Vicarious acquisition of learned helplessness in humans.
    Journal of Personality & Social Psychology, 36,
    894-899.

DeVries, H.A. (1980). Physiology of exercise (third
    edition). Dubuque: Brown.

Dean, A. & Lin, N. (1972). The stress buffering role of
    social support: Problems and prospects for systematic
    investigation. Journal of Nervous and Mental
    Disease,165, 403-417.

Deci,E.L. (1975). Intrinsic motivation. New York:
    Plenum.

Deci,E.L. (1980). Intrinsic motivation and personality.
    In Staub,E. (Ed.), Personality. Basic aspects and
    current research (pp. 35-80). Englewood Cliffs:
    Prentice Hall.

Deci,E.L. (1980). The psychology of self-determination.
    Lexington: Heath.

Deci, E.L. & Ryan, R.M. (1984). Self-regulation and self-control: The dynamics of self-determination in personality and development. In R. Schwarzer (Ed.), Self-Related Cognitions in Anxiety and Motivation. Hillsdale: Erlbaum.

Defares, P.B., Grossman, P. & de Swart, C.G. (1983). Test anxiety, cognitive primitivation and hyperventilation. In R. Schwarzer, H.M. van der Ploeg & C.D. Spielberger (Eds.), Advances in test anxiety research (Vol. 2) (pp. 87-98). Lisse/ Hillsdale, N.Y.: Swets & Zeitlinger/ Erlbaum.

Deffenbacher,J.L. (1980). Worry and emotionality in test anxiety. In Sarason, I.G. (Ed.), Test anxiety (pp. 111-128). Hillsdale: Erlbaum.

Denney, D. (1980). Self-control approaches to the treatment of test anxiety. In I.G. Sarason (Ed.), Test anxiety (pp. 209-244). Hillsdale, N.Y.: Erlbaum.

Depreeuw, E. (1982). From test anxiety research to treatment. Some critical considerations and propositions. In R. Schwarzer, H.M. van der Ploeg & C.D. Spielberger (Eds.), Advances in test anxiety research (Vol. 1) (pp. 155-163). Lisse/Hillsdale, N.Y.: Swets & Zeitlinger/ Erlbaum.

Depreeuw, E. & Duyck, J. (1983). The adaptation of a German anxiety questionnaire to a Dutch speaking population. In R. Schwarzer, H.M. van der Ploeg & C.D. Spielberger (Eds.), Advances in test anxiety research (Vol. 2) (pp. 169-181). Lisse/ Hillsdale, N.Y.: Swets & Zeitlinger/ Erlbaum.

Derogatis, L.S., Lipman, L.C. & Rickles, K. (1971). Neurotic symptoms dimensions (Archives of General Psychiatry (24th ed.). : 454-464.

Derry, P.A. & Kuiper, N.A. (1981). Schematic processing and self-reference in clinical depression. Journal of Abnormal Psychology, 90, 286-297.

Dessonville, C., Gallagher, D., Thompson, L.W., Finell, K. & Lewinson, P.M. (1981). Relation of age and health status of depressive symptoms in normal and depressed older adults. Essence, 83, 191-196.

Diener,C.I. & Dweck,C.S (1981). An analysis of learned helplessness: II.The processing of success. Journal of Personality and Social Psychology, 39, 940-952.

Diener,C.I. & Dweck,C.S. (1978). An analysis of learned helplessness: Continuous changes in performance, strategy and achievement cognitions following failure. Journal of Personality and Social Psychology, 36,

451-462.

Dohrenwend, B.S., Krasnoff, L., Askenasy, A.R. &
    Dohrenwend, B.P. (1978). Exemplifications of a method
    for scaling life events: The PERI Life Events Scale.
    Journal of Health and Social Behavior, 9, 205-229.

Dolan, S. & Arsenault, A. (1979). The organizational and
    individual consequences of stress at work: A new
    frontier to human resources administration. In V.V.
    Vesey & G. Jr. Hall (Eds.), The New World of Managing
    Human Resources (Vol. 2) (pp. 4-22). Pasadena:
    California Inst. of Technology.

Dolan, S. & Arsenault, A. (1980). Stress, health and
    performance at work. Montreal: University of Montreal,
    186pp.

Dolan, S., Arsenault, A. & Abenhaim, L. (1981). Stress and
    performance at work: An empirical test. Stress, 2,
    29-34.

Dorn, N. (1983). Alcohol, youth and the state: Drinking
    practices, controls and health education. Beckenham:
    Croom Helm.

Durlak, J.A. (1983). Social problem-solving as a primary
    prevention strategy. In R.D.Felner, L.A.Jason,
    J.N.Moritsugu, S.S.Farber (Ed.), Preventive Psychology:
    Theory, Research and Practice (pp. 31-49). New York:
    Pergamon Press.

Dusek, J.B. & Flaherty, J.F (1981). The development of the
    self-concept during the adolescent years. Monographs
    of the Society for Research in Child Development,
    46.

Dweck, C.S., Davidson, W., Nelson, S. & Enna, B. (1978).
    Sex differences in learned helplessness: II. The
    contingencies of evaluative feedback in the classroom
    and III. An experimental analysis. Developmental
    Psychology, 14, 268-276.

Dörner, D. (in press). Verhalten, Denken und Emotionen.
    Sprache und Kognition. .

Easly, A.H. (1967). Involvement as a determinant of
    response to favorable and unfavorable information.
    Journal of Personality and Social Psychology.
    Monograph, 7, 1-15.

Eckenrode, J. (1983). The mobilization of social supports:
    Some individual constraints. American Journal of
    Community Psychology, 5, 509-528.

Edwards, G., Arif, A. & Jaffe, J. (Eds.) (1983). Drug use

and misuse: Cultural perspectives. Beckenham: Croom Helm.

Eelen, P. (1981). Experimental study of the self-schema in depressives. Abstract. Scandinavian Journal of Behavior Therapy, 10, 41.

Eliot, R. (1977). Stress and cardiovascular disease. European Journal of Cardiology, 5, 97-104.

Elkind, D. & Bowen, R. (1979). Imaginary audience behavior in children and adolescents. Development Psychology, 15, 38-44.

Ellis, A. & Grieger, R. (1979). Praxis der rational-emotiven Therapie. München: Urban & Schwarzenberg.

Epstein, S. (1976). Anxiety, arousal, and the self-concept. In C.D. Spielberger & I.G. Sarason (Eds.), Stress and anxiety (Vol. 3). New York: Wiley.

Epstein, S. (1979). The stability of behavior: I. On predicting most of the people much of the time. Journal of Personality and Social Psychology, 37, 1097-1124.

Epstein,S. (1979). Entwurf einer integrativen Persönlichkeitstheorie. In Filipp, S.-H. (Ed.), Selbstkonzept-Forschung (pp. 15-45). Stuttgart: Klett-Cotta.

Erikson, E. (1950). Childhood and society. New York: W.W. Norton.

Eysenck, H.J. (1956). The questionnaire measurement of neuroticism and extraversion. Revista de Psicologia, 50, 113-140.

Eysenck, H.J. & Eysenck, S.B.G. (1964). Manual of the Eysenck Personality Inventory. London: University of London Press.

Eysenck, M.W. (1982). Attention and arousal. New York: Springer.

Eysenck, M.W. (1983). Anxiety, stress and performance. In G.R. Hockey (Ed.), Stress and fatigue. London: Wiley.

Fairbank, D. & Hough, R. (1979). Life event classifications and the event-illness relationship. Journal of Human Stress, 5, 41-47.

Falger, P.R.J. (1983). Behavioral factors, life changes,

and the development of vital exhaustion and depression
in myocardial infarction patients. International
Journal of Behavioral Development, 6, 405-425(a).

Falger, P.R.J. (1983). Pathogenic life changes in middle
adulthood and coronary heart disease: A life-span
developmental perspective. International Journal of
Aging & Human Development, 16, 7-27(b).

Falger, P.R.J. & Appels, A. (1982). Psychological risk
factors over the life course of myocardial infarction
patients. Advances in Cardiology, 29, 132-139.

Falger, P.R.J., Appels, A. & Lulofs, R. (1984).
Ontogenetic development and 'breakdown in adaptation'. A
review on psychosocial factors. In J. Siegrist & H.
Cullen (Eds.), Breakdown im human adaptation to
'stress' (Vol. 1) (pp. 159-187). Den Haag/ Boston:
Martinus Nijhoff.

Felner, R.D., Ginter, M. & Primavera, J. (1982). Primary
prevention during school transitions: Social support and
environmental structure. American Journal of Community
Psychology, 3, 277-290.

Fend,H.& Helmke,A. (1983). Selbstkonzepte und
Selbstvertrauen - 10 Jahre Selbstkonzeptforschung in den
Konstanzer pädagogisch-psychologischen Wirkungsstudien.
Zeitschrift für Personenzentrierte Psychologie und
Psychotherapie, 1.

Fenigstein, A., Scheier, M.F. & Buss, A.H. (1975). Public
and private self-consciousness: Assessment and theory.
Journal of Consulting and Clinical Psychology, 43,
522-527.

Fennell, M.J.V. (1983). Cognitive therapy of depression:
The mechanism of change. Behavioral Psychotherapy,
11, 97-108.

Ferguson, T.J., Rule, B.G. & Carlson, D. (1983). Memory
for personally relevant information. Journal of
Personality and Social Psychology, 44, 251-261.

Festinger, L. (1957). A theory of cognitive dissonance.
Evanston, Illinois: Row Peterson.

Festinger,L. (1954). A theory of social comparison
processes. Human Relations, 7, 117-140.

Filipp, S.- H. (1983). Die Rolle von Selbstkonzepten im
Prozeß der Auseinandersetzung mit und Bewältigung von
kritischen Lebensereignissen. In Schwarzer, Ralf (Ed.),
Zeitschrift für personenzentrierte Psychologie und
Psychotherapie. Themenheft Selbstkonzept (Vol. 2) (pp.
39-47).

Filipp, S.-H., Aymanns, P. & Braukmann, W. (1984). Coping with life events: When the self comes into play. In Schwarzer, R. (Ed.), Self-related cognitions in anxiety and motivation. Hillsdale: Erlbaum.

Filipp,S.-H.(Ed.) (1979). Selbstkonzept-Forschung. Stuttgart: Klett.

Findley, M. J. & Cooper, H.M. (1983). Locus of control and academic achievement. Journal of Personality and Social Psychology, 44, 419-428.

Fineman, S. (1977). The achievement motive construct and its measurement: Where are we now? British Journal of Psychology, 68, 1-22.

Firth, S. & Narikawa, O. (1972). Attitudes toward school. Los Angeles: Instructional Objective Exchange.

Fischer,M., Stein,F. & Stephan,E. (1982). Prüfungsangstforschung in der kognitiven Sackgasse? Eine empirische Studie und ihre kritische Reflexion. Trierer Psychologische Berichte, 9, 12.

Fitzgerald, K.C. (1980). Revisiting sex differences in the expresssion of depression. Journal of Abnormal Psychology, 89, 194-202.

Flavell, J.H. (1981). Monitoring social cognitive enterprises: something else that may develop in the area of social cognition. In J.H. Flavell & L. Ross (Eds.), Social cognitive development frontiers and possible futures (pp. 272-287). Cambridge, Mass.: Cambridge University Press.

Folger, R., Rosenfield, D. & Robinson, T. (1983). Relative deprivation and procedural justifications. Journal of Personality and Social Psychology, 45, 268-273.

Fornell, C. (1982). Second generation in multivariate analysis. New York: .

Foulds, G.A. & Bedford, A. (1975). Hierarchy of classes of personal illness. Psychological Medicine, 5, 181-192.

Fox, J.E. & Houston, B.K. (1983). Distinguishing between cognitive and somatic trait and state anxiety in children. Journal of Personality and Social Psychology, 45, 862-870.

Frankenhaeuser, M. & Gardell, B. (1976). Underload and overload in working life: Outline of a multidisciplinary approach. Journal of Human Stress, 2, 35-45.

Franzoi, S.L. (1983). Self-concept differences as a function of private self-consciousness and social anxiety. Journal of Research in Personality, 17, 275-287.

Fraser, B.J. & Fisher, D.L. (1983). Use of actual and preferred classroom environment scales in person-environment fit research. Journal of Educational Psychology, 75, 303-313.

Fredricks, A.J. & Dossett, D.L. (1983). Attitude-behavior relations: A comparison of the Fishbein-Ajzen and the Bentler-Speckart models. Journal of Personality and Social Psychology, 45, 501-512.

French, J.R.P. Jr. (1976). Job demands and worker health: Introduction. Paper presented at the 84th Annual Convention of the APA, Washington D.C.. .

French, J.R.P. Jr., Rodgers, W. & Cobb, S. (1974). Adjustment as person-environment fit. In G.V. Coelho, D.A.Hamburg & J.E. Adams (Eds.), Coping and Adaptation (pp. 316-333). New York: Basic Books.

Friedman, D. & Jaffe, A. (1983). Anxiety disorders. Journal of Family Practice, 16, 145-152.

Friedman, G.H., Lehrer, B.E. & Stevens, J.P. (1983). The effectiveness of self-directed ad lecture/discussion stress management approaches ad the locus of control of teachers. American Educational Research Journal, 20, 563-580.

Friedman, M. & Rosenman, R.H. (1959). Association of a specific overt behavior pattern with blood and cardiovascular findings. Journal of the American Medical Association,169, 1286-1296.

Friedman, M. & Rosenman, R. (1977). The key-cause - Type A behavior pattern. In H. Monat & R.S. Lazarus (Eds.), Stress and coping (pp. 203-212). New York: Columbia University Press.

Friedman, M. & Rosenman, R.H. (1974). Type A behavior and your heart. New York: Knopf.

Friedman, M., Byer, S.O., Diamants, J. & Rosenman, R.H. (1975). Plasma catecholamine response of coronary-prone subjects (type A) to a specific challenge. Metabolism Clinical and Experimental, 24, 205-210.

Fry, P.S. (1982). Social affective andcognitive mediators of depression in the elderly. Paper presented at the Twentieth Int. Congress of Applied Psychology.... .

Fry, P.S. (1983). Correlates of cognitive failure in the elderly. Unpublished paper. Calgary, Alberta, Canada:
.

Fry, P.S. (1983). Structured and unstructured reminiscence training and depression in the elderly. Clinical Gerontologist, 1, 15-37.

Fry, P.S. (in press). The development of a geriatric scale of hopelessness: Implications for counseling and intervention with the depressed elderly. Journal of Counseling Psychology.

Fry, P.S. & Grover, S (1982). Cognitive appraisals of life stress and depression in the elderly: A cross-cultural comparisons of Asians and Caucasians. International Journal of Psychology, 17, 437-454.

Fry, P.S. & Leahey, M. (in press). Positive and negative attributions of longevity: A cross-sectional study of the perceptions of the elderly from three socio-economic conditions. International Journal of Psychology.

Fry, P.S. & Trifiletti, R.J. (in press). Cognitive training and cognitive-behavioral variables in the treatment of depression in the elderly. Clinical Gerontologist.

Fry,P.S. (1974). The development of differentiation in self-evaluations: A cross-cultural study. Journal of Psychology, 89, 194-202.

Fry,P.S. & Coe,K.J. (1980). Achievement performance of internally and externally oriented black and white high school students. British Journal of Educational Psychology, 50, 162-167.

Fry,P.S. & Coe,K.J. (1980). Interaction among dimensions of academic motivation and classroom social climate: A study of the perceptions of junior high school pupils. British Journal of Educational Psychology, 50, 33-42.

Galassi,J.P., Frierson,H.T. & Sharer,R. (1981). Behavior of high, moderate and low test anxious students during an actual test situation. Journal of Consulting and Clinical Psychology, 49, 51-62.

Gallagher, D. & Thompson, L.W. (1982). Treatment of major depressive disorders in older adult outpatients with brief psychotherapies. Psychotherapy: Theory, Research and Practice, 19, 482-490.

Gallagher, D. & Thompson, L.W. (1983). Cognitive therapy for depression in the elderly. In L. Beslau & M. Haug

(Eds.), Depression in the elderly: Causes, care and consequences (pp. 168-192). New York: Springer Press.

Gallagher, D., Slife, B., Rose, T. & Okarma, T. (1982). Psychological correlates of immunologic disease in older adults. Clinical Gerontologist, 1, 51-58.

Gallant, D.M. & Simpson, G.M. (1976). Depression: Behavioral, Biochemical, Diagnostic and Treatment Concepts. New York: Spectrum Publications, Inc..

Gambrill, E.D. & Richey, C.A. (1975). An assertion inventory for use in assessment and research. Behavior Therapy, 6, 550-561.

Garber,J. & Seligman,M.E.P.(Eds.) (1980). Human helplessness. New York: Academic Press.

Gaudry, E. & Fitzgerald, D. (1971). Test anxiety, intelligence and academic achievement. In E. Gaudry & C.D. Spielberger (Eds.), Anxiety and educational achievement (pp. 155-162). Sydney: Wiley.

Geller,V. & Shaver,P. (1976). Cognitive consequences of self-awareness. Journal of Experimental Social Psychology, 13, 99-108.

Gergen,K.J. (1971). The concept of self. New York: Holt.

Ghiselli, E.E., Campbell, J.P. & Zedeck, S. (1981). Measurement theory for the behavioral sciences. San Francisco: W.H. Freeman & Co., 154-182.

Gibbons,F.X. (1976). Self-focused attention and enhancement of response awareness. Unpublished doctoral dissertation, University of Texas.

Gibbons,F.X. & Wicklund,R.A. (1976). Selective exposure to self. Journal of Research in Personality, 10, 98-106.

Glass, D. (1977). Behavior patterns, stress, and coronary disease. Hillsdale, N.Y.: Erlbaum, 72-140.

Glass, D. & Carver, C. (1980). Helplessness and the coronary-prone personality. In J. Garber & M.E.P. Seligman (Eds.), Human helplessness: Theory and applications (pp. 223-243). New York: Academic Press.

Goldberg, D.P. (1972). The detection of psychiatric illness by questionnaire. In Institute of Psychiatry (Ed.), Mandsley Monographs Nr. 21. London: Oxford University Press.

Goodwin, A.M. & Williams, J.M.G. (1982). Mood-induction

research: Implications for clinical depression. Behavior Research and Therapy, 20, 373-382.

Gottlieb, B.H. (1978). The development and application of a classification scheme of informal helping behaviors. Canadian Journal of Behavioral Science, 10, 105-115.

Gottlieb, B.H. (1983). Social support strategies. Guidelines for mental health practice. Beverly Hills: Sage Publications.

Gough H.G., Fioravanti, M. & Lazzari, R. (1983). Some implications of self versus ideal-self congruence on the revised Adjective Check List. Journal of Personality and Social Psychology, 44, 1214-1220.

Gough, H. & Heilbrun, A.B. (1965). The adjective check list manual. Palo Alto, California: Consulting Psychologists Press.

Graham, S.H. (in press). Communicating sympathy and anger to black and white children: The cognitive (attributional) consequences of affective cues. Journal of Personality and Social Psychology.

Graham, S.H. & Weiner, B. (1983). Some educational implications of sympathy and anger from an attributional perspective. Unpublished paper. Los Angeles: University of California, L.A..

Grant, M. & Ritson, B. (1983). Alcohol: The prevention debate. Beckenham: Croom Helm.

Greenwald, A.G. & Pratkanis, A.R. (in press). The self. In R.S. Wyer & T.K. Srull (Eds.), Handbook of Social Cognition. Hillsdale, N.Y.: Erlbaum.

Grinker, R.R., Sr. & Robbins, F.B. (1954). Psychomatic Case Book. New York: McGraw-Hill (Blakston).

Grobe, R. & Hofer, M. (1983). Kognitiv-motivationale Korrelate von Schulnoten: Typen motivierter Schüler. Zeitschrift für Entwicklungspsychologie und Pädagogische Psychologie, 15, 292-316.

Groebel, J. & Schwarzer, R. (1982). Social comparison, expectations and emotional reactions in the classroom. School Psychology International, 3, 49-56.

Gupta, N. & Beehr, T.A. (1979). Job stress and employee behaviors. Organizational Behavior and Human Performance, 23, 373-387.

Haan, N. (1977). Coping and defending: Processes of self-environment organization. New York: Academic

Press.

Haas, H., Fink, H. & Hartfelder, G. (1963). The placebo problem. Psychopharmacology Service Centre Bulletin, 1-65.

Hackfort, D. (1983). Theorie und Diagnostik sportbezogener Ängstlichkeit. Köln: Deutsche Sporthochschule.

Hackman, J.R. (1970). Task and task performance in research on stress. In J.E. McGrath (Ed.), Social and Psychological Factors in Stress. New York: Holt.

Haertel, G.D., Walberg, H.J. & Weinstein, T. (1983). Psychological models of educational performance: A theoretical synthesis of constructs. Review of Educational Research, 53, 75-91.

Hagtvet, K. (1984). Fear of failure, worry and emotionality: Their suggestive causal relationship to mathematical performance and state anxiety. In Ploeg, H. van der, Schwarzer, R. & Spielberger, C.D. (Eds.), Advances in Test Anxiety Research (Vol. 3). Lisse / Hillsdale: Swets / Erlbaum.

Hagtvet, K.A. (1983). A construct validation study of test anxiety: A discriminant validation of fear of failure, worry and emotionality. In R. Schwarzer, H.M. van der Ploeg & C.D. Spielberger (Eds.), Advances in test anxiety research (Vol. 2) (pp. 15-34). Lisse/ Hillsdale, N.Y.: Swets & Zeitlinger/ Erlbaum.

Hagtvet,K.A. (1976). Worry and emotionality components of test anxiety in different sex and age groups of elementary school children. Psychological Reports, 39, 1327-1334.

Hakmiller,K.L (1966). Threat as a determinant of downward comparison. Journal of Experimental Social Psychology, 1, 31-39.

Hamilton, V. (1975). Socialization, anxiety and information processing. In I.G. Sarason & C.D. Spielberger (Eds.), Stress and anxiety (Vol. 2). New York: Wiley.

Hammen, C. & Mayol, A. (1982). Depression and cognitive characteristics of stressful life-event types. Journal of Abnormal Psychology, 91, 165-174.

Hammen, C.L. (1978). Depression, distortion and life stress in college students. Cognitive Therapy and Research, 2, 189-192.

Hammen, C.L. & Krantz, S. (1976). Effect of success and

failure on depressive cognition. Journal of Abnormal Psychology, 85, 577-586.

Hammen, C.L. & Padesky, C.A. (1977). Sex differences in the expression of depressive responses on the Beck depression inventory. Journal of Abnormal Psychology, 86, 609-614.

Hammer, M. (1980). Social supports, social networks and schizophrenia. Schizophrenia Bulletin, 7, 45-57.

Hansen,R.D. (1980). Commonsense attribution. Journal of Personality and Social Psychology, 39, 996-1009.

Hansford,B.C. & Hattie,J.A. (1982). The relationship between self and achievement/performance measures. Review of Educational Research, 52, 123-142.

Hanusa,B. & Schulz,R. (1977). Attributional mediators of learned helplessness. Journal of Personality and Social Psychology, 35, 602-611.

Harter,S. (1978). Effectance motivation reconsidered: Toward a developmental model. Human Development, 21, 34-64.

Harter,S. (1982). The Perceived Competence Scale for Children. Child Development, 53, 87-97.

Harvey, O.J., Hunt, D.E. & Schroder, H.M. (1961). Conceptual systems and personality organization. New York: John Wiley and Sons.

Harvey,J.H. & Weary,G. (1981). Perspectives on attributional processes. Dubuque: Brown Company.

Haynes, S. & Feinleib, M. (1982). Type A behavior and the incidence of coronary heart disease in the Framingham Heart Study. Advances in Cardiology, 29, 85-95.

Heckhausen, H. (1980). Motivation und Handeln. Heidelberg: Springer.

Heckhausen,H. (1982). Task-irrelevant cognitions during an exam: Incidence and effects. In Krohne,H.W. & Laux,L. (Eds.), Achievement,stress and anxiety. Washington: Hemisphere.

Heiby, E.M. (1983). Assessment of frequency of self-reinforcement. Journal of Personality and Social Psychology, 44, 1304-1307.

Heineman, W. (1983). Die Erfassung dispositioneller Selbstaufmerksamkeit mit einer deutschen Version der Self-Consciousness Scale (SCS). Bielefelder Arbeiten zur Sozialpsychologie, Nr. 106. Bielefeld: Universität

Bielefeld.

Heinemann,W. (1979). The assessment of private and public
self-consciousness: A German replication. European
Journal of Social Psychology, 9, 331-337.

Heinrich, D.L. & Spielberger, C.D. (1982). Anxiety and
complex learning. In H.W. Krohne & L. Laux (Eds.),
Achievement, stress and anxiety. Washington:
Hemisphere.

Heller, K. (1979). The effects of social support:
Prevention and treatment implications. In A.P.
Goldstein & F.H. Kanfer (Eds.), Maximizing treatment
gains: Transfer enhancement in psychotherapy. New
York: Academic Press.

Heller, K. & Swindle, R.W. (1983). Social networks,
perceived social support, and coping with stress. In
R.D. Felner, L.A. Jason, J.N. Moritsugu & S.S. Farber
(Eds.), Preventive psychology. Theory, research and
practice. New York: Pergamon Press.

Hellpach, W. (1913). Vom Ausdruck der Verlegenheit.
Archiv für die gesamte Psychologie, 27, 1-62.

Helmke, A. (1982). Schulische Leistungsangst:
Erscheinungsformen und Entstehungsbedingungen.
Dissertation an der Universität Konstanz. Konstanz: .

Helmke, A. & Fend, H. (1982). Diagnostic sensitivity of
teachers and parents with respect to the test anxiety of
students. In R. Schwarzer, H.M. van der Ploeg & C.D.
Spielberger (Eds.), Advances in test anxiety research
(Vol. 1) (pp. 115-128). Lisse/ Hillsdale, N.Y.: Swets
& Zeitlinger/ Erlbaum.

Henderson, S., Byrne, D.G. & Duncan-Jones, P. (1981).
Neurosis and the social environment. Sydney: Academic
Press.

Hillia, J.W., Crano, W.D. (1973). Additive effects of
utility and attitudinal supportiveness in the selection
of information. Journal of Social Psychology, 89,
257-269.

Hirsch, B.J. (1980). Natural support systems and coping
with major life changes. American Journal ofCommunity
Psychology, 8, 159-172.

Hirsch, B.J. (1980). Natural support systems and coping
with major life change. American Journal of Community
Psychology, 8, 159-172.

Hobfoll, S.E., Anson, O. & Bernstein, J. (1983). Anxiety
reactions in two ego-threat situations of varying

intensity. In R. Schwarzer, H.M. van der Ploeg & C.D. Spielberger (Eds.), Advances in test anxiety research (Vol. 2) (pp. 81-86). Lisse/ Hillsdale, N.Y.: Swets & Zeitlinger/ Erlbaum.

Hodapp, V. & Henneberger, A. (1983). Test anxiety, study habits, and academic performance. In R. Schwarzer, H.M. van der Ploeg & C.D. Spielberger (Eds.), Advances in test anxiety research (Vol. 2) (pp. 119-127). Lisse/ Hillsdale, N.Y.: Swets & Zeitlinger/ Erlbaum.

Hodapp, V., Laux, L. & Spielberger, C.D. (1982). Theorie und Messung der emotionalen und kognitiven Komponente der Prüfungsangst. Zeitschrift für Differentielle und Diagnostische Psychologie, 3, 169-184.

Hodapp,V. (1982). Causal inference from nonexperimental research on anxiety and educational achievement. In Krohne,H.W. & Laux,L. (Eds.), Achievement, stress and anxiety. Washington: Hemisphere.

Hogan, R., Jones, W.H. & Cheek, J.M. (in press). Socioanalytic theory: An alternative to armadillo psychology. In B. Schlenker (Ed.), Self and identity: Presentations of self in social life. New York: McGraw-Hill.

Holahan, C.J. & Moos, R.H. (1982). Social support and adjustment: Predictive benefits of social climate indices. American Journal of Community Psychology, 4, 403-415.

Hollan, S.D. (1981). Comparisons and combinations with alternative approaches. In L.P. Rehm (Ed.), Behavior therapy for depression (pp. 33-71). New York: Academic Press.

Holmes, B.S. & Houston, B.K. (1974). Effectiveness of situation redefinition and affective isolation in coping with stress. Journal of Personality and Social Psychology, 29, 212-218.

Holmes, T.H. & Rahe, R.H. (1967). The Social Readjustment Rating Scale. Journal of Psychosomatic Research, 11, 213-218.

Horan, J.J. & Williams, J.M. (1982). Longitudinal study of assertion training as a drug abuse prevention strategy. American Educational Research Journal, 19, 341-351.

Horner, M. (1968). Sex differences in achievement motivation and performance in competitive and noncompetitive situations. Unpublished doctoral dissertation. University of Michigan.

Hornke, L. (1983). Computerunterstütztes Testen - Eine

bewertende empirische Untersuchung. Zeitschrift für Differentielle und Diagnostische Psychologie, 4, 323-334.

Horowitz, L.M., French, R., Lapid, J.S. & Weckler, D.A. (1982). Symptoms and interpersonal problems: The prototype as an integrating concept. In Anchin, J.C. & Kiesler, D.J. (Eds.), Handbook of Interpersonal Psychotherapy. New York: Pergamon.

House, J.S. (1974). Occupational stress and coronary heart disease: A review and theoretical integration. Journal of Health and Social Behavior, 15, 17-27.

House, J.S., Wells. J.A., Landerman, L.R., McMichael, A.J. & Kaplan, B.H. (1979). Occupational stress and health among factory workers. Journal of Health and Social Behavior, 20, 139-160.

Houston, B.K. (1977). Dispositional anxiety and the effectiveness of cognitive coping strategies in stressful laboratory and classroom situations. In C.D. Spielberger & I.G. Sarason (Eds.), Stress and anxiety (Vol. 4). Washington: Hemisphere.

Howarth, E. (1980). Major factors of personality. Journal of Psychology,104, 171-183.

Howe, Michael J. A. (1982). Biographical evidence and the development of outstanding individuals. American Psychologist.

Hrebeniak, L.G. & Alltto, J.A. (1972). Personal and role related factors in the development of organizational commitment. Administrative Science Quarterly, 17, 555-573.

Hull, J.G. & Levy, A.S. (1979). The organizational functions of the self: An alternative to the Duval and the Wicklund model of self-awareness. Journal of Personality and Social Psychology, 37, 756-768.

Hull, J.G. & Young, R.D. (1983). Self-consciousness, self-esteem, and success-failure as determinants of alcohol consumption in male social drinkers. Journal of Personality and Social Psychology, 44, 1097-1109.

Hull, J.G., Levenson, R.W., Young, R.D. & Shar, K.J. (1983). Self-awareness-reducing effects of alcohol consumption. Journal of Personality and Social Psychology, 44.

Hunter, J.E., Schmidt, F.L. & Jackson, G.B. (1982). Meta-analysis. Cumulating research findings across studies.. Beverley Hills: Sage.

Hyman,H.H. (1942). The psychology of status. Archives of Psychology,269.

Hyman,H.H. & Singer,E.(Eds.) (1968). Readings in reference group theory and research. New York: Free Press.

Ingenkamp, K. (Ed.) (1984). Sozial-emotionales Verhalten in Lehr-und Lernsituationen. Landau: Erz.wiss. Hochsch. Rh.-Pfalz.

Ingram, R.E., Smith, T.W. & Brehm, S.S. (1983). Depression and information processing: Self-schemata and the encoding of self-referent information. Journal of Personality and Social Psychology, 45, 412-420.

Ivancevich, J.M. & Matteson, M.T. (1979). Organizations and coronary heart disease: The stress connection. In J.L. Gibson, J.M. Ivancevich & J.M. Donnely Jr. (Eds.), Readings in Organizations, 3rd ed. (pp. 103-113). Dallas: BPI, Inc..

Jacobs,B. (1982). Die Fachspezifität der Prüfungsängstlichkeit. In Strittmatter (Ed.), Arbeitsberichte aus der Fachrichtung Allgemeine Erziehungswissenschaften. Saarbrücken: Universität.

Janis, I.L. & Field, P.B. (1959). The Janis-Field Feelings of Inadequacy Scale. In I.L. Janis & C.I. Hovland (Eds.), Personality and persuasibility. New Haven, Connect.: Yale University Press.

Janis,I.L. (1983). Stress inoculation in health care: Theory and research. In D.Meichenbaum & M.E.Jaremko (Eds.), Stress Reduction and Prevention (pp. 67-101). New York: Plenum Press.

Jaremko,M.E. (1983). Stress R. .

Jaremko,M.E. (1983). Stress inoculation training for social anxiety,with emphasis on dating anxiety. In D.Meichenbaum & M.E.Jaremko (Eds.), Stress Reduction and Prevention (pp. 419-451). New York: Plenum Press.

Jenkins, C.D. (1976). Recent evidence supporting psychologic and social risk factors of coronary disease. New England Journal of Medicine,294, 987-994/1033-38.

Jerusalem, M. (1984). Kumulative Mißerfolge und Hilflosigkeit in der Schule: Ein Entwicklungsmodell und erste empirische Hinweise. In Ingenkamp, K. (Ed.), Sozial-emotionales Verhalten in Lehr-und Lernsituationen (pp. 223-235). Landau: Erz.wiss. Hochsch. Rh.-Pfalz.

Jerusalem, M. & Schwarzer, R. (1983). Die Entwicklung des
    Selbstkonzepts in schulischen Bezugsgruppen: Eine
    dynamische Mehrebenenanalyse. In G. Lüer (Ed.),
    Bericht über den 33. Kongreß der Deutschen Gesellschaft
    für Psychologie in Mainz 1982. Göttingen: Hogrefe.

Johnson, J.H. & Sarason, I.G. (1979). Recent developments
    in research on life stress. In V. Hamilton & D.M.
    Warburton (Eds.), Human stress and cognition: An
    information processing approach (pp. 205-236). London:
    Wiley.

Jones, W.H. (1982). Loneliness and social behavior. In
    L.A. Peplau & D. Perlman (Eds.), Loneliness: A
    sourcebook of current theory, research and therapy.
    New York: Wiley-Interscience.

Jones, W.H. & Russell, D.W. (1983). Personality congruent
    analysis of situations. Unpublished manuscript. Tulsa,
    Ok.: University of Tulsa, Ok..

Jones, W.H., Cavert, C. & Indart, M. (1983). Impressions
    of shyness. In J.M. Cheek (Ed.), Progress in research
    on shyness. Anaheim, Ca.: Symposium at APA meeting,
    Anah..

Jones, W.H., Freemon, J. & Goswick, R. (1981). The
    persistence of loneliness: Self and other determinants.
    Journal of Personality, 49, 27-48.

Jöreskog, K.G. (1977). Statistical models and methods for
    analysis of longitudinal data. In D.V. Aigner & A.S.
    Goldberg (Eds.), Latent variables in socioeconomic
    models. Amsterdam: No. Holland.

Jöreskog, K.G. & Sörbom, D. (1978). LISREL Analysis of
    linear structural relationships by the method of maximum
    likelihood (Version IV). Chicago:: NER.

Kagan, J., Rosman, B.L., Day, D., Albert, J. & Phillips, W.
    (1964). Information processing in the child:
    Significance of analytic and reflective attitudes.
    Psychological Monographs, 78, WholeNo.578.

Kahn, R.L., Wolf, D., Quinn, R., Snock, J. & Rosenthal, R.
    (1964). Organizational stress: Studies in the role
    conflict and ambiguities. New York: Wiley.

Kahnemann, D. (1973). Attention and effort. New Yersey:
    Prentice-Hall.

Kammer, D. (1983). Eine Untersuchung der psychometrischen
    Eigenschaften des deutschen Beck-Depressionsinventars
    (BDI). Diagnostica, 24, 48-60.

Kanfer, F.H., Stifter, E. & Morris, S.J. (1981).

Self-control and altruism: Delay of gratification for another. Child Development, 52, 674-682.

Kaplan, H.B. (1980). Deviant behavior in defense of self. New York: Academic Press.

Kasl, S.V. (1974). Work and mental health. In J. O'Toole (Ed.), Work and quality of life (pp. 171-194). Cambridge, Mass.: The MIT Press.

Kasl, S.V. (1978). Epidemological contribution to the study of work stress. In C.L. Cooper & R. Payne (Eds.), Stress at work (pp. 3-48). New York: Wiley.

Kasl. S.V. (1973). Mental health and the work environment: An examination of the evidence. Journal of Occupational Medicine, 15, 509-518.

Keenan, A. & McBain, G.D.M. (1979). Effects of type A behavior, intolerance to ambiguity, and locus of control on the relationship between role stress and work related outcomes. Journal of Occupational Psychology, 52, 277-285.

Kelley,H.H. (1967). Attributional theory in social psychology. In Levine,D. (Ed.), Nebraska Symposium on Motivation (pp. 192-238).

Kelley,H.H. (1968). Two functions of reference groups. In Hyman,H.H. & Singer,E. (Eds.), Readings in reference group theory and research (pp. 77-83). New York: Free Press.

Kelley,H.H. (1973). The process of causal attribution. American Psychologist, 28, 107-128.

Kelley,H.H. & Michela,J.L. (1980). Attribution theory and research. Annual Review of Psychology, 31, 457-501.

Kendall, P.C. & Korgeski, G.P. (1979). Assessment and cognitive-behavioral interventions. Cognitive Therapy and Research, 3, 1-21.

Kenny,D.A. (1979). Correlation and causality. New York: Wiley.

Kenrick, D.T. & Stringfield, D.O. (1980). Personality traits and the eye of the beholder: Crossing some tradit.philosoph. boundaries in the search for consistency in all of the people. Psychological Review, 87, 88-104.

Kifer,E. (1975). Relationships between academic achievement and personality characteristics, a quasi-longitudinal study. American Educational

Research Journal, 12, 191-210.

Kirk, R.E. (1968). Experimental design: Procedure for the
behavioral sciences. Belmont: Wadsworth.

Klauer,K.J. (1982). Bezugsnormen zur Leistungsbewertung:
Begriffe, Konzepte, Empfehlungen. In Rheinberg,F.
(Ed.), Bezugsnormen zur Schulleistungsbewertung.Jahrbuch
für Empirische Erziehungswissenschaften 1982 (pp. 21-38).
Düsseldorf: Schwann.

Kleijn, W.C., Ploeg, H.M van der & Kwee, M.G.T. (1983).
Construct validation of test anxiety: An exploration of
relationships with anxiety, anger and irrational
thinking. In R. Schwarzer, H.M. van der Ploeg & C.D.
Spielberger (Eds.), Advances in test anxiety research
(Vol. 2) (pp. 203-214). Lisse/ Hillsdale, N.Y.: Swets
& Zeitlinger/ Erlbaum.

Knoke, D. & Kuklinski, J. H. (1982). Network analysis.
Beverly Hills: Sage.

Kobasa, S.C.O. & Puccetti, M.C. (1983). Personality and
social resources in stress resistance. Journal of
Personality and Social Psychology, 45, 839-850.

Kornitzer, M., Kittel, F., de Backer, G. et al. (1981).
The Belgian Heart Disease Prevention Project: Type A
behavior pattern and the prevalence of coronary heart
disease. Psychosomatic Medicine, 43, 133-145.

Korte, C. (1978). Helpfulness in the urban environment.
In A. Baum, J.E. Singer & S. Valins (Eds.), Advances in
environmental psychology, 1. The urban environment.
Hillsdale, N.Y.: Erlbaum.

Kovacs, M. & Beck, A.T. (1978). Maladaptive cognitive
structures in depression. American Journal of
Psychiatry,135, 525-533.

Krantz, S. (1983). Cognitive appraisals and
problem-directed coping: A prospective study of stress.
Journal of Personality and Social Psychology, 44,
638-643.

Kroeber, T.C. (1963). The coping functions of the ego
mechanisms. In R.W. White (Ed.), The study of lives:
Essays on personality in honor of Henry A. Murray. New
York: Atherton Press.

Krohne, H.W. (1978). Individual differences in coping with
stress and anxiety. In C.D. Spielberger & I.G. Sarason
(Eds.), Stress and anxiety (Vol. 5). New York:
Wiley.

Krohne, H.W. & Schaffner, P. (1980). Anxiety, coping

strategies, and test performance. Invited paper pres. at
Fourth Int. Symp. on Educational Testing (ISET IV), June
24-27, 1980. Antwerp, Belgium: .

Krohne, H.W., Wiegand, A. & Kiehl, G.E. (in press).
Konstruktion eines multidimensionalen Instruments zur
Erfassung von Angstbewältigungstendenzen. In H.W.
Krohne (Ed.), Angstbewältigung in Leistungssituationen.
Weinheim: Edition Psychologie.

Krohne,H.W. & Laux,L.(Eds.) (1982). Achievement, stress
and anxiety. Washington: Hemisphere.

Krug, S. (1983). Motivförderungsprogramme: Möglichkeiten
und Grenzen. Zeitschrift für Entwicklungspsychologie
und Pädagogische Psychologie, 15, 317-346.

Krüger, J., Möller, H. & Meyer, W.-U. (1983). Das Zuweisen
von Aufgaben verschiedener Schwierigkeit: Auswirkungen
auf Leistungsbeurteilung und Affekt. Zeitschrift für
Entwicklungspsychologie und Pädagogische Psychologie,
15, 280-291.

Krüger, J., Möller, H. & Meyer, W.-U. (1983). Das Zuweisen
von Aufgaben verschiedener Schwierigkeit: Auswirkungen
auf Leistungsbeurteilungen und Affekt. Zeitschrift für
Entwicklungspsychologie und Pädagogische Psychologie,
15, 280-291.

Krüger, J., Möller, H. & Meyer, W.-U. (1983). Das Zuweisen
von Aufgaben verschiedener Schwierigkeit: Auswirkungen
auf Leistungsbeurteilung und Affekt. Zeitschrift für
Entwicklungspsychologie und Pädagogische Psychologie,
15, 280-291.

Kugle, C.L., Clements, R.O. & Powell, P.M. (1983). Level
and stability of self-esteem in relation to academic
behavior of second-graders. J. Pers. and Soc.
Psych., 44, 201-219.

Kuhl, J. (1981). Motivational and functional helplessness:
The moderating effect of state versus action
orientation. Journal of Personality and Social
Psychology, 40, 155-171.

Kuhl, J. (1982). Kurzanweissung zum Fragebogen KAKEMP.
Manuskript. .

Kuhl, J. (1983). Motivation, Konflikt und
Handlungskontrolle. Berlin: Springer, (a).

Kuhl, J. (1983). Volitional aspects of achievement
motivation and learned helplessness: Toward a
comprehensive theory of action control. In B.A. Maher
(Ed.), Progress in experimental personality research
(Vol. 12) (pp. (b)). New York: Academic Press.

Kuhl, J. & Blankenship, V. (1979). Behavioral change in a
   constant environment: Shift to more difficult tasks with
   constant probability of success. Journal of
   Personality and Social Psychology, 37, 551-563.

Kuiper, N.A. (1978). Depression and causal attributions
   for success and failure. Journal of Personality and
   Social Psychology, 3, 236-246.

Kuiper, N.A. & Derry, P.A. (1980). Encoding personal
   adjectives: The effects of depression on self-reference.
   Unpublished manuscript. Western Ontario: University of
   Western Ontario.

Kuiper, N.A. & Derry, P.A. (1982). Depressed and
   nondepressive content self-reference in mild
   depressives. Journal of Personality, 50, 67-80.

Kuiper, N.A. & MacDonald, M.R. (1982). Self and other
   perception in mild depressives. Social Cognition,
   13, 223-239.

Kuiper, N.A. & Rogers, T.B. (1979). Encoding of personal
   information: Self-other differences. Journal of
   Personality and Social Psychology, 37, 499-512.

Kuiper, N.A., Derry, P.A. & MacDonald, M.R. (1981).
   Self-reference and person perception in depression: A
   social cognition perspective. In G. Weary & H. Mirels
   (Eds.), Integration of Clinical and Social Psychology.
   New York: Oxford University Press.

Kuiper,N.A. & Derry,P.A. (1981). The self as a cognitive
   prototype: An application to person perception and
   depression. In Cantor,N. & Kihlstrom.J.F. (Eds.),
   Personality, cognition and social interaction (pp.
   215-232). Hillsdale: Erlbaum.

Kulik, J.A. (1983). Confirmatory attribution and the
   perpetuation of social beliefs. Journal of Personality
   and Social Psychology, 44, 1171-1181.

Kuller, L. (1978). Prodromata of sudden death and
   myocardial infarction. Advances in Cardiology, 25,
   61-72.

Kuller, L., Cooper, M. & Perper, J. (1972). Epidemiology
   of sudden death. Archives of Internal Medicine,129,
   714-719.

Lader, M. & Marks, I.M. (1971). Clinical anxiety.
   London: Heineman.

Lange,B. (1982). Situationsspezifische Entwicklung von
   Schülern nach dem Übergang in die Sekundarstufe I.

Dissertation, RWTH Aachen.

Lantermann, E.D. (1982). Integration von Kognitionen und
Emotionen in Handlungen. In H.W. Hoefert (Ed.), Person
und Situation. Göttingen: Hogrefe.

Lantermann, E.D. (1983). Kognitive und emotionale Prozesse
beim Handeln. In G. Huber & H. Mandl (Eds.), Kognition
und Emotion. München: Urban & Schwarzenberg.

Laux, L. (1983). Psychologische Streßkonzeptionen. In
Theorien und Formen der Motivation. Serie Motivation
und Emotion der Enzyklopädie der Psychologie.
Göttingen: Hogrefe, 1, 453-535.

Laux, L. & Vossel, G. (1981). Paradigms in stress
research: Laboratory versus field and traits versus
processes. In L. Goldberger & S. Breznitz (Eds.),
Handbook of stress: Theoretical and clinical aspects.
New York: The Free Press.

Lazarsfeld, P.F. (1948). The use of panels in social
research. Proceedings of the American Philosophical
Society. .

Lazarus, A.-A. (1968). Learning theory and the treatment
of depression. Behavior Research and Therapy, 6,
83-89.

Lazarus, P.J. (1982). Incidence of shyness in
elementary-school age children. Psychological
Reports, 51, 904-906.

Lazarus, R.S. (1966). Psychological stress and the coping
process. New York: McGraw-Hill.

Lazarus, R.S. (1982). Thoughts on the Relations
Between Emotion and Cognition. American
Psychologist.

Lazarus, R.S. (1983). The costs and benefits of denial.
In S. Breznitz (Ed.), The denial of stress. New York:
International Universities Press.

Lazarus, R.S. & Cohen, J.B. (1978). Environmental stress.
In I. Altman & J.F. Wohlwill (Eds.), Human behavior and
the environment: Current theory and research. New
York: Plenum.

Lazarus, R.S. & DeLongis, A. (1983). Psychological stress
and coping in aging. American Psychologist, 38,
245-254.

Lazarus, R.S., Averill, J.R. & Opton, E.M. Jr. (1974). The
psychology of coping: Issues of research and assessment.
In G.V. Coelho, D.A. Hamburg & J.E. Adams (Eds.),

Coping and adaptation. New York: Basic Books.

Lazarus, R.S., Coyne, J.C. & Folkman, S. (1982).
Cognition, emotion and motivation: The doctoring of
humpty-dumpty. In R.W.J. Neufeld (Ed.), Psychological
stress and psychopathology. New York: McGraw-Hill.

Lazarus,R.S. & Launier,R. (1978). Stress related
transactions between person and environment. In
Pervin,L.A. & Lewis,M. (Eds.), Perspectives in
international psychology (pp. 287-327). New York:
Plenum.

Lazarus,R.S., Kanner,A. & Folkman,S. (1980). Emotions: A
cognitive-phenomenological analysis. In Plutchik,R. &
Kellerman,H. (Eds.), Emotion.Vol.1 (pp. 189-217). New
York: Academic Press.

Leary, M.R. (1982). Social anxiety. In L. Wheeler (Ed.),
Review of personality and social psychology (Vol. 3).
Beverly Hills: Sage.

Leary, M.R. & Schlenker, B.R. (1981). The social
psychology of shyness: A self-presentation model. In
J.I. Tedeschi (Ed.), Impression management: Theory and
social psychological research (pp. 335-358). New York:
Academic Press.

Lee, B. & Noam, G. G. (Ed.) (1983). Developmental
approaches to the self. New York: Plenum Press.

Leventhal, H. (1980). Toward a comprehensive theory of
emotion. In L. Berkowitz (Ed.), Advances in
experimental social psychology (Vol. 13) (pp. 139-207).
New York: Academic Press.

Levey, A.B. (1980). Measurement units in psychophysiology.
In I. Martin & P.H. Venables (Eds.), Techniques in
psychophysiology. New York: Wiley.

Levine, J.M. & Moreland, R.L. (1984). Outcome comparisons
in group contexts: Consequences for the self and others.
In R. Schwarzer (Ed.), Self-Related Cognitions in
Anxiety and Motivation. Hillsdale: Erlbaum.

Levine, M. (1966). Hypothesis behavior by humans during
discrimination learning. Journal of Experimental
Psychology, 71, 331-338.

Levine,J.M. (1982). Social comparison and education. In
Levine,J.M. & Wang,M.C. (Eds.), Teacher and student
perceptions: Implications for learning.
Hillsdale,N.J.: Erlbaum.

Levine,J.M., Snyder,H.N. & Mendez-Caratini,G. (1982). Task
performance and interpersonal attraction in children.

Child Development, 53, 359-371.

Lewicki, P. (1983). Self-image bias in person perception. *Journal of Personality and Social Psychology, 45*, 384-393.

Lewin, K. (1946). Behavior and development as a function of the total situation. In L. Carmichael (Ed.), *Manual of Child Psychology*. New York: Wiley.

Lewin, K., Dembo, T., Festinger, L. & Sears, P.S. (1944). Level of aspiration. In J. McV. Hunt (Ed.), *Personality and the behavior disorders*. New York: Ronald.

Lewinsky, H. (1941). The nature of shyness. *British Journal of Psychology, 32*, 105-113.

Lewinsohn, P.M. (1974). A behavioral approach to depression. In R.M. Friedman & M.M. Katz (Eds.), *The psychology of depression: Contemporary theory and research* (pp. 157-178). Washington, D.C.: Winston/ Wiley.

Lewinsohn,P.M., Mischel,W., Chaplin,W. & Bartin,R. (1980). Social competence and depression: The role of illusory self-perceptions. *Journal of Abnormal Psychology, 89*, 202-212.

Libermann, R.P. (1981). A model for individualizing treatment. In Rehm, L.P. (Ed.), *Behavior Therapy for Depression: Present Status and Future Directions*. New York: Academic Press.

Lieberman, M.A. (1983). The effects of social supports on responses to stress. In L. Goldberger & S. Brezinitz (Eds.), *Handbook of stress: Theoretical and clinical aspects* (pp. 764-784). New York: The Free Press.

Liebert,R.M. & Morris,L.W. (1967). Cognitive and emotional components of test anxiety: A distinction and some initial data. *Psychological Reports, 20*, 975-978.

Likert, R. (1961). *New patterns of management*. New York: McGraw-Hill.

Lissmann,U. & Paetzold,B. (1982). Achievement feedback and its effects on pupils - a quasi-experimental and longitudinal study. *Studies in Educational Evaluation*.

Littig, L.W. (1963). Effects of motivation on probability preferences. *Journal of Personality, 31*, 417-427.

Lord, C.G. (1980). Schemas and images as memory aids: Two modes of processing social information. *Journal of*

Personality and Social Psychology, 38, 257-269.

Loreto, G. (1982). Dimensao conceitual da ansiedade/
Conceptual dimension of anxiety. Neurobiologia, 45,
3-12.

Ludwig, R.P. & Lazarus, P.J. (1983). Relationship between
shyness in children and constricted cognitive control as
measured by the Stroop Color-Word Test. Journal of
Consulting and Clinical Psychology, 51, 386-389.

Lundberg, U. & Theorell, T. (1976). Scaling of life
changes: Differences between three diagnostic groups and
between recently experienced and non-experienced events.
Journal of Human Stress, 2, 7-17.

Lundberg, U., Theorell, T. & Lind, E. (1975). Life changes
and myocardial infarction: Individual differences in
life change scaling. Journal of Psychosomatic
Research, 19, 27-32.

Lyons, T.F. (1971). Role clarity, need for clarity,
satisfaction, tension and withdrawal. Organizational
Behavior and Human Performance, 6, 99-110.

Mackay, C.J. (1980). The measurement of mood and
psychophysiological activity using self-report
techniques. In I. Martin & P.H.Venables (Eds.),
Techniques in Psychophysiology. New York: Wiley.

Mackenzie, D. E. (1983). Research for school improvement:
An appraisal of some recent trends. Educational
Researcher, 12, 5-17.

Mahoney, M.J. & Arnkoff, D. (1978). Cognitive and
self-control therapies. In S.L. Garfield & A.E. Bergin
(Eds.), Handbook of psychotherapy and behaviour change,
2nd ed.. New York: Wiley.

Mandel, N.M. & Shrauger, J.S. (1980). The effects of
self-evaluative statements on heterosocial approach in
shy and nonshy males. Cognitive Therapy and
Research, 4, 369-381.

Mandl,H. & Huber,G.L.(Eds.) (1982). Kognition und
Emotion. München: Urban & Schwarzenberg.

Mandler, G. & Sarason, S.B. (1952). A study of anxiety and
learning. Journal of Abnormal and Social Psychology,
47, 166-173.

Marks, I.M. (1969). Fears and phobias. London:
Heineman.

Markus,H. & Smith,J. (1981). The influence of
self-schemata on the perception of others. In Cantor,N.

& Kihlstrom,J.F. (Eds.), Personality, cognition and social interaction (pp. 233-262). Hillsdale,N.J.: Erlbaum.

Marmot, M. (1982). Socio-economic and cultural factors in ischaemic heart disease. Advances in Cardiology, 29, 68-76.

Maroldo, G.K. (1982). Shyness and love on a college campus. Perceptual and Motor Skills, 55, 819-824.

Marsella, A.J. & Snyder, K.K. (1981). Stress, social supports and schizophrenic disorders: Toward an interactional model. Schizophrenia Bulletin, 7, 152-163.

Marsh, H., Smith, I.D. & Barnes, J. (1983). Multitrait-multimethod analyses of the Self-Description Questionnaire: Student-Teacher agreement on multidimensional ratings of self-concept. American Educational Research Journal, 20, 333-358.

Marsh, H.W., Relich, J.D. & Smith, I.D. (1983). Self-concept: The construct validity of interpretations based upon the SDQ. Journal of Personality and Social Psychology, 45, 173-187.

Marsh, H.W., Smith, I.D., Barnes, J. & Butler, S. (1983). Self-concept: Reliability, stability, dimensionality, validity and the measurement of change. Journal of Educational Psychology, 75, 772-789.

Martin, I. & Venables, P.H. (Eds.) (1980). Techniques in psychophysiology. New York: Wiley.

Matarazzo, J.D., Herd, J.A., Miller, N.E. & Weiss, S.M. (Eds.) (1983). Behavioral health: A handbook of health enhancement and disease prevention. New York: Wiley.

Matlin, M.W. & Stang, D.J. (1978). The Pollyanna principle: Selectivity in language, memory and thought. Cambridge: Schenkman Publish. Comp..

Matthews, K. (1982). Psychological perspectives on the Type A behavior pattern. Psychological Bulletin, 91, 293-323.

McCarthy, J.D. & Hoge, D.R. (1982). Analysis of age effects in longitudinal studies of adolescent self-esteem. Development Psychology, 372-379.

McCroskey, J.C. & Sheahan, M.E. (1978). Communication apprehension, social preference and social behavior in a college environment. Communication Quarterly, 26, 41-45.

McGrath, J. (1976). Stress and behavior in organizations.
     In M. Dunnette (Ed.), Handbook of Industrial and
     Organizational Psychology (pp. 1351-1395). Chicago:
     Rand McNally.

McReynolds, P. (1975). Changing conceptions of anxiety: A
     historical review and proposed integration. In I.G.
     Sarason & C.D. Spielberger (Eds.), The Series in
     Clinical Psychology. New York: John Wiley and Sons.

Mead, G.H, (1934). Mind, self and society. Chicago:
     University of Chicago Press.

Mechanic, D. (1974). Social structure and personal
     adaptation: Some neglected dimensions. In G.V. Coelho,
     Hamburg, D.A. & J.E. Adams (Eds.), Coping and
     adaptation. New York: Basic Books.

Mehrabian, A. (1968). Male and female scales of the
     tendency to achieve. Educational and Psychological
     Measurement, 28, 493-502.

Meichenbaum, D. (1976). A cognitive-behaviour modification
     approach to assessment. In M. Herson & A. Bellack
     (Eds.), Behavioural Assessment: A practical handbook.
     New York: Pergamon.

Meichenbaum, D. & Goodman, J. (1971). Training impulsive
     children to talk to themselves: A means of developing
     self-control. Journal of Abnormal Psychology, 77,
     115-126.

Meichenbaum, D. & Goodman, J. (1971). Training impulsive
     children to talk to themselves: A means of developing
     self-control. Journal of Abnormal Psychology, 77,
     115-126.

Melges, F. & Bowlby, J. (1969). Types of hopelessness in
     psychopathological process. Archives of General
     Psychiatry, 20, 690-699.

Messe, L.A. & Watts, B.L. (1983). Complex nature of the
     sense of fairness: Internal standards and social
     comparison as bases for reward evaluations. Journal of
     Personality and Social Psychology, 45, 84-93.

Meyer,W.-U. (1972). Überlegungen zur Konstruktion eines
     Fragebogens zur Erfassung von Selbstkonzepten der
     Begabung. Ruhr-Universität Bochum.

Meyer,W.-U. (1983). Das Konzept der eigenen Begabung als
     ein sich selbst stabilisierendes System. Zeitschrift
     für Personenzentrierte Psychologie und Psychotherapie,
     1.

Meyer, W.-U. (1982). Indirect communications about perceived ability estimates. Journal of Educational Psychology, 74, 259-268.

Meyer, W.-U. (1983). Prozesse der Selbstbeurteilung: Das Konzept von der eigenen Begabung. Zeitschrift für Entwicklungspsychologie und Pädagogische Psychologie, 15, 1-25.

Meyer, W.-U. (1984). Das Konzept von der eigenen Begabung. Bern: Huber.

Meyer, W.-U. & Plöger, F.O. (1979). Scheinbar paradoxe Wirkungen von Lob und Tadel auf die wahrgenommene eigene Begabung. In S.-H. Filipp (Ed.), Selbstkonzept-Forschung: Probleme, Befunde, Perspektiven (pp. 221-235). Stuttgart: Klett-Cotta.

Meyer, W.-U., Bachmann, M., Biermann, U., Hempelmann, M., Plöger, F.-O. & Spiller, H. (1979). The informational value of evaluative behavior: Influences of praise and blame on perceptions of effort and ability on achievement evaluation. Journal of Educational Psychology, 71, 259-268.

Meyer, W.-U., Engler, U. & Mittag, W. (1982). Auswirkungen von Tadel auf die Beurteilung des eigenen Leistungsstandes und auf das Interesse an Aufgaben. Zeitschrift für Entwicklungspsychologie und Pädagogische Psychologie, 14, 263-276.

Michelson, W. (1970). Man and his urban environment: A sociological approach. Reading, Mass.: Addison-Wesley.

Miettinen, O. (1982). Principles of epidemiologic research. Unpublished manuscript. Cambridge, Harvard University: Dep. of Epidemiology & Biostat..

Miller, G.A., Galanter, E. & Pribram, K.H. (1960). Plans and the structure of behavior. New York: Holt.

Miller, L.C., Berg, J.H. & Archer, R.L. (1983). Openers: Individualy who elicit intimate self-disclosure. Journal of Personality and Social Psychology, 44, 1234-1244.

Miller, S.M. & Mangan, C.E. (1983). Interacting effects of information and coping style in adapting to gynecologic stress: Should the doctor tell all ? Journal of Personality and Social Psychology, 45, 223-236.

Minsel, B. & Schwarzer, C. (1983). Nonlinear relationships of worry and emotionality to school achievement. In R. Schwarzer, H.M. van der Ploeg & C.D. Spielberger (Eds.), Advances in test anxiety research (Vol. 2) (pp.

159-166). Lisse/ Hillsdale, N.Y.: Swets & Zeitlinger/
Erlbaum.

Mischel, H.N. & Mischel, W. (1983). The development of
children's knowledge of self-control strategies. Child
Development, 54, 603-619.

Mischel, W. (1966). Theory and research on the antecedents
of self-imposed delay of reward. In B.A. Maher (Ed.),
Progress in experimental personality research (Vol.
3). New York: Academic Press.

Mischel, W. & Ebbesen, E.B. (1970). Attention in delay of
gratification. Journal of Personality and Social
Psychology, 16, 329-337.

Mischel, W. & Metzner, R. (1962). Preference for delayed
reward as a function of age, intelligence, and length of
delay interval. Journal of Abnormal and Social
Psychology, 64, 425-431.

Mischel, W. & Mischel, H.N. (1977). Essentials of
psychology. New York: Random House.

Mischel, W. & Moore, B. (1973). Effects of attention to
symbolically presented rewards upon self-control.
Journal of Personality and Social Psychology, 28,
172-179.

Mischel, W., Ebbesen, E.B. & Zeiss, A.R. (1972). Cognitive
and attentional mechanisms in delay of gratification.
Journal of Personality and Social Psychology, 21,
204-218.

Mollon, P. & Pary, G. (1983). The fragile self:
Narcissistic disturbance and the protective function of
depression. British Journal of Medical Psychology.

Monat, A. (1976). Temporal uncertainty, anticipation time
and cognitive coping under threat. Journal of Human
Stress, 2, 32-43.

Monge, R.H. (1973). Developmental trends in factors of
adolescent self-concept. Developmental Psychology,
8, 382-393.

Monroe, S.E. (1983). Social support and disorder: Toward
an untangling of cause and effect. American Journal of
Community Psychology, 1, 81-98.

Moore, B., Mischel, W. & Zeiss, A.R. (1976). Comparative
effects of the reward stimulus and its cognitve
representation in voluntary delay. Journal of
Personality and Social Psychology, 34, 419-424.

Moos, R.H. (1974). Family Environment Scale preliminary

manual. Palo Alto: Consulting Psychologists Press.

Moos, R.H. (1975). Evaluating correctional and community settings. New York: Wiley.

Moos, R.H. (1979). Evaluating educational environment: Procedures, measures, findings, and policy implications. San Francisco: Jossey Bass.

Moos, R.H. & Finney, J.W. (1983). The expanding scope of alcoholism treatment evaluation. American Psychologist, 38, 1036-1044.

Moos, R.H. & Insel, P. (1974). Work Environment Scale preliminary manual. Palo Alto: Consulting Psychologists Press.

Moreland,R., Miller,J. & Laucka,F. (1981). Academic achievement and self-evaluations of academic performance. Journal of Educational Psychology, 73, 335-344.

Morgan, W.P., Roberts, J.A. & Feinerman, A.D. (1971). Psychological effect of acute physical activity. Archives of Physical Medicine & Rehabilitation, 52, 422-425.

Morris,L.W. & Engle,W.B. (1981). Assessing various coping strategies and their effects on test performance and anxiety. Journal of Clinical Psychology, 37, 165-171.

Morris,L.W. & Fulmer,R.S. (1976). Test anxiety (worry and emotionality) changes during academic testing as a function of feedback and test importance. Journal of Educational Psychology, 68, 817-824.

Morris,L.W., Davis,M.A. & Hutchings,C.H. (1981). Cognitive and emotional components of anxiety: Literature review and a revised worry-emotionality scale. Journal of Educational Psychology, 73, 541-555.

Morris, L.W., Franklin, M.S. & Ponath, P. (1983). The relationship between trait and state indices of worry and emotionality. In H.M. van der Ploeg, R. Schwarzer & C.D. Spielberger (Eds.), Advances in test anxiety research (Vol. 2) (pp. 3-13). Lisse/ Hillsdale: Swets & Zeitlinger/ Erlbaum.

Morris, L.W., Harris, E.W. & Rovins, D.S. (1981). Interactive effects of generalized and situational expectations on the arousal of cognitive and emotional components of social anxiety. Journal of Research in Personality, 15, 302-311.

Morris, L.W. & Ponath, P.M. (1984). Differences in

anxiety among androgynous women: Relation to achievment
motivation variables. In R. Schwarzer (Ed.),
Self-Related Cognitions in Anxiety and Motivation.
Hillsdale: Erlbaum.

Moulton, R.W. (1965). Effects of success and failure on
level of aspiration as related to achievement motives.
Journal of Personality and Social Psychology, 1,
399-406.

Mueller, J.H. & Thompson, W.B. (1984). Test anxiety and
distinctiveness of personal information. In Ploeg, H.
van der, Schwarzer, R. & Spielberger, C.D. (Eds.),
Advances in Test Anxiety (Vol. 3). Lisse /
Hillsdale: Swets / Erlbaum.

Murphy, L.B. & Moriarty, A.E. (1976). Vulnerability,
coping, and growth. New Haven and London: Yale Univ.
Press.

Musante, L., MacDougall, J.M., Dembroski, T.M. & Van Horn,
A.E. (1983). Component analysis of the Type A
coronary-prone behavior pattern in male and female
college students. Journal of Personality and Social
Psychology, 45, 1104-1117.

Muuss, R.E. (1975). Theories of adolescence. New York:
Random House.

Neufeld, R.W. (ed.) (1982). Psychological stress and
psychopathology. New York: McGraw-Hill.

Neugarten, B., Havighurst, R. & Tobin, S. (1961). The
measurement of life satisfaction. Journal of
Gerontology, 16, 134-143.

Nicholls, J. & Miller, A. (1983). The differentiation of
the concepts of difficulty and ability. Child
Development, 54, 951-959.

Nicholls, J.G., Jagacinski, C.M. & Miller, A.T. (1984).
Conceptions of ability in children and adults. In R.
Schwarzer (Ed.), Self-Related Cognitions in Anxiety and
Motivation. Hillsdale: Erlbaum.

Niemelä, P. (1967). Coping patterns in shock anticipation
and in everyday stress. Scandinavian Journal of
Psychology, 23, 446-448.

Nisbett, R.E., Caputo, C., Legant, P. & Maracek, J. (1973).
Behavior as seen by the actor and as seen by the
observer. Journal of Personality and Social
Psychology, 27, 154-164.

Nisbett,R. & Ross,L. (1980). Human inference: Strategies
and shortcomings of social judgment. Englewood Cliffs:

Prentice Hall.

Nitsch, J.R. (1981). Stress. Theorien, Untersuchungen, Maßnahmen. Bern: Huber.

Nowlis, V. (1970). Mood: Behavior and experiences. In M. Arnold (Ed.), Feelings and Emotions. New York: Academic Press.

O'Malley, P.M. & Bachman, J.G. (1983). Self-esteem: Change and stability between ages 13 and 23. Developmental Psychology, 19, 257-268.

OBanion, K. & Arkowitz, H. (1977). Social anxiety and selective memory for affective information about the self. Social Behavior and Personality, 5, 321-328.

Obrist, P.A. (1976). The cardiovascular-behavioral interaction - as it appears today. Psychophysiology, 13, 95-107.

Obrist, P.A. (1981). Cardiovascular Psychophysiology. New York: Plenum.

Oliver, J.M. & Burkham, R. (1979). Depression in university students: Duration, relation to calendar time, prevalence and demographic corelates. Journal of Abnormal Psychology, 88, 601-623.

Otto, J. (1981). Regulationsmuster in Warte- und Vollzugssituationen. München: Minerva.

Otto, J. (1983). Experiments in multidimensional activation (arousal): The effects of mild exercise. Research report. Deutsche Forschungsgemeinschaft.

Oxley, D., Barrera, M. & Sadalla, K.E. (1981). Relationships among community size mediators, and social support variables: A path analytic approach. American Journal of Community Psychology, 9, 637-651.

Palys, T.S. & Little, B.R. (1983). Perceived life satisfaction and the organization of personal project systems. Journal of Personality and Social Psychology, 44, 1221-1230.

Parsons,J.E., Midgley,C. & Adler,T.F. (1983). Age-related changes in the school environment: Effects on achievement motivation. In Nicholls,J.H. (Ed.), The development of achievement motivationJAI Press.

Paulhus, D. (1983). Sphere-specific measures of perceived control. Journal of Personality and Social Psychology, 44, 1253-1265.

Paykel, E.S. (1973). Life Events and Acute Depression. In
    J.P. Scott & E.C. Senay (Eds.), Separation and
    Depression (pp. 224-25). Washington, D.C.:
    Amer.Assoc.f.t.Advanc.o.Science.

Payne, R., Jick, T.D. & Burke, R.J. (1982). Whither stress
    research: An agenda for the 1980's. Journal of
    Occupational Behavior, 3, 131-145.

Pedhazur,E.J. (1982). Multiple regression in behavioral
    research. Explanation and prediction. New York: Holt.

Pekrun, R. (1983). Schulische Persönlichkeitsentwicklung.
    Frankfurt: Lang.

Pekrun, R. (1984). An expectancy-value model of anxiety.
    In Ploeg, H. van der, Schwarzer, R. & Spielberger, C.D.
    (Eds.), Advances in Test Anxiety Research (Vol. 3).
    Lisse / Hillsdale: Swets / Erlbaum.

Pekrun,R. (1983). Wie valide ist das
    attributionstheoretische Motivationsmodell ? In Lüer,G.
    (Ed.), Bericht über den 33.Kongreß der Deutschen
    Gesellschaft für Psychologie in Mainz 1982. Göttingen:
    Hogrefe.

Peplau, L.A. & Perlman, D. (Eds.) (1982). Loneliness: A
    sourcebook of current theory, research and therapy.
    New York: Wiley-Interscience.

Peterson,C., Schwartz,S.M. & Seligman,M.E.P. (1981).
    Self-blame and depressive symptoms. Journal of
    Personality and Social Psychology, 41, 253-259.

Pettigrew,T.F. (1967). Social evaluation theory. In
    Levine,D. (Ed.), Nebraska Symposium on Motivation (pp.
    241-311)Lincoln.

Phillips, D.C. (1967). Mental health status, social
    participation, and happiness. Journal of Health and
    Social Behavior, 8, 285-291.

Pilkonis, P.A. (1977). The behavioral consequences of
    shyness. Journal of Personality, 45, 596-611.

Ploeg, H.M. van der (1981). Zelf-Beoordelingsvragenlijst,
    Handleiding Addendum 1981. Lisse: Swets & Zeitlinger.

Ploeg, H.M. van der (1982). Examen/ Toets Attitude
    Vragenlijst. Lisse: Swets & Zeitlinger.

Ploeg, H.M. van der (1982). The relationship of worry and
    emotionality to performance in Dutch school children.
    In R. Schwarzer, H.M. van der Ploeg & C.D. Spielberger
    (Eds.), Advances in test anxiety research (Vol. 1)
    (pp. 55-66). Lisse/ Hillsdale, N.Y.: Swets &

Zeitlinger/ Erlbaum.

Ploeg, H.M. van der (1983). Test anxiety and anger: Some empirical considerations. In R. Schwarzer, H.M. van der Ploeg & C.D. Spielberger (Eds.), Advances in test anxiety research (Vol. 2) (pp. 67-80). Lisse/ Hillsdale, N.Y.: Swets & Zeitlinger/ Erlbaum.

Ploeg, H.M. van der (1983). The validation of the Dutch form of the Test Anxiety Inventory. In R. Schwarzer, H.M. van der Ploeg & C.D. Spielberger (Eds.), Advances in test anxiety research (Vol. 2) (pp. 191-202). Lisse/ Hillsdale, N.Y.: Swets & Zeitlinger/ Erlbaum.

Ploeg, H. van der (1984). Worry, emotionality, intelligence and academic performance in male and female Dutch secondary school children. In Ploeg, H. van der, Schwarzer, R. & Spielberger, C.D. (Eds.), Advances in Test Anxiety Research (Vol. 3). Lisse / Hillsdale: Swets / Erlbaum.

Ploeg, H.M. van der (in press). The development and validation ot the Dutch State-Trait Anxiety Inventory: " De Zelf-Beoordelings Vragenlijst". In C.D. Spielberger, I.G. Sarason & P.B. Defares (Eds.), Stress and anxiety (Vol. 9). New York: Wiley.

Ploeg, H.M. van der, Defares, P.B. & Spielberger, C.D. (1979). Zelf-Beoordelings Vragenlijst. STAI-versie DY-2. Lisse: Swets & Zeitlinger.

Ploeg, H.M. van der, Defares, P.B. & Spielberger, C.D. (1980). Handleiding bij de Zelf-Beoordelings Vragenlijst. ZBV Een nederlandstalige bewerking van de Spielberger State-Trait Anxiety Inventory, STAI-DY. Lisse: Swets & Zeitlinger.

Ploeg, H.M. van der, Schwarzer, R. & Spielberger, C.D. (Eds.) (1983). Advances in test anxiety research (Vol. 2). Lisse/ Hillsdale: Swets & Zeitlinger/ Erlbaum.

Ploeg, H.M. van der, Schwarzer, R. & Spielberger, C.D. (Eds.) (1984). Advances in test anxiety research (Vol. 3). Lisse/ Hillsdale: Swets & Zeitlinger/ Erlbaum.

Ploeg-Stapert, J.D. van der & Ploeg, H.M. van der (1984). A multifacetted treatment program of test anxiety. Leiden: Paper in preparation.

Plomin, R. & Rowe, D.C. (1979). Genetic and environmental etiology of social behavior in infancy. Developmental Psychology, 15, 62-72.

Porter, L.W. & Steers, R.M. (1973). Organizational work and personal factors in employee turnover and absenteeism. Psychological Bulletin, 80, 151-176.

Posner, B.Z. & Randolph, W.A. (1980). Moderators of role
  stress among hospital personnel. The Journal of
  Psychology,105, 215-224.

Posner, M.J. (1978). Chronometric explorations of mind.
  Hillsdale, N.Y.: Erlbaum.

Powers, W.T. (1973). Behavior: The control of
  perception. Chicago: Aldine.

Powers, W.T. (1978). Quantitative analysis of purposive
  systems - Some spadework at the foundations of
  scientific psychology. Psychological Review, 85,
  417-435.

Pribram, K.H. & McGuinness, D. (1975). Arousal, activation
  and effort in the control of attention. Psychological
  Review, 82, 116-149.

Procidano, M.E. & Heller, K. (1983). Measures of perceived
  social support from friends and familiy: Three
  validation studies. American Journal of Community
  Psychology, 11, 1-24.

Pruyn, A., Vlek, C. & Aaten, J. (1984). Heart rate
  variability and public task performance:
  Psychophysiological expressions of test anxiety. In
  Ploeg, H. van der, Schwarzer, R. & Spielberger, C.D.
  (Eds.), Advances in Test Anxiety Research (Vol. 3).
  Lisse / Hillsdale: Swets / Erlbaum.

Prystav, G. (1982). Vorhersagbarkeit von
  Streß-Ereignissen und Angstbewältigung.
  Forschungsbericht Nr.6 des Psychologischen Inst. der
  Albert-Ludwigs-Univ., Freiburg. Freiburg/ Breisgau: .

Quinn, R.P. & Shepard, L.J. (1964). The 1962-1963 quality
  of employment survey. Ann Arbor: Soc. Res. Inst.,
  Michigan Univ..

Rachman, S.J. & Hodgson, R.J. (1980). Obsessions and
  compulsions. New Yersey: Prentice-Hall.

Rahe, R. & Romo, M. (1974). Recent life changes and the
  onset of myocardial infarction and coronary death in
  Helsinki. In H. Gunderson & R. Rahe (Eds.), Life
  stress and illness (pp. 105-120). Springfield:
  Thomas.

Ramsay, R. (1977). Flooding with grief: A treatment for
  depression. Paper presented at the International
  Congress of Behavior Therapy, Uppsala, Sweden. .

Rangell, L. (1967). The metapsychology of psychic trauma.
  In S.S. Furst (Ed.), Psychic trauma. New York: Basic

Books.

Reason, J.T. (1977). Skill and error in everyday life. In
M. Howe (Ed.), Adult learning (pp. 77-89). London:
Wiley Press.

Reckman, R.F. & Goethals, G.R. (1973). Deviancy and group
orientation as determinants of group composition
preferences. Sociometry, 36, 419-423.

Rheinberg, F. (1982). Reducing anxiety in classroom
settings: Some theoretical observations. In R.
Schwarzer, H.M. van der Ploeg & C.D. Spielberger (Eds.),
Advances in test anxiety research (Vol. 1) (pp.
131-137). Lisse/ Hillsdale, N.Y.: Swets & Zeitlinger/
Erlbaum.

Rheinberg,F. (1980). Leistungsbewertung und
Lernmotivation. Göttingen: Hogrefe.

Rheinberg,F. & Peter,R. (1982). Selbstkonzept,
Ängstlichkeit und Schulunlust von Schülern: Eine
Längsschnittstudie zum Einfluß des Klassenlehrers. In
Rheinberg,F. (Ed.), Bezugsnormen zur
Schulleistungsbewertung. Jahrbuch für Empirische
Erziehungswissenschaft 1982 (pp. 143-159). Düsseldorf:
Schwann.

Rheinberg,F.(Ed.) (1982). Bezugsnormen zur
Schulleistungsbewertung. Jahrbuch für Empirische
Erziehungswissenschaften 1982. Düsseldorf: Schwann.

Richardson, F.C. & Woolfolk, R.L. (1980). Mathematics
anxiety. In Sarason, I.G. (Ed.), Test anxiety.
Hillsdale: Erlbaum.

Rissanen, V., Romo, M. & Siltanen, P. (1978). Premonitory
symptoms and stress factors preceding sudden death from
ischaemic heart disease. Acta Medica
Scandinavica,204, 389-396.

Ritchie, F.K. & Toner, I.J. (in press). Direct labeling,
tester expectancy and delay maintenance behavior in
Scottish preschool children. International Journal of
Behavioral Development.

Rizley, R. (1978). Depression and distortion in the
attribution of causality. Journal of Abnormal
Psychology, 87, 32-48.

Rogers, T.B. (1981). A model of the self as an aspect of
the human information system. In N. Cantor & J.F.
Kihlstrom (Eds.), Personality, Cognition and Social
Interaction. Hillsdale, N.Y.: Erlbaum.

Rogers, T.B., Kuiper, N.A. & Kirker, W.S. (1977).

Self-reference and the encoding of personal information. <u>Journal</u> <u>of</u> <u>Personality</u> <u>and</u> <u>Social</u> <u>Psychology</u>, <u>35</u>, 677-688.

Rogers,C.M., Smith,M.D. & Coleman,J.M. (1978). Social comparison in the classroom: The relationship between academic achievement and self-concept. <u>Journal</u> <u>of</u> <u>Educational</u> <u>Psychology</u>, <u>70</u>, 50-57.

Ronis, D.L., Hansen, R.H. & O'Leary, V.E. (1983). Understanding the meaning of achievement attributions: A test of derived locus and stability scores. <u>Journal</u> <u>of</u> <u>Personality</u> <u>and</u> <u>Social</u> <u>Psychology</u>, <u>44</u>, 702-711.

Rose, R.M., Jenkins, C.D. & Hurst, M.W. (1978). Health change in air traffic controllers: A prospective study I. Background und description. <u>Psychosomatic</u> <u>Medicine</u>, <u>40</u>, 142-165.

Rosenberg,M. (1979). <u>Conceiving</u> <u>the</u> <u>self</u>. New York: Basic Books, 99-127.

Rosenman, R. (1978). The interview method of assessment of the coronary prone behavior pattern. In H. Dembroski, S. Weiss & F. Shields et al. (Eds.), <u>Coronary-prone</u> <u>behavior</u> (pp. 55-69). New York: Springer.

Roth, M., Gurney, C., Garside, R.F. & Kerr, T.A. (1972). Studies in the classification of affective disorders: The relationship between anxiety states and depressive illnesses. <u>British</u> <u>Journal</u> <u>of</u> <u>Psychiatry</u>,<u>121</u>, 147-161.

Rotter,J.B. (1966). Generalized expectancies for internal versus external control of reinforcement. <u>Psychological</u> <u>Monographs</u>, <u>1</u>, wholeno.609.

Rush, A.J. & Giles, D.E. (1982). Cognitive therapy: Theory and research. In Rush, A.J. (Ed.), <u>Short-term</u> <u>psychotherapies</u> <u>for</u> <u>depression</u>. Chichester: Wiley.

Rushton, J.P., Brainerd, C.J. & Pressley, M. (1983). Behavioral development and construct validity: The principle of aggregation. <u>Psychological</u> <u>Bulletin</u>, <u>94</u>, 18-38.

Rustemeyer, R. (1982). <u>Wirkungen</u> <u>von</u> <u>Emotionen</u> <u>auf</u> <u>die</u> <u>Wahrnehmung</u> <u>der</u> <u>eigenen</u> <u>Fähigkeiten</u>. <u>Unveröffentlichte</u> <u>Diplom-Arbeit</u>. Bielefeld: Universität Bielefeld, Abt. Psy..

Sanders, A.F. (1983). Towards a model of stress and human performance. <u>Acta</u> <u>Psychologica</u>, <u>53</u>, 61-97.

Sandler,I.N. & Lakey, B. (1982). Locus of control as a stress moderator: The role of control perceptions and social support. American Journal of Community Psychology, 10, 65-80.

Sarason, B. (1984). Social support, social behavior, and cognitive processes. In R. Schwarzer (Ed.), Self-Related Cognitions in Anxiety and Motivation. Hillsdale: Erlbaum.

Sarason, I.G. (1960). Empirical findings and theoretical problems in the use of anxiety scales. Psychological Bulletin, 57, 403-415.

Sarason, I.G. (1975). Test anxiety, attention, and the general problem of test anxiety. In C.D. Spielberger & I.G. Sarason (Eds.), Stress and anxiety (Vol. 1). New York: Wiley.

Sarason, I.G. (1978). The Test Anxiety Scale: Concepts and research. In C.D. Spielberger & I.G. Sarason (Eds.), Stress and anxiety (Vol. 5) (pp. 193-216). Washington: Hemisphere.

Sarason, I.G. (1980). Life stress, self-preoccupation, and social supports. In I.G. Sarason & C.D. Spielberger (Eds.), Stress and anxiety (Vol. 7) (pp. 73-91). Washington: Hemisphere.

Sarason, I.G. (1981). Test anxiety, stress, and social support. Journal of Personality, 49, 101-114.

Sarason, I.G. (1984). Test anxiety, worry, and cognitive interference. In R. Schwarzer (Ed.), Self-Related Cognitions in Anxiety and Motivation. Hillsdale: Erlbaum.

Sarason, I.G. & Sarason, B.R. (1981). The importance of cognition and moderator variables in stress. In D. Magnusson (Ed.), Toward a psychology of situations: An interactional perspective. Hillsdale, N.Y.: Erlbaum.

Sarason, I.G., Johnson, J.H. & Siegel, J.M. (1978). Assessing the impact of life changes: Development of the life experiences survey. Journal of Consulting and Clinical Psychology, 46, 932-946.

Sarason, I.G., Levine, H.M., Basham,R.B. & Sarason, B. (1983). Assessing social support: The Social Support Questionnaire. Journal of Personality and Social Psychology, 44, 127-139.

Sarason,I.G.(Ed.) (1980). Test anxiety. Hillsdale,N.J.: Erlbaum.

Schachter, S. (1959). The psychology of affiliation: Experimental studies for the sources of gregariousness. Stanford: Stanford University Press.

Schaefer, C., Coyne, J.C. & Lazarus, R.S. (1981). The
health-related functions of social support. Journal of
Behavioral Medicine, 4, 381-406.

Schaie, K. (1973). Methodological problems in descriptive
developmental research on adulthood and aging. In J.
Nesselroade & S. Reese (Eds.), Life-span developmental
psychology: Methodological issues (pp. 253-280). New
York: Academic Press.

Schlenker, B.R. & Leary, M.R. (1982). Social anxiety and
self-presentation: A conceptualization and model.
Psychological Bulletin, 92, 641-669.

Schlenker, Barry R. & Leary, Mark R. (1982). Social
Anxiety and Self-Presentation: A Conceptualization and
Model. Psychological Bulletin, 92, 641-669.

Schmalt, H.-D. (1982). Two concepts of fear of failure
motivation. In R. Schwarzer, H.M. van der Ploeg & C.D.
Spielberger (Eds.), Advances in test anxiety research
(Vol. 1) (pp. 45-52). Lisse/ Hillsdale, N.Y.: Swets &
Zeitlinger/ Erlbaum.

Schmidt, N. & Sermat, V. (1983). Measuring loneliness in
different relationships. Journal of Personality and
Social Psychology, 44, 1038-1047.

Schneewind, K.A. & Cattell, R.B. (1970). Zum Problem der
Faktoridentifikation: Verteilungen und
Vertrauensintervalle von Kongruenzkoeff. für Pers.fakt.
i.Bereich objektiv-analyt. Tests. Psychologische
Beiträge, 12, 214-226.

Schuler, R.S. (1982). An integrative transactional process
model of stress in organizations. Journal of
Occupational Behavior, 3, 5-19.

Schulz, P. (1983). Regulation und Fehlregulation im
Verhalten VII. Entstehungsbedingungen und
Erscheinungsweisen der emotionalen Belastung in
Leistungssituationen. Psychologische Beiträge, 24,
498-522.

Schunk, D.H. (1983). Reward contingencies and the
development of children's skills and self-efficacy.
Journal of Educational Research, 75, 511-518.

Schwarz, N. & Clore, G.L. (1983). Mood, misattribution,
and judgments of well-being: Informative and directive
functions of affective states. Journal of Personality
and Social Psychology, 45, 513-523.

Schwarzer, C. (1983). Lehrer als ein Bestimmungsfaktor
curricularer Lernereignisse. In Hameyer, U., Frey, K. &

Haft, H. (Eds.), Handbuch der Curriculumforschung (pp. 387-398). Weinheim: Beltz.

Schwarzer, C. & Cherkes-Julkowski, M. (1982). Determinants of test anxiety and helplessness. In R. Schwarzer, H.M. van der Ploeg & C.D. Spielberger (Eds.), Advances in test anxiety research (Vol. 1) (pp. 33-43). Lisse/ Hillsdale, N.Y.: Swets & Zeitlinger/ Erlbaum.

Schwarzer, C. & Kim, M.-J. (1984). Adaptation of the Korean form of the Test Anxiety Inventory. In Ploeg, H. van der, Schwarzer, R. & Spielberger, C.D. (Eds.), Advances in Test Anxiety Research (Vol. 3). Lisse / Hillsdale: Swets / Erlbaum.

Schwarzer,R. (1981). Streß, Angst und Hilflosigkeit. Stuttgart: Kohlhammer.

Schwarzer,R. (1983). Unterrichtsklima als Sozialisationsbedingung für Selbstkonzeptentwicklung. Unterrichtswissenschaft, 11, 129-148.

Schwarzer,R. & Jerusalem,M. (1982). Selbstwertdienliche Attributionen nach Leistungsrückmeldungen. Zeitschrift für Entwicklungspsychologie und Pädagogische Psychologie, 14, 47-57.

Schwarzer,R. & Schwarzer,C. (1982). Test anxiety with respect to school reference groups. In Schwarzer,R., van der Ploeg,H.M. & Spielberger,C.D. (Eds.), Advances in test anxiety research.Vol.1 (pp. 95-104). Lisse: Swets & Zeitlinger.

Schwarzer,R., Jerusalem,M. & Lange,B. (1982). A longitudinal study on worry and emotionality. In Schwarzer,R., van der Ploeg,H.M. & Spielberger,C.D. (Eds.), Advances in test anxiety research.Vol.1 (pp. 67-81). Lisse: Swets & Zeitlinger.

Schwarzer,R., Lange,B. & Jerusalem,M. (1982). Die Bezugsnorm des Lehrers aus der Sicht des Schülers. In Rheinberg,F. (Ed.), Bezugsnormen zur Schulleistungsbewertung. Jahrbuch für Empirische Erziehungswissenschaft 1982 (pp. 161-172). Düsseldorf: Schwann.

Schwarzer,R., Lange,B. & Jerusalem,M. (1982). Selbstkonzeptentwicklung nach einem Bezugsgruppenwechsel. Zeitschrift für Entwicklungspsychologie und Pädagogische Psychologie, 14, 125-140.

Schwarzer,R., van der Ploeg,H.M. & Spielberger,C.D.(Eds.) (1982). Advances in test anxiety research.Vol.1. Lisse: Swets & Zeitlinger.

Schwarzer, R. (1984). Self-related cognitions in anxiety
    and motivation: An introduction. In R. Schwarzer (Ed.),
    Self-Related Cognitions in Anxiety and Motivation.
    Hillsdale: Erlbaum.

Schwarzer, R. & Jerusalem, M. (1983).
    Selbstkonzeptentwicklung in schulischen Bezugsgruppen –
    eine dynamische Mehrebenenanalyse. Zeitschrift für
    personenzentrierte Psychologie und Psychotherapie,
    2, 79-87.

Schwarzer, R. & Lange, B. (1983). Test anxiety development
    from grade 5 to grade 10: A structural equation
    approach. In R. Schwarzer, H.M. van der Ploeg & C.D.
    Spielberger (Eds.), Advances in test anxiety research
    (Vol. 2) (pp. 147-157). Lisse/Hillsdale, N.Y.: Swets &
    Zeitlinger/ Erlbaum.

Schwarzer, R. & Schwarzer, C. (1983). The validation of
    the German form of the State-trait Personality
    Inventory: A pilot study. In R. Schwarzer, H.M. van der
    Ploeg & C.D. Spielberger (Eds.), Advances in test
    anxiety research (Vol. 2) (pp. 215-221). Lisse/
    Hillsdale, N.Y.: Swets & Zeitlinger/ Erlbaum.

Schwarzer, R., Jerusalem, M. & Schwarzer, C. (1983).
    Self-related and situation-related cognitions in test
    anxiety and helplessness: A longitudinal analysis with
    structural equations. In R. Schwarzer, H.M. van der
    Ploeg & C.D. Spielberger (Eds.), Advances in test
    anxiety research (Vol. 2) (pp. 35-43). Lisse/
    Hillsdale, N.Y.: Swets & Zeitlinger/ Erlbaum.

Schwarzer, R., Jerusalem, M. & Stiksrud, H.A. (1984). The
    developmental relationship between test anxiety and
    helplessness. In Ploeg, H.M. van der, Schwarzer, R. &
    Spielberger, C.D. (Eds.), Advances in Test Anxiety
    Research (Vol. 3). Lisse/ Hillsdale: Swets &
    Zeitlinger/ Erlbaum.

Schwarzer, R., Ploeg, H.M. van der & Spielberger, C.D.
    (1982). Test anxiety: An overview of theory and
    research. In R. Schwarzer, H.M. van der Ploeg & C.D.
    Spielberger (Eds.), Advances in test anxiety research
    (Vol. 1) (pp. 3-9). Lisse/ Hillsdale, N.Y.: Swets &
    Zeitlinger/ Erlbaum.

Schönpflug, W. (1979). Regulation und Fehlregulation im
    Verhalten I. Verhaltensstruktur, Effizienz und Belastung
    – theoretische Grundlagen eines Untersuchungsprogramms.
    Psychologische Beiträge, 21, 174-203.

Schönpflug, W. (1982). Aspiration level and causal
    attribution under noise stimulation. In H.W. Krohne &
    L. Laux (Eds.), Achievement, stress and anxiety. New
    York: Wiley.

Schönpflug, W. (1983). Coping efficiency and situational demands. In G.R.J. Hockey (Ed.), Stress and fatigue in human performance. New York: Wiley.

Schönpflug, W. (1983). Stress, fatigue and the economics of behavior. In G.R. Hockey (Ed.), Stress and fatigue. London: Wiley.

Schönpflug, W. (1984). Activity style of anxious individuals. In Ploeg, H. van der, Schwarzer, R. & Spielberger, C.D. (Eds.), Advances in Test Anxiety Research (Vol. 3). Lisse / Hillsdale: Swets / Erlbaum.

Schönpflug, W. (1984). Goal directed behavior as a source of stress: Psychological origins and consequences of inefficiency. In M. Frese & J. Sabini (Eds.), Goal directed behavior: The concept of action in psychology. Hillsdale, N.Y.: Erlbaum.

Schönpflug, W. (in press). Anxiety, prospective orientation, and preparation. Invited paper, presented at the conference "Stress and Anxiety", Warszawa, Sept. 26-29, 1983. .

Schönpflug, W. & Heckhausen, H. (1976). Lärm und Motivation. Forschungsbericht des Landes Nordrhein-Westfalen. Opladen: Westdeutscher Verlag.

Schönpflug, W. & Schulz, P. (1979). Lärmwirkungen bei Tätigkeiten mit komplexer Informationsverarbeitung. Forschungsbericht Nr. 79-10501201. Berlin: Umweltbundesamt.

Seligman, M.E.P. (1971). Phobias and preparedness. Behaviour-therapy, 2, 307-320.

Seligman, M.E.P. (1981). A learned helplessness point of view. In L.P. Rehm (Ed.), Behavior Therapy for Depression (pp. 123-141). New York: Academic Press.

Seligman, M.E.P., Abramson, L.Y., Semmel, A. & Von Baeyer, C. (1979). Depressive attributional style. Journal of Abnormal Psychology, 88, 242-247.

Seligman, M.E.P. (1975). Helplessness. San Francisco: Freeman.

Sells, S.B. (1970). On the nature of stress. In J. McGrath (Ed.), Social and psychological factors in stress (pp. 134-139). New York: Holt Rinehart & Winston.

Selye, H. (1974). Stress without distress. Toronto: McClelland & Stewart.

Selye, H. (1976). <u>The</u> <u>Stress</u> <u>of</u> <u>Life</u>. New York:
    McGraw-Hill Book Co..

Shapiro, D.A. (1980). Science and psychotherapy: The state
    of the art. <u>British</u> <u>Journal</u> <u>of</u> <u>Medical</u> <u>Psychology</u>,
    <u>53</u>, 1-10.

Sharma, S. & Rao, U. (1983). Academic performance in
    different school courses as related to self-acceptance,
    test anxiety and intelligence. In R. Schwarzer, H.M.
    van der Ploeg & C.D. Spielberger (Eds.), <u>Advances</u> <u>in</u>
    <u>test</u> <u>anxiety</u> <u>research</u> (Vol. 2) (pp. 111-118). Lisse/
    Hillsdale, N.Y.: Swets & Zeitlinger/ Erlbaum.

Sharma, S., Sud, A. & Spielberger, C.D. (1983).
    Development of the Hindi form of the Test Anxiety
    Inventory. In R. Schwarzer, H.M van der Ploeg & C.D.
    Spielberger (Eds.), <u>Advances</u> <u>in</u> <u>test</u> <u>anxiety</u> <u>research</u>
    (Vol. 2) (pp. 183-189). Lisse/ Hillsdale, N.Y.: Swets
    & Zeitlinger/ Erlbaum.

Shavelson, R.J. & Marsh, H.W. (1984). On the structure of
    self-concept. In R. Schwarzer (Ed.), <u>Self-Related</u>
    <u>Cognitions</u> <u>in</u> <u>Anxiety</u> <u>and</u> <u>Motivattion</u>. Hillsdale:
    Erlbaum.

Shirom, A. (1982). What is organizational stress? A facet
    analytic conceptualization. <u>Journal</u> <u>of</u> <u>Occupational</u>
    <u>Behavior</u>, <u>3</u>, 21-37.

Siegrist, J., Dittman, K., Rittner, K. et al. (1980).
    <u>Soziale</u> <u>Belastungen</u> <u>und</u> <u>Herzinfarkt</u>. Stuttgart:
    Enke.

Siegrist, J., Dittman, K., Rittner, K. et al. (1982). The
    social context of active distress in patients with early
    myocardial infarction. <u>Social</u> <u>Science</u> <u>&</u> <u>Medicine</u>,
    <u>16</u>, 443-453.

Silbereisen, R.K. & Eyferth, K. (eds.) (in press).
    <u>Development</u> <u>as</u> <u>action</u> <u>in</u> <u>context</u>. New York:
    Springer.

Silver, R.L. & Wortman, C.B. (1980). Coping with
    undesirable life events. In J. Garber & M.E.P. Seligman
    (Eds.), <u>Human</u> <u>helplessness.</u> <u>Theory</u> <u>and</u> <u>applications</u>
    (pp. 279-340). New York: .

Simmons, R.G., Rosenberg, F. & Rosenberg, M. (1973).
    Disturbance in the self-image at adolescence. <u>American</u>
    <u>Sociological</u> <u>Review</u>, <u>38</u>, 553-568.

Sivacek, J. & Crano, W.D. (1982). Vested interest as a
    moderator of attitude-behavior consistency. <u>Journal</u> <u>of</u>
    <u>Personality</u> <u>and</u> <u>Social</u> <u>Psychology</u>, <u>43</u>, 210-221.

Snyder, M. (1974). Self-monitoring of expressive behavior. Journal of Personality and Social Psychology, 30, 526-537.

Sörbom, D. (1974). A general method for studying differences in factor structure between groups. British Journal of Mathematical and Statistical Psychology, 27, 229-239.

Sörbom, D. & Jöreskog, K.G. (1976). COFAMM: Confirmatory factor analysis with model modifications: A Fortran IV program. Chicago, III.:: National Educat. Resources, Inc..

Spielberger, C.D. (1966). The effects of anxiety on complex learning and academic achievement. In C.D. Spielberger (Ed.), Anxiety and Behavior. New York: Academic Press.

Spielberger, C.D. (1966). Theory and research on anxiety. In C.D. Spielberger (Ed.), Anxiety and Behavior. New York: Academic Press.

Spielberger, C.D. (1972). Anxiety as an emotional state. In C.D. Spielberger (Ed.), Anxiety: Current trends in theory and research (Vol. 1) (pp. 23-49). New York: Academic Press.

Spielberger, C.D. (1972). Anxiety: Current trends in theory and research (Vol. 1). New York: Academic Press.

Spielberger, C.D. (1972). Conceptual and methodological issues in anxiety research. In Spielberger, C.D. (Ed.), Anxiety: Current Trends in Theory and Research (Vol. 2). New York: Academic Press.

Spielberger, C.D. (1975). Anxiety: State-Trait-Process. In C.D. Spielberger & I.G. Sarason (Eds.), Stress and anxiety (Vol. 1) (pp. 115-143). New York: Wiley.

Spielberger, C.D. (1976). The nature and treatment of test anxiety. In M. Zuckerman & C.D. Spielberger (Eds.), Emotion and anxiety. New York: Wiley.

Spielberger, C.D. (1980). Test Anxiety Inventory. Preliminary professional manual. Palo Alto, Ca.: Consulting Psychologists Press.

Spielberger, C.D. (1983). Manual for the State-Trait Anxiety Inventory (STAI Form Y). Palo Alto, Ca.: Consulting Psychologists Press.

Spielberger, C.D. & Diaz-Guerrero, R.(Eds.) (1976). Cross-cultural anxiety (Vol. 1). Washington:

Thayer, R.E. (1970). Activation states as assessed by
   verbal report and four psychophysiological variables.
   Psychophysiology, 7, 86-94.

Thayer, R.E. (1978). Toward a psychological theory of
   multidimensional activation (arousal). Motivation and
   arousal, 2, 1-34.

Thayer, R.E. (1978). Towards a psychological theory of
   multidimensional activation (arousal). Motivation and
   Emotion, 2, 1-34.

Thayer, R.E. (in press). Activation (arousal): The shift
   from a single to a multidimensional perspective. In J.
   Strelau, T. Gale & F, Farley (Eds.), Biological
   foundations of personality and behavior. Washington:
   Hemisphere.

Thayer, R.E. (in press). Energy, tiredness and tension
   effects of a sugar snack vs. moderate exercise.
   Journal of Personality and Social Psychology.

Theorell, T. (1980). Life events and manifestations of
   ischaemic heart disease: Epidemiological and
   psychophysiological aspects. Psychotherapy &
   Psychosomatics, 34, 135-148.

Thiel, H., Parker, D. & Bruce, T. (1973). Stress factors
   and the risk of myocardial infarction. Journal of
   Psychosomatic Research, 17, 43-57.

Titchener, J.L.& Ross, W.D. (1974). Acute or chronic
   stress as determinants of behavior, character, and
   neurosis. In S. Arieti (Ed.), American handbook of
   psychiatry (Vol. 3) (2nd ed.). New Yor: Basic Books.

Tobias, S. (1984). Anxiety and cognitive processing of
   instruction. In R. Schwarzer (Ed.), Self-Related
   Cognitions in Anxiety and Motivation. Hillsdale:
   Erlbaum.

Toner, I.J. (1981). Role involvement and delay maintenance
   behavior in preschool children. Journal of Genetic
   Psychology,138, 245-251.

Toner, I.J. & Hagan, M.S. (1983). The effects of child
   age and label on instructor expectation and performance.
   Paper pres. at Biennial Meet. of Soc. for Research in
   Child Dev.. Detroit, Michigan: , a.

Toner, I.J. & Hagan, M.S. (1983). The effects of
   instructor expectation and performance on child
   comprehension and performance. Paper pres. Meet. Int.
   Soc. for Study of Beh. Dev.. In . (Ed.), München: .

Toner, I.J. & Ritchie, F.K. (in press). Signed statements and delay of gratification in hearing-impaired and non-handicapped children. Journal of General Psychology.

Toner, I.J. & Smith, R.A: (1977). Age and overt verbalization in delay maintenance behavior in children. Journal of Experimental Child Psychology, 24, 123-128.

Toner, I.J., Holstein, R.B. & Hetherington, E.M. (1977). Reflection-impulsivity and self-control in preschool children. Child Development, 48, 239-245.

Toner, I.J., Lewis, B.C. & Gribble, C.M. (1979). Evaluative verbalization and delay maintenance behavior in children. Journal of Experimental Child Psychology, 28, 205-210.

Toner, I.J., Moore, L.P. & Emmons, B.A. (1980). The effect of being labeled on subsequent self-control in children. Child Development, 51, 618-621.

Totman, R. (1979). The social cause of illness. New York: Partheon Books.

Trautmann, R.D. (1983). Depression as a 'final common pathway' of cognitions. Paper presented at the conference 'Anxiety and Self Related Cognitions. Berlin: .

Tricket, E.J. & Moos, R.H. (1973). The social environment of junior high and senior high school classrooms. Journal of Educational Psychology, 65, 93-102.

Trower, P. (1980). Situational analysis of the components and processes of behavior of socially skilled and unskilled patients. Journal of Consulting and Clinical Psychology, 48, 327-339.

Trower, P., Bryant, B. & Argyle, M. (1978). Social skills and mental health. London: Methuen & Co..

Tucker, L.R. & Lewis, C.A. (1973). A reliability coefficient for maximum likelihood factor analysis. Psychometrika, 38, 1-10.

Tukey, J.W. (1977). Exploratory data analysis. Reading, Mass.: Addison-Wesley.

Tupes, E.D. & Christal, R.C. (1961). Recurrent personality factors based on trait ratings. Lackland Air Force Bases, Texas: Personnel Laboratory ASD.

Turner, R.G. (1978). Consistency, self-consciousness, and the predictive validity of typical and maximal personality measures. Journal of Research in Personality, 12, 117-132c.

Turner, R.G. (1978). Effects of differential request procedures and self-consciousness on trait attributions. Journal of Research in Personality, 12, 431-438a.

Turner, R.G. (1978). Self-consciousness and speed of processing self-relevant information. Personality and Social Psychology Bulletin, 4, 456-460b.

Turner, R.G. (1980). Self-consciousness and memory of trait terms. Personality and Social Psychology Bulletin, 6, 273-277.

Turner, R.G., Scheier, M.F., Carver, C.S. & Ickes, W. (1978). Correlates of self-consciousness. Journal of Personality Assessment, 42, 285-289.

Ullrich, R. & Ullrich de Muynck, R. (1978). Das Emotionalitätsinventar: EMI-Befinden. In R. Ullrich & R. Ullrich de Muynck (Eds.), Soziale Kompetenz. München: Pfeifer.

Ullrich, R. & Ullrich de Muynck, R. (1979). Das Situationsbewertungssystem SB-EMI-S, Teil III, Testmanual. München: Pfeiffer.

Uytdenhoef, P. & Linkowski, P. & Mendlewicz, J. (1982). Marqueurs biologiques et prediction de la reponse au traitement dans la depression. Acta Psychiatrica Belgica, 82, 229-242.

Van Sell, M., Brief, A.P. & Schuler, R.S. (1981). Role conflict and role ambiguity: Integration of the literature and directions for future research. Human Relations, 34, 43-71.

Velten, E.A. (1968). A laboratory task for induction of mood states. Behavior Research and Therapy, 6, 473-482.

Vlek, C. & Pruyn, A. (1984). Evaluative stress and human performance: The case of test anxiety. In Ploeg, H. van der, Schwarzer, R. & Spielberger, C.D. (Eds.), Advances in Test Anxiety Research (Vol. 3). Lisse / Hillsdale: Swets / Erlbaum.

Voss, H.-G. (1984). Curiosity, exploration and anxiety. In Ploeg, H. van der, Schwarzer, R. & Spielberger, C.D. (Eds.), Advances in Test Anxiety Research (Vol. 3). Lisse / Hillsdale: Swets / Erlbaum.

Wagner,H. (1982). Bezugsnormspezifische Lehrerunterschiede im Urteil von Schülern. In Rheinberg,F. (Ed.), Bezugsnormen zur Schulleistungsbewertung. Jahrbuch für

Empirische Erziehungswissenschaft 1982 (pp. 173-191). Düsseldorf: Schwann.

Waldron, I., Zyzanski, S., Shekelle, R. et al. (1977). The coronary-prone behavior pattern in employed men and women. Journal of Human Stress, 3, 2-18.

Walls, R.T. & Smith, T.S. (1970). Development of preference for delayed reinforcement in disadvantaged children. Journal of Educational Psychology, 61, 118-123.

Wallston, B.S., Wallston, K.A., Kaplan, G.D. & Maides, S.A. (1976). Development and validation of the Health Locus of Control Scale (HCL). Journal of Consulting and Clinical Psychology, 44, 580-585.

Wanberg, K.W. & Horn, J.L. (1983). Assessment of alcohol use with multidimensional concepts and measures. American Psychologist, 38, 1055-1069.

Wang, M.C. & Walberg, H.J. (1983). Adaptive instruction and classroom time. American Educational Research Journal, 20, 601-626.

Warren, L.W. & McEachren, L. (1983). Psychosocial correlates of depressive symptomatology in adult women. Journal of Abnormal Psychology, 92, 151-160.

Washburne, J.N. (1929). An experiment in character measurement. Journal of Juvenile Research, 13, 1-18.

Watson, D. (1982). The Actor and the Observer: How Are Their Perceptions of Causality Divergent? Psychological Bulletin, 92, 682-.

Watson, D. & Friend, R. (1969). Measurement of social-evaluatiive anxiety. Journal of Consulting and Clinical Psychology, 33, 448-457.

Weary,G. (1979). Self-serving attributional biases: Perceptual or response distortions ? Journal of Personality and Social Psychology, 37, 1418-1420.

Wegner,D.M. & Vallacher,R.R.(Eds.) (1980). The self in social psychology. New York: Oxford Press.

Weinberger, D.A., Schwartz, G.E. & Davidson, R.J. (1979). Low-anxious, high-anxious and repressive coping styles: Psychometric patterns and behavioral and physiological responses to stress. Journal of Abnormal Psychology, 88, 369-380.

Weiner, B. (1980). Human motivation. New York: Holt, Rinehart & Winston.

Weiner, B. (1980). The role of affect in rational (attributional) approaches to human motivation. Educational Researcher, 9, 4-11.

Weiner, B. (1982). An attribution theory of motivation and emotion. In H.W. Krohne & L. Laux (Eds.), Achievement, stress and anxiety. Washington: Hemisphere.

Weiner, B. (1982). The emotional consequences of causal ascriptions. In Clark, M.S. & Fiske, S.T. (Eds.), Affect and cognition. The 17th Annual Carnegie Symposium on Cognition. Hillsdale: Erlbaum.

Weiner, B. (1983). Some methodological pitfalls in attributional research. Journal of Educational Psychology, 75, 530-543.

Weiner, B., Graham, S.H., & Chandler, C. (1982). An attributional analysis of pity, anger, and guilt.. Personality and Social Psychology Bulletin, 8, 226-232.

Weiner, B., Graham, S.H., Stern., W. & Lawson, M. (1982). Using affective cues to infer causal thoughts. Developmental Psychology, 18, 278-286.

Weiner, B., Russell, D. & Lerman, D. (1978). Affective consequences of causal ascriptions. In J.H. Harvey, W.J. Ickes & R.F. Kidd (Eds.), New directions in attribution research (Vol. 2). Hillsdale, N.Y.: Erlbaum.

Weiner, B., Russell, D. & Lerman, D. (1979). The cognition-emotion process achievement-related contexts. Journal of Personality and Social Psychology, 37, 1211-1220.

Weiner,B. (1982). An attributionally based theory of motivation and emotion - focus, range and issues. In Feather,N.T. (Ed.), Expectations and actions: Expectancy-value models in psychology. Hillsdale,N.J.: Erlbaum.

Weingartner, H., Cohen, R.M., Murphy, D.L., Martello, J. & Gerdt, C. (1981). Cognitive processes in depression. Archives of General Psychiatry, 38, 42-47.

Weinraub, M. & Wolf, B.M. (1983). Effects of stress and social supports on mother-child interactions in sngle- and two-parents families. Child Development, 54, 1297-1311.

Weinshel, E.M. (1970). Some psychoanalytic consideration on moods. International Journal of Psychoanalysis, 51, 313-320.

Weismann, M.M. (1980). Use of self report symptom scale to detect depression in a community sample. American Journal of Psychiatry,137.

Weiss, W. (1982). Familienstruktur und Selbständigkeitserziehung. Göttingen: Hogrefe.

Weissman, A.W. & Beck, A.T. (1978). Development and validation of the dysfunctional attitude scale. Paper pres. at annual meet. of the Assoc. for Advancement of Behav. Therapy. Chicago: .

Weitz, J. (1970). Psychological research needs on the problems of human stress. In J. McGrath (Ed.), Social and psychological factors in stress (pp. 124-133). New York: Holt Rinehart & Winston.

Wells, K.C., Hersen, M., Bellack, A.S. & Himmelhoch, J.M. (1979). Social skills training in unipolar nonpsychotic depression. American Journal of Psychiatry,136, 1331-1332.

Wertheim, E.H. & Schwarz, J.C. (1983). Depression, guilt and self-management of pleasant and unpleasant events. Journal of Personality and Social Psychology, 45, 884-889.

Wetzel, R.D., Cloninger, C.R., Hong, B. & Reich, T. (1980). Personality as a subclinical expression of the affective disorders. Comprehensive Psychiatry, 21, 197-205.

Wheeler, L. (Ed.) (1982). Review of personality and social psychology. Volume 3. London: Sage.

White, J. (1982). The masks of melancholy. Downers Grove, Ill.: InterVarsity Press.

White,R.W. (1959). Motivation reconsidered: The concept of competence. Psychological Review, 66, 297-333.

Wicker, A.W. (1979). An introduction to ecological psychology. Monterey, Calif.: Brooks/Cole.

Wicklund, R. A. & Gollwitzer, P. M. (1983). The fallacy of the private-public self-focus distinction. Draft. .

Wicklund, R.A. (1979). Objektive Selbstaufmerksamkeit: Ein theoretischer Ansatz der Persönlichkeits- und Sozialpsychologie. In S.E. Hormuth (Ed.), Sozialpsychologie der Einstellungsänderung. Hain: Königstein.

Wicklund, R.A. (1982). Self-focused attention and the validity of self-reports. In Zanna, M.P., Higgins, E.T.

& Herman, C.P. (Eds.), Consistency in social behavior:
The Ontario Symposium, Vol. 2 (pp. 149-172).
Hillsdale: Erlbaum.

Wicklund, R.A. (1984). Fitting to the environment and the
use of dispositions. In R. Schwarzer (Ed.),
Self-Related Cognitions in Anxiety and Motivation.
Hillsdale: Erlbaum.

Wicklund, R.A. & Gollwitzer, P.M. (1982). Symbolic
self-completion. Hillsdale: Erlbaum.

Wicklund,R.A. (1975). Objective self-awareness. In
Berkowitz.L. (Ed.), Advances in experimental social
psychology. Vol 8 (pp. 233-275). New York: Academic
Press.

Wicklund,R.A. & Frey,D. (1980). Self-awareness theory:
When the self makes a difference. In Wegner,D.M. &
Vallacher,R.R. (Eds.), The self in social psychology
(pp. 31-54). New York: Oxford University Press.

Wieland, R. (1980). Strukturanalyse von Tätigkeiten
längerer Dauer. In W. Michaelis (Ed.), Bericht über
den 32. Kongreß der Deutschen Gesellschaft für
Psychologie, Zürich 1980. Göttigen: Hogrefe.

Wieland, R. (1981). Schwankende Schallpegel,
Leistungshandeln und der Wechsel von Arbeit und
Erholung. Zeitschrift für Lärmbekämpfung, 28,
117-122.

Wieland, R. (in press). Anxious-defensive,
anxious-sensitive, and non-anxious coping style:
Temporal patterns and behavioral regulation in
achievement-related stress. In C.D. Spielberger & J.
Strelan (Eds.), Stress and anxiety. Washington/ New
York: Hemisphere/ McGraw-Hill.

Wilcox, B. (1980). The role of social support in
adjustment to marital disruption. Paper presented at the
annual meeting of the Western Psychological
Association. Honolulu, Hawai: .

Wilcox, B.L. (1981). Social support, life stress, and
psychological adjustment: A test of the buffering
hypothesis. American Journal of Community
Psychology, 4, 371-386.

Wilkinson, I.M. & Blackburn, I.M. (1981). Cognitive style
in depressed and recovered depressed patients. British
Journal of Clinical Psychology, 20, 283-292.

Williams, J.M.G. (1982). Experimental and control tapes on
mood induction. Personal Communication.

Wilmotte, C.G. & Mendlewicz, J. (1982). Le test de freination a la dexamethasone dans les troubles de l' humeur: Une revue. Acta Psychiatrica Belgica, 82, 349-362.

Winer, B.J. (1971). Statistical principles in experimental design, 2nd ed.. New York: McGraw-Hill.

Wing, J.K., Cooper, J.E. & Sartorius, N. (1974). The measurement and classification of psychiatric symptoms. Cambridge: Cambridge University Press.

Winne, P.H. & Marx, R.W. (1981). Convergent and discriminant validity in self concept measurement. Paper presented at AERA meeting in Los Angeles 1981. .

Wolpe, J. (1979). The experimental model and treatment of neurotic depression. Behavior Research and Therapy, 17, 555-565.

Wortman, C.B. & Brehm, J.W. (1975). Responses to uncontrollable outcomes: An integration of reactance theory and the learned helplessness model. In L. Berkowitz (Ed.), Advances in Experimental Social Psychology (Vol. 8) (pp. 277-336). New York: Academic Press.

Wrzesniewski, K. (1984). Development of the Polish form of the State-Trait Personality Inventory. In Ploeg, H. van der, Schwarzer, R. & Spielberger, C.D. (Eds.), Advances in Test Anxiety Research (Vol. 3). Lisse / Hillsdale: Swets / Erlbaum.

Wylie, R.C. (1979). The self-concept: Vol. 2. Theory and research on selected topics. Lincoln: University of Nebraska Press.

Yates, B.T. & Mischel, W. (1979). Young children's preferred attentional strategies for delaying gratification. Journal of Personality and Social Psychology, 37, 286-300.

Zajonc, R.B. (1965). Social facilitation. Science, 149, 269-274.

Zeiss, A., Lewinsohn, P. & Munoz, R. (1979). Nonspecific improvement effects in depression using interpersonal skills training, pleasant activity schedules, or cognitive training. Journal of Consulting and Clinical Psychology, 47, 427-439.

Zerssen, D. von (1976). Die Befindlichkeitsskala (Bf-S). Weinheim: Beltz.

Zimbardo, P.G. (1977). Shyness. New York: Jove.

Zuckerman, M. (1976). General and situation-specific traits and states: New approaches to assessment of anxiety and other constructs. In C.D. Spielberger (Ed.), Emotions and anxiety. New concepts, methods and applications. Hillsdale, N.Y.: Erlbaum.

Zuckermann, M. & Lubin, B. (1965). Manual for the Multiple Affect Adjective Check List. San Diego, Calif.: Educat.& Industr.Testing Service.

Zung, W W.K. (1965). A self-rating depression scale. Archives of General Psychiatry, 12, 63-70.

Zyzanski, S. (1978). Coronary-prone behavior pattern and coronary heart disease. Epidemiological evidence. In H. Dembroski, S. Weiss, F. Shields et al. (Eds.), Coronary-prone behavior (pp. 25-38). New York: Springer.

Zyzanski, S., Wrzesniewski, K. & Jenkins, D. (1979). Cross-cultural validation of the coronary-prone behavior pattern. Social Science & Medicine, 13, 405-412.

ADDRESSES OF AUTHORS

William J. Alagaratnam
Department of Clinical Psychology
Knowle Hospital
Fareham, Hampshire PO17 5NA
Great Britain

Andre Arsenault
Industrial Relations and Work Psychology
University of Montreal
P.O.Box 6128
Montreal PQ H3C 3J7
Canada

Jens Asendorpf
Max-Planck-Institut für Psychologische Forschung
Leopoldstr. 24
8000 München 40
Federal Republic of Germany

Anna Maria Asprea
Istituto di Sociologia
Corso Umberto I 40
University of Naples
80138 Naples
Italy

Riva Bartell
Department of Educational Psychology
The University of Manitoba
Winnipeg, Manitoba R3T 2N2
Canada

Virginia Blankenship
Department of Psychology
Oakland University
Rochester, Michigan 48063
USA

Stephen R. Briggs
Henry Kendall College of Arts and Sciences
The University of Tulsa
600 South College Avenue
Tulsa, Oklahoma 74104
USA

Willem Claeys
Faculteit der Psychologie
Katholieke Universiteit te Leuven
Tiensestraat 102
3000 Leuven
Belgium

Suellen L. Crano
Department of Psychology
Michigan State University
East Lansing, Michigan 48824
USA

William D. Crano
Department of Psychology
Michigan State University
East Lansing, Michigan 48824
USA

Shimon L. Dolan
Industrial Relations and Work Psychology
University of Montreal
P.O.Box 6128
Montreal PQ H3C 3J7
Canada

Stephan Dutke
Institut für Psychologie
Freie Universität Berlin
Habelschwerdter Allee 45
1000 Berlin 33
Federal Republic of Germany

Paul R.J. Falger
Department of Medical Psychology
State University of Limburg
P.O.Box 616
6200 MD Maastricht
The Netherlands

Joachim Faulhaber
Institut für Psychologie
Freie Universität Berlin
Habelschwerdter Allee 45
1000 Berlin 33
Federal Republic of Germany

Angelika M. Frenzel
Institut für Psychologie
Freie Universität Berlin
Habelschwerdter Allee 45
1000 Berlin 33
Federal Republic of Germany

Prem S. Fry
Department of Educational Psychology
The University of Calgary
2500 University Drive N.W.
Calgary, Alberta T2N 1N4
Canada

Matthias Jerusalem
Institut für Psychology
Freie Universität Berlin
Habelschwerdter Allee 45
1000 Berlin 33
Federal Republic of Germany

Warren H. Jones
Henry Kendall College of Arts and Sciences
The University of Tulsa
600 South College Avenue
Tulsa, Oklahoma 74104
USA

Daniele Kammer
Fakultät Psychologie und Sport
Universität Bielefeld
Postfach 8640
4800 Bielefeld
Federal Republic of Germany

Mary Ann MacDougall
Department of Educational Research and Evaluation
University of Virginia
405 Emmet Street, Ruffner Hall
Charlottesville, Virginia 22903
USA

Chris J.S. Nekanda-Trepka
Bangour Village Hospital
West Lothian EH52 6LW, Scotland
Great Britain

Jürgen Otto
Psychologisches Institut
Johannes-Gutenberg-Universität
Saarstr. 21
6500 Mainz
Federal Republic of Germany

Hans-Henning Quast
Institut für Psychologie
Freie Universität Berlin
Habelschwerdter Allee 45
1000 Berlin 33
Federal Republic of Germany

Henk van der Ploeg
Stress-Groep Leiden
University of Leiden
Postbus 1251
2340 BG Oegstgeest
The Netherlands

Arne Raeithel
Institut für Psychologie
Freie Universität Berlin
Habelschwerdter Allee 45
1000 Berlin 33
Federal Republic of Germany

Wolfgang Royl
Fachbereich Pädagogik
University of the Armed Forces
Werner-Heisenberg-Weg 39
8014 Neubiberg
Federal Republic of Germany

Ruth Rustemeyer
Institut für Psychologie
Universität Gesamthochschule Paderborn
Warburger Straße 100, Gebäude H
4790 Paderborn
Federal Republic of Germany

Wolfgang Schönpflug
Institut für Psychologie
Freie Universität Berlin
Habelschwerdter Allee 45
1000 Berlin 33
Federal Republic of Germany

Christine Schwarzer
Institut für Erziehungswissenschaften II
Universität Düsseldorf
Universitätsstraße
4000 Düsseldorf
Federal Republic of Germany

Ralf Schwarzer
Institut für Psychologie
Freie Universität Berlin
Habelschwerdter Allee 45
1000 Berlin 33
Federal Republic of Germany

Rainer K. Silbereisen
Institut für Psychologie
Technische Universität
Dovestr. 1-5
1000 Berlin 10
Federal Republic of Germany

Ignatius J. Toner
Department of Psychology
The University of North Carolina
UNCC Station
Charlotte, North Carolina 28223
USA

Giulia Villone-Betocchi
Istituto di Sociologia
Corso Umberto I 40
University of Naples
80138 Naples
Italy

Rainer Wieland
Psychologisches Institut
Freie Universität Berlin
Habelschwerdter Allee 45
1000 Berlin 33
Federal Republic of Germany

Susanne Zank
Institut für Psychologie
Technische Universität
Dovestr. 1-5
1000 Berlin 10
Federal Republic of Germany